Working Time

Working time is a crucial issue for both research and public policy. It is a focal point for discussions about social values, family decision-making, economic competitiveness, and the very nature of economic growth and sustainable development. A growing number of workers around the world are reporting they are overworked, fatigued and unable to achieve the desired balance between work and family. The erstwhile standard working week appears to be disintegrating, and no one knows precisely what will replace it.

This book presents the first comprehensive analysis of both paid and unpaid work time, integrating a unique discussion of overwork, underwork, shortening the working week, and flexible work practices. From the broad perspective of social economics, time at work is determined within a complex web of evolving culture and social relations, as well as market, technological, and macroeconomic forces, and institutions such as collective bargaining and government policy. Using a variety of new data sources, the authors review the latest trends on working time in numerous countries, provide theoretical perspectives on both overwork and underemployment, and appraise various public and workplace policies.

This international and interdisciplinary volume will be of great interest to both scholars and students, as well as practitioners and advocates in the policy arena.

Lonnie Golden is Associate Professor of Economics at Pennsylvania State University. **Deborah M. Figart** is Professor of Economics at Richard Stockton College, New Jersey.

Advances in social economics

Edited by John B. Davis

Marquette University

This series presents new advances and developments in social economics thinking on a variety of subjects that concern the link between social values and economics. Need, justice and equity, gender, cooperation, work poverty, the environment, class, institutions, public policy, and methodology are some of the most important themes. Among the orientations of the authors are social economist, institutionalist, humanist, solidarist, cooperatist, radical and Marxist, feminist, post-Keynesian, behaviouralist, and environmentalist. The series offers new contributions from today's most foremost thinkers on the social character of the economy.

Published in conjunction with the Association of Social Economics.

Books published in the series include:

Social economics
Premises, findings and policies
Edited by *Edward J. O'Boyle*

The environmental consequences of growth
Steady state economics as an alternative to ecological decline
Douglas Booth

Economics for the common good
Two centuries of social economic thought in the humanistic tradition
Mark A. Lutz

The human firm
A socio-economic analysis of its behavior and potential in a new economic age
J. Tomer

Working Time

International trends, theory and policy perspectives

Edited by
Lonnie Golden and Deborah M. Figart

London and New York

First published 2000
by Routledge
11 New Fetter Lane, London EC4P 4EE

Simultaneously published in the USA and Canada
by Routledge
29 West 35th Street, New York, NY 10001

Routledge is an imprint of the Taylor & Francis Group

Typeset in Garamond by
Keyword Publishing Services Ltd.
Printed and bound in Great Britain by
St Edmundsbury Press, Bury St Edmunds, Suffolk

British Library Cataloguing in Publication Data
A catalogue record for this book is available from the British Library

Library of Congress Cataloging in Publication Data
Working time: international trends, theory, and policy perspectives / edited by Lonnie Golden and Deborah M. Figart.
p. cm. – (Advances in social economics)
Includes bibliographical references and index.
1. Hours of labor. 2. Labor supply. I. Golden, Lonnie. II. Figart, Deborah M. III. Series.
HD5106.W63 2000
331.25′72 – dc21 00-035314

ISBN 0-415-22834-4 (hbk)

Contents

Figures

Tables

Contributors

Linda A. Bell is Associate Professor of Economics at Haverford College. She has held visiting positions at Princeton University and Harvard University, and was a senior economist at the Federal Reserve Bank in New York. She has held varied consultancies at institutions such as the World Bank, the US Labor Department, and the Federal Reserve Bank of Philadelphia. Her recent research includes several papers on work hour intensity, earnings inequality, faculty salary trends, and the impact of children and marriage on men and women in the labor market over time.

Barry Bluestone is the Stearns Trustee Professor of Political Economy at Northeastern University in Boston, Massachusetts and director of the University's Center for Urban and Regional Policy. His work has appeared in numerous economics and policy journals. He is coauthor of *The Deindustrialization of America* and *The Great U-Turn* (with Bennett Harrison) and *Negotiating the Future* (with Irving Bluestone), published by Basic Books.

Gerhard Bosch is Professor of Sociology at the University of Duisburg. He is also Director of the Labor Market Department of the Institute for Work and Technology, Science Center North-Rhine Westphalia in Gelsenkirchen, Germany. He is an expert on labor markets and has published several books. He is working on a European comparison of working time arrangements in the service economy and on an international study on the labor market in the construction industry.

Tanya Brubaker received her M.Phil. in Industrial/Organizational Psychology in August 1999 from the George Washington University. She is finishing her Ph.D., which investigates value congruence as a means of maximizing charismatic leader effectiveness. She currently works as a management consultant.

Paul Burkett teaches Economics at Indiana State University, Terre Haute. His research centers on Marxism and ecology; finance, development, and crises; and the political economy of the working class. He is the author of

Marx and Nature: A Red and Green Perspective (St. Martin's Press, 1999); "Insiders and Outsiders, Unemployment, and Worktime," *Review of Radical Political Economics*, Summer 1998; and "Critical Notes on the Insider/Outsider Approach to Unemployment," *Review of Radical Political Economics*, Summer 1997.

Robert Caplan has been Professor and Director of the Doctoral Program in Applied and Organizational Psychology and member of the Center for Family Research in Psychiatry at the George Washington University and Program Director at ISR's Survey Research Center at the University of Michigan. His numerous publications deal with stress and coping in the areas of organizational behavior, health care, and work–family relationships and with preventive intervention. He is a consultant in Redondo Beach, California.

Darnell L. Cloud received his M.A. in Economics from the University of Wisconsin – Milwaukee in 1995. He is currently finishing his Ph.D. in Economics at the University of Wisconsin – Milwaukee, specializing in industrial organization and labor economics.

David Costanza is an Assistant Professor of Administrative Sciences and of Psychology at the George Washington University in Washington, DC. He received his doctorate in Industrial/Organizational Psychology from George Mason University in 1996. His primary areas of research include leadership and its impact on organizational performance and policies, including in the work–family domain, and the creation and use of new job analysis and performance appraisal techniques.

Robert Drago is Professor of Labor Studies at Penn State University. A Fulbright Scholar, Dr. Drago has published 3 books and over 60 articles. He moved into the work–family area in 1995, initiating the work–family newsgroup <http://www.la.psu.edu/lsir/workfam>, and undertaking a major study of teachers and time pressures for the Alfred P. Sloan Foundation. Findings from the study first appeared in the *Monthly Labor Review*. His latest research analyzes ways in which organizations and employees respond to the demands of work and unpaid care for children.

Deborah M. Figart is Professor of Economics at Richard Stockton College in Pomona, New Jersey. She teaches courses in labor relations, work and family, women's studies, economic theory, and political economy. She is an Associate Editor of the *Encyclopedia of Political Economy* (Routledge). Her work has appeared in numerous journals, including *Review of Social Economy, Work and Occupations, Feminist Economics, Journal of Economic Issues*, and *Industrial Relations Journal*.

David George is Associate Professor of Economics at La Salle University in Philadelphia. His main research interests are in rational choice theory and the rhetorical practices of economists. Articles that he has written have appeared in the *International Journal of Social Economics*, *Review of Social Economy*, *Journal of Economic Issues*, and the *Eastern Economic Journal*. He is currently finishing a book, *Preference Pollution*, in which he further develops his argument that markets fail in the shaping of our tastes.

Kathleen Gerson is Professor of Sociology at New York University, where she specializes in the study of gender, work, family, the life course and social change processes. Her books include *No Man's Land: Men's Changing Commitments to Family and Work* (Basic Books) and *Hard Choices: How Women Decide About Work, Career and Motherhood* (University of California Press). Her current projects include studies of work–family conflict.

Lonnie Golden holds a Ph.D. in Economics and is Associate Professor of Economics at Penn State University Delaware County, Business and Economics Division of the Commonwealth College. His research primarily focuses on the economics of the labor market. In particular, it analyzes both the theory of and empirical trends in labor market flexibility, working hours, and the contingent workforce. He is also coeditor of *Nonstandard Work: The Nature and Challenge of Emerging Employment Arrangements* (Cornell University Press, 2000).

Naomi Harris is a doctoral student in Industrial/Organizational Psychology at the George Washington University. Her research focuses on helping families and organizations cope with increasing home–work time demands. She is employed at the Marasco Newton Group, Ltd, where she specializes in performance measurement and organizational development.

Jerry A. Jacobs is Professor of Sociology and Chair of the Graduate Program in Sociology at the University of Pennsylvania. He has studied a number of aspects of women's employment, including authority, earnings, working conditions, part-time work, and entry into male-dominated occupations. His current research includes a study of women in higher education, funded by the Spence Foundation, and a study of work–family conflict, funded by the Sloan Foundation.

Russell Kashian received his Ph.D. from the University of Wisconsin – Milwaukee (1999) in Economics. He also holds an M.A. in Economics (University of Wisconsin – Milwaukee 1994) and an M.S. in Urban Studies (Cleveland State University 1992). He currently teaches economics at the University of Wisconsin – Whitewater.

Laura Leete is Director of the Public Policy Research Center and Associate Professor of Economics and Management at Willamette University in Salem, Oregon. She holds a Ph.D. in Economics from Harvard University and engages in research in the areas of poverty and welfare reform, work time, family policy, temporary and contingent work arrangements, and race and gender wage discrimination.

Steffen Lehndorff is an economist and Senior Researcher at the Labor Market Research Department of the Institute for Work and Technology IAT (Institut Arbeit und Technik im Wissenschaftszentrum Nordrhein-Westfalen), Gelsenkirchen, Germany. His major research interests include working time and industrial relations in an international comparative perspective, and working time and work organization in various manufacturing and service industries.

Ellen Mutari is Assistant Professor in the General Studies Division at Richard Stockton College in Pomona, New Jersey. She is coeditor of *Gender and Political Economy: Integrating Diversity into Theory and Policy* (M. E. Sharpe) and an Associate Editor of the *Encyclopedia of Political Economy* (Routledge). Her research has been published in the *Journal of Economic Issues, Review of Social Economy, Feminist Economics*, and other journals. She is working on a new book about wage policies in the twentieth century.

Robert E. Prasch is Visiting Assistant Professor of Economics at Middlebury College. Most of his recent work on labor economics has been on the history and theory of minimum wage legislation, and has appeared in such journals as *Journal of Economic Perspectives, Journal of the History of Economic Thought, Review of Social Economy* and the *Journal of Economic Issues.*

T. Lynn Riggs holds a Ph.D. in Economics from the University of Wisconsin – Milwaukee. Her dissertation consisted of an evaluation of an accelerated, year-round school and the impact these programs had on teacher stress levels. She is currently involved in research in health economics.

Stephen Rose is a Senior Economist with the Educational Testing Service in Washington, DC. His research on working time has been published by the *Review of Social Economy, The American Prospect,* and the Jerome Levy Economics Institute at Bard College. He has also served as an economist with the former National Commission for Employment Policy.

Juliet B. Schor is an economist currently teaching in the Women's Studies Program at Harvard University. She is also Professor of the Economics of Leisure at Tilburg University in the Netherlands. She is the author of *The*

Overworked American: The Unexpected Decline of Leisure, The Overspent American: Upscaling, Downshifting and the New Consumerism, and *The Consumer Society: A Reader*, which is forthcoming in 2000. Schor is a founding member of the Center for a New American Dream, an organization which is attempting to foster more environmentally and temporally sustainable lifestyles.

Tom Walker is a social policy analyst and advocate for shorter work time. Since 1995 he has maintained the TimeWork Web <http://www.vcn.bc.ca/timework> on the internet, a resource for information and analysis on the working time issue. He lives in Vancouver.

Acknowledgments

Working time has been a focus in our own research agenda as labor economists. In 1997, we assembled a group conducting research on working time to present their work at the 1998 Allied Social Science Association meetings in Chicago, Illinois, a session sponsored by the Association for Social Economics. John B. Davis, Editor of the *Review of Social Economy*, sensed that this would now be a very "timely topic." At his urging and encouragement, we collected and edited additional papers into one of the journal's annual symposium issues, "Special Issue on the Social Economics of Work Time" (Volume LVI, Winter 1998). Its theoretical and empirical analyses focused largely on working hours, paid and unpaid, in the United States. The present book expands the scope to a more global perspective. The chapters in this volume present new research by scholars studying working hours, both across time and across several post-industrial countries.

We have enjoyed the collective work process, both with each other and with the authors. We would like to thank each contributor in this volume for their efforts, cooperation and timeliness. We are very grateful to John B. Davis for his support throughout the last few years, and for suggesting this volume for Routledge's "Advances in Social Economics" series. Several current (and former) staff members at Routledge have helped shepherd the manuscript through the various stages of production, including Alison Kirk, Andreja Zivkovic, Emma Davis, Heidi Bagtazo, and our Editor, Robert Langham. Finally, we received unending support from our families. Considerable unpaid work time and family time was sacrificed over the past year, to complete this project on schedule. Thank you Ellen, Deborah S. Meyer, Carla and Talia!

1 Introduction and overview

Understanding working time around the world

Deborah M. Figart and Lonnie Golden

An increasing number of workers around the world are reporting they are overworked, fatigued, and unable to achieve a desired balance in their lives between paid work, family life, personal, and civic time. Millions of workers – salaried and hourly, professional, technical, and blue-collar – are regularly clocking work weeks well in excess of the venerable 40-hour standard, and often without receiving overtime compensation. Some labor unions in the USA have begun to defy these trends, seeking limits on mandatory overtime in certain manufacturing and service sectors, although not as aggressively as their counterparts in Germany, France, Sweden, and other European Union countries. Other workers pursue individualized solutions such as "downshifting" to careers allowing more free time. Pioneering US corporate managers are beginning to recognize the issue of employee "burnout," innovating such work redesign programs, beyond flexitime and child-care assistance, that have employees set their own goals not only for productivity and but also for leisure time. But these pockets of resistance and innovation remain the exceptions. Even in Europe, growing overtime and the emerging 24-hour, 7-day economy have led to workers experiencing work well in excess of their number of preferred hours and wishing a change in their schedules, to preserve valued cultural norms such as family holidays, meal times, and days of rest.[1]

As it stands, workers in the United States and Japan have the highest average annual hours on the job, about 30 percent more than their European counterparts. The nearly 2000 annual hours per capita worked by US workers translates into 15 weeks longer on the job each year. While economists generally regard this is a sign of economic vigor and diligence, the climbing number of paid work hours to levels beyond standard work weeks nevertheless is of concern. It is no doubt diminishing the extent of workers' non-income-producing time and productivity per hour. The degree of work beyond 40 hours per week is also prevalent in the Czech Republic, Turkey, Korea, Iceland, and Switzerland. In emerging market economies such as Singapore, Mexico, and Chile, weekly hours of work in the manufacturing sector are also rising. While many of the world's workers complain of excess overtime, other workers remain underemployed, employed at very low or fewer than desired hours. Switzerland, the Netherlands, Australia, and the United Kingdom are among the countries that have the highest percentage of workers employed for less than ten hours per week. Both between and within countries, there appears to be an increasing polarization – an escalation in working time for some and a reduction in weekly hours for others.[2]

Another trend across the globe is the growing flexibility and differentiation in the duration and organization of paid working time, especially in Western and Central Europe, Australia, New Zealand, and the United States. Statutory and collectively bargained limits to the length of the work week, a hallmark of the postwar period "social contract," are either fading, neglected, or irrelevant.[3] A social organization of time that served to synchronize hours of work and leisure for much of the 20th century is gradually disintegrating. Working time is becoming more differentiated and variable, triggered by a combination of economic, technological, and cultural influences (see Hinrichs, Roche, and Sirianni 1991; Boulin 1993; ILO 1995; Hamermesh 1996). The "standard" work week is giving way to schemes of hours averaging over longer intervals of time.[4] For example, exceptions allowed in the Working Time Directive in the European Union allow for the annualization of hours. In addition, proposals are pending in the United States Congress to extend the time period applied for the calculation of overtime pay from one to two weeks. Employers are already implementing various nonstandard hours and shift arrangements and extending operating times, some of it worker friendly such as telework and flexitime but much of it furthering "unsocial" hours. It is not yet clear what configuration of hours will emerge in the 21st century to replace the erstwhile standard of the late 20th century. Nor is it clear whether this will largely be to workers' benefit or to their detriment. What is clear is that work hour patterns and institutions will touch ever more households as growing proportions of the population join the labor force.

The authors in this volume all explore some aspect of the trend toward longer or more differentiated hours, overwork and underemployment, and the "time squeeze" among many workers in post-industrial countries. There are so many different dimensions to work time itself. Largely for this reason, measuring the actual level and trends in work hours is controversial. There is its duration, which may be observed either daily, weekly or annually, by family or individual. There is its distribution – the extent to which workers are getting the slice of the total work time pie they prefer - among workers by gender, race, or job type, as well as within households. There is the degree of flexibility and control workers may possess regarding its duration, as well as its timing and its pace. The implications one draws for worker well-being, productivity, or equity may well depend upon which of these dimensions is highlighted. What this volume reveals is that the level, distribution, and alterations in individuals' hours of work reflects their responses to trends in wages, inequality, consumerism, or balance of power. Working time is determined within a complex web of evolving culture and social relations as well as traditionally conceived market, technological, and macroeconomic forces, and institutions such as collective bargaining and government policy.

This volume not only presents the major trends in working time. It provides alternative theoretical and historical perspectives to analyze these trends and public policies proposed to restructure work either to foster a better balance between work and non-work life or promote employment opportunities. Among neoclassical economists, time tends to be conceived of as a scarce resource that, when commodified as labor, serves as both a factor of production for optimizing firms and as a means to the end, for consumption according to the individual's or family's "preferences" (Rottenberg 1995, for example). Because such a model can always be relied upon to generate some unique prediction involving an equilibrium, it continues to have value in exchange, even while it may lack value in use (Golden 1999: 428). In stark contrast, radical political economists view working time as both the yardstick measuring the value created by labor and an indicator of managerial control over the labor process (see Nyland 1986; Yates 1994). Yet working time means more than these conceptions. Time spent on the job is all at once a source of income, personal identity, and relative status within society, the workplace and household, and a constraint on individuals' ability to pursue self-directed activities and social reproduction. Each chapter addresses at least one aspect of the multi-dimensional character of work time and emerging patterns of its organization.

WORKING TIME REDUCTIONS IN THE INDUSTRIAL ERA

There is considerable variability in working time across the globe and within countries by industry and occupation, by gender and race, by family type, and by time period. In the last 100 years, though, the overall propensity among industrialized economies has been to take a portion of productivity gains achieved in the form of a reduced work week (van Ginneken 1984; Nyland 1986; Hunnicutt 1988). Far from being an unswerving, downward linear trend, there have been waves of both stability and fluctuation in hours.

Economic historian E.P. Thompson (1967) sought to understand the general role of working time in the formation of the industrial revolution. The rise of employment in the industrial sector created a sharper distinction between the "employer's time" and a worker's "own" time, which became more central to the employment relationship. Industrialization and mechanization led to the precise measurement of time. In Thompson's oft-quoted phrase: "Time is now currency; it is not passed but spent" (61). Workers fought a losing battle against this new, strict time-discipline. Throughout the 19th century, the nascent labor movement took up the struggle to reduce the standard hours in paid employment in order to increase hours for leisure and to prevent feared technological unemployment (Hunnicutt 1988; Roediger and Foner 1989; Schor 1991a). The shorter hours issue spawned the first wave of strike and organization activity including the Ten Hours Movement in the UK. It also led to governmental reform establishing maximum hours, beginning with the Factory Acts of 1833 in England and state hours legislation in the United States. At first, regulation limited work hours for women and children only. Considered weak, dependent, and too vulnerable to negotiate their own working conditions, women and children were targets of this so-called protective legislation (Wikander, Kessler-Harris, and Lewis 1995). There is some evidence that protective legislation reduced work hours for male workers as well (see Goldin 1990).

In the USA, Europe, Canada, Australia, and New Zealand, reduction of working hours through gender-neutral legislation and collective bargaining had became standard practice by the 1920s. But the shorter hours movement was attenuated by the Depression (Hinrichs, Roche, and Sirianni 1991; Bosch, Dawkins, and Michon 1993; ILO 1995). Regular, standardized work schedules for full-time workers became one of the institutional arrangements of Fordism, along with "business unionism," the spread of internal labor market practices, job security, and systems for on-the-job training. The work time bargain struck by capital and labor also facilitated a gender division of labor between home and waged work, enabling working class male breadwinners to support full-time female homemakers.

Stability in the level of work hours is a general feature of postwar economies (Hart 1987; Hunnicutt 1988; Roediger and Foner 1989; Golden 1990; Schor 1991b; Glickman 1997). According to historian Benjamin Kline Hunnicutt, some economists argue that there has been no increase in leisure since World War II (1984: 375; see also Winston 1966). While some research has found a continuing gradual decline in *annual* hours of work since the 1940s (see Northrup and Greis 1983), due in part to the growth in paid holiday and vacation time off, average *weekly* hours remained virtually constant through 1970 (Kniesner 1976; Owen 1989). The level of median weekly hours was most constant for white men in their prime earning years, while they declined somewhat for young men, older men, and black men of all ages (Coleman and Pencavel 1993a).

IS WORKING TIME ON THE RISE AGAIN?

Evidence suggesting average hours per worker may be lengthening over the last few decades has reignited intense discussion and debate about the present and future course of working time and its public policy implications. There is so very much at stake, not only for scholars but for workers and societies, in determining whether the nature of post-industrial economic growth is to deliver shorter or longer hours of work. For a variety of reasons, it is difficult to definitively establish recent trends in work hours. One is that different samples and methodologies are used. For instance, findings are affected by whether a study considers only full-time workers or production workers.[5] Average work hours may be suppressed by the growing percentage of the labor force working in nonstandard, less than full-time or year-round employment, such as temporary work, contingent work, or voluntary and particularly involuntary part-time jobs (Nollen 1989; ILO 1995; Tilly 1996). Also critical is whether data collection is from time diaries, from surveys of households or individuals, or from surveys of establishments (employers).[6] It is advantageous to consider and weigh the data selected and methodologies employed, especially when considering cross-country trends. Fortunately, with few exceptions, the official statistical gathering agencies of most countries use a consistent definition of employment and household surveys that ensure complete coverage of workers (see ILO 1999 for more information).

For much of the 20th century, annual and weekly work hours in Japan have remained higher than those in other industrialized countries, despite a declared 40-hour work week in 1977. However, hours have gradually declined since 1980 (ILO 1999), in part due to government and trade union confederation efforts (ILO 1995; Hoffman and Fajertag 1996), linking reductions to expansion of flexible work schedules (Takagi 1993). An opposite trend has been observed in the USA (see Rones, Ilg, and Gardner 1997). On an annual basis, US workers now average two weeks more on the job than Japanese workers.

Many scholars focusing on the USA have pointed to an increase in either average work hours or a growing share of the work force working long hours. Juliet Schor's (1991a) book *The Overworked American* argues that both paid and total (including unpaid) annual work hours are increasing, creating a "time-squeeze" (see also Leete and Schor 1994). In addition, paid market hours rose more than non-market work hours declined for most families (see also Blau 1998; Heath, Ciscel, and Sharp 1998). Some contradictory evidence is derived from surveys of worker-completed time diaries. In *Time for Life*, Robinson and Godbey (1997) find that total work load, paid and unpaid, has fallen between 1965 and 1985 (see also Rupert and Roberts 1995). Several studies note that increases in average weekly hours, on the other hand, are negligible (Nollen 1989; Coleman and Pencavel 1993a,b; Rones, Ilg, and Gardner 1997).[7]

While there is debate about the length of the average work week, the evidence is clearer with regard to overtime, a potential indicator of overwork. Once exclusively an indicator of cyclical trends, such as tight labor markets and economic expansion, overtime has undergone a secular increase since the late 1970s (Golden 1998). While 20 percent of the work force covered by overtime pay laws now work over 40 hours per week, up to 45 percent of "exempt" workers do (USGAO 1999). Excessive hours (49 hours or more) are well documented for higher-educated white men in their prime earning years (Coleman and Pencavel 1993a; Hedges 1993), for the highest wage-earners (Costa 1998), particularly in managerial, professional, sales, and transportation occupational classifications (Rones, Ilg, and Gardner 1997).

In contrast with the USA, annual and weekly hours in continental Western Europe declined in recent decades. Several social and institutional factors account for the cross-country differences, including statutory and collectively bargained restrictions on standard and overtime hours in the countries of the European Union. From 1960 to 1985, the Netherlands, Belgium, and West Germany experienced a reduction in annual hours of over 20 percent, even higher than the 15 percent decline for Western Europe as a whole (Di Martino 1995). The trend toward shorter hours slowed in the 1980s and early 1990s (Hart 1987; Blyton 1989; Hinrichs, Roche, and Sirianni 1991; Bosch, Dawkins and Michon 1993; ILO 1995; Rubin and Richardson 1997), as employers and government have pursued greater flexibility such as annualization of hours. In the European Union, there has been a renewed interest by governments and unions in reducing working time, largely as an employment policy tool. Some countries in western Europe are cutting the standard work week, perhaps even to a 35-hour work week, and at the same time they are closing their productivity gap with the USA.

There is evidence also of a proliferation of jobs with nonstandard hours of work and variability of scheduled hours, a departure from the historical standardization. Fewer workers work five-day work weeks, and the proportion working seven days has risen in the last thirty years (Hamermesh 1996, 1998). In the USA and throughout Europe especially, there is an increasing diversity of work patterns, across sectors, industries, and even individual workers (Hinrichs, Roche and Sirianni 1991; Bosch, Dawkins, and Michon 1993; ILO 1995; OECD 1995). Canada exhibits similar trends: declining annual hours due to increased vacations and the expansion of part-time jobs, as well as increasing diversity of work schedules (ILO 1995).

These transitions in the social organization of time raise considerable issues that remain unresolved. What are the forces behind the trends? Can working time reductions be introduced without a loss in pay? Does working time reduction stimulate employment and, if so, by how much? Do countries that have shorter work weeks enable workers to budget more time for leisure, for family, and for civic activity? Is the greater diversity in work redesign, including the proliferation of part-time and nonstandard work schedules, as helpful to workers as it appears to be for industry?

PERSPECTIVES ON TRENDS, THEORY AND POLICY

The fourteen succeeding chapters reflect the reemergence of working time as a provocative issue for both research and public policy. The issue is a focal point for discussions about social values, family dynamics, economic competitiveness, and the very nature of economic growth and development. The book is organized into three sections. Presented first are analyses of the recent trends in working time in the US and Western Europe. Section two considers both theoretical and empirical perspectives about working time. The final part evaluates innovations and prospective policies regarding working time, especially shortening the standard work week.

In "The Enigma of Working Time Trends," Barry Bluestone and Stephen Rose open the first section by demonstrating that average paid work hours in the USA have indeed risen for prime-age workers over the last two decades. The authors rely upon a resourceful longitudinal household survey, the Panel Study of Income Dynamics (PSID), plus the Current Population Survey (CPS) to portray trends in working time. They find that average hours declined significantly between 1967 and 1982, but hours have increased ever since, marking a reversal of prior trends. This escalation in annual hours is comprised of both an increase in weeks worked per worker and an increase in hours worked per year. Moreover, Bluestone and Rose view one segment of the labor force as "overemployed," consisting mainly of those possessing higher levels of education, while another is underemployed. Similar polarization of hours has been documented in Canada (Morissette, Myles and Picot 1994), where it is reinforcing rising income inequality. Bluestone and Rose suggest both may often involve the same workers, experiencing an irregular work pattern through time. Workers engage in overwork to make up for past or expected future unemployment, underemployment, or wage erosion. This leads the authors to develop a hypothesis that labor supply is increasing at the micro level, driven by greater job insecurity and lower real wage rates, contributing to the non-inflationary growth experienced in the macro economy during the 1990s.

Steffen Lehndorff continues by analyzing the pressures contributing to working time changes in the European Union in "Working Time Reduction in the European Union: A Diversity of Trends and Approaches." The author argues that in the latter half of the 1980s, the West German engineering trade union, IG Metall, provided an impetus for the 35-hour work week. Collective agreements across Europe contained provisions to shorten the work week. The movement slowed a decade later, but has reemerged due to the persistently high unemployment rates in the European Union. The newer initiatives, Lehndorff asserts, are from the state, including implementation of a statutory 35-hour work week in France. Workers in Spain, Sweden, Finland, and Denmark, for example, have called for similar responses from their own governments.[8] In addition to reductions in the working week, the author demonstrates the reorganization of working time, especially the increasing trend toward flexibilization – variable hours, nonstandard hours, and part-time work. European companies are achieving their long sought after flexibility. As in the USA, the preferences of most people in EU countries is for more flexible hours, according to a survey of working time preferences. A fundamental portion of added flexibility, however, has been the increase in part-time work for European women, although the degree varies among EU countries (O'Reilly and Fagan 1998). This is not a promising development for gender equity (see Bruegel, Figart, and Mutari 1998). A remaining priority of most people in EU countries, according to Lehndorff, is a shorter standard work week that would increase employees' time sovereignty.

One group of workers whose time demands seem to expand every year is school teachers. This is the topic explored in a case study of a major profession, "The Longest Day: Working Time for Teachers," by Robert Drago, Robert Caplan, David Costanza, Tanya Brubaker, Darnell Cloud, Naomi Harris, Russell Kashian, and T. Lynn Riggs. The authors present findings of the first detailed study of how teachers' working time is organized. Their methodology extends time diary research to include various dimensions of working time, not merely contractual time or even "face time." They find that teachers are physically present at work 30 percent more than their contractual hours of 6.5 hours per day. The total working day is longer, nearly ten hours, and even more when "work invasiveness" is considered. The authors contrast total working time for teachers who are parents and teachers who are not; teachers who are also parents have a slighter longer work day than non-parents. The authors assert that school policies need to recognize that almost half of the teacher working day is unpaid and voluntary.

In "Working Hours and Time Pressure: The Controversy About Trends in Time Use," Juliet B. Schor follows upon her important contributions to the debate over working time. Here she contrasts the methodologies of and evidence provided by household surveys and time-diaries. Specifically, she focuses on issues such as the consistency of data, sample selection issues, potential biases in responses, defining work versus non-work time, and annual versus weekly hours. She argues that, contrary to the critique of time-diary researchers, average work hours are indeed rising. This is what is driving the speed up of time experienced by a growing number of people, not a misperception due to the acceleration of technology or a growing "entitlement" mentality. The increase in work hours is crowding out time for community and children and requires policy action to achieve a more sustainable balance of time use.

The five chapters in Part Two seek to provide both empirical and theoretical foundations for the trends in overwork and underemployment. Whether it is pressure from consumerism (see also Schwartz 1994; Haight 1997), managers (see also Hochschild 1997), or fellow workers (see Eastman 1998), it is clear that a non-negligible segment of the world's labor force is overemployed while another subset is underemployed. Samuel Gompers, founder of the American Federation of Labor, was quoted as saying if one worker is unemployed then work hours are too long.

Jerry A. Jacobs and Kathleen Gerson seek to identify a source of the problem in their chapter titled "Who Are the Overworked Americans?" Relying on an international archive of data sets from industrialized countries, the Luxembourg Income Study (LIS), the authors conclude that overwork is apparent at the upper tail of the work time distribution, especially among professional and managerial workers in the USA. Long hours for both men and women are more prevalent in Australia and the USA than in all comparable countries. For a sample of US workers from the Families and Work Institute's National Study of the Changing Workforce, Jacobs and Gerson also contrast actual hours worked with "ideal" hours. The longer the average total hours usually worked, the greater is the tendency for such workers – male and female – to indicate dissatisfaction with their hours. At the lower end of the hours spectrum, though, workers are getting less than their preferred amount of work hours. Jacobs and Gerson link the rise in work hours to demographic shifts in the labor force. Specifically, between 1970 and 1997, the escalation of joint hours worked by dual earner, husband–wife families, has created time pressures; working time of male breadwinner families or families headed by women with no husband present has hardly budged.

In the following chapter, "The Incentive to Work Hard: Differences in Black and White Workers Hours and Preferences," Linda A. Bell finds that the differences in work hours between black women and white women are small, but that black men work about 20 percent fewer hours than white men. Black men are underemployed relatively more, desiring more hours than they are actually working, largely due to more limited opportunities and expectations regarding advancement. Additionally, using 1985 and 1995 CPS data, Bell tests an innovative hours–inequality hypothesis framed in earlier research on US and German workers with Richard B. Freeman (Bell and Freeman 1995): there is a strong link between individual black worker hours and earnings inequality measured at the occupational level. That is, the average hours of work and extent of underemployment in a nation, racial group, or occupation are increased by the degree of wage inequality and absence of a social safety net.

To provide a theoretical interpretation of the increase in overwork, David George's chapter, "Driven to Spend: Longer Hours as a Byproduct of Market Forces," points to the central role of shifting cultural norms. George evaluates three possible reasons for the decline in leisure. First, the minimalist explanation, based in neoclassical economic theory, offers that individuals prefer additional income to additional leisure, despite increased affluence. However, he argues that the rise in paid hours of work is more complex than this. The second two explanations are more concerned with the social context that shapes individuals' preferences. The "work-and-spend" explanation asserts that workers, pressured by employers into longer hours, became accustomed to rising material expectations. According to Schor (1991a, 1998), under the dual pressures of employers and consumerism, people have gotten into a "squirrel cage," "trapped by the cycle of work-and-spend" (Schor 1991a: 126). A "spend-and-work" hypothesis, favored by the author, suggests that modern marketing and advertising initiated the change in workers' preferences. These preferences are shaped by relentless advertising and marketing, leading workers to spend more than they initially preferred, thus raising their hours of labor supply. Utilizing the concept of "metapreferences," George argues that we do not always like our preferences; so-called workaholics wish that they wanted more leisure but are addicted to work and consumption.

Paul Burkett constructs an argument that Marx's historical examination of class struggle over the working day is relevant to today's working time issues. In "Natural, Social, and Political Limits to Work Time: The Contemporary Relevance of Marx's Analysis," Burkett draws from Marx's writings to dispute the contention that under capitalism there is a tendency toward increased leisure. Instead, the author asserts that capital infringes upon the social and natural limits to humans' capacity to work. From this theoretical analysis, Burkett draws policy implications about the need for a worker/community-based movement to promote government policies to shorten the working day. The policy implications of Burkett's chapter also share some commonalities with a "green" or environmental approach to work: "Shorter working hours with less exploitation of nature extends labour's century-long struggle for better living conditions" (Sanne 1998a: 95).

The relationship between labor time and leisure time is analyzed in a different manner by Robert E. Prasch in "Revising the Labor Supply Curve: Implications for Work Time and Minimum Wage Legislation." Prasch offers a competing explanation for the relationship between the wage and the value of leisure. Specifically, at very low wages, leisure becomes less preferable to income, forcing workers to substitute labor time for leisure. This means that a lower segment of the labor supply curve is backward-bending, or negatively sloped. Unlike George, who provides the hours-push effect of advertising and consumerism for longer hours, both Prasch and Burkett apply a model where labor suffers from an inherent disadvantage in their bargaining power relative to employers.

Part Three of the volume investigates working time innovations and public policy. Three social forces have influenced the social organization of time in the late 20th century. First, the labor-led movement for shorter hours in the European Union has achieved significant reductions in the standard work week. The latest is a legislated decrease to 35 hours in France by the year 2002, primarily as a means of worksharing, or spreading employment opportunities (see Freyssinet 1998). Second, new manufacturing technologies, a 24-hour service economy, and the globalization of organizations, production, and competition are leading employers to create more nonstandard and flexible work hour practices, more at the behest of customers than employees. Third, flexible hours scheduling at the discretion of employees has been proposed as means of enabling workers to meet their responsibilities outside of work.

Working time reduction has generally received mediocre ratings among economists in terms of its ability to generate employment. However, Gerhard Bosch regards the empirical evidence of "elasticity of employment" with respect to hours more favorably. The author reviews recent literature on the employment effects of working time reductions, effects estimated with a variety of methodologies, including case studies, econometric regression analysis, and macroeconomic simulations. He outlines the specific conditions under which working time reduction will be a successful employment policy, in the opening to Part Three, "Working Time Reductions, Employment Consequences and Lessons from Europe: Defusing a Quasi-Religious Controversy." According to Bosch, it is not just a question of whether work reorganization and/or reductions in working time create jobs, but how employment and productivity growth are generated. For example, Bosch contrasts the Netherlands, where the lion's share of working time reductions have been in the form of swelling part-time work with, for instance, Germany, Finland, Denmark, and France, who have shortened the work day or work week. Like any other employment policy instrument, working time reductions can be used successfully or unsuccessfully. By reviewing recent experiences in OECD countries in general and European countries in particular, the author evaluates the kind of policy implementation that can be productive (see also Roche, Fynes, and Morrissey 1996).

Tom Walker also defends worksharing policies from their critics. Mainstream economists accuse worksharing advocates of subscribing to an assumption that there is only a fixed amount of work to be done, "a lump of labor." The neoclassical case against shortening the work week rests on exposing this assumption as a "fallacy." In "The Perennial 'Lump of Labor' Case Against Worksharing: Populist Fallacy or Marginalist Throwback?" Walker maintains that arguments against this so-called "lump of labor," "lump of work" or "lump of output" fallacy set up a straw person. By reviewing texts from the history of economic thought, Walker deconstructs the lump of labor fallacy, tracing discussions of the controversy back over 100 years. His key point of departure from neoclassical models is that the "optimal" work week may be below the free-market established work week. Next, using a model of a production function that allows for the fact that productivity is affected by the length of the work day, the author projects the possible net employment effects of reducing working time without an assumption of a fixed amount of labor. His estimates are based upon productivity and hours in Canada and the USA. According to Walker, preoccupation with the lump of labor fallacy is unfortunate, because its reliance on simplistic textbook models and resultant short-sightedness discourages serious consideration of public policies to increase productivity and stimulate job growth.

In Lonnie Golden's chapter, "Better Timing? Work Schedule Flexibility Among US Workers and Policy Directions," the author analyzes 1997 CPS data regarding the timing of paid work activity, including the distribution of starting and ending times and whether workers are able to vary them. Flexible daily scheduling of work hours was available to only 27 percent of the US workforce, although this is a marked rise since the 1980s. There is substantial variation in access to flexibility by industry, occupation, and demographic characteristic. For example, nonwhite workers, women workers, government employees, less-educated workers, workers in the skilled construction trades, and food and building service occupations have more limited access to flexitime. Workers working the standard 40-hour work week have a significantly lower likelihood of having flexitime. In order to gain greater access to flexibility in work timing, full-time workers must put in no less than 50 hours per week. Alternatively, they would have to change job status to part-time or self-employment. Taking a cue from the European Union Work Time Directive, a policy that potentially opens the door to the annualization of hours, the US Congress continues to pursue landmark reform of working time regulation through amendments to the Fair Labor Standards Act (FLSA) that govern overtime pay and through which workers are covered by the pay premium. The author resolves that the proposals are misguided since they do not promote the kind of hours and schedule flexibility desired most by workers, more discretion over the timing of their use of compensatory (comp) time, nor a reduction in overtime hours.

The next two chapters analyze the interaction of gender relations in the household with labor market trends, highlighting the importance of looking at the distribution of paid and unpaid work within families. One model has been a perpetuated, unequal, gendered division of working time within the household, with men working full time or overtime, and women working part time, as shown in the contribution by Ellen Mutari and Deborah M. Figart. Their chapter, "The Social Implications of European Work Time Policies: Promoting Gender Equity?" demonstrates that in paid employment, it is men, for the most part, who are overworked and women who are underemployed. Mutari and Figart weave comparative scholarship on welfare state regimes with an analysis of European policies to identify four distinct regimes of work time: (1) male breadwinner; (2) liberal flexibilization; (3) solidaristic gender equity; and (4) high road flexibilization. The authors show where EU countries fit into this framework. They also identify a possible fifth type, Transitional Flexibilization, or hybrid case that appears to be in transition toward increased flexibility. They conclude that countries such as Finland, with a shorter hours standard for full-time jobs, have relatively greater gender equity.

Overwork hampers gender equity in the household and the labor force by interfering with time necessary for marriage, parenting, caregiving, community, and civic work. Laura Leete, in the final chapter, "History and Housework: Implications for Work Hours and Family Policies in Market Economies," sheds new light on the issues of time squeeze and hours of work and suggests a re-consideration of family policies. Leete does this by tracing the historical shift from home to market economic activity, including the gender division of labor. She points out that the provision of child-care does not share in the productivity increases that have occurred in most other types of economic activity. Providing child-care entails an ever-higher opportunity cost, and greater relative cost for lower income families. Leete proposes that work hours and family leave policies should be reconstructed.

European policies have been more successful than US schemes at lowering the costs incurred by families of child-care, especially care for children under five years old.

WORK TIME AS AN ISSUE FOR SOCIAL ECONOMICS

A holistic, social economics perspective recognizes that working time is influenced by and influences an array of cultural norms as well as economic forces. The supply of hours depends upon individual and joint preferences within families that reflect societal expectations, roles, and values. The decisions made by members of households generate feedback effects from peer pressure or positioning within the organization as well as organizational policies. The demand for hours is clearly related to the strategic choices and time-horizons of managers.

The repercussions of working time, especially overwork and under-employment, affect the economy and society. Longer hours can impede average productivity of labor and thus competitiveness, or restrain job creation and workers' investment in their own human capital. Too many hours or too few hours can further polarize the income distribution. Moreover, excessive work hours have been shown to have demonstrable adverse effects on physical and mental health and well-being by producing stress, illness, and unhealthy lifestyles (Sparks, Cooper, Fried and Shirom 1997). Finally, longer hours of paid work clearly must come at the expense of at least one component of non-income-producing time. If an increase in paid working time does not reduce the quantity then it must surely lower the quality of time spent off the job. Either it reduces the amount of socially productive activities, such as time for parenting, civic volunteering or life-long learning, or it diminishes non-productive leisure, such as recuperation and recreation. The social cost of overwork and time-pressured leisure will come back to haunt an entire economy, in addition to the individuals or family members who bear the brunt of it.

Developing a coherent, humanistic working time policy is therefore a pressing challenge for social economists. As social economists, our own plea is for recognizing the complex web of forces that determine paid and unpaid hours of work, and then for broader policies that acknowledge feed-back effects. A comprehensive policy could lower both the hours demanded by employers and the paid work hours deemed necessary by workers to maintain a rising standard of living. Specifically, components of such a policy might include reducing the standard work week while incorporating living wages and universal benefits, pay equity for part-time jobs, and ensuring access to quality, affordable child-care for households with children. A social economics approach would ensure that workers be able to participate in a process that affects these policy decisions about working time and labor flexibility.

NOTES

1 Among the most developed experimental programs is the Hewlett-Packard corporation. See ILO (1995: 21), Wells (1997), Saltzman (1997), Clarkberg (1999), Kaufman (1999), Greenhouse (1999), Shellenbarger (1999), and "Americans Working Longer Hours" (1999) for the anecdotal and empirical evidence introduced here.

2 These global trends are part of a new statistical study, *Key Indicators of the Labour Market*, published by the International Labour Office in 1999 (see also ILO 1995: Part II).

3 For a summary of laws in states within the USA, see Coil and Rice (1997). For a summary of cases involving the violation of overtime compensation and employee exemption rules, see US General Accounting Office (USGAO 1999).

4 See ILO (1995: 7) in particular for the risks to health and safety posed to workers by having their work hours established on an annual rather than weekly basis.

5 See Figart and Golden (1998), Table 1, for a summary of research on US trends.

6 In the USA, household surveys would include the Current Population Survey (CPS), the Panel Survey of Income Dynamics (PSID), and self-reports in the General Social Survey (GSS). With few exceptions for those using an establishment survey, data on working hours are typically collected through household or labor force surveys (see ILO 1999: Ch. 6).

7 For a further discussion of measurement issues, especially the accuracy of self-reported measures of working time, see Jacobs (1998).

8 The German case is elaborated upon in Seifert (1998). Sanne (1998b), Madsen (1998), and Peltola (1998), respectively, present the recent Swedish, Danish, and Finnish experience with working time policies.

REFERENCES

"Americans Working Longer Hours" (1999) *New York Times*: < http://www.nytimes.com/aponline/f/AP-America-the-Grindstone.html >.

Bell, L. A. and Freeman, R. B. (1995) "Why Do Americans and Germans Work Different Hours?" in F. Buttler, W. Franz, R. Schettkat, and D. Soskice (eds), *Institutional Frameworks and Labor Market Performance*, London: Routledge.

Blau, F. (1998) "Trends in the Well-Being of American Women," *Journal of Economic Literature* 36(1): 112–165.

Blyton, P. (1989) "Work Time Reductions and the European Work-Sharing Debate," in A. Gladstone (ed.), *Current Issues in Labour Relations: An International Perspective*, New York: Walter de Gruyter.

Bosch, G., Dawkins, P., and Michon, F. (eds) (1993) *Times Are Changing: Working Time in 14 Industrialised Countries*, Geneva: International Institute for Labour Studies.

Boulin, J.-Y. (1993) "The Social Organization of Time," *Futures* June: 511–520.

Bruegel, I., Figart, D., and Mutari, E. (1998) "Whose Full Employment? A Feminist Perspective on Work Redistribution," in J. Wheelock and J. Vail (eds), *Work and Idleness: The Political Economy of Full Employment*, Dordrecht: Kluwer Academic Publishers: 69–83.

Clarkberg, M. (1999) "The Time-Squeeze: Married Couples' Work-Hours Patterns and Preferences," *Proceedings of the 51st Annual Meeting*, Madison, WI: Industrial Relations Research Association: 15–23.

Coil, J. H. and Rice, C. M. (1997) "Give Me a Break! State Laws on Meal Periods, Rest Breaks and Maximum Working Hours," *Employment Relations Today*, Autumn: 113–121.

Coleman, M. T. and Pencavel, J. (1993a) "Changes in Work Hours of Male Employees, 1940–1988," *Industrial and Labor Relations Review* 46(2): 262–283.

Coleman, M. T. and Pencavel, J. (1993b) "Changes in Work Hours of Female Employees, 1940–1988," *Industrial and Labor Relations Review* 46(4): 653–676.

Costa, D. L. (1998) "The Unequal Work Day: A Long-Term View," *American Economic Review* 88(2): 330–334.

Di Martino, V. (1995) "Megatrends in Working Time," *Journal of European Social Policy* 5(3): 235–249.

Eastman, W. (1998) "Working for Position: Women, Men, and Managerial Work Hours," *Industrial Relations* 37(1): 51–66.

Figart, D. M. and Golden, L. (1998) "The Social Economics of Work Time: Introduction." *Review of Social Economy* 56(4): 411–424.

Freyssinet, J. (1998) "France: A Recurrent Aim, Repeated Near-Failures and a New Law," *Transfer* 4(4): 641–656.

Glickman, L. B. (1997) *A Living Wage: American Workers and the Making of Consumer Society*, Ithaca, NY: Cornell University Press.

Golden, L. (1990) "The Insensitive Workweek: Trends and Determinants of Average Hours in U.S. Manufacturing, 1929–1987," *Journal of Post Keynesian Economics* 13(1): 79–110.

Golden, L. (1998) "Working-Time Policy, Hours Determination, and Regulatory Reforms in the United States and Other Industrialized Countries," *International Review of Comparative Public Policy* 10: 51–75.

Golden, L. (1999) "Integrating Social Economics into Analysis of the Labor Market: Causes and Consequences of Hours of Work and Leisure as an Application," in E. O'Boyle (ed.), *Teaching the Social Economics Way of Thinking: Selected Papers from the Ninth World Congress of Social Economics*, Lewiston, NY: The Edwin Mellen Press: 423–454.

Goldin, C. (1990) *Understanding the Gender Gap: An Economic History of American Women*, New York: Oxford University Press.

Greenhouse, S. (1999) "So Much Work, So Little Time," *New York Times* (September 5, Section 4): 1, 4.

Haight, A. D. (1997) "Padded Prowess: A Veblenian Interpretation of the Long Hours of Salaried Workers," *Journal of Economic Issues* 31(1): 29–38.

Hamermesh, D. S. (1996) *Workdays, Workhours and Work Schedules: Evidence for the United States and Germany*, Kalamazoo, MI: W. E. Upjohn Institute for Employment Research.

Hamermesh, D. S. (1998) "When We Work," *American Economic Review* 88(2): 321–325.

Hart, R. A. (1987) *Working Time and Employment*, Boston: Allen and Unwin.

Heath, J. A., Ciscel, D. H., and Sharp, D. C. (1998) "The Work of Families: The Provision of Market and Household Labor and the Role of Public Policy," *Review of Social Economy* 56(4): 501–521.

Hedges, J. N. (1993) "Worktime Levels and Trends: Differences Across Demographic Groups," *Industrial Relations Research Association 45th Proceedings*: 321–329.

Hinrichs, K., Roche, W., and Sirianni, C., (eds) (1991) *Working Time in Transition: The Political Economy of Working Hours in Industrial Nations*, Philadelphia: Temple University Press.

Hochschild, A. R. (1997) *The Time Bind: When Work Becomes Home and Home Becomes Work*, New York: Metropolitan Books.

Hoffmann, R. and Fajertag, G. (1996) "Working-Time Policy in Europe," in N. Levine (ed.), *The US and the EU: Economic Relations in a World of Transition*, Lanham, MD: University Press of America: 221–235.

Hunnicutt, B. K. (1988) *Work Without End: Abandoning Shorter Hours for the Right to Work*, Philadelphia: Temple University Press.

ILO (1995) *Working Time Around the World*, Conditions of Work Digest, Vol. 14, Geneva: International Labour Office.

ILO (1999) *Key Indicators of the Labour Market*, Geneva: International Labour Office.

Jacobs, J. (1998) "Measuring Time at Work: Are Self-Reports Accurate?" *Monthly Labor Review* 121(12): 42–53.

Kaufman, L. (1999) "Some Companies Derail the 'Burnout' Track," *New York Times* (May 4).

Kniesner, T. J. (1976) "The Full-Time Workweek in the United States, 1900–1970," *Industrial and Labor Relations Review* 30(1): 3–15.

Leete, L. and Schor, J. (1994) "Assessing the Time-Squeeze Hypothesis: Hours Worked in the United States, 1969–89," *Industrial Relations* 33(1): 25–43.

Madsen, P. K. (1998) "Working Time Policy and Paid Leave Arrangements: The Danish Experience in the 1990s," *Transfer* 4(4): 692–714.

Morissette, R., Myles, J., and Picot, G. (1994) "Earnings Inequality and the Distribution of Working Time in Canada," *Canadian Business Economics* 2(3): 3–16.

Nollen, S. D. (1989) "Changes in Work Time in the United States," in A. Gladstone (ed.) *Current Issues in Labour Relations: An International Perspective*, New York: Walter de Gruyter.

Northrup, H. and Greis, T. D. (1983) "The Decline in Average Annual Hours Worked in the US, 1947–1979," *Journal of Labor Research* 4(2): 95–113.

Nyland, C. (1986) "Capitalism and the History of Worktime Thought," *British Journal of Sociology* 37(4): 513–534.

OECD (1995) *Flexible Working Time: Collective Bargaining and Government Intervention*, Paris: Organisation for Economic Co-operation and Development.

O'Reilly, J. and Fagan, C. (1998) *Part-Time Prospects: An International Comparison of Part-Time Work in Europe, North America and the Pacific Rim*, London: Routledge.

Owen, J. D. (1989) *Reduced Working Hours: Cure for Unemployment or Economic Burden?* Baltimore, MD: Johns Hopkins University Press.

Peltola, P. (1998) "Working Time Reduction in Finland," *Transfer* 4(4): 729–746.

Robinson, J. and Godbey, G. (1997) *Time For Life: The Surprising Ways Americans Use Their Time*, University Park, PA: Penn State Press.

Roche, W. K., Fynes, B., and Morrissey, T. (1996) "Working Time and Employment: A Review of International Evidence," *International Labour Review* 135(2): 129–157.

Roediger, D. R. and Foner, P. S. (1989) *Our Own Time: A History of American Labor and the Working Day*, London: Verso.

Rones, P. L., Ilg, R. E., and Gardner, J. M. (1997) "Trends in Hours of Work Since the mid-1970s," *Monthly Labor Review* 120(4): 3–14.

Rottenberg, S. (1995) "Regulation of the Hours of Work and Its 'Externalities' Defenses," *Journal of Labor Research* 16(1): 97–103.

Rubin, M. and Richardson, R. (1997) *The Microeconomics of the Shorter Working Week*, Aldershot: Ashgate.

Rupert, P. and Roberts, K. (1995) "The Myth of the Overworked American," *Economic Commentary*, Federal Reserve Bank of Cleveland, January 15: 1–4.

Saltzman, A. (1997) "When Less Is More," *U.S. News & World Report* (October 27): 79–84.

Sanne, C. (1998a) "A Green Approach to Work and Idleness," in J. Wheelock and J. Vail (eds), *Work and Idleness: The Political Economy of Full Employment*, Dordrecht: Kluwer Academic Publishers: 85–96.

_____ (1998b) "The Working Hours Issue in Sweden," *Transfer* 4(4): 715–728.

Schor, J.B. (1991a) *The Overworked American: The Unexpected Decline of Leisure*, New York: Basic Books.

_____ (1991b) "Global Equity and Environmental Crisis: An Argument for Reducing Working Hours in the North," *World Development* 19(1): 73–84.

_____ (1998) *The Overspent American*, New York: Basic Books.

Schwartz, B. (1994) *The Costs of Living: How Market Freedom Erodes the Best Things in Life*, New York: Norton.

Seifert, H. (1998) "Working Time Policy in Germany: Searching for New Ways," *Transfer* 4(4): 621–640.

Shellenbarger, S. (1999) "Are Saner Workloads Key to Greater Productivity?" *The Wall Street Journal* (March 10).

Sparks, K., Cooper, C., Fried, Y., and Shirom, A. (1997) "The Effects of Hours of Work on Health: A Meta-Analytic Review," *Journal of Occupational and Organizational Psychology* 70: 391–408.

Takagi, I. (1993) "Japan," in G. Bosch, P. Dawkins, and F. Michon (eds), *Times Are Changing: Working Time in 14 Industrialised Countries*, Geneva: International Institute for Labour Studies: 213–228.

Thompson, E. P. (1967) "Time, Work-Discipline, and Industrial Capitalism," *Past and Present* 38: 56–97.

Tilly, C. (1996) *Half a Job: Bad and Good Part-Time Jobs in a Changing Labor Market*, Philadelphia: Temple University Press.

USGAO (1999) *Fair Labor Standards Act: White Collar Exemptions in the Modern Work Place*, GAO/HEHS-99-164, Report to the Subcommittee on Workforce Protections, Committee on Education and the Workforce, US House of Representatives, September, United States General Accounting Office.

van Ginneken, W. (1984) "Employment and the Reduction of the Work Week: A Comparison of Seven European Macro-Economic Models," *International Labour Review* 123(1): 35–52.

Wells, S. J. (1997) "Honey, They've Shrunk the Workweek," *New York Times* (June 15): Sec. 3.

Wikander, U., Kessler-Harris, A., and Lewis, J., (eds) (1995) *Protecting Women: Labor Legislation in Europe, the United States, and Australia*, 1880–1920, Urbana, IL: University of Illinois Press.

Winston, G. C. (1966) "An International Comparison of Income and Hours of Work," *Review of Economics and Statistics* 48: 28–39.

Yates, M. (1994) *Longer Hours, Fewer Jobs*, New York: Monthly Review Press.

Part I

Current trends and patterns in work hours

What is the evidence?

2 The enigma of working time trends

Barry Bluestone and Stephen Rose

Beginning in the 1980s, there was a growing sense that Americans were working "too much." Juliet Schor's book *The Overworked American* tapped into a strong popular sentiment, becoming the unusual economics book to reach the best-seller list. In it, she estimated that Americans worked an average of 163 more hours a year in 1990 than they had in 1970 – the equivalent of nearly an extra month of full-time work (Schor 1991). Men were working two and a half more weeks per year and women an average of seven and a half more weeks. This increase reversed over a century of declining working time.[1] Many people identified with the quandary of spending more and more time on the job, with too few hours left in the day for family and chores. Workers were being tuckered out, if not burned out, by the sheer amount of time on the job. Children and community were suffering as a consequence. Few knew how to get off the treadmill of having to work long hours to support the lifestyle to which they aspired.

But, other labor market phenomena have also filled the headlines: corporate downsizing has undermined long-term job stability; the average work week reported by employers is down; and more workers have alternative working arrangements as part-timers, contract workers, employees of temp firms, and as multiple-job holders. For some, these are indications that workers are having trouble finding full-time jobs that they would want to keep indefinitely.

So, are workers over- or underworked? Or, maybe some workers are overworked and others are underworked? Or, perhaps some workers go through alternating years of short hours and years of long hours? In this last scenario, the same individuals face both underemployment and overworking at different points in their careers. These are some of the questions we will address in this chapter.

IS AVERAGE WORKING TIME RISING OR FALLING IN THE USA?

Research by Larry Mishel and Jared Bernstein of the Economic Policy Institute support Schor's claims of increased *annual* working hours, but

Table 2.1 Average weekly hours, total private sector employment

1947–1958	39.5
1959–1972	38.2
1973–1978	36.2
1979–1988	35.0
1989–1996	34.5

Source: Bureau of Labor Statistics.

for a comparable period (1973–1992) their estimate is only three-fifths as large as Schor's 163 hours (Mishel and Bernstein 1994). Hence, annual average hours had risen to 1 759, an increase of 100 hours or 6 percent – 63 hours less than Schor's estimate. *Three-quarters* of the increase, they estimate, can be attributed to more weeks worked per year; one-quarter to increased hours per week.

Some researchers suggest no such increase in working time has actually occurred. Employer surveys – the very ones the Bureau of Labor Statistics use to measure working time when it reports the monthly unemployment rate each month – show weekly hours in manufacturing and weekly hours in the rest of the economy going in opposite directions. It is true that in much of manufacturing the use of overtime is becoming the norm. But, as Table 2.1 shows, average weekly hours for the entire private sector workforce have actually declined steadily from 39.5 hours (1947–1958) to 34.5 hours (1989–1997). Shorter work weeks in services and retail trade have more than offset increases in overtime in manufacturing.

Moreover, data from "diary" studies, where respondents keep 24-hour time diaries of everything they do, suggest no historical increase in work time at all (Robinson and Bostrom 1994). Using the diary studies for 1965, 1975, and 1985, which are presumably more accurate than CPS estimates because they rely less on recall, Robinson and Bostrom find a systematic increase in the size of the CPS-diary hours gap over time. The gap rises from just 1 hour in 1965 to 4 hours in 1975 to 6 hours in 1985. This increase is allegedly large enough to account for the "overwork" that Schor and Mishel and Bernstein claim.

But neither the employer surveys nor the diary studies are definitive themselves. Since the employer surveys count the hours on individual jobs, the hours worked by multiple-job holders and those who supplement regular work with self-employment are not measured. If a worker loses a full-time 40-hour a week job and takes two 25 hour part-time jobs in its place, the employer survey would signal shorter average working time while the CPS would signal just the opposite. As for the diary surveys, even if they do produce a more accurate count of weekly hours, they do not measure weeks worked. Thus, the diary estimates cannot be used for measuring changes in annual hours. Finally, diary studies in their quest for accuracy count workers talking at the water cooler with coworkers as time not working. This rather unusual procedure is inconsistent with the more commonsense approach that working consists of time spent at the job or at the workplace.

Trends in work hours

One of the standard sources for most labor market studies is the annual Census Bureau's March Current Population Survey (CPS). Approximately 60 000 households are surveyed and asked detailed questions about their last year's employment, family status, and income. However, prior to 1974, the normal weekly working hours question was based on a categorical answer (e.g., from 30 hours to 40 hours per week) rather than a single figure. Therefore we can not construct a time series on annual hours worked prior to 1974 using the CPS. However, in previous research, we showed that the Panel Study on Income Dynamics (PSID) gives consistent results with the CPS on the reporting of annual hours worked. Given this close relationship, we are able to combine data from the two surveys to produce a single series for 1967 through 1996. Through 1974, the series is based on PSID; the remainder of the series is taken from CPS. Based on this concatenated data set, Figure 2.1 tracks the working time of the prime age workforce.

The data reveal two distinct trends in annual hours since the late 1960s. While there is a clear cyclical component in the data, there is a sharp decline in annual hours from 1967 through 1982 and thereafter an even sharper monotonic increase through the business cycle peak in 1989. Following a brief dip during the 1990–1991 recession, the growth in hours began to climb

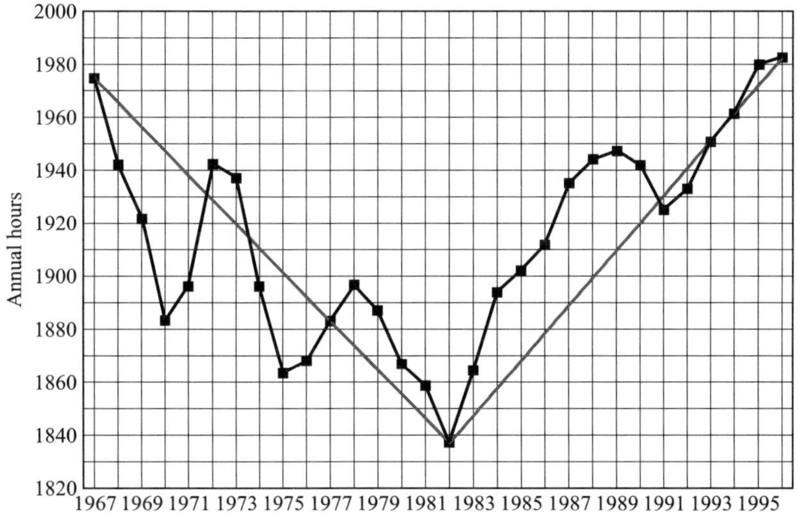

Figure 2.1 Working time as average annual hours for the prime-age workforce (age 25–54) for the years 1967–1996. (Source: Panel Study on Income Dynamics 1967–1974 and Current Population Survey 1975–1996.)

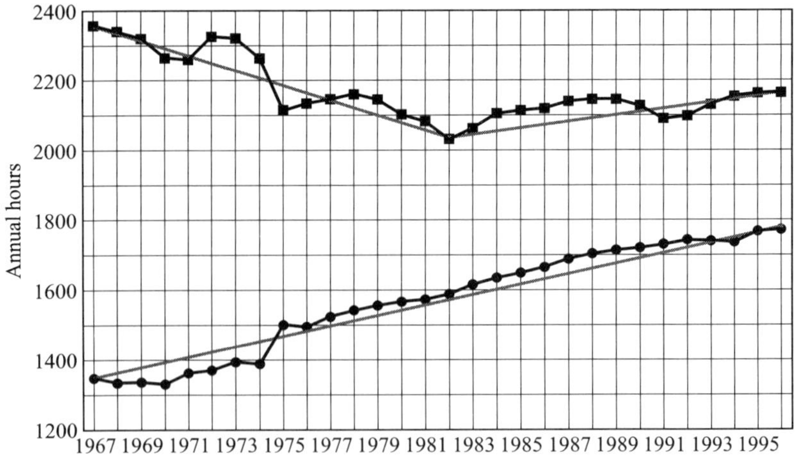

Figure 2.2 Trends in average annual hours worked by men (■) and women (●) of prime age (25–54) between 1967 and 1996. (Source: Panel Study on Income Dynamics 1967–1974 and Current Population Survey 1975–1996.)

again. In 1996, average annual hours reached a new peak, surpassing its 1967 level. Since the last business cycle peak in 1989, annual hours have increased by another 35 hours – a 1.8 percent increase in labor supply from incumbent workers. The upward trend in working time shows no sign of reversing.

Decomposing this trend, we find that the overall decline in annual hours from 1967 through 1982 was due to a collapse in men's hours that could not be fully offset by increases in those of women. After 1982, however, even men's hours began to increase and they continued to do so right through the 1989–1996 period. Since 1989, the average men's work year has increased by 20 hours – half a full-time equivalent employee (FTE) work week or 0.9 per cent, while women's annual hours continued to increase at a rapid pace. Just between 1989 and 1996, the average work year for women increased by 61 hours or 3.4 percent. Furthermore, there was a sharp cyclical recovery in men's hours since the recession of 1991–1992. These series are depicted in Figure 2.2.

Changes in annual hours can be decomposed into two components: (1) changes in annual weeks worked and (2) changes in average hours worked per week. The former includes the effect of changes in the official unemployment rate while the latter does not. As we have measured them here, weekly hours are estimated only for those who are already counted as employed. In the 1970s, the average weeks worked per year of prime age workers bounced between 45.5 and 46.0. After the recession of 1981–1982, weeks of work per year rose steadily to 47.1 in 1989. After another dip during the 1990–1991 recession, weeks worked continued to rise to 47.8. In other words, over the last 20 years, each worker has averaged an additional 2 weeks worked per year.

The same pattern is also evident with average weekly hours of prime-age workers. In the late 1970s, each worker spent about 40.2 hours on the job. This fell to 39.5 hours during the recession of 1981–1982. During the economic expansion through 1989, weekly hours increased by 0.16 hour per year reaching 40.7 in 1989. The recession that followed interrupted this upward trend, but it continued after 1991 to reach almost 41 hours per week.

Increased work effort in the total workforce

To this point, we have focused attention on the prime-age workforce, age 25–54, in order to assure that estimates of changes in working time were independent of changes in the age composition of the workforce. However, measuring work time trends among *all workers* is important for studies of the macro economy.

As Figure 2.3 demonstrates, the 1975–1996 trend in weekly hours for all workers age 16 and older closely resembles the trends we found for prime-age workers. Weekly hours have expanded from a low of 37.6 in 1982 to a present level of close to 39. From a labor supply perspective, this is equivalent to increasing the number of workers in the economy by 3.6 percent. Given that the workforce was just about 100 million strong in 1982, this increase in weekly hours represents approximately the same addition to labor supply as if we had added 3.6 million new workers to the total workforce – or had reduced the official unemployment rate by 3.6 percentage points. Between 1982 and 1996, the workforce as conventionally measured

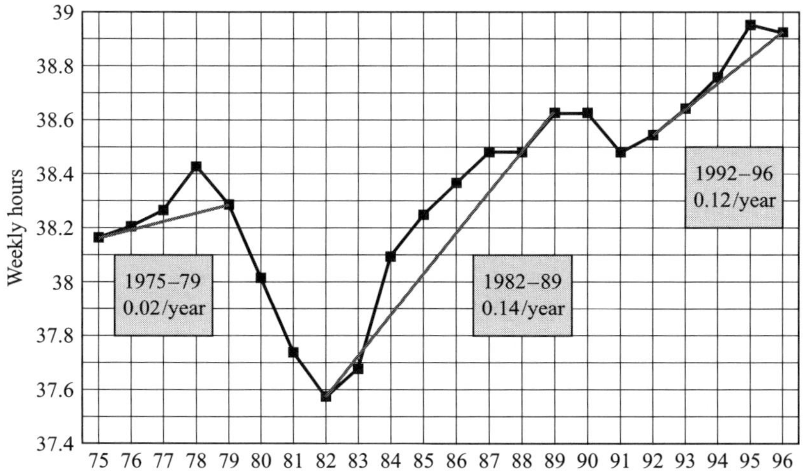

Figure 2.3 Trend in average weekly hours of all workers (16+) between 1975 and 1996. (Source: Current Population Survey 1975–1996.)

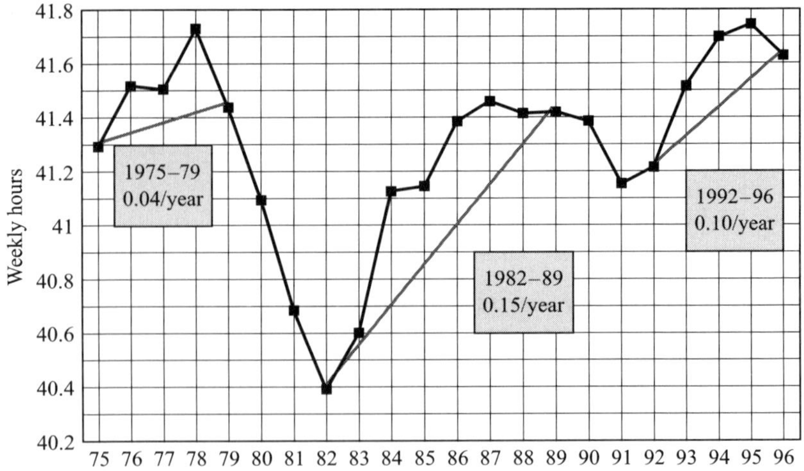

Figure 2.4 Trend in average weekly hours worked by men of all ages (16+) between 1975 and 1996. (Source: Current Population Survey 1975–1996.)

increased by 27.2 million. Hence, the increase in weekly hours among incumbent workers was equivalent to about 13 percent of the hours available from new workers. This is hardly a trivial amount, yet it is overlooked in measures of labor supply based on official unemployment rates.

The weekly hours trends for the past three recoveries are also depicted in this figure. Note that in the 1975–1979 recovery, weekly hours increased by only 0.02 hour per year. In the subsequent recovery (1982–1989), the rate increased to 0.14 hour per year. Finally, in the current recovery, weekly work time has been rising at 0.12 hour per year. Again, the evidence is consistent with a labor supply regime change beginning in the 1980s and continuing right up to the present.

For men, the hours recovery since 1982 is particularly noteworthy. By 1996, the average work week was back up to the peak level reached in 1979 – 41.6 hours (see Figure 2.4). In the current recovery, weekly hours are increasing by 1/10 of an hour per year, about double the rate of the 1970s expansion. For women, there has been a nearly continuous increase in weekly hours. Despite reports of women reaching a plateau in terms of labor force participation and workforce attachment, the shift from part-time to full-time work seems to continue – although not as strongly as during the 1982–1989 period (see Figure 2.5).

There is a distinct racial and ethnic pattern to the weekly hours trend as well. Non-Hispanic whites, non-Hispanic blacks, and Hispanics have all seen increases in the length of their work weeks, but at different rates. Whites still work the longest work week, but the gap between whites and blacks is closing. In 1975, whites worked 1.6 hours more per week than blacks; by

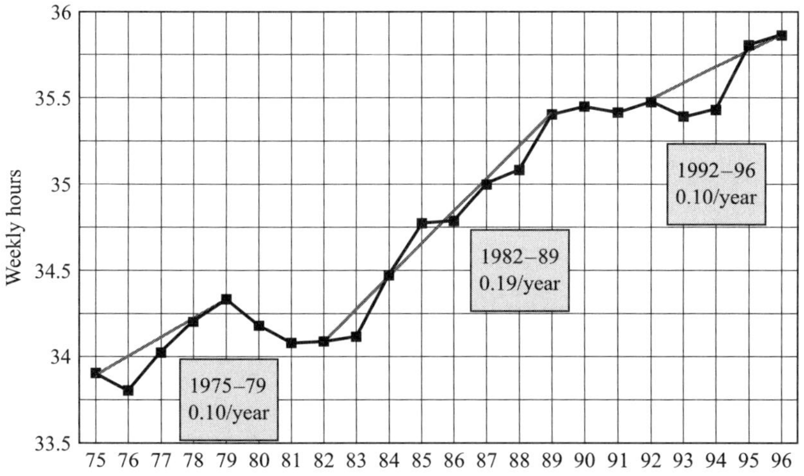

Figure 2.5 Trend in average weekly hours worked by women of all ages (16+) between 1975 and 1996. (Source: Current Population Survey 1975–1996.)

1996, the gap had closed by more than half to 0.64 hour. Hispanics had the slowest increase in weekly hours, having started out at the white level. They kept pace with whites throughout most of the period, but began to fall behind after 1989. This may reflect recent immigration patterns and, as we shall presently demonstrate, the role of education.

In terms of educational attainment, the general pattern is that the more educated the worker, the longer the work week. College educated workers averaged 41.8 hours per week in 1996 compared to only 35.1 hours for high school dropouts. High school graduates and those with 1–3 years of college fell near the middle of these two extremes. These results help explain the overall upward trend in weekly hours. As the labor force has become better educated, a larger proportion of the workforce falls into schooling categories which normally work longer hours. By 1996, 25 percent of the workforce had a college degree. By contrast, back in 1975, only 16.1 percent was this well educated. If the level of education had not increased over these 20 years, average work time would have increased by only about 9 minutes (from 38.16 to 38.31 hours) between 1975 and 1996.[2] As is, the actual increase in work time was 45 minutes. Hence, 80 percent of the long-run increase in average weekly hours over the past 20 years can be associated with the increased education level of the workforce. Schooling not only contributes to faster economic growth by improving labor productivity, but by adding to the overall level of labor supply.

The contribution of increased education to increased weekly hours varies substantially across the last three business cycles. During the 1975–1979 recovery, nearly 90 percent (88.5 percent) of the small total (7 minutes)

Table 2.2 Sources of additional hours of work: total added hours of work due to these factors

Period	*Changes in population*	*Changes in labor force participation rate*	*Changes in the unemployment rate*	*Changes in average hours worked per week*	*Change in total hours worked*
1975–1979	51.0%	27.2%	19.7%	2.2%	100%
1982–1989	41.4%	19.7%	24.6%	14.2%	100%
1992–1996	51.2%	7.6%	28.8%	12.4%	100%

Source: *Economic Report of the President* (*ERP* 1997); special tabulations on hours from Current Population Survey data.

increase in the average workweek is associated with rising schooling levels. This leaves very little of the increase to be explained by other factors, including worker response to changing wage rates or expectations about job insecurity. In the two most recent recoveries, however, these other factors clearly dominate. Only 17 percent of the 65 minutes total increase in weekly hours between 1982 and 1989 can be attributed to rising education levels. In the most recent recovery, only 22 percent of the total 25 minutes increase is associated with schooling. Thus, while over the long run, education plays a critical role in explaining increased labor supply, in the short run other factors are more important. Stagnating wages and increased job security are natural candidates.

The growing importance of work hours as a factor in total hours worked in the economy is revealed in Table 2.2. Here the total number of additional hours supplied to the labor market during the past three expansionary cycles is decomposed into four factors: (1) the growth in the civilian population age 16 and above; (2) changes in labor force participation; (3) changes in the unemployment rate; and (4) changes in average weekly hours per worker as estimated in this chapter.[3]

According to this analysis, somewhere between two-fifths and half of the additional work hours worked during the past three expansionary periods were supplied as a result of simple population growth. This increase in supply is, of course, independent of the business cycle. The contributions of the other three elements, however, vary over the cycle and have varied rather dramatically in their relative importance from one period to the next. More than a fourth of the additional hours worked in the 1970s can be attributed to increases in labor force participation. By the 1990s, this source accounted for less than 5 percent of the total additional hours. After decades of rising participation rates, particularly as a result of increased women's participation, the trajectory reached a plateau in the first years of the current recovery. It has only begun to grow again at a faster pace in 1996 and 1997.

In sharp contrast, the role of declining unemployment and, even more importantly, average weekly hours, has increased remarkably over time. In the late 1970s, less than one-fifth of additional work time was due to workers being called back to work from unemployment. By the 1990s, this one factor accounted for nearly a third of the addition to total work time. The increased contribution from longer work weeks was even more significant. In the 1970s growth cycle, practically none of the total increase in work time came from existing workers putting in more hours. But in the next two business cycle recoveries, in the 1980s and 1990s, more than one-eighth of the additional labor supply came from incumbent workers. Together, the combined contribution of unemployed workers returning to work and incumbent workers putting in longer work weeks is accounting for *over two-fifths* of the increased labor supply, helping to sustain non-inflationary economic growth in the early 1990s.

Back in the 1970s, these two factors accounted for only about *one-fifth* of the total – the rest coming from new labor force participants. This is the essence of the labor supply regime shift we have witnessed over the past two decades. We are now obtaining much more labor supply from experienced workers rather than new labor force recruits *and* a good share of this added supply is forthcoming when the official unemployment rate signals little slack in the economy.

Family working time and earnings

We have also investigated what has happened to family work time and family earnings. In this case, we began by estimating the combined hours of work for "prime age" families in which both husband and wife were working.[4] There was, as expected, a clear and nearly unbroken trend toward much greater work effort, interrupted only modestly by the recessions of 1971, 1974–1975, and 1980–1982. By 1988, prime-age working couples were putting in an average of 3 450 hours per year in combined employment, up from 2 850 two decades before.[5]

This increase equals approximately 32 hours *per year* more working time each year during the 1970s and 1980s – the equivalent of adding nearly another month of full-time work *effort* every five years (160 hours). Hence, in the span of just two decades, working husband–wife couples increased their *annual* market work input by a cycle-adjusted 684 hours or *four months* of full-time work. Put still another way, the typical dual-earner couple at the end of the 1980s was spending an additional day and half on the job *every week*.

Increases in family work effort were found to differ significantly by race and by education. The increase in working hours among white working couples was 60 percent larger than the increase for black couples – a reflection of both the sharp decline in black men's hours at least through the late 1980s and the large increase in white female work effort. More educated working couples also increased their work effort more than those with less schooling. Those in which the husband had at least a four-year college degree increased their combined work effort by nearly 730 hours compared

Table 2.3 Percentage growth in annual hours worked versus percentage change in real annual earnings, prime-age working husband–wife couples, 1973–1988

	All	*White*	*Black*	*HS dropouts*	*HS grads*	*Some college*	*BA+*
Hours	16.3	17.1	11.8	11.6	16.1	17.4	16.6
Real earnings	18.5	19.8	15.8	−8.2	3.7	3.8	32.5
"Family" hourly wage	1.8	2.2	3.6	−17.7	−10.7	−11.5	13.6

Source: Authors' calculations based on data from the Panel Study on Income Dynamics.

to an increase of only 490 hours for couples headed by a high school dropout.

How much did this enormous increase in work effort pay off in terms of increased family earnings? Are families working longer hours to improve their standard of living, or simply to maintain it? The results for this inquiry are found in Table 2.3. Here the growth in real combined earnings is compared to the change in combined work hours for the period 1973 to 1988.[6]

For prime-age working couples as a group, combined real earnings rose by 18.5 percent between 1973 and 1988. (This represents an increase from $43 851 to $51 955 in 1991 dollars). These families saw their material standard of living increase by just a little bit better than 1 percent per year. Most of this modest increase, however, did not come from improved wages, but from increased work effort. The 18.5 percent increase in real earnings was purchased with a 16.3 percent increase in hours worked. Over the entire sixteen year period, the combined average husband–wife hourly wage increased by only 1.8 percent – the equivalent of a real hourly wage increase of less than 2 cents each year! From a purely material perspective, the "average" working family with two earners appears to have been able to increase its consumption over time, but only by working much longer to enjoy what is basically a modest improvement in the amount of goods and services they can buy. The story is much the same for both white and black families, with real earnings rising but chiefly because of increased work effort.

However, when the data are disaggregated by education group, we find an even more telling story than that of workers sacrificing family time in order to indulge in a cornucopia of material consumption. For all families – with the notable exception of those headed by a worker with at least a college degree – the enormous increase in work effort over the past twenty years has accomplished no more than permit families to maintain their *old* standard of living. For high school dropout families, the situation has been even tougher. Between 1973 and 1988, these families increased their annual work effort by nearly 12 percent yet ended up with 8 percent *less* annual income. For families headed by high school graduates or some college, work effort was up by 16–17.4 percent. All of these added hours of work left such families with less than a 4 percent increase in total earnings. These families are trapped in an Alice in Wonderland world, running faster and faster just to stay in the same place. For all of these families, the "family" hourly wage has fallen precipitously, by as much as 17 percent in the case of the high school dropout.

The one great exception to the Alice in Wonderland world is found among families headed by a college graduate. These families increased their work effort by about the same percentage as those headed by high school graduates or those with some college. But this added work effort paid off, permitting their material consumption standard to increase by nearly a full third between 1973 and 1988. In this one case, hard work apparently has its reward. Unfortunately, such well-educated families comprise less than a third (31 percent) of all families. For most other families, the increase in work time can be understood as a response to falling wage rates – evidence of workers exhibiting behavior consistent with being on the backward bending portion of the labor supply curve.

VARIATION IN WORKING TIME AND JOB INSECURITY

In the previous section, we showed how families increased their working time in response to stagnant and falling male wage rates. Another reason for working longer is that workers face greater job instability – they might voluntarily work as much overtime as they can when work *is available* in order to cushion the blow of depressed income when joblessness strikes. To answer this question, we turn to the full longitudinal capacity of the PSID.

Working in a longitudinal mode requires making a number of decisions about how to classify individuals, for their status can change over time. Individuals marry and divorce, for example. Over a ten year period, how should one classify an individual who was single for 6 years and married for 4? An individual's occupation and industry may change over time. In what labor market categories should we place them? An individual's income changes over time. In what quintile should we place an individual? Essentially, what would be point estimates in cross-section data become ranges in longitudinal data sets.

For the purposes at hand, we separate the PSID into two 10-year time frames corresponding to the 1970s (1969–1979) and the 1980s (1979–1989). Both of these 10-year periods had similar growth rates in real output per person and in job creation, and each encompasses two complete business cycles. This helps make for an appropriate comparison. We restrict our analysis to prime-age workers in order to exclude those who would normally be moving from part-time work to full-time work as they leave school and those who might be moving from full-time work to part-time work as they approach retirement. Given the longitudinal nature of the

Table 2.4 "Strong" employment continuity in the 1970s and 1980s (in percent) – men

	1970s	*1980s*
All	79	71
Race		
White	79	71
Black	73	51
Education		
HS dropout	52	30
HS graduate	84	72
Some college	87	70
College graduate +	77	79
10-year earnings quintile		
Lowest	52	30
Fourth	76	66
Middle	82	75
Second	90	87
Top	94	91

Source: Rose (1994).

data, our analysis of each decade is restricted to individuals who began at age 24–48 and ended the decade aged 34–58.

Our first task here is to investigate continuity of employment – the ability to hold a full-time, full-year job consistently over 10 years. We define "strong continuity" as working at least 1 750 hours (50 weeks at 35 hours per week) in eight out of ten years and never working less than 1 000 hours in any single year. Using this definition, the results are very clear. Job stability is declining. In the 1970s, 79 percent of prime-age men met this criteria, but only 71 percent did so in the 1980s (see Table 2.4).

Individual demographic groups had varying degrees of employment continuity, but for every group *except* college graduates continuity declined between the 1970s and the 1980s. The decline for black prime-age men was the most precipitous, from 73 percent to 51 percent, indicating that nearly half of these men either had a year in which they worked less than half-time (<1 000 hours) or had at least three years out of ten in which they worked only part-time (<35 hours/week on average). Persistent low-earners (those with 10-year earnings histories putting them in the lowest earnings quintile) went from over one in two having strong continuity to under one in three. Finally, the share of high school dropouts with strong attachment declined from 68 percent to 51 percent. These declines show the added difficulty faced by men at the lower end of the labor force distribution, a finding fully consistent with other studies showing a sharp deterioration in the labor market fortunes of less-educated men in general (Mishel and Bernstein 1994; Bluestone 1990a,b; Levy and Murnane 1992).

For women, the 10-year analytical approach accentuates the difference they have from men in terms of their labor force attachment (see Table 2.5). In the

Table 2.5 "Strong" and "weak" employment continuity in the 1970s and 1980s (in percent) – women

	Strong		*Weak*	
	1970s	*1980s*	*1970s*	*1980s*
All	11	20	59	38
Race				
White	10	20	61	39
Black	13	22	48	33
Education				
HS dropout	8	13	65	56
HS graduate	12	22	60	38
Some college	15	25	56	35
College grad +	8	19	48	29
Marital status				
Never married	29	35	33	20
Sometimes	13	24	45	26
Always married	8	15	67	48

Source: Rose (1994).

1970s, prime-age women averaged only 870 hours of paid labor per year. This level increased to 1 243 hours per year in the 1980s but still lagged considerably behind the male average of over 2 100 hours. In the 1970s only one in nine prime-age women met the criteria of strong labor market continuity. By the 1980s, this ratio had risen to one in five.

Another way of measuring the degree of labor force participation of prime-age workers is to define "weak continuity" as working full-time, full-year in three or fewer years and working less than 1 000 hours in each of five or more years during a decade. Only 2 percent of prime-age men in the 1970s had such little labor force activity and only 4 percent in the 1980s. For prime-age women, by contrast, nearly three out of five had this low level of labor market participation in the 1970s. That is, by the definition we have adopted here, nearly 60 percent of women would be considered "part-time" in the 1970s. Only a decade later, this proportion had plummeted to 38 percent. The important story here is that the overall supply of labor in the USA has increased sharply, not only because of the rising labor force participation rates of women, but also because many more of the women participating in the workforce are now working full-time. This critical shift in labor supply regime is missed in the standard measures of participation and unemployment rates.[7]

Furthermore, greater job instability may be accompanied by more variance in hours worked – a "feast or famine" phenomenon in working time. In this case, increased job insecurity could explain a number of labor market phenomena: increased voluntary overtime, increased moonlighting; *and* higher rates of underemployment. Job instability may mean that the same Americans are both overworked *and* underemployed.

To examine this possibility, we estimate the proportion of workers who experience large year-to-year variation in annual hours worked (see

Table 2.6 HiLo analysis of hours variance for individual workers – men

	% of individuals in group with at least one year >2 400 hours and at least one year <1 750 hours		
	1970s	*1980s*	*% Difference*
All	26.4	28.5	7.9
Race			
White	25.7	27.9	8.5
Black	37.1	37.2	0.3
Education			
HS dropout	32.1	38.2	19.0
HS graduate	22.5	24.7	10.2
Some college	31.0	28.6	−7.7
College graduate +	22.9	26.6	16.1
Earnings quintile			
Lowest Q	41.6	39.2	−5.8
Fourth Q	35.6	37.3	4.6
Middle Q	25.3	28.6	13.1
Second Q	19.2	21.3	10.7
Top Q	10.4	16.3	56.6

Source: Authors' calculations based on data from the Panel Study on Income Dynamics.

Table 2.6). We defined a "HiLo" statistic to measure the proportion of individuals in a demographic group who, during a decade, experience at least one year in which they work more than 2 400 hours and at least one year of 1 750 hours or less. The Hi value is equivalent to an average work week of approximately 46 hours or more. The Lo value is equivalent to less than 35 hours per week. These cutoffs were arbitrarily set, but correspond to a reasonable definition of "overtime" work and "part-time" work.[8]

Among all prime-age males, more than 28 percent experienced substantial year-to-year variation in hours worked during the 1980s. Nearly three out of ten workers had at least one year of substantial "overtime" (>46 hours/week) and at least one year of significant "underemployment" (<35 hours/week) during the 1980s. Compared to the 1970s, the proportion of such individuals experiencing such hours variation was up by nearly 8 percent.

For black men, the incidence of HiLo variation is substantially higher than among white men, with well more than one-third of all black men experiencing this type of "feast and famine" working hours. While white men experience less inter-year variation in hours worked, over the two decades they moved closer to the black average. Those who have completed a high school diploma or college degree appear to experience less hours variation than those who drop out of high school or do not complete college. But by the far the strongest correlates with elevated inter-year hours variation can be found in terms of earnings levels and number of job changes. Among those with the lowest average quintile earnings, four out of ten experience HiLo hours variation – more than double those in the top quintile. Simply put, those who confront "feast and famine" work experience are more likely to have low average earnings. Similarly, those who change employers often face the highest rates of HiLo activity. More than half of prime-age men who change employers at least four times in a decade end up with years of "overtime" and years of "underemployment."

Which men have experienced the greatest *increases* in hours variation? According to Table 2.6, there is no clear pattern. High school dropouts have clearly seen a substantial rise in HiLo activity between the two decades. But so have college graduates and the top quintile earners. One might conjecture from these findings that those with the fewest skills and those in the ranks of middle managers have been particular victims of downsizing. Future research with the PSID should be able to provide more evidence to test this hypothesis.

The HiLo analysis does not apply as well to women because so few of them meet the high criteria of working more than 2 400 hours in a year. Virtually all prime-age women have some years with fewer than 1 750 hours, and therefore the increase in their HiLo value from 12 percent in the 1970s to 21 percent in the 1980s is the result of more women having at least some years with very high working hours. The differences among women by race and education were not large, and the key change for women was the decrease in the amount of time they left the labor market for child-rearing. Therefore, their yearly variation in hours worked in the 1980s was actually considerably less than the corresponding figure in the 1970s.

CONCLUSION

There has been much controversy in the last decade over Schor's research showing that Americans were working 163 hours more in 1990 than in 1970. In our approach, average annual hours worked of prime-age workers in the labor force at some point during a calendar year decreased steadily from 1967 to 1982 and then rebounded thereafter to return to its original level in 1995. For men, the decline through 1982 was much greater than the increase in the ensuing years. Women's experiences were different, with a trend that was basically montonic – increasing in virtually every year through 1995.

Where the overworked theme is most clearly evident is in families. Our data show a remarkable 600 hour increase in the joint working time of husband–wife couples in which they both worked during the course of the year. How much of this was voluntary and how much was driven by the labor market difficulties of many men (shorter hours and lower pay) can not be known with certainty. But we do show that the family average wage decreased for all families except for those headed by someone with at least a four-year degree. This gives some credence to the notion that many working wives increased their time in the paid labor force to maintain rather than improve the family's standard of living.

We also showed various ways in which hours worked varied considerably from year to year. Comparing the 1980s with the 1970s, fewer prime-age men (particularly African Americans) were able to consistently work full-time, full-year. In addition, greater than one in four men had at least one year of long hours and one year of short hours. We speculate that this boom and bust pattern accentuates the desire to accept overtime hours when they are available. This may help explain why the current low unemployment rate has not resulted in high inflation. Increased labor demand has been met by the increased supply of those willing to work longer hours.

In any case, the long-term trend of translating economic growth at least partially into shorter working time has been reversed. American workers seem committed to putting in long hours and demanding less vacation time than their European or Japanese counterparts. Not surprisingly, a recent ILO study found that Americans worked more hours per year than workers in other countries: while Americans worked 1 966 hours per year, Canadians put in only 1 732 hours, the hardworking Japanese 1 889 hours, the British 1 731, the French 1 656, and the Germans only 1 560. So, when many commentators clamor about the success of the "American model," perhaps they should temper their enthusiasm given the high level of working time we are forced to bear in order to achieve our economic "success."

NOTES

1 According to a recent survey by the British news magazine *The Economist*, Americans have now surpassed even the Japanese in annual work time, and toil 15 percent longer than the typical German. See "Workaholics Anonymous: Why do Americans work so hard?" *The Economist*, October 22, 1994, p. 20.

2 This value was calculated by weighting the 1995 weekly hours for each education group by the 1975 share of the workforce in each of these education groups. The difference between the actual 1995 weekly hours estimate and this 1975 education-weighted 1995 weekly hours estimate was then divided by the actual weekly hours increase between 1975 and 1995. This yields the percentage associated with increased education level (80.8 percent).

3 This analysis was carried out by decomposing the changes in total hours of work according to the following formulas:

Added hours due to changes in population growth:

$$\text{Pop}_{(t-(t-1))} \times \text{LFPR}_{t-1} \times (1 - \text{UR}_{t-1}) \times (\text{HRS/Worker})_{t-1}$$

Added hours due to changes in the labor force participation rate:

$$\text{LFPR}_{(t-(t-1))} \times \text{Pop}_{t-1} \times (1 - \text{UR}_{t-1}) \times (\text{HRS/Worker})_{t-1}$$

Added hours due to changes in the unemployment rate:

$$(1 - \text{UR})_{(t-(t-1))} \times \text{Pop}_{t-1} \times \text{LFPR}_{t-1} \times (\text{HRS/Worker})_{t-1}$$

Added hours due to changes in hours worked per worker:

$$(\text{HRS/Worker})_{(t-(t-1))} \times \text{Pop}_{t-1} \times \text{LFPR}_{t-1} \times (1 - \text{UR})_{t-1}$$

Here Pop = civilian noninstitutional population, LFPR = labor force participation rate, UR = unemployment rate, and HRS/Worker = average annual hours worked per worker.

4 This analysis is limited to intact husband–wife families in which the husband is "prime-age" (age 25–54) and in which both husband and wife worked at least 1 hour in the survey year.

5 Because of incomplete family hours and earnings data for 1989 in the PSID we used for conducting this study, the following analysis is for the period ending in 1988.

6 The year 1973 was chosen as the base year for this analysis for that year represents the end of the postwar boom in real average hourly wages.

7 One might also note that Table 2.5 indicates the racial difference among prime-age women in labor force continuity is the reverse of that for men. In both decades, black women have both higher levels of strong attachment and lower levels of weak attachment to the labor market – although both gaps are closing. In general, more educated women have stronger attachment, as expected, with the one anomaly being the drop-off in attachment among college-educated women. At this point, we do not have a good explanation for this finding. It is possible that this may reflect a contingent of better-educated women who have gone back to school during their "prime working years" to complete additional education. Another possibility is that this reflects delayed child-bearing among college educated women and therefore more part-time employment in the early prime working years.

8 We also computed the coefficient of variation of annual hours worked for individuals over the course of 10 years, and found the same pattern of increasing unevenness.

REFERENCES

Bluestone, B. (1990a) "The Great U-Turn Revisited: Economic Restructuring, Jobs, and the Redistribution of Earnings," In John D. Kasarda (ed.) *Jobs, Earnings, and Employment Growth Policies in the United States* (Boston: Kluwer Academic Publishers): 7–37.

_____ (1990b) "The Impact of Schooling and Industrial Restructuring on Recent Trends in Wage Inequality in the United States," *American Economic Review*, 80(2): 303–307.

ERP (1997) *Economic Report of the President*, Council of Economic Advisers, Washington, DC: Government Printing Office.

Levy, F. and Murnane, R. (1992) "US Earnings Levels and Earnings Inequality: A Review of Recent Trends and Proposed Explanations." *Journal of Economic Literature* 30: 1333–1381.

Mishel, L. and Bernstein, J. (1994) *The State of Working America 1994–95*, Armonk, New York: M. E. Sharpe.

Robinson, J. P., and Bostrom, A. (1994) "The Overestimated Workweek? What Time Diary Measures Suggest," *Monthly Labor Review*, 117(8): 11–24.

Rose, S. J. (1994) *On Shaky Ground: Rising Fears About Incomes and Earnings*, Report No. 94-02, Washington, DC: National Commission for Employment Policy.

Schor, J. B. (1991) *The Overworked American*, New York: Basic Books.

3 Working time reduction in the European Union

A diversity of trends and approaches

Steffen Lehndorff

Western Europe is well known for its short working hours compared with Japan and, even more so, the United States. Working times in major European countries, counted as average annual hours actually worked per employee, dropped continuously throughout the 1980s and 1990s. In contrast, the average annual working time of US employees in 1997 surpassed some counterparts in Europe by several hundred hours (see Table 3.1). Recent initiatives for shorter working hours in two European countries fit wonderfully in this picture. In Denmark, one of the countries with the shortest working times in Europe, the spring of 1998 saw an eleven-day general strike in favor of the introduction of a sixth week of holiday entitlement. In France, the government has just introduced a statutory 35-hour working week from the year 2000 in companies with more than 20 employees (in smaller firms from 2002) as an important element in its fight against unemployment.[1]

It is true that these two examples expose major motives behind an apparently never ending story of initiatives for shorter working hours in European Union (EU) member states. General working time reductions, so many people feel, provide for a better reconciliation of work and personal life and may also be an important remedy for unemployment.[2] However, if one takes a look at the working times of full-time workers that are negotiated between the unions and the employers' associations or regulated by the state, the picture of continuous working time reductions in Europe is less clear. In fact, the tempo of reductions in the normal work week in EU member states has been slowing since the 1970s, whereas part-time work is getting more and more important. This observation gives rise to the idea that the era of collectively negotiated working time reductions may have come to end. Among European policy makers, for example, it has become a widely shared view that "collective" working time reductions are being (and ought to be) replaced by what may be called "individual" reductions, in particular part-time working, a view that has the attractive side aspect of being very much in line with the neo-liberal *Zeitgeist*.

Is this view in accordance with the actual working time trends? This chapter seeks an answer to this question. First, it describes the most

Table 3.1 Average annual hours actually worked per employee[a]

	1979	*1983*	*1990*	*1997*
France	1 667	1 558	1 539	1 519
Germany (W)	1 699	1 686	1 557	1 498
Netherlands	1 591	1 530	1 433	1 365
Spain	1 936	1 837	1 762	1 748
UK	1 750	1 652	1 704	1 701
Japan	2 114	2 098	2 052	1 900
US	1 884	1 866	1 936	1 966

Source: OECD (1998).

Note

a The concept used is the total number of hours worked over the year divided by the average numbers of people in employment including part-timers. The data are intended for comparisons of trends over time; they are unsuitable for comparisons of the level of hours worked for a given year because of differences in their sources.

significant working time changes in the European Union in the 1980s and 1990s. Second, the importance of differing paths to greater female labor market participation is discussed as one of the basic factors behind changing working time patterns. Finally, major challenges faced by those responsible for formulating working time policies are outlined.

EUROPEAN TRENDS IN WORKING TIME

For decades, working time reductions in Western Europe have been based primarily on collective bargaining between employers' associations and trade unions or, in some countries, triggered by government intervention. In recent years, however, as will be shown in this section, this process has been outweighed or even replaced by a trend of differentiation of working times.

As can be demonstrated by the example of Germany, collectively agreed reductions in standard working time[3] were still of great significance for developments in working time in some EU countries in the 1980s and early 1990s. Figure 3.1 is based on what male and female employees answered when asked about how many hours they usually worked per week.[4] The effects of the collectively bargained working time reductions on the actual weekly working hours is clearly reflected. Note that usual weekly working hours for both men and women have declined, especially between 1987 and 1990.

This finding was emphasized by the Organization for Economic Cooperation and Development (OECD) that measured the strength of collective bargaining systems on the basis of the four indicators: unionization; trade union density; coverage rate of collective agreements; and degree of centralization of bargaining processes. It thus identified "a tendency for those countries where collective bargaining is more developed to have shown a faster decline in working hours" (OECD 1998: 167).[5] In this respect, the United Kingdom may serve as an example for the importance of a virtual

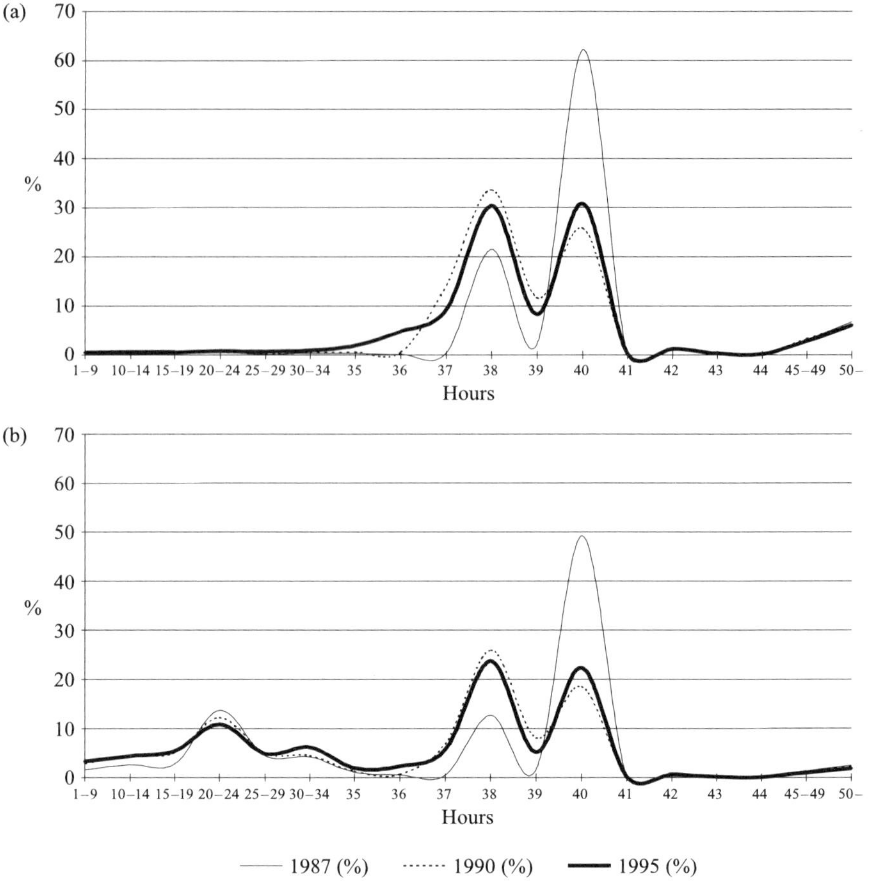

Figure 3.1 Usual weekly working hours reported by (a) male and (b) female German employees for the years 1987, 1990 and 1995. (Source: Eurostat.)

non-existence of industry-wide or even nationwide collective bargaining for the development of working hours. As shown in Figure 3.2, working times in the UK are neither standardized nor have they been reduced since the early 1980s. In fact, working time has risen a little for workers of both genders.

A broader look at the development of working times of full-time employees between the early 1980s and the early 1990s in Table 3.2 reveals the differentiated trends among twelve EU countries. Only full-timers in three countries, Denmark, Western Germany and the Netherlands, saw a substantial reduction in their annual working hours (at least 70 hours annually). The working time of their British counterparts even increased nearly 50 hours. Plasman (1997) identified the mid-1970s as the turning point from which the process of collectively negotiated working time reductions in the EU started to slow down. Before that, various forms of agreement had brought about

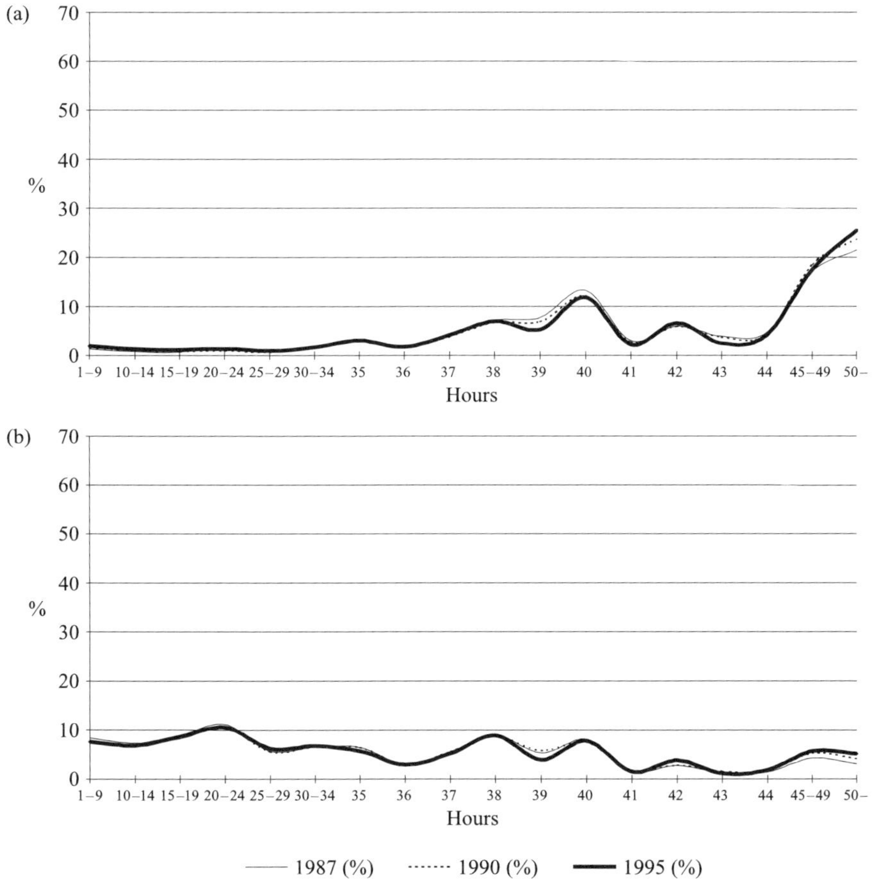

Figure 3.2 Usual weekly working hours reported by (a) male and (b) female UK employees for the years 1987, 1990 and 1995. (Source: Eurostat.)

reductions of working hours to under 40 per week in most cases, but since then one country after another has broken ranks. Even in West Germany, where the engineering trade union IG Metall had provided the main driving force during the second half of the 1980s, the call for shorter hours lost its momentum. Since the early 1990s, just as the deal on the 35-hour week in the metalworking industry was struck, there was no other union but one willing or able to follow on that route. Thus, as the "locomotives" of working time reductions in EU countries obviously have run out of power, it must be stated that the influence of collective agreements on working time trends has weakened substantially as compared with earlier decades.

Moreover, not only is there a differentiation of working times *between* countries, but also working time *within* certain European countries exhibits what may be called a "spread" of working hours. At the top of the scale there

Table 3.2 Estimates of actual annual working hours for full-time employees (1983/1987/1993)

	1983	*1987*	*1993*
Belgium	1739.0	1711.3	1711.2
Denmark	1833.6	1784.0	1746.8
Germany (W)	1808.2	1777.7	1738.7
France	1785.3	1789.9	1790.0
Greece	1852.9	1821.1	1835.4
UK	1903.8	1942.7	1952.7
Ireland	1870.9	1879.1	1859.1
Italy	1741.1	1718.6	1709.7
Luxembourg	1778.6	1767.9	1769.0
Netherlands	1863.3	1787.5	1788.4
Portugal	no data	1904.8	1857.7
Spain	no data	1831.2	1807.1
EUR 12	no data	1809.7	1797.1

Source: Eurostat (1995).

are signs that in particular unpaid overtime working is on the rise (OECD 1998). This is even true for a country such as Germany with its comparatively strong collective bargaining (Wagner 1998) and fed by the increasing proportion of self-employed people among the working population.[6] If the bottom end of the scale is included, a gender-specific aspect in all fifteen EU countries can be seen clearly. The proportion of employed persons with very short hours (fewer than 15 hours per week) is considerably higher for women than for men, whereas many more men work more than 45 hours per week than women (see Table 3.3).

Another aspect of differentiation which can be found behind the figures on length of working time is an increasingly irregular distribution of working hours over the week, month, or year. This trend is rarely reflected in the statistics. Company surveys on the use of flexible forms of work and approaches to working time provide just a rough impression, as shown in Table 3.4. In Finland, the Netherlands, and West Germany, at least 43 percent of companies increased their use of flexible working time in the mid-1990s. In Germany, the increase of flexibility is reflected in a form of working time organization called "working time accounts" which is largely, though not only, used as a tool of adaptation of individual working times to business fluctuations. In 1999, 37 percent of German employees declared that they used these working time accounts (Gross and Munz 1999).

These observations also indicate that the data on trends in working time reflect shifts in the political balance of power. Of course employees also have an interest in a more flexible approach to working time, but the driving force behind the changes outlined here is primarily the pressure of competition between companies. Above all, firms are interested in lowering unit costs and extending contact and opening hours, leading to an extension of the framework of regular working hours into the late evenings and weekends. They

Table 3.3 Short working hours for women, long hours for men (in percentages of total employees, 1996)

	1–14 hours per week		*45+ hours per week*	
	Men	*Women*	*Men*	*Women*
Belgium	0.5	3.7	5.7	2.1
Denmark	7.4	9.6	13.3	4.5
Germany (1995)	1.0	7.7	8.8	2.8
Finland (1995)	1.9	2.7	5.2	2.7
France	0.8	4.3	14.5	5.9
UK (1995)	3.3	14.4	43.0	10.9
Greece (1995)	0.4	1.2	20.0	12.1
Italy	0.8	2.0	14.6	5.9
Ireland (1995)	1.2	6.0	20.4	5.7
Luxembourg (1995)	0.2	5.3	7.2	3.8
Netherlands	6.3	23.0	2.1	0.4
Austria	0.7	3.5	5.8	2.2
Portugal	0.3	2.6	28.8	13.3
Sweden (1995)	2.2[a]	4.5[a]	8.9	3.9
Spain	2.9	5.6	3.6	1.8
EU 15 (1995)	1.8	8.3	17.8	5.9

Source: Eurostat special tabulation.

Note
a 1–15 hours.

Table 3.4 Percentage of companies that have changed their use of flexible forms of working time over the last three years

	Increased	*Unchanged*	*Reduced*	*Not used*
Denmark	16	53	1	25
Finland	62	24	0	12
France	19	46	1	24
Germany (W)	55	27	1	14
Ireland	25	27	1	31
Italy	32	22	0	36
Netherlands	43	38	0	14
Norway	23	59	1	10
Sweden	35	52	1	10
UK	30	31	1	32

Source: Cranfield School of Management (1995).

are also concerned to increase the efficiency of capital use and avoid paid working time that is not directly productive. The result is a variation of working time to better match fluctuations in orders and transport flows. All in all, the initiative in formulating working time policy, that for decades lay largely with the unions, has to a large extent passed into the hands of the companies (Lehndorff 1999).

What is the reason, then, for the ongoing decline in average working hours in the bulk of the EU countries as indicated at the beginning of this chapter? A major cause behind this trend to be observed in the statistics is the increase in

Table 3.5 Contribution of full-time and part-time working to recent changes in average annual hours of employees (average change in hours from year to year)

			Change attributable to:		
	Period	*Average annual change*	*Change in hours of full-timers*	*Change in hours of part-timers*	*Change in share of part-timers*
Belgium	1983–1993	−7.5	−2.5	0.2	−4.9
Denmark	1985–1993	−6.6	−7.1	−0.9	1.4
France	1983–1993	−4.1	0.4	0.7	−4.4
Germany	1983–1993	−10.9	−6.1	−0.9	−3.9
Italy	1983–1993	−3.7	−3.0	0.4	−0.9
Netherlands	1987–1993	−6.6	0.0	3.2	−11.3
Spain	1987–1993	−6.0	−3.8	−0.4	−1.8
Sweden	1987–1994	7.7	1.8	3.6	2.3
UK	1983–1993	−1.5	3.8	−0.5	−5.0
USA	1983–1993	7.3	4.7	1.3	1.2

Source: OECD (1998).

part-time working, as seen in Table 3.5. In all but three countries (Denmark, Sweden, and the USA), an increase in the percentage of workers who are in part-time jobs contributed to a decline in average annual hours. The expansion of part-time employment was the most important determinant of declining hours in Belgium, France, the Netherlands, and the UK. The hidden message of these statistics is that "individual" working time reductions are gradually replacing "collective" ones.

Such a conclusion is based, however, on a phenomenon that could be described as an illusion created by statistical snapshots. What appears to be a shift from "collective" to "individual" working time reductions, in fact, reflects the growing labor force participation of women, most of whom took up part-time employment. Part-time working by women is the most dynamic factor on European labor markets and accounted for the largest element in the growth in employment within the EU in the last cycle, from 1983 to 1992 (Rubery *et al.* 1998).[7] This means that, statistically speaking, annual working time per person has, on average, declined, but in most cases this has had nothing to do with reduction of the work week for individuals. Indeed, for most women, it is more likely to be related to an increase in working time – for example from 0 to 20 hours part-time work. Thus the working time trends described here in averages or statistical means must always be seen against a background of an increasing number of women devoting more paid time toward paid employment.

To conclude, the momentum of working time policy based on collective agreements is slowing down. That is, working time reality for an increasing proportion of employees – especially women – is hardly influenced by the regulation of standard working hours. In what follows we look at some aspects of the problems related to this shift of emphasis.

WOMEN AT WORK AND WORKING TIME TRENDS

The pattern of changes occurring in the proportion of women in employment and the proportion working on a part-time basis varies considerably within the EU, as can be seen from Table 3.6. Country-specific institutions and models as to female labor market participation play a major role behind these differences. This has very different implications for working time trends in individual countries.[8] A number of examples illustrate these implications.

For many years the UK has had a proportion of women in work and in employment that is well above the EU average, and this is fed by a similarly above-average rate of part-time working. Women are prompted to take up work because of the low wages earned by their husbands; however, poor child-care provisions prevent them from accepting full-time employment

Table 3.6 Female employment rates and part-time working in selected EU countries (in percent)[a]

	1975	*1985*	*1990*	*1996*	*1985–1996*[b]
EU 15					
Employment rate	44.0	45.0	49.4	50.2	+5.2
Part-time rate	no data	23.4	28.1	31.6	+8.2
Denmark					
Employment rate	60.6	69.9	72.0	68.6	−1.3
Part-time rate	no data	43.9	38.4	34.6	−9.3
Germany					
Employment rate	47.5	48.5	53.6	53.8	+5.3
Part-time rate	no data	29.6	33.8	33.6	+4.0
Finland					
Employment rate	65.6	71.4	71.5	59.5	−11.9
Part-time rate	no data	12.1	9.6	15.7	+3.6
France					
Employment rate	51.4	50.7	52.6	52.8	+2.1
Part-time rate	no data	21.8	23.6	29.5	+7.7
UK					
Employment rate	53.8	55.0	62.6	63.1	+8.1
Part-time rate	no data	44.8	43.2	44.8	±0
Italy					
Employment rate	30.6	33.5	36.2	36.6	+3.1
Part-time rate	no data	10.1	9.6	12.7	+2.6
Netherlands					
Employment rate	33.4	39.7	47.5	54.3	+14.6
Part-time rate	no data	51.6	59.4	68.5	+16.9
Sweden					
Employment rate	67.6	76.4	80.7	69.0	−7.4
Part-time rate	no data	45.6	40.9	41.8	−3.8

Source: European Commission (1997).

Notes

a Employment rate for women as the number of female employees in percent of women of working age, part-time rate for women as part-time workers in percent of total women in employment. European and German numbers for 1996 include East Germany.

b Change in percentage points.

(leaving aside the question of whether full-time jobs are even available). There are also particularly high wage differentials between men and women, which means that the household income can best be increased by the husband working longer hours (see, for example, Rubery 1998). In Britain there are particularly strong grounds for fearing that women could end up in a "part-time trap." A combination of these factors leads to the polarization of working times between men and women mentioned above and also to an increase in average overall working times.

For a long time Sweden has been the EU country with the highest rate of employment among women. There is also a strong tradition of part-time work by women, though with a considerably higher number of hours than in the UK. In 1996, the number of hours usually worked by female employees per week averaged 24.9 in Sweden and 18.0 in the UK (Eurostat 1997: 171). Furthermore, part-time work by women in Sweden declined considerably during the 1980s, whereas the employment rate rose sharply (see Table 3.6). These figures illustrate a well-known fact: that it is regarded as the norm for women to work in Sweden, and even full-time working by women is supported and encouraged by institutionalized provisions (comprehensive child-care, tax system). Against such a background, the positive economic developments up to 1990 meant that more women than before took up full-time work. Even in the subsequent years of declining employment prospects, the high rate of full-time employment hardly dropped at all. However, reductions in weekly working time had no longer been on the trade union agenda since the 40-hour working week was achieved, likely due to the widely accepted view that a full use of labor capacity was needed for maintaining the Swedish Welfare State. The inevitable result was an increase in average working times – a development that is likely to have been counter-productive during the years when unemployment was increasing by leaps and bounds. It would be only a slight exaggeration to say that for as long as there was no pressure to introduce collectively negotiated working time reductions, the entire Swedish economy had fallen into a sort of "full-time trap." Against this background it is understandable that in recent years there has been a distinct increase in societal pressure to introduce collectively negotiated reductions in working times (see also Sanne 1998).

Denmark, too, saw a distinct decline in the number of women working on a part-time basis during the mid-1980s. As in Sweden, this trend started from a well established high base figure for women workers, so it can be viewed as a sign of the widespread acceptance and institutional encouragement of women working full time in Denmark. Here, too, it is likely that comprehensive availability of child care facilities played a crucial role. In the early 1990s, almost every other woman in her twenties or thirties with a child under the age of 15 worked full-time (Rubery, Smith, and Fagan 1997). As in Sweden, part-time work by women in Denmark proves to be a historically transitional phase on the road to equal status for both sexes in terms of paid employment. In contrast to Sweden, however, the average working time in Denmark has nevertheless not increased, because unions have at various stages achieved comprehensive reductions in this respect. The fact that the employment situation is also distinctly better in Denmark than in Sweden is probably not exclusively a result of the way working time has developed, but should at least be mentioned in this context.

France, too, has had a high proportion of working women, but unlike Denmark, full-time employment has always been the predominant model. Comprehensive provision of child-care facilities has a long tradition in France, so a tradition of full-time working for women, with only brief interruptions, is relatively well established in French society (Gauvin and Silvera 1997). As can be seen in Table 3.6, the rate of employment among women has remained almost unchanged since the mid-1970s, whereas part-time working among women has increased significantly. In many cases it is correct to speak here of "individual working time reduction." But, to a large extent, it would seem to be a case of enforced reductions. This is indicated by the fact that, in 1996, 36.9 percent of French women in part-time employment gave as the reason for working part-time the fact that they were not able to find a full-time job. This degree of so-called "involuntary" part-time working is exceeded only by Finnish women, with 43.9 percent. (By way of comparison, in Germany the figure was 11.3 percent, and in the Netherlands 4.7 percent (Eurostat 1997: 138)). The low levels of reductions of average working hours in France since the early 1980s are to a considerable extent due to this factor.

Whereas throughout the 1990s French governments have tried with some success to use financial incentives to entice women away from full-time jobs into part-time employment or even to persuade them to leave the labor market completely, the "part-time offensive" in the Netherlands made it possible for some women to enter employment in the first place and resulted in the Dutch employment rate for women rapidly reaching (and overtaking) the EU average during the mid 1990s. The collectively negotiated working time reductions that followed on from a national tripartite agreement (state – trade unions – employers associations) on wages and working times policies in the early 1980s and the subsequent rapid growth in part-time working resulted, together, in a significant redistribution of work within Dutch society, with the employment rate rising faster than the volume of work generated by the economy (Boulin and Cette 1997; Plantenga and Dur 1998). However, the full-time employment rate of mothers with children under the age of 15 was, at the beginning of the 1990s, still at 5.3 percent, the lowest level within the European Union (Rubery, Smith, and Fagan 1997). Moreover, the Netherlands, too, is experiencing increasing resistance on the part of companies to any more collectively negotiated working time reductions. It is therefore doubtful whether the process of a relatively low-conflict redistribution of work can be continued.

In a nutshell, institutional backgrounds and the country-specific routes of female labor market participation come out in the differing employment and working time patterns by gender in particular industries, even under conditions of comparable labor demand strategies on the part of companies (see the example of food retailing, in Baret, Lehndorff, and Sparks 2000). A very simple conclusion can be derived from these observations: only when part-time working is no longer associated with particular groups – mainly, of course, women – but rather takes on the character of a form of employment that can be chosen for a certain *period*, can it be referred to correctly as an "individual working time reduction."

ALTERNATIVE ROUTES TO "PART-TIME TRAPS" AND "FULL-TIME TRAPS"

The impact of the dual trend described here – weakening momentum of collective working time regulation on the one hand and growing female labor market participation on the other – may be further polarization of working times and excess labor supply. Nevertheless, the preferences of most people in EU countries where working time is concerned continue to shift towards shorter working hours (Table 3.7). "Countries in which average annual hours of work per person are already relatively low tend to be those in which the average preference for fewer hours is relatively strong," according to the OECD (1998: 166), a link that, incidentally, can be the result of a mutual interaction effect.

Table 3.7 Working hours and earnings preferences of workers, European Union, 1985 and 1994[a]

	Percentage of employees preferring:				
	More earnings		*Fewer hours*		
	1985	*1994*	*1985*	*1994*	
Belgium	58	48	36	40	↑
Denmark	38	32	51	66	↑
Germany	56	54	30	34	↑
France	62	53	34	40	↑
Greece	68	84	26	14	↓
UK	77	62	19	32	↑
Ireland	78	59	19	37	↑
Italy	55	54	39	39	→
Netherlands	46	43	47	52	↑
Portugal	82	58	11	35	↑
Spain	64	70	31	24	↓

Source: OECD (1998).

Note

a The question asked, which was identical at both points in time, was: If the choice were offered in the next pay round between an increase in pay for the same hours of work and shorter working time for the same pay you get now, which would you prefer? Respondents could choose between answering "increase in pay" or "shorter working time." "Don't knows" are not detailed here.

A basic conclusion can be drawn from these studies. From the point of view of an increasing proportion of working people in the EU, reductions in working time are by no means out of the question; they are indeed regarded as a relevant issue for the future. On the other hand, the momentum of traditional policies aimed at regulating and reducing standard working hours is slowing down. Thus, as will be outlined in what follows, EU working time policy makers face the challenge of finding new ways to further working time reductions by re-calibrating the balance of collective regulation and individual choice. This challenge includes aspects such as the need of what many people call "a new work – family balance," the conflict over firms' sustainable use of knowledge workers, and, finally, the redefinition of the role of governments in the field of working time.

A new work–family balance

Against a background of a further increase in women's work as the basic social development, one can identify certain competing perspectives, with the ultimate resolution being governed by political factors. Sweden and the UK to some extent represent two poles, with other countries including Germany somewhere in between. Under social conditions that tend to hinder women's work as a basis for making an independent living (the British way), there is a risk that the spread of part-time working as a replacement for further shortening standard working time will lead into the vicious circle of a gender-specific polarization of working time. The result could then even be an average lengthening of working time. On the other hand, under conditions conducive to women working as a basis for making an independent living (the Swedish way), part-time work by women increasingly takes on the character of a (historically and individually) transitional stage, so that doing without cuts in standard working time sooner or later can also lead to a lengthening of working time. Neither way offers a solution to the problem that, as the amount of labor available continues to increase but economic growth remains limited, the total volume of paid work has to be (re)distributed in such a way that all women and men who wish and need to have an independent basis for making a living should be granted one.

The alternative to such routes – that sooner or later can lead to extremely problematic increases in working time – is to attempt to take coordinated action in three areas of policy: first, to encourage expansion of the system of institutions, with the aim of achieving equal status for women's work as a method of making an independent living; second, to make individual working time reductions easier so as to create a greater degree of individual choice during a person's working life (in contrast to a policy that, for example, effectively allocates part-time working to women as a group); and third, a return to collectively negotiated working time reductions. In the absence of institutional reforms that both improve the relative status of employed women and provide more viable options for individuals to choose reduced work hours, a collectively negotiated reduction in working time will be rendered ineffective or irrelevant.

Seen in this light, the strike for longer holiday entitlement in Denmark that was mentioned at the beginning of this chapter lies very much at the heart of present working time problems in Europe. As a matter of fact, the strike was brought to an end by the government with a compulsory arbitration process that resulted in all employees receiving one additional day of holiday entitlement, and employees with children three additional "child-care days." Thus, the call for shorter *standard* working hours (and the way government reacted to this call) in one of the countries with the shortest working times in Europe and the highest shares of women in total employment signalled a further shift away from the model of the male as the single or major breadwinner.

Working time flexibility and firms' sustainable use of knowledge workers

As the initiative with regard to working time policy is coming much more from the companies themselves than was the case twenty years ago, complex questions of flexible working time organization have to be solved in many companies and – assuming the existence of workforce representative bodies – negotiated. A collective bargaining policy aimed at working time reductions that to some extent "takes on board" a compromise within the company has a certain tradition, especially in the Netherlands but to some extent also in Germany. The problem today, however, seems to consist in the fact that the original configuration of compromises – working time reduction plus flexibilization – has shifted in both countries towards flexibilization without any reduction in working time. Thus, a "bilateral" approach that tries to reconcile firms' interest in flexible working hours with the interest of employees in gaining a certain degree of control over their individual working time is getting even harder to attain.

It is therefore all the more interesting, as can be seen particularly by the case of France, that tangible reductions in working time can help to achieve a sort of strategic compromise at the company level between various different interests where working time is concerned.[9] Agreement on training times represents an important possibility of finding a compromise within companies that at the same time brings with it considerable medium-term scope for reducing working time. There is an interaction between working time reduction and further training. The latter is facilitated by working time reductions (or indeed can be made explicitly the purpose of reductions). But working time reductions can at the same time trigger further training, as they encourage the reorganization of work procedures and the overcoming of the strict divisions between highly specialized areas of responsibility that have existed in the past. This is one of the reasons for the French government to favor, in the framework of the 35-hour law, the use of the working time reduction for training purposes.

Sabbaticals dedicated to training and to other forms of reproductive time off are becoming one of the key strategic questions for future working time reductions. The more that production and services are knowledge-based, the greater the danger that working time reductions will fail because of a lack of trained staff. And the more it is exclusively left up to the companies to invest in training their workforce, the greater the problem of high fixed staff costs becomes for them – an insurmountable hurdle for agreeing on working time reductions within the company. Anyone who invests a lot of money into the "intellectual plant" in their company is interested in rapid amortization and therefore wants, as far as possible, round-the-clock operating hours for this type of plant as well as for their machines. Of course the comparison is not entirely accurate, for unlike a machine, human intelligence is more like a "renewable resource." Ongoing investment in knowledge can lead to decades of "intellectual capital operating time," provided, of course, that it is not worn out before its time by excessively long operating hours. But is it realistic to expect companies (at least the majority of companies) to act according to such a concept of *sustainable* growth of intellectual capital, that is, invest on their own initiative in the long-term, ongoing training of their workforce and at the same time agree to shorter working times? Here the limits of a purely company-oriented perspective on the finding of strategic compromises that include working time reductions become evident. Only if subsidization of further training is also seen as a public task can one avoid this barrier to working time reductions.

Collective bargaining policy and the state

In order to prevent the key role of collective bargaining for the regulation of standard working time from dwindling further, it is the French working time policy in particular that gives fresh impetus to the discussion of the future relationship between collective bargaining and the state. As a matter of fact, experience in various European countries yields a series of important examples of the scope that the state has to promote collective bargaining on shorter standard hours or even to provide for working time reductions by public support:

- A basic element in any government policy aimed at promoting women's work as a basis for earning a living is an adequate supply of child-care facilities and all-day schooling. Child-care provision, incidentally, not only improves the prospects of both genders working on an equal basis but also increases demand for labor within society.
- The state can remove institutional hurdles blocking the way to developing work as a basis on which women can earn a living. Such hurdles usually take the form of regulations that favor small "additional earnings"

for women who are otherwise financially dependent on their husbands, and therefore perpetuate gender-specific discrepancies in working times and incomes. Thus, for example, there is a clear correlation between the frequency of working times below 15 hours a week and the existence of institutions such as "low-paid employment," in Germany or the UK for example (Dingeldey 1999).

- The state can facilitate individual working time reductions. On the one hand it can soften the penalty of part-time phases during individuals' working lives on their pensions (see the examples of Denmark, Austria and the Netherlands). Second, this also usually involves financial cushioning of interrupted professional careers, as in Sweden or Denmark or an extended and financially secure possibility of interrupting one's career, e.g. for child-rearing or further training (see Madsen (1998) on Denmark).

The present government policy in France, however, may provide an interesting example on the possibilities of state intervention exerting *direct* impact on collective bargaining on shorter working hours. It is true that the French initiative, mentioned at the beginning of this chapter, to introduce a statutory 35-hour work week will by no means prevent companies from having their employees work more than 35 working hours. In fact, the upper legal limit for working time is 46 hours per week as an average in 3 months. However, every hour worked beyond 35 per week or beyond an annualized 1 600 hours roster is subject to overtime bonuses. Moreover, companies that make an agreement with the trade unions or workforce representatives on the organization of the 35-hour week benefit from substantial government subsidies.[10] Such subsidies make it easier for companies to carry out the reorganization that is often associated with working time reductions, and help avoid loss of income on the part of the employees. The main justification is the savings that then result in terms of state expenditure on unemployment benefits. Moreover, such subsidies are of particular interest when, as is at present the case in France, they are aimed at stimulating collectively agreed working time reductions.

It should be noted that by this law the government of France, that is the government of the European country with perhaps the most powerful initiating role of the state in working time issues, recognizes the fact that however great the weight of the state may have been in recent decades, in the last event working time reductions are implemented in real life only if they have the support of society. As the experience of the preparatory phase of the law has shown, the importance of collective bargaining on the level of industries and, much more so, on the firm level has already been promoted substantially.

These considerations on the responsibility of the state for working time developments may sound strange for a US or UK audience. Nevertheless, for many European countries, to ignore the impact of government actions would, in the final event, mean overloading collective bargaining policy with unrealistic expectations. This would be just as dubious an approach as the attitude that – given the difficulties being experienced with collective bargaining on working time policy and the weakening of trade union power in most industrialized countries – one just has to put one's hopes in the state as a *deus ex machina*.

CONCLUSION

As described in this chapter, the decline of average working times per employee during earlier decades in EU countries was to a large extent attributable to regulations of the standard work day, in particular to collective bargaining between employers' organizations and trade unions. Since the 1980s, however, the key role of collective bargaining for working time reductions has been subject to a gradual decline, whereas part-time work is gaining importance for the statistical average of working time per employee.

In contrast to a widely accepted view, it was argued here that it is misleading to interpret this shift as a move from "collective" to "individual" forms of working time reductions. It should rather be seen as concomitant with increasing female labor market participation that may lead either into the "part-time trap" of growing polarization of working times between men and women or into the "full-time trap" of general working time increases. Those in charge of working time policy who look for alternatives to this dual trap will have to find ways to revitalize collective bargaining in the working time field that include, rather than replace, individual working time choices.

Some initiatives in EU countries in recent years with respect to working time – taken more often by the state than by the trade unions – are, in our view, far from being the dawn of a new wave of working time reductions. A realistic assessment should be that the crisis which those attempting to achieve comprehensive reductions have been faced with for some time now is unlikely to be resolved quickly. One major reason for this difficulty can be seen in the lack of consistent and widely shared views on the future status of women in employment, or, more generally, on the division of paid and unpaid work of men and women in society in many European countries.

In this respect, the recent initiatives of the French government may influence working time policies in other European countries in more than one way. France is, on the one hand, a country with comparatively favorable institutional conditions for female labor market participation. On the other hand, working time reductions were stuck until recent years in the deadlock of weak collective bargaining. Government policy aims at breaking up this deadlock by particularly promoting bargaining on shorter working hours on the firm and establishment levels. Initial experience is rather encouraging, but it has yet to be seen whether decentralized bargaining and active support by employees will continue to gain ground in the years to come.

The powerful action taken by the French government will undoubtedly back the attempts to renew collective bargaining on working time reductions in other European countries, provided it is successful in terms of reduced actual working hours and the promotion of employment growth. If it proves to be a failure in these respects, however, the backlash will be experienced all over Europe.

NOTES

1 For details on working time policies in Denmark, France and other EU member states see the current reports in *European Industrial Relations Review* (*EIRR*).
2 It is unfortunately beyond the scope of this chapter to discuss the relationship between collectively negotiated working time reductions and employment. For an overview of theoretical problems and empirical research see Bosch and Lehndorff (1998) and Gerhard Bosch's Chapter 11 in the present book.
3 For the sake of clarity I will continue to use the term "standard working times" in connection with collectively agreed working times for full-time employees, even though the blurring of such standards is part of the problem under discussion here.
4 Working times are recorded and estimated using a number of different methods, with the result that some of the resulting data varies considerably. The concept of "hours usually worked per week" is used by Eurostat, the European Bureau of Statistics, to assess the average actual working hours, that is including overtime, whether it be paid or unpaid, but without singular incidents such as absenteeism due to illness. Eurostat has been surveying working time in all EU member states on a uniform basis using this method since 1983. The estimates of actual annual working times in Table 3.1 are also based on this approach. Of course the figures gained in this way differ from the individual national statistics and other sources. But the uniform method of calculating them means that they have the great advantage that they are comparable across the EU countries.
5 Sweden is a significant exception here for reasons mentioned later.
6 In Western Germany, highly skilled employees (who make up roughly 25 percent of all white collar employees) who are covered by collective bargaining worked 41.8 hours per week in 1984 and 45.6 hours in 1996 (actual working time), whereas their contractual hours fell from 40.2 hours to 36.8 hours. However, the share of those highly skilled employees who by definition are not covered by collective bargaining rose in the same period of time, from 12.1 percent to 16.5 percent. Their working time soared from 47.0 hours to 54.5 hours per week (Wagner 1998).
7 Part-time work of women accounted for about 43 percent of the employment growth in that period, whereas the numbers for full-time work of women, part-time work of men and full-time work of men were 33 percent, 11 percent and 13 percent, respectively.
8 For detailed treatment of this issue, see O'Reilly and Fagan (1997), Rubery, Smith, Fagan and Grimshaw (1998).
9 See Boulin and Silvera (1999) for case studies on French firms with 10 percent reductions in working time.
10 One precondition for government subsidies that may soar up to one quarter of the wage costs in the case of low-wage employees is an agreement on the number of workers to be hired. In the preparatory phase of the new working time law in numerous firms, particularly in larger ones, collective agreements on the 35-hour

week were signed that have covered, at the end of 1999, about one quarter of the full-time employees in the private sector. The initial employment effect of these measures is estimated by the government at some 100 000 persons, with an additional 600 000 expected to come after the law is fully applied. For the political background and economics and concept behind the government plan, see Freyssinet (1998), Cette and Taddei (1998), and Lehndorff (2000).

REFERENCES

Baret, C., Lehndorff, S., and Sparks, L. (2000) *Flexible Working in Food Retailing. A Comparison between France, Germany, the United Kingdom and Japan*. London: Routledge.

Bosch, G. and Lehndorff, S. (1998) "Arbeitszeitverkürzung und Beschäftigung – Erfahrungen in Europa und wirtschaftspolitische Empfehlungen," *DIW Vierteljahreshefte zur Wirtschaftsforschung* 4: 300–325.

Boulin, J. Y. and Cette, G. (1997) "Réduire la Durée du Travail: l'Exemple des Pays Bas," *Futuribles*, Nos 222, 226.

Boulin, J. Y. and Silvera, R. (1999) "France – 'Breakfast' Food Processing and 'Beta' Consultancy," In S. Lehndorff. (ed.), *New Working Time Systems, Work Organisation and Re-distribution of Work*, Final Report for the European Commission, Gelsenkirchen: Graue Reihe des Instituts Arbeit und Technik 1999–03.

Cette, G. and Taddei, D. (1998) *Réduire la Durée du Travail. Les 35 Heures*, Paris: Librairie Générale Française.

Cranfield School of Management (1995) *Price Waterhouse Cranfield Project 1995 Survey Results*, Centre for European Human Resource Management, Cranfield School of Management.

Dingeldey, I. (1999) *Begünstigungen und Belastungen familialer Erwerbs- und Arbeitszeitmuster in Steuer- und Sozialversicherungssystemen – Ein Vergleich zehn europäischer Länder*, Graue Reihe des Instituts Arbeit und Technik 1999–04, Gelsenkirchen.

EIRR (1998a) "Employers Change Tack on 35-hour Week," *European Industrial Relations Review* 291: 5.

_____ (1998b) "Company Agrees Provisional Deal Ahead of 35-hour Week Law," *European Industrial Relations Review* 292: 5.

_____ (1998c) "Government Publishes 35-hour Week Bill," *European Industrial Relations Review* 292: 9.

_____ (1998d) "Survey Reveals Flexible-Working Trend," *European Industrial Relations Review* 293: 19f.

_____ (1998e) "UGT Asks for Law on Working Time Reduction," *European Industrial Relations Review* 292: 12.

_____ (1998f) "Draft Working Time Legislation," *European Industrial Relations Review* 292: 13.

_____ (1998g) "General Strike Ends," *European Industrial Relations Review* 293: 5.

European Commission (1997) *Employment in Europe 1997*, Luxembourg.

Eurostat (1995) "Die Arbeitszeit in der Europäischen Union. Schätzung der tatsächlichen Jahresarbeitszeit 1983–1993," *Statistik kurzgefaßt* 4, Luxembourg.

_____ (1997) *Erhebung über Arbeitskräfte, Ergebnisse 1996*, Luxembourg.

Freyssinet, J. (1997) *Le Temps de Travail en Miettes. 20 Ans de Politique de l'Emploi et de Négociation Collective*, Paris.

Freyssinet, J. (1998) "France – a recurrent aim, repeated near-failures and a new law," *Transfer* 4(4): 641–656.

Gauvin, A. and Silvera, R. (1997) "La Flexibilité du Temps de Travail au Féminin: Poursuite des Tendances Antérieures ou Inflexions des Pratiques et des Enjeux?" in G. Bosch, D. Meulders, and F. Michon (eds), *Working Time: New Issues, New Norms, New Measures*, Brussels: Editions du DULBEA: 301–327.

Gross, H. and Munz, E. (1999) *Erste Ergebnisse einer 1999 durchgeführten repräsentativen Beschäftigtenbefragung zu Arbeitszeitformen und -wünschen*, Köln: ISO Institut zur Erforschung sozialer Chancen.

Lehndorff, S. (ed.) (1999) *New Working Time Systems, Work Organisation and Redistribution of Work. Final report for the European Commission*, Gelsenkirchen: Graue Reihe des Instituts Arbeit und Technik 1999–03.

Lehndorff, S. (2000) "Mut und Kalkül. Der französische Weg zur 35-Stunden-Woche," *Blätter für deutsche und internationale Politik* 45(1): 53–63.

Madsen, P. K. (1998) "Working Time Policy and Paid Leave Arrangements: The Danish Experience in the 1990s," *Transfer* 4(4): 692–714.

OECD (1998) *Employment Outlook*, Paris.

O'Reilly, J. and Fagan, C. (eds) (1997) *Part-time Prospects – An International Comparison of Part-time Work in Europe, North-America and the Pacific Rim*, London: Routledge.

Plantenga, J. and Dur, R. A. J. (1998) "Working Time Reduction in the Netherlands: Past Developments and Future Prospects," *Transfer* 4(4): 678–691.

Plasman, R. (1997) "Working Hours and Economic Growth: An Analysis by Decomposition into Trend and Cycle," in G. Bosch, D. Meulders, and F. Michon (eds), *Working Time: New Issues, New Norms, New Measures*, Brussels: Editions du DULBEA: 111–138.

Rubery, J. (1998) "Working Time in the UK," *Transfer* 4(4): 657–677.

Rubery, J., Smith, M., and Fagan, C. (1997) "Explaining Working Time Patterns by Gender: Societal and Sectoral Effects," in G. Bosch, D. Meulders, and F. Michon (eds), *Working Time: New Issues, New Norms, New Measures*, Brussels: Editions du DULBEA: 329–372.

Rubery, J., Smith, M., Fagan, C., and Grimshaw, D. (1998) *Women and European Employment*, London: Routledge.

Sanne, C. (1998) "The Working Hours Issue in Sweden," *Transfer* 4(4): 715–728.

Wagner, A. (1998) "Working Times of High-Level White-Collar Workers in Germany. An Evaluation of the SOEP," paper presented at the International Working Party on Labour Market Segmentation 20th Conference, July 9–14, Arco, Italy.

4 The longest day

Working time for teachers

Robert Drago, Robert Caplan, David Costanza, Tanya Brubaker, Darnell Cloud, Naomi Harris, Russell Kashian and T. Lynn Riggs

There is much anecdotal evidence that teachers are overburdened and experience significant time pressures. Recent works suggest that the demands on public school teachers as employees continue to grow (Kimball 1999), leading to associated "self-help" books designed to help teachers cope with the stresses of work and family (McGrath 1995). The problem is that, to date, no detailed study of the working time of teachers had been undertaken. We present the results of the first such study below. The data are drawn from the "Time, Work and Family" or TWF project.[1]

In the course of generating such a study, we found that estimating the amount of time that teachers spend in their work is a complex task. Different indicators convey different types of information and are biased toward one set of activities or another. Furthermore, what may be an appropriate indicator for one demographic group may not be appropriate for another – an issue which is particularly pertinent to teachers who also provide unpaid care for their own children. This study describes the approach we used to uncover this richness, considers the implications for the study of working time across occupations, and provides the first appropriately detailed consideration of the length of a teacher's working day.

We specifically address different indicators of working time: (1) contractual working time as specified in collective bargaining agreements; (2) the standard time diary measure of working time; (3) time physically present at the workplace, or face time; (4) the amount of time work invades an individual's time, or work invasiveness; (5) the amount of time spent on housework; and (6) the total hours of housework and teaching-related activities. For each indicator of working time, we compare a variety of demographic groups within our sample of teachers. These comparisons allow us to see how individuals in diverse circumstances structure their working time to meet the demands of work and family.

Below we provide further background to the study and then explain our reliance upon time diaries for the study. The methods section discusses the sampling, administration of the time diaries, and the ways in which we calculate working time. Results follow, and we conclude with a summary and a discussion of why the working day for teachers appears to be so long.

BACKGROUND

Recent interest in working time stems from the assertion that, due to a variety of structural changes in the nature of employment and its relationship to the family, the workforce in many countries has become increasingly overworked. This argument has sparked intense debate.[2] Two arguments are offered for why American society in particular is overworked and time pressured. One is that families are increasingly dual-earners, a phenomenon currently applying to 78 percent of all married employees (Bond, Galinsky and Swanberg 1998: 36). Dual-earner families are largely the result of women entering the workforce. For women in particular, this shift has likely created attendant pressures to manage work responsibilities as well as more traditional household tasks. Public, elementary school teachers in urban schools fit this mold quite well: 87 percent of such teachers are women, 71.5 percent are members of dual-earner couples, and 57 percent are parents of dependent children.[3]

A second argument is that time pressures have resulted from attempts by American industry to become more competitive in the global economy. In response to a variety of economic pressures, many firms have introduced high-commitment work systems (Appelbaum and Batt 1994) which, in turn, increase demands on employees (Appelbaum and Berg 1997). Similar initiatives and related demands on employees have been mirrored in teachers' jobs. Poverty and accompanying decreases in tax bases in urban centers have motivated school administrators to introduce their own versions of high-commitment work systems. There is some evidence that these initiatives, such as "accelerated schooling" and site-based management, may be adding to the demands already placed on teachers.[4] Increasing levels of urban poverty also function as an additional source of workload and stress on teachers, carrying increased behavioral and performance problems among students. In the average school in our sample, 58.2 percent of the children are from families near or below the poverty line. The higher the poverty level, the more the teacher is called upon to deal with difficult discipline problems and other conditions antithetical to a good learning environment. For all of these reasons, our expectations are that the Time, Work and Family sample experiences substantial time pressures.

Of course, there are elements of teaching that may offset such pressures. Public school teachers are not typically in the classroom with students for eight hours per day. Further, summer holidays are far longer than for other occupations, a job characteristic which motivates a sizeable minority to enter the teaching profession.[5] In examining the time allocation of teachers, however, we focus on periods when school is in session.

RATIONALE FOR AND DEVELOPMENT OF THE TWF TIME DIARY

Previous estimates of working time for teachers used broad survey questions to obtain reports of teacher time allocation. For example, a yearly survey administered by the National Education Association, the largest teacher union in the United States, asked teachers about the "exact length of your required school day," time per week spent "after the required work day – evenings and weekends – on instruction-related activities," and about additional time per week on "compensated noninstructional activities," and "noncompensating noninstructional activities" related to school. Summing the resulting figures suggests that public, elementary school teachers averaged 46.6 hours of work per week in the 1996–1997 school year (National Education Association 1997: 164). Roughly comparable items included in a survey undertaken by the National Center for Education Statistics (NCES) provide a figure of 44.4 hours per week for full-time, public, elementary school teachers during the 1993–1994 school year (National Center for Education Statistics 1996: 74).

Such estimates may be biased upwards for two reasons. First, leisure time at school may be counted as part of the required school day. If, for example, teachers received one hour per day of non-prep, duty-free time, then the workweek figures could be overestimated by a full five hours.[6] Second, there is evidence that broad survey questions about usual or typical hours of work tend to produce biased estimates. Particularly for individuals working long hours, researchers have suggested that overestimation in response to such survey questions is the norm (Robinson and Bostrom 1994). However, there is at least one plausible reason to believe that the teacher survey results underestimate working time. If a teacher feels guilty about spending too much time at home performing work related tasks and ignoring family matters, then he or she might underestimate this type of working time in response.

Time diaries have the potential to overcome under- or overestimates. In a time diary study, respondents are requested to provide detailed information regarding primary and secondary activities for a 24-hour period. Robinson and Godbey's review of objective checks of time diary data support their superior validity, and show that different methods of administering the diaries (e.g., written or oral), tend to yield similar, reliable data (1997: 74–77).

For the TWF project, respondents were asked to complete a written diary at the end of a day. The diary covered the period from the previous midnight to "just before you go to sleep." For each activity, respondents were asked to describe the primary activity ("What were you doing?") and to indicate when they began and ended the activity. In addition, respondents were requested to describe secondary activities ("Were you doing anything else?") that may have occurred along with the primary activity. The respondent indicated, in a box, if the activity was "at school" or not during the time period covered.

Respondents were also asked to check boxes, separately, for whether their youngest child and for whether their spouse or partner was present for the activity.

The major drawback of the time diary methodology stems from the time commitment required to complete the diary. As a result, response rates for diaries covering an entire week are typically low (around 40 percent; Robinson and Godbey 1997: 62). To avoid such low response rates, the majority of diary studies sample each respondent for only one 24 hour period. To make inferences about the work week then requires that individual responses be grouped according to measured characteristics (e.g., age, gender) so that a synthetic work week can be constructed for each group by using information drawn from diaries for *similar* respondents across *different* days of the week. The synthetic work week approach poses problems of measurement error, since the accuracy of within-group estimates varies across groups (Juster and Stafford 1991). Further, since individual observations on the working week are not statistically independent within a particular group, comparisons of working time across small groups are not meaningful.

To avoid these problems, TWF respondents completed all diaries at the end of a Tuesday which was also a working day. The Tuesday diary strategy has the disadvantage of selecting an arbitrary, though standardized, day. To address this issue, we obtained ratings for whether the respondent performed "less than usual," "about the usual," or "more than usual" teaching-related work that day. The latter item permits us to control for unusual days.[7]

METHODS

The TWF sample

The sample was constructed to provide three levels of information: district, school, and individual teacher/family.[8] We selected four urban school districts from a list of the 30 largest cities in the USA, providing a sample with two cities along the Eastern seaboard, and two in the Midwest. The smallest city had a population of just under one-half million, while the largest ranked in the top five of all US cities.

The second level of sampling was at the elementary school level. Within each district, we sought to maximize variance in working pressures on teachers, this time across schools. One type of relevant information that is standardized across districts and collected regularly at the school level is the percentage of students qualifying for free or reduced-price lunch programs as a result of low family income levels. The measure is set by the National School Lunch Program such that children from families with incomes at or below 185 percent of the poverty level are eligible for free or reduced price meals.

Assuming that work pressures on teachers are greater in schools with a higher percentage of students from low income families, all schools in each district were ranked according to the relevant statistics for 1995. The middle 20 percent of schools in each district were eliminated from consideration, and six schools in each district were selected randomly from the resulting list of high-poverty schools, and another six schools in each district were selected from the list of low-poverty schools.

Principals on the resulting list of 48 schools were contacted to invite participation in the study. Random resampling (within the relevant district/group) due to refusals resulted in a total of 57 schools being contacted and 46 schools participating in the study for a school level response rate of 80.7 percent. Attempts to achieve the projected sample of 48 schools fell short by two due to time constraints.

The third level of sampling was at the teacher level. A maximum of 17 teachers were asked to participate at each school. Criteria for inclusion in the sample included full-time teaching status, and teaching a "regular" class of students from grades kindergarten through fifth.[9] Given the small percentage of male teachers in such schools, to maximize variance on gender, all teachers who were identified as male from the school faculty roster were included in the study. Female teachers were then randomly selected from rosters to achieve a maximum of 17 eligible teachers per school. Of 627 eligible teachers contacted, 324 time diaries were completed and codable for a 24-hour day on a working Tuesday, for a response rate of 51.7 percent.[10]

Demographic information for the TWF sample of teachers was compared to figures from a larger sample of teachers from urban, elementary, public schools in the USA produced by the National Center for Education Statistics (NCES) for the 1993–1994 school year. The comparison suggested that the TWF sample characteristics were fairly close to the national averages (Drago *et al.* 1999: 33–34). However, the percentage of parents in the TWF data was over 12 full percentage points below the national average. We suspect this low figure is due to response bias, with relatively fewer parents willing to add to their already demanding schedules by committing to participate in the project (see Hochschild 1989: 279). Given various differences, we urge caution in treating the precise figures below as representative.[11] It is more important to focus on the patterns of findings across groups and methods of time estimation.

Administration of time diaries

The TWF time diaries were administered by the Institute for Survey and Policy Research at the University of Wisconsin-Milwaukee. After selection of potential respondents as described earlier, teachers received a letter informing them of the purpose of the project and informing them to expect a telephone call at the school. During the telephone call, a contact telephone number at home and time to call the teacher were requested. During the at-home telephone contact, teachers were given more details and requested to formally agree to participate in the study. Teachers who agreed were scheduled for a telephone interview and mailed a packet including the time diary, a $10 subject payment, and other materials. An attempt was made to schedule the telephone interview at least one full day after the diary should have been completed. If the diary had not been completed at the time scheduled for the telephone interview, respondents were requested to reschedule the telephone interview for one week later, and to complete the time diary in the meantime.[12]

To ensure that the diary and diary coding were standardized against extensively tested procedures, the diary was largely a replication of one from the Child Development Supplement of the Panel Study of Income Dynamics study at the Survey Research Center (SRC) at the University of Michigan. Coding and data entry methods were also replicated from SRC materials and practices.

Estimation methods

The data resulting from the procedures described above permit the development of six distinct measures of working time for teachers: contractual, standard diary, face, work invasiveness, housework, and total working time. These measures can be compared to determine whether different measurement approaches yield similar or distinct estimates of working time. Additionally, we are able to compare working time estimates across demographic categories to determine whether different measures of working time might mask or highlight demographic divergence.

Contractual working time. Contractual working time is a potentially important estimate of working time because it may influence public perceptions of teacher working time and help to determine expectations held by teachers and administrators regarding the appropriate length of the working day. A majority of respondents, 76.1 percent, are union members, but all respondents are covered by collective bargaining agreements. Such agreements specify the minimum amount of time the teacher is required to work each day. To ensure uniformity, contractual working time is measured to include all required time, whether in the classroom or in preparation, while excluding any duty-free lunch period.

Standard diary time. The standard diary approach captures working time both at the workplace and in the home, while excluding leisure time at work (e.g., Robinson and Godbey 1997). Commuting to work is also included as working time.[13] Conceptually, the standard approach is intended to represent time when the respondent's efforts are devoted to work for the employer.

Face time. This indicator refers to the amount of time the respondent is physically present in the workplace on the day in question. At a general conceptual level, face time is important because pressures to perform may be higher when customers, coworkers, and supervisors are present.

Moreover, organizational cultures that emphasize face time may deny the flexibility necessary for employees to meet family commitments and emergencies. Regarding teachers specifically, face time is important because it may have a closer relationship to public perceptions of teacher working time than does either the standard diary measure or contractual working time. Note that, because the TWF diaries include a check box for whether an activity is performed at the school of employment, face time is measured directly.

Work invasiveness. Theoretically, for professional occupations, work can "invade" an employee at any time. A telephone call or email may arrive at home, problems at work may be discussed at the family dinner table, leisure time may involve the company of fellow employees with work issues emerging as topics of discussion, or parents might attend events for their children and end up conversing about work. Particularly as the internet and telecommuting have become more pervasive, the interface between work and family time has become more porous, and the possibilities for work invading time at home have expanded.

The standard diary measure of working time goes part of the way towards capturing work invasiveness, because the standard measure includes commuting and work for the employer while off the job site. Nonetheless, the standard measure can understate invasiveness for two reasons. First, work arguably can invade an employee's time whenever he or she is physically present at work, even while engaging in leisure activities. Having a lunch break in a quiet classroom is not the same as a picnic in the park or dinner with the family, because the workplace constrains the set of activities an employee may engage in, even during nominally "free" time. We include such free time in our measure of work invasiveness.

Second, the performance of multiple activities leads to the understatement of work invasiveness in the standard diary measure. This problem stems from the 24-hour day constraint applied in diary coding. For example, if a teacher spends 1 hour simultaneously grading papers and helping a child with homework, coders are instructed to "divide the time evenly between the activities listed" (Survey Research Center 1997: 6). As a result, only one half hour would be attributed to work, and the other half hour would be attributed to helping one's child with homework. While this rule may be reasonable for many purposes, it also can lead to a systematic understatement of the time that work invades family.

To recover a portion of the information lost in the standard process, the research team created a "work multiplier" variable which allows us to capture work invasiveness while maintaining a 24-hour day. The structure of the variable is such that when all time variables are multiplied by the term we recover all working time regardless of whether another activity was performed at the same time. To preserve a 24-hour day, activities performed along with work were given multiplier values of zero. For the example provided above, the half hour attributed to grading papers in the standard diary measure would be given a value of '2' such that we capture the full hour of work invasion, while the half hour of helping a child with homework would be given a multiplier value of '0,' and the latter would drop out of the data set. All time at work, along with the standard diary count of commuting and working time at home, as modified by the work multiplier, yields the measure of work invasiveness.

Housework. In addition to time devoted to employment, most adults spend time on housework, suggesting our fifth measure of working hours: housework time. Housework is fundamentally different from work as conceptualized in the measures discussed above, since neither an employer nor wages are typically involved. This difference provides a reason for measuring housework separately. Nonetheless, as economist Gary Becker (1965) argues, tasks typically performed in the home, such as cleaning, cooking, and child-care, are similar to duties performed for wages in that they require time and effort.

Time diaries permit straightforward calculation of housework as broadly defined. Child-care and care for others (including partner or elder or neighbor) receive specific categories, as does travel related to these activities. In addition, housework such as cooking and cleaning receive separate codes. Adding time spent on errands yields housework figures for the TWF sample.

We are interested in housework *per se* for two reasons. First, Becker's work is built on an assumed trade-off between time devoted to household work and time provided to an employer. If this assumption is correct, then we would expect to see an identifiable trade-off between time devoted to the two sets of activities. Second, there may exist a gender division of labor in the household such that women disproportionately bear the burden of housework (Folbre 1994). If so, then the other measures of working time may understate the contributions of women to the economy.

Total working time. To the extent both housework and work for an employer involve time and effort, a global measure of total working time should include both sets of activities. The latter argument leads to our final measure of working time, labeled "total working time," which is obtained by summing housework and the standard diary measure of working time.[14]

RESULTS

We apply the measures of working time to the TWF data to ascertain how the different indicators alter measured working time.

Contractual working time. Analysis of the collective bargaining agreements covering our sample indicates that the average teacher in the sample was under contract to work 6.5 hours per day or 32.5 hours per week. Demographic comparisons of contractual working time exhibited minimal differences except with respect to race. White respondents were contracted to work an average of around 10 minutes longer than non-white respondents, a difference which is significant ($p < 0.01$, eta = 0.24).[15] A deeper look into the data reveals that white respondents were simply concentrated in school districts with the longest hours requirements. We ran a simple regression with contracted hours as the dependent variable, and independent variables including a dummy for white respondents, a dummy for union membership, and the percentage of children at the school receiving free and reduced price lunches. The regression explained just under 40 percent of the variance, but the race dummy was insignificant (beta = 0.067), while union membership had a significant negative effect on contracted hours (beta = 0.258), and the percentage of students from poor families had an even larger negative effect (beta = 0.489). These results point towards the dangers of using simple correlations to infer causation.

Standard diary time. Estimates of the standard diary measure of working time are provided in the first column of Table 4.1. As shown there, the average teacher in the sample worked just under 10 hours per day, or 9 hours and 41 minutes (table figures are given in decimal form). Analysis of variance reveals only two significant disparities: age exhibited a U-shaped relationship with working time ($p < 0.01$, eta = 0.22), and parents worked significantly fewer hours than non-parents ($p < 0.01$, eta = 0.21). The quantitative difference is such that respondents over 50 years of age worked 1 full hour longer than those in their 30's, while non-parents worked slightly over 45 minutes per day longer than parents. In sum, standard diary time

Table 4.1 Working hours by demographics: time-use diary measures[a]

Characteristic	*Standard diary time*	*Face time*	*Work invasiveness*
Average for entire sample	9.69	8.26	10.28
Men	10.12	8.22	10.70
Women	9.63	8.26	10.22
White	9.72	8.33	10.33
Black	9.60	8.00	10.16
Hispanic	9.42	7.92	9.89
Other	10.12	8.40	10.57
Age			
23–30	9.63	8.32	10.13
31–40	9.30	8.18	9.80
41–50	9.48	8.17	10.21
51+	10.32	8.40	10.89
No partner	9.76	8.06	10.42
Have partner	9.66	8.34	10.22
Not parent	10.03	8.34	10.55
Parent of dependent child	9.25	8.16	9.93

Source: TWF Project.

Note
a 324 observations except 322 observations on race, and 323 observations on gender and age.

produces age and family status differences, but no race differences. In contrast, contracted time yields only race differences.

Face time. The second column of Table 4.1 provides measures of face time. The average amount of face time for the TWF sample is 8.26 hours. Relative to contractual time, the average teacher was present in the school a full hour and three-quarters longer than was required. Relative to the standard diary indicator, face time understated the working day by just under one and one-half hours per day. Although the standard diary time varied substantially by demographic category, face time did not. This finding is sensible given that the contractual working day for teachers in these four school districts only ranges from a minimum of 6 to a maximum of 6.83 hours per day, and face time should be linked fairly closely to contractual time.

Analysis of variance reveals one significant difference in face time between groups. Teachers with partners exhibited face time around one-third of an hour longer than single respondents ($p < 0.05$, eta $= 0.12$). One possible explanation for this difference is that teachers with partners may often use school as a place to escape from the pressures of home.[16] If this was the case, we would expect teachers with partners to work longer hours overall. In fact, standard diary working time for partners is actually shorter by 6 minutes. It may be more plausible to suggest that these teachers are increasing their face time in an effort to erect a barrier between work and home, thereby improving the quality of time spent with the partner.

Work invasiveness. The third column of Table 4.1 presents work invasiveness figures. The average work invasiveness figure of 10.28 hours is a full one-half hour longer than working time as measured by standard diary procedures, and is 2 hours beyond average face time.[17] Analysis of variance reveals that significant differences exist here according to the age of the respondent, with respondents over the age of 50 appearing to permit work to invade over one hour more of their time relative to teachers in the 31–40 age group ($p < 0.01$, eta $= 0.22$). Parents appeared to allow work to invade their time significantly less than non-parents ($p < 0.01$, eta $= 0.17$), with a difference of just under 40 minutes. Perhaps the most striking aspect of the work invasiveness figures, however, is that for every demographic group the work invasiveness figures were at least a full hour and a half above the face time figures. To the extent perceptions of teacher working time are based on face or contractual time, a substantial underestimation of workload may exist.

Housework. Turning to housework, relevant figures are provided in the first column of Table 4.2. There we find an average of 2 hours and 14 minutes spent on such activities across the sample. As expected, women spent an average of over one-half hour more than men on household tasks, a difference which is significant in an analysis of variance ($p < 0.05$, eta $= 0.13$). This large difference for a single day is notable given that all of the respondents taught full-time the same day. Other significant differences are found according to age ($p < 0.01$, eta $= 0.29$). Teachers

Table 4.2 Housework and total working hours by demographics: time-use diary measures[a]

Characteristic	*Housework time*	*Total working hours*
Average for entire sample	2.23	11.92
Men	1.74	11.86
Women	2.31	11.93
White	2.35	12.07
Black	1.84	11.44
Hispanic	1.74	11.16
Other	2.06	12.18
Age		
23–30	1.50	11.13
31–40	2.63	11.94
41–50	2.55	12.02
51+	1.89	12.22
No partner	2.04	11.80
Have partner	2.31	11.96
No child	1.69	11.72
Have child	2.91	12.16

Source: TWF Project.

Note

a 324 observations except for 322 observations on race, and 323 observations on gender and age.

in the child-rearing years of their 30's added over 2.6 hours to their employment time; those in their 20's added only 1.5 hours; and those older than 50 added 1.89 hours. Teachers with children generated household production time well over an hour longer than non-parents ($p < 0.01$, eta $= 0.41$).

These findings support Becker's belief that there is a trade-off between paid employment and home production. Parents devoted less time to work as a teacher and more time to their families. However, the findings also suggest that parents appeared to compensate their employer for time spent on household matters: teachers who are parents spent an additional 73 minutes per day on their families, but in response only reduced employment time by between 17 and 47 minutes depending upon the measure used for work (see Table 4.1).

Total working time. The second column of Table 4.2 provides total working time figures for the sample, where total working time is the sum of housework and the standard diary measure of working time. For the entire sample, average total working time was just under 12 hours for the day. Gender differences were no longer significant, suggesting in connection with our other results that men may still be expected to devote more time than women to paid employment, and less time than women to housework. Racial differences in total working time were significant ($p < 0.05$, eta $=$ 0.16), with blacks and Hispanics showing shorter hours than others. This result achieves significance when insignificant differences in standard diary and housework measures are added together.[18] Differences in total working time were directly linked to age ($p < 0.05$, eta $= 0.19$). Due to longer standard diary working time, respondents over 50 years of age put in over 1 hour more on work of various sorts as compared to respondents in their 20's.

Recall our finding that the extra housework of parents is not totally offset by reductions in time devoted to employment. Relatedly, we find that the total working time of parents was higher by almost 30 minutes per day than that for non-parents ($p < 0.05$, eta $= 0.16$).

CONCLUSIONS

This paper presented initial results from a time diary study of full-time, public, elementary school teachers in four urban school districts. The demographics are similar to those from larger teacher samples in some ways, but with enough divergence so that caution is urged in generalizing the demographic results to teachers as a whole. Despite such cautions, the differences in work hours produced by these different estimation methods are so substantial that they deserve exploration in other occupational groups.

Six indicators of working time were developed and applied to the data to ascertain whether the method chosen to measure working time changes the results. Our major conclusion is that the choice of method exerts an important influence over measured working time. Specifically, the average teacher in the sample was under contract to work six and one-half hours per day. The amount of time spent at the school of employment, or face time, averaged eight and one-quarter hours per day, or over one and three-quarters hours longer than required by the contract. Standard time diary methodology suggests the working day was even longer, around twenty minutes shy of a ten hour day. Considering all time, either at school or performing work related tasks, even if performed simultaneously with others, yielded an average of approximately ten and one-quarter hours per day of work invasiveness. Work invaded these teachers' lives for almost four hours beyond that which is explicitly required. If perceptions of teacher working time are based upon contract stipulations or upon the amount of time teachers spend at school, such perceptions may substantially underestimate the actual time teachers devote to their jobs. In addition to teaching related work, respondents reported spending around two and one-quarter hours per day on housework. Adding housework to the standard diary measure of working time yielded an average total working day of just under twelve hours.

Demographic analyses reinforce our conclusion that the choice of measurement method exerts a strong influence over the results found. For example, contractual and total working time were significantly linked to race, while other measures were not. By way of contrast, standard diary time, work invasiveness, housework, and total working time were significantly associated with differences in age and parental status. Gender differences were only significant for housework, while teachers with partners or spouses only significantly diverged from others according to the face time measure.

Cutting across most measures of working time is the parental status of respondents. Parents worked less according to either the standard diary or work invasiveness measure. Parents devoted all of this time, and more, to their families and housework in general. The net result of parents performing more housework and less teaching related work is that parents spent almost one-half hour more per day on teaching and housework. These results again highlight the value of employing an assortment of working time measures: without the measure of housework, our results could have led us to conclude that parents work less than non-parents. The housework and total working time figures point to the opposite conclusion.

To the extent that these findings are shown to generalize, they may have important implications for policy and practice. For policy-makers in the field of education, the results may suggest that teaching is already an occupation involving long hours of work. Initiatives which involve lengthening the school day might therefore lead to a reduction in teaching-related work performed at home (e.g., preparation). Alternatively, lengthening the school day may increase teacher working time and possibly increase the stress associated with the job. In either case, problems of teacher retention could intensify if the long hours of teachers in this sample are typical for the profession.

Not addressed in this chapter is the question of causality: why do teachers work such long hours, much unpaid? Three potential culprits, any of which might well apply to other occupations and industries, can be discounted. First, Juliet Schor (1991) has argued that employers provide economic incentives for employees to work long hours. Second, Schor has suggested more recently (1999) that a work-and-spend mentality drives people to work long hours in order to support high consumption expenditures. Given that the teachers in the sample were salaried and covered by collective bargaining agreements which tightly control salaries and provide a high degree of job security, it seems unlikely that either type of economic motivation is at work. Third, Arlie Hochschild (1997) suggests that the workplace is now relatively more enjoyable or attractive than home, leading employees to work long hours in order to minimize time at home. Given the hours of work for the employer that our teachers provide *at home*, this argument also seems implausible.

Recent research suggests two related but distinct dynamics may be responsible for the long hours of teachers both as employees and family members. The first dynamic, posited by Folbre (1994), concerns the social devaluation of women's work in general. Such devaluation can explain why teachers and mothers are expected to work long hours for low or no pay. The specific context for such devaluation includes considerable institutional pressures on teachers to improve student performance along a variety of dimensions without expanded resources to achieve those ends (Rogers 1999). The second dynamic, posited by Garey (1999), suggests that many women are driven by the internalization of social understandings regarding the meaning of being a "good mother" and a "good employee." Such internalization leads working mothers to demand much of themselves in terms of both work and family.[19]

Although we do not test these hypotheses here, we believe they offer promising directions for future research. What we do know, without question, is that if society were to pay for the currently unremunerated work of these teachers, and particularly those who are parents, the bill would be enormous.

NOTES

1 This chapter is largely drawn from Drago *et al.* (1999). The authors thank the Alfred P. Sloan Foundation for financial support for this research, the Institute for Survey and Policy Research for adminstering the survey, and the editors and Juliet Schor and Frank Stafford for valuable advice along the way.
2 On the possibility of overwork, see Schor (1991, 1997). For contrary evidence, see Robinson and Bostrom (1994) or Robinson and Godbey (1997).
3 Gender and parenting figures for the 1993–1994 school year are from the National Center for Education Statistics (1998). Dual earner figures are estimated from the Bureau of the Census (1992).
4 On high commitment work systems in schools, see US General Accounting Office (USGAO 1995). On the effects of such initiatives on teachers, see Drago *et al.* (1996).
5 Although multiple answers were permitted, a 1996 survey of teachers reveled that slightly over 20 percent of respondents entered the profession at least in part due to the long summer vacation (National Education Association 1997: 59).
6 The issue is unambiguous in the National Center for Education Statistics survey, where respondents are asked about time "required to be at school," which clearly includes break time (1996: 74), but is ambiguous in the National Education Association survey, which asks about the "length of your required school day" (1997: 150).
7 Comparing the subsamples of respondents who reported a usual as opposed to an unusual workload revealed no significant ($p < 0.01$) differences according to any of the demographic variables employed here or in any of the five measures of working time. However, regressions for the relationship between measures of working time are affected by the variable (see discussion of Figure 1).
8 Technical detail on sampling and the sample is provided in Drago *et al.* (1999: 33–34).
9 Teachers with at least one-half of their students defined as "special needs" were also excluded from the study. Our supposition was that the number of special needs teachers that would naturally emerge without the restriction would be too small for statistical analysis.
10 An overlapping set of 438 teachers completed a telephone interview, for a response rate of 69.9 percent. Telephone interview survey data are used for the demographic information employed here.
11 Even though the 12.6 percent difference in parental status is large, calculations suggest the effects of such response bias are small. Applying the NCES proportion

of parents to the working time figures for parents and non-parents (reported in Tables 4.1 and 4.2) finds the standard diary time estimate falling from 9.69 hours to 9.58 hours per day, housework time rising from 2.23 hours to 2.38 hours, with a net increase in the total working time estimate of 0.04 hour.

12 Given the difficulty of scheduling some telephone interviews, rescheduling was only requested and not required of those who had not completed the time diary. Additionally, for respondents who requested an immediate telephone interview, the interview was performed prior to completion of the time diary.

13 See, e.g., Juster and Stafford (1991: 475).

14 By adding housework and the standard diary measure of working time, we avoid double-counting. If instead we added housework and face time, time spent at school on a phone call to a sick partner or child would be double-counted. If we added housework to work invasiveness, the same problem would exist.

15 The specific figures for contractual working time by race are: whites 6.55 hours, blacks 6.36 hours, Hispanics 6.39 hours, and other respondents 6.34 hours.

16 This argument is suggested by Arlie Hochschild (1997).

17 Recall that work invasiveness differs from the standard diary measure only by the inclusion of leisure at work and the application of the work multiplier to recover working time which was shared with other activities. Most of the difference between the standard diary measure and work invasiveness is due to leisure time at work, with an average of only 0.1 hour difference accounted for by the work multiplier.

18 Note that we make no causal arguments regarding race, since race is closely linked to other demographic variables and to contractual working time.

19 By extension, the men in the sample may select into this female-dominated occupation because they hold similar beliefs. This possibility could be explored in future studies.

REFERENCES

Appelbaum, E. and Batt, R. (1994) *The New American Workplace*, Ithaca, NY: ILR Press.

Appelbaum, E. and Berg, P. (1997) "Balancing Work and Family: Evidence from Surveys of Manufacturing Workers," In *Proceedings of the Forty-Ninth Annual Meeting, Industrial Relations Research Association*, Madison, Wisconsin: IRRA: 115–122.

Becker, G. (1965) "A Theory of the Allocation of Time," *Economic Journal* 75(299): 493–517.

Bond, J. T., Galinsky, E., and Swanberg, J. (1998) *The 1997 National Study of the Changing Workforce*, New York: Families and Work Institute.

Bureau of the Census (1992) *Census of Population and Housing, 1990: Public Use Microdata Samples U.S.* [machine-readable data files], Washington: The Bureau.

Drago, R., Caplan, R., Costanza, D., Brubaker, T., Cloud, D., Harris, N., Kashian, R., and Riggs, T. L. (1999) "New Estimates of Working Time for Teachers," *Monthly Labor Review* 122(4): 31–40.

Drago, R., Caplan, R., Markowitz, A., Spiros, R., and Riggs, T. L. (1996) "Is Participatory Decision Making Family-Friendly?" *Journal for Quality and Participation* 19(5): 90–93.

Folbre, N. (1994) *Who Pays for the Kids? Gender and the Structures of Constraint*, New York: Routledge.

Garey, A.I. (1999) *Weaving Work and Motherhood*, Philadelphia: Temple University Press.

Hochschild, A. (1989) *The Second Shift*, New York: Avon Books.

Hochschild, A. (1997) *The Time Bind: When Work Becomes Home and Home Becomes Work*, New York: Metropolitan Books.

Juster, T. F. and Stafford, F. P. (1991) "The Allocation of Time: Empirical Findings, Behavioral Models, and Problems of Measurement," *Journal of Economic Literature* 29(2): 471–522.

Kimball, G. (1999) *Twenty-First Century Families: Blueprints of Family-Friendly Schools and Governments*, Chico, CA: Equality Press.

McGrath, M. Z. (1995) *Teachers Today: A Guide to Surviving Creatively*, Thousand Oaks, CA: Corwin Press.

National Center for Education Statistics (1998) *Schools and Staffing Survey and Teacher Follow-up Survey*, Washington, DC: US Department of Education (CD-Rom).

National Center for Education Statistics (1996) *Schools and Staffing in the United States: A Statistical Profile, 1993–94*, Washington, DC: US Department of Education.

National Education Association (1997) *Status of the American Public School Teacher, 1995–1996*, Washington, DC.

Robinson, J. P. and Bostrom, A. (1994) "The Overestimated Workweek? What Time Diary Measures Suggest," *Monthly Labor Review* 117(8): 11–23.

Robinson, J. P. and Godbey, G. (1997) *Time for Life: The Surprising Ways Americans Use Their Time*, University Park: Pennsylvania State Press.

Rogers, J. K. (1999) *There's No Substitute: Time Transfer in the Teaching Profession*, University Park: Penn State University Department of Labor Studies and Industrial Relations, working paper (September).

Schor, J. B. (1991) *The Overworked American: The Unexpected Decline of Leisure*, New York: Basic Books.

Schor, J. B. (1997) "Civic Engagement and Working Hours: Do Americans Really Have More Free Time Than Ever Before?" paper presented at the Conference on Civic Engagement in American Democracy, Portland, Maine.

Schor, J. B. (1999) *The Overspent American: Upscaling, Downshifting, and the New Consumer*, New York: HarperCollins.

Survey Research Center (1997) 1997 Child Development Supplement of the Panel Study of Income Dynamics, *Time Diary Coding Manual*, University of Michigan, Project 721.

USGAO (1995) *Schools and Workplaces. An Overview of Successful and Unsuccessful Practices*, No. GAO/PEMD-95-28, Washington DC: US Government Accounting Office.

5 Working hours and time pressure

The controversy about trends in time use

Juliet B. Schor

THE ACCELERATION OF DAILY LIFE

If there is anything on which Americans can agree these days, it may be the experience of hurry. There seems to be an omnipresent feeling of speed-up; Americans are busier, have more to do, experience time pressure, stress, and even burnout. There are no comprehensive statistics on the "speed of daily life," but attitudinal evidence indicates that "time pressure" has increased. Over the period from 1965 to 1995 the fraction of the urban population aged 18–64 reporting that they "always feel rushed" rose from 24 percent to 33 percent. Similarly, the fraction of Americans reporting that they "almost never" have time on their hands has risen from 47 percent in 1971 to 56 percent in 1995 (Robinson and Godbey 1999: Table 22, 232). Stress levels have also risen, and by the mid-1990s a majority of Americans reported that in the two weeks prior to being asked they had experienced a lot or moderate stress (Robinson and Godbey 1999: 235). Forty-five percent of all Americans report that they have less free time today than they had five years ago (Robinson and Godbey 1999: 239).

One popular view of the acceleration of daily life is that technology is responsible. First put forward by Jeremy Rifkin in his 1987 book *Time Wars*, the technological argument says that computers are fast, and they transmit that sense of speed to us. Immersed for hours in the world of the nanosecond, we become impatient with the minute (see also Gleick 1999). While there is much that is appealing in this technological view, it is ultimately of limited explanatory power. On the one hand, it does not account for the demographic pattern of time pressure. Particular groups, such as women, employed people, and 35–54 year olds, feel more time pressure than other types of people. However, these are not the population segments which spend most time with the new technologies. (Men and children, for example, are heavy electronic media users.) One problem with the technological explanation is that it has no gender analysis, yet the phenomenon of time famine is highly gendered. Furthermore, the technological view has a simplistic vision of both human action and technological impact. The human being is seen as an automaton unreflexively adopting the speed of whatever screen he or she is in front of. But an informative scholarly literature suggests the impact of technology is much more nuanced, depending greatly on context.

A second argument about time pressure is that it is due mainly to the phenomenon of "the overworked American," that is, long and growing hours of work (Schor 1991). People feel more pressure and stress because their hours on the job have increased, while the temporal responsibilities of the household economy have not declined commensurately. Leete and Schor (1994) found that annual hours of paid employment rose slightly in the 1970s, and substantially in the 1980s.

This view has been directly challenged by time-use researchers John Robinson and Geoffrey Godbey. Although they find a considerable growth in time pressure, they argue it is mainly a "a perceptual problem." Based on their research with time diaries, they find that free time has risen, not declined. They argue that Americans work less than ever, and that time pressure is a purely subjective phenomenon, caused by escalating desires for various activities. They believe Americans have developed a "psychology of entitlement," and that feelings of time pressure are part of an "increasing tendency to feel victimized" (Robinson and Godbey 1999: 304–305).[1]

CONTESTED SCHEDULES: ARE AMERICANS WORKING MORE HOURS?

The debate about time pressure which has been carried on in the 1990s came after a long period of inattention to the question of average hours of work. Indeed, the work week was generally considered to be a solved issue, because working hours were thought to be either falling or stable. This view was challenged when Laura Leete and I presented estimates from the Current Population Survey which showed that annual hours had risen appreciably (Leete and Schor 1992, 1994; Schor 1991). "Working harder for less" became a popular mantra in the public discourse. Quickly, researchers from the Universities of Michigan and Maryland argued the contrary. Relying on time diary data, they claimed that Americans were enjoying more leisure time than ever before (Robinson 1989a,b, 1994; Juster and Stafford 1991). Subsequent studies ensued, but considerable disagreement about trends in worktime persists.

In the pages that follow, I will confine the discussion about hours in two ways. First, most of the debate has been about hours of paid employment, rather than trends in household hours, which are available only from the time diaries.[2] Therefore in the text, I will be discussing only hours of paid employment. As a consequence, I will mainly be discussing hours for labor force participants, in order to exclude effects on average hours which are due to trends in participation rates.

Types of data on hours of paid work

There are three major sources of data on hours of work. The first is data provided by business establishments to the government. These data have rarely figured in the public debates because they measure hours per job rather than per person. While establishment data are extremely important for some issues (i.e., measurements of productivity per hour), they are less well suited to trends in individual or household time use, particularly because the importance of multiple jobholding and the underground economy have been growing. The second type of data is household surveys such as the Current Population Survey (CPS), the Census, and the Panel Study of Income Dynamics (PSID). These are large government data sets which provide representative samples of the population. They use recall questions about weekly hours and weeks of work per year such as "how many hours did you work last week?" These data cover only hours worked at paid jobs, and do not include unpaid work in the home. The third type of data is time diaries.[3] In these surveys respondents are asked to record, at fifteen minute intervals, how they are using their time over a 24-hour period. The US diary studies vary in methodology. Some are recorded at the time of activity, others use telephone surveys and ask respondents to recall yesterday's activities. The diary surveys have been carried out by university survey research centers at various points in time. They include both market and household work. Here I will be discussing only the evidence from the household surveys and the diary studies.

Findings from the household surveys

A number of estimates from the household surveys, such as the CPS, the PSID, and the National Survey of the Changing Workforce (NSCW) show clear evidence of rising hours. My own estimates with those of Laura Leete (Leete and Schor 1992, 1994; also reported in Schor 1991 for a shorter period) show that annual hours of market work as measured by the Current Population Survey rose substantially for the labor force between 1969 and 1989, and particularly since 1979 (see Table 5.1).[4] Because there has been confusion about exactly what our estimates measured, it may be worth clarifying two points. First, the large increase in market hours for women is *not* due to increases in married women's labor force participation. These estimates include only labor force participants. This is a point on which there has been considerable misinterpretation, including by Bluestone and Rose (1997).

Second, the estimates which show the largest increases in hours are those which exclude those labor force participants who are either unemployed or involuntarily under-employed (i.e., working part-week or part-year, but preferring to work longer hours). We differentiate between the "unconstrained labor force," that is, employed persons who are not involuntarily

Table 5.1 Annual market hours

	1969	*1979*	*1989*	*Change 1969–1989*
All labor market participants				
All	1751	1731	1804	53
Men	2007	1962	1987	−20
Women	1385	1451	1593	208
Unconstrained labor force only				
All	1786	1855	1924	138
Men	2054	2093	2126	72
Women	1406	1558	1693	287

Source: Leete and Schor (1994).

underemployed, and the "constrained labor force." The trends in hours between these two groups are quite marked, as the unconstrained group has seen quite substantial increases in their annual hours, and the latter the reverse. Indeed, although subsequent authors (Bluestone and Rose 1997; Jacobs and Gerson 1998) have made similar points, sometimes to "refute" the idea of the average "overworked American," we believe this finding was one of our most important. While the majority of Americans did experience an increase in hours of work over this time, a growing minority found themselves unable to find adequate amounts of work.

A longer series from the CPS, which includes the underemployed, is provided by Mishel *et al.* (1999). They find that average annual hours have increased by 110 since 1967. Notably, they find that hours have continued to rise since 1989, increasing by 45 (from 1823 to 1868) between 1989 and 1996 (Table 3.1, 123).

Using the Panel Study of Income Dynamics (PSID), Bluestone and Rose (1997) find similar trends. In response to Robinson's criticisms that the CPS weekly hours series is plagued by overestimation bias (see below), Bluestone and Rose have argued that the PSID is a more accurate measure because respondents are asked to provide more detail about vacation days, leaves, primary and second jobs, and so on. Looking at prime-age workers (ages 25–54), Bluestone and Rose find considerable business cycle fluctuation in hours. After controlling for the cyclical effects, they find annual hours have increased on average 3.3 hours per year, for a total rise of 66 hours between 1969 and 1989. This is similar to Leete and Schor's finding of a 2.75 yearly increase for those years for all labor force participants. The 0.65 hour difference may be attributable mainly to the exclusion of the 55+ age group from Bluestone and Rose's sample.[5]

The 1997 National Survey of the Changing Workforce conducted by the Families and Work Institute (Bond *et al.* 1997) also has found substantial increases in weekly hours of work among wage and salaried workers between 1977 and 1997. On average, weekly hours (for those working 20 or more hours per week) increased by 2.8 hours for men and 5 hours for women.[6]

Findings from the time diaries

Results from the household surveys are disputed by researchers who rely on time diaries. Juster and Stafford of the University of Michigan (1991) have claimed that Americans' free time has risen, on the basis of data covering the period 1965–1981. John Robinson, from the University of Maryland, using the Michigan data for 1965 and 1975, and his own diary surveys for 1985 and 1992–95, has disputed the findings that hours of work were increasing. Robinson's findings have been published in a variety of places, including a monograph for the Office of Technology Assessment (1988), articles in *American Demographics* (1989a,b), in a *Monthly Labor Review* article (Robinson and Bostrom 1994), and most comprehensively in his coauthored book with Geoffrey Godbey, *Time for Life: The Surprising Ways Americans Use Their Time*, in both a 1997 and a 1999 edition.

In *Time for Life*, Robinson and Godbey present diary estimates of trends in paid work for the period 1965 to 1985, and in the second edition, include less detailed updates for 1992–1995 (Robinson and Godbey 1999: 95). They find that hours of paid work fell for both men and women between 1965 and 1985. Weekly hours of employed women declined from 36.8 to 30.8 while men's weekly hours declined from 46.5 to 39.7. In the period between 1985 and 1992–95, the trends are more consistent with the household surveys. Hours of paid work for employed women increased by 3 per week, while men's hours remained unchanged (Table 37, 346; no average figure is provided).

It is worth noting the path of decline during the 1965–85 period, however, in light of the sample issues which I address below. In the aggregate, Robinson finds that virtually all the decline in hours comes between 1965 and 1975. For women, there is a weekly 2.5-hours rise after 1975, and for men a 4.2-hours decline.[7]

Who is correct? Has free time increased, as the diaries show, or are hours of work rising, the picture we get from the household surveys? As is usual in debates of this kind, some of the differences are due to the fact that we are not dealing with uniform time periods, uniform measures of work, labor force coverage, and the like. Leete and Schor's estimates include the 18+ age group, Robinson's cover 25–65, Bluestone and Rose's cover 25–54, and the NSCW include only those working 20 hours per week. But the discrepancies are due also to other factors. Robinson's critique centers on the quality of answers to the weekly hours question in the CPS. The economists (Leete and Schor, Mishel, Rose and Bluestone) emphasize the importance of measuring annual hours and accounting for business cycle and labor market trends. I turn to these issues now, in more detail.

A statistical artifact?

One of the major sources of disagreement between Robinson and myself continues to be the usefulness of the 1965 survey that forms his benchmark year. The importance of the 1965 data is clear from Robinson's (1989a: 34–35) discussion: "Most gains in free time have occurred between 1965 and 1975. Since then, the amount of free time people have has remained fairly stable, with some loss for certain groups."

The 1965 survey, like the 1975 and its 1981 follow-up, was carried out at the University of Michigan. It was part of a pioneering international comparative project in time-use organized by Alexander Szalai. In order to conform to the requirements of that project, certain sample restrictions were put in place. Thus, the 1965 sample includes only employed heads of households and their spouses, it includes only respondents from Standard Metropolitan Statistical Areas (SMSAs), and it excludes all farmers. These restrictions in themselves are not a problem if either (1) future samples are similarly restricted or (2) the restrictions are not correlated with trends in time use.[8]

Leete's and my analysis of the 1965 sample found that the sample restrictions, while not always significant in uncontrolled comparisons (as for example, the rural/urban comparison that Robinson reports), *are* correlated with hours of work. Compared to the representative population measures (as measured by the CPS), the 1965 sample is higher-income, it is more white, and it is more employed. These characteristics are all correlated with hours of work. (Income and hours are positively correlated, being white is positively correlated, and obviously, being employed is positively correlated.) Thus, the fact that Robinson finds a substantial decline in hours of work between 1965 and 1975 is not surprising from this perspective: it is in part caused by comparing a sample of high-hours people with a representative sample.

Labor market and macroeconomic conditions

Perhaps the major source of difference between the estimates of the economists and Robinson is in their respective treatments of differences in labor market and macroeconomic conditions. It is well-known among economists that average hours of work fluctuate with the business cycle, rising in expansions, as firms increase production more rapidly than employment, and falling in recessions as production shrinks. For this reason, trends in hours worked should be calibrated at consistent points in the business cycle, or should be corrected by the inclusion of a cyclical variable in a trend regression. Such corrections are now standard procedure among economists who study trends in hours.[9] By contrast, the time diary studies have never taken these factors into account, despite the fact that cyclical adjustments are possible.[10]

In Robinson's 1965–1985 estimates, this problem is not as severe as in other studies, because both 1965 and 1985 are expansion years. However, GDP growth in 1965 was almost twice as high as in 1985, so that some cyclical bias does exist. However, his middle year (1975) was a recession. On the other hand, Robinson's latest estimates cover three years (1992–1995) during which the economy was recovering from recession and unemployment was declining substantially. Estimates later in the decade show larger increases in hours.

A second problem is more serious. Typically, time diary studies of working hours divide the population into the employed and nonemployed. This is a reasonable procedure in a world where there is no unemployment or underemployment. However, if unemployment and underemployment are large and/or growing, the failure to differentiate among these states leads to a conflation of voluntary and involuntary leisure time. By extension, it also results in estimates of work time which are downward biased in a substantive, although not literal sense. This is probably the most important source of difference between the estimates of Leete and Schor and Robinson. During the period under question, there was a pronounced upward trend in unemployment and, more importantly for the estimates of hours among employed persons, in underemployment, defined as involuntary part-time and part-year work. Involuntary part-time and part-year workers are those individuals who identified themselves to the CPS surveyer as having only part-week work but wanting full-time weekly work or as being employed only a fraction of the year but wanting to work all year, or both. As noted above, Leete and Schor call these people "labor market constrained."

The time diary questionnaires do not contain questions about labor market constraints, so these individuals cannot be identified. However, their inclusion in the average estimates has a large impact on hours, for two reasons. First, their numbers have increased steadily over the period in question. Between 1969 and 1989, the fraction of the labor force which was underemployed rose from 7.16 percent to 13.9 percent (Leete and Schor 1994: Table 4, 32).[11] Furthermore, their average hours of work have fallen precipitously, from 1 312 in 1969 to 1 066 in 1989, a drop of 246 hours (Leete and Schor 1992: Figure 1, 8). Inclusion of these individuals imparts a downward bias to estimates of hours. Comparing the trends for the entire labor force and the unconstrained labor force, Leete and Schor found that the rise in hours was 85 hours greater among the latter (138 compared to 53). Our correction for the growth of the underemployed explains our larger estimates of hours rise than other CPS studies which correct only for business cycle fluctuations. The estimates of Coleman and Pencavel (1993a,b) using Census Data (and for 1988, the CPS) are revealing in this respect. They find that hours of work have fallen for individuals of low educational attainment, and risen for those of high attainment. The growth in underemployment has been considerably more pronounced among those of lower educational attainment level, and also among black males.[12]

Which is the right category for measuring trends in time use? If average hours of work fall because involuntary underemployment is rising, the general conclusion that Americans have more free time, while strictly speaking true, is misleading. The growth of a bimodal distribution in hours which has emerged since the late 1960s is perhaps *the* major development in time-use trends which cannot be illuminated by the time diaries. The labor force was increasingly comprised of an overworked segment of full-time workers and a growing group of underemployed whose annual hours are shrinking. (On these points, see also Bluestone and Rose 1997 and Jacobs and Gerson 1998). Failure to account for this development, rather than the psychological processes they invoke, may well be the most important source of the disconnect between Robinson and Godbey's claim that the average American has more free time than ever before, and the pervasive sense of overwork, stress, and a speeded-up pace of life that everyone agrees has taken hold.

Overestimation in the recall data

The core of Robinson's critique of the CPS is that individuals overestimate their working hours when asked about them in the standard recall format, but give true estimates when they fill out a time diary. (There may be some overestimation in cases where diaries are filled out retrospectively, as roughly 40 percent of the 1985 sample were, but I set aside this issue.) This view is supported by at least one study which found the diary method to be the most accurate measure of time use (Juster and Stafford 1985). Robinson and Bostrom (1994) and Robinson and Godbey (1997) treat this issue in detail, arguing that with recall methods, individuals with high hours overestimate their worktime, and those with low hours underestimate. This claim has been challenged by Jacobs (1998) who finds that self-reports correlate well with alternative measures of working hours, such as the times at which people leave home and return on work days. Jacobs also finds that errors in the self-reports are random, rather than patterned, and that longer reference periods (i.e., hours worked last year) are more accurate than weekly estimates. Finally, Jacobs argues that Robinson and Bostrom's findings of under- and overestimation are caused by the phenomenon of "regression to the mean" associated with responses measured with error rather than a true phenomenon of exaggeration.

Before leaving the issue of exaggerated self-reports, it is important to note that the relevance of this issue to trends in worktime depends on those trends themselves. Even if Robinson and Bostrom are correct about exaggeration, that is an argument about a bias in *levels* of working hours rather than *trends*. The question for trends is whether the extent of overestimation is changing over time. Robinson and Bostrom (1994) argue that the amount of bias is in fact growing over time. That is because higher hours individuals engage in more overestimation than those who work less. (There is relatively little overestimation bias in the 20–44 hours per week range, but high exaggeration in the 55+ category.) But if the size of the bias is growing, it is most likely due to precisely the trend Robinson contests – the rise in working hours. Because more people are working longer hours there is more overestimation. Overestimation may inflate the magnitude of the increase, but does not account for the basic upward trend itself.

Response bias in the time diary estimates: do busy people refuse to participate?

Nearly a decade ago, Arlie Hochschild (1989) in her classic work, *The Second Shift*, rejected the time diary findings of equal work burdens between employed wives and husbands on the grounds that high rates of attrition from the sample were caused by disproportionate drop-out rates among the busiest women. Robinson rejected this argument on the grounds that, in the 1975 survey, diary respondents were not statistically different in their time use than those who dropped out. This question has been revisited more recently by Robert Drago and his colleagues, who conducted a large diary survey of teachers. Drago *et al.* found a statistically significant decision not to participate among the most time-pressed teachers (Drago *et al.* 1998; Drago *et al.* Chapter 4 in this volume). Drago *et al.* differ from Robinson in a number of ways. First, their study was done more than twenty years after Robinson's, and in a period of high and rising levels of work and stress for teachers. Recall that 1975 was a recession year, well before the rise in major increases in work time occurred. Furthermore, Robinson's drop-outs were individuals who had participated in the first wave of the diary survey, rather than those who refused initially. Finally, Drago *et al.* had a sample consisting entirely of teachers.

A Finnish study also found that those who refused to participate in the diary studies worked longer hours than those who did participate, and that the difference was especially marked for the self-employed. Furthermore, non-participation was also shown to be correlated with variables such as educational level and taxable income. Middle-aged persons with higher educational levels were most likely to participate (Pääkkönen 1998). However, an analysis of the high rate of non-response in Dutch time-budget surveys did not support the busy bias hypothesis (Knulst and van den Broek 1998).

"Time at work" versus "time actually working"

Another source of difference among the findings concerns the measurement of work. In the household surveys, respondents are asked how many hours they worked last week. It is likely that they respond with an answer which covers "time at work," that is, the hours they are officially on the job.[13] However, as Robinson and Godbey point out, not all hours at work are spent actually working. Employees whose jobs permit it congregate around the water cooler, make personal phone calls, and go to the bathroom during company time. In their estimates, Robinson and Godbey subtract some of this "on-the-job leisure." They also subtract time spent in on-the-job-training.

Which measure is preferable? It depends on the questions one is interested in answering. For measurements of productivity, clearly the time working measure is the right one. For larger social concerns, such as work–family pressure, or the trend in civic engagement, time on the job is preferable, because it measures time that is formally committed to the employer and not available for many other uses. These differences account for some of the divergence in the estimates.

Annual versus weekly hours

As I have noted, time diaries give us estimates of weekly hours, whereas the CPS and PSID allow us to construct estimates of annual hours.[14] One reason it is important to look at annual hours is that two-thirds of the increase in working time in Leete and Schor's estimates occurred as a result of a growth in weeks of work per year. (Our total labor force measure of weekly hours finds relatively little change over the period.) Among the unconstrained labor force, weeks worked per year rose by 1.4 for men and 6.1 for women. These substantial increases are unlikely to be adequately reflected in the smaller samples of the time diaries, which measure only 24-hour periods, and have not been carried out during the summer, when we suspect much of the increase in women's work has occurred.

SUMMARY AND CONCLUSION

While it is generally agreed that time diaries are the most accurate measures of individuals' time use *at* a point in time, it is by no means clear that they are superior for assessing trends in working hours *over* time. This is a task they were not designed for, and for which the available US diary studies have serious drawbacks. Unlike the diary studies, the household surveys offer population samples which are consistent over time and representative. Because trends in hours of work are to a significant extent driven by demographic and socioeconomic factors, such representativeness is crucial to any analysis of trends. The household surveys also include weeks of work per year, which the diary studies do not. The household surveys allow us to account for macroeconomic and labor market variables which have strong effects on hours, which the diary estimates do not. Furthermore, the argument of exaggeration in the recall data appears not to be as compelling as originally thought. For the foregoing reasons, I continue to be skeptical about the time diary results which find that Americans have more free time than ever before, and to believe that trends in worktime remain best measured by large, representative household surveys.[15] That having been said, I believe everyone concerned in this debate agrees that large sample, government-sponsored time diary surveys, such as those which exist in Western Europe, are preferable to existing modes of data collection.

The controversy about trends in time use has mainly been of a technical nature, revolving around issues of data quality, sample selection, and so forth. However, its significance is of far more than academic interest, in part because it has important political, social and gender dimensions. If time-squeeze is only a "perceptual" or "entitlement" problem it can be solved merely by lowering expectations. There is no need for public policy, institutional change, or a renegotiation of household work between men and women. Corporations (as employers) play no role here, nor does government. We only think we do not have time for our children, or our communities. By contrast, if work has indeed become more demanding, crowding out family and community time, there is a larger public interest involved. Achieving a sustainable and optimal balance between various uses of time will require fundamental restructuring of the basic institutions which govern market, household and community work.

NOTES

1 Robinson and Godbey do not offer a comprehensive explanation for why time pressure has increased, beyond a brief discussion of the standard, neoclassical economics theory of time allocation. But that theory predicts that wage levels and the productivity of non-marketed activities determine time pressure. *Ceteris paribus*, individuals with rising wages should experience increasing time pressure (because the opportunity cost of leisure is higher), and those with declining wages should be less pressured. If Robinson and Godbey are correct, the substantial fraction of the population whose real wages have fallen since the mid-1970s should have experienced a decline in time pressure. Furthermore, among those whose wages have been stagnant, time pressure should have remained constant. Only individuals who experienced upward wage movements should have become more harried. Robinson and Godbey's findings on stress (that report education levels) are at variance with this prediction. The rise in stress levels was greatest for respondents with low educational attainment; college-educated individuals had very slight (1–2 percent increases) and those with graduate school had a decline in stress levels. Similar findings were obtained by income level (Robinson and Godbey 1999: 234–235). The fact that the data repudiate the standard neoclassical prediction is not surprising from a heterodox perspective in which income effects dominate, and "stress" is caused by overall income rather than wage levels. In addition, a rising quality of leisure activity could have raised the quantity of leisure activities attempted, which would also raise time pressure.

2 Our basic methodology follows that of Victor Fuchs (1986), and uses CPS data to construct annual hours of paid work. It intends to avoid the shortcomings we were concerned about in the time diary data. Robinson and Godbey's comments (1999: 50) concern the way we calculated household hours. For household hours we created predicted estimates from the 1975 Michigan Time Diary Survey and the CPS. (Time diaries provide the only existing estimates of household hours.) Using the 1975 and 1981 survey, we constructed an econometric model to predict average amounts of weekly housework for various demographic and socioeconomic groups. The coefficients from that model are applied to the CPS in order to construct estimated trends in household work. We presumed that trends in housework are driven largely by demographic and socioeconomic trends, that are well captured by the CPS data. Like Robinson and Godbey, we also find significant declines in women's and rises in men's hours of housework, so their suggestion to the contrary is somewhat puzzling. Robinson and Godbey take exception to the fact that we used only the 1975 survey, although we did use the 1981 survey as well. They did not make the 1985 survey available to us.

3 In the time diary studies, respondents are asked to record, for every 15-minute interval, how they spent their time. Analysts then choose a particular definition of "work" or "leisure," in order to produce the kinds of measures that are used in debates on time allocation. Time budgets are always weekly, either because the diaries are filled out for an entire week, or because a synthetic week is created from daily diaries. In a classic diary study, respondents receive the diary before it is to be filled out. In Robinson's 1985 survey, some respondents were called on the telephone and asked to recall in 15-minute intervals how they used their time in the previous day. In the 1992 data (which was actually collected over the period 1992–95), all respondents were contacted by telephone and asked about yesterday's activities.

4 Our estimates were derived by combining respondents' estimates of their actual hours last week and the number of weeks they worked in the previous year. We found similar trends using the "usual weekly hours" question which has been available since 1979.

5 There are differences in the trends once they are broken down by gender, however. Bluestone and Rose report (but do not present) that in their estimates male hours declined slightly, after controlling for the business cycle. This may be due partly to the large declines in hours (7.7 per year) registered for black men, a finding which accords with that of Coleman and Pencavel (1993a). But note also that Leete and Schor find a 20-hour decline in market hours for men before underemployment and unemployment are taken into account. By contrast, Bluestone and Rose find even larger increases in female hours than Leete and Schor, recording a rise of 18.8 hours per year, or 376 hours over the period.

6 The NSCW estimates include work at all jobs, including work taken home.

7 It is not clear why these figures differ from Robinson's earlier estimates, as all calculations are based on the same survey. In two papers for the Office of Technology Assessment (OTA) (a mimeo entitled preliminary in 1986, and the other published in 1988: 69), significant differences with the 1999 figures appear. Levels of worktime are significantly higher in the 1988 table, and there is a rise in both male and female hours between 1975 and 1985 (see Table 5.2). Other discrepancies exist between the 1989 *American Demographics* (*AD*) article on free time and *Time for Life* (Table 5.3). One possible explanation of these differences is variations in the handling of the missing categories of the 1965 sample. Finally, there are discrepancies within *Time for Life*. In Table 2, employed women are reported to work 30.8 hours per week, but in Figure 16 they are reported to work 34.3 hours.

Table 5.2 Weekly hours of paid work

	1975	*1985*	*Change in worktime*
Women (1988, OTA)	13.4	19.3	+5.9
Women (1997, *TFL*)	17.8	20.3	+2.5
Men (1988, OTA)	30.0	29.6	−0.4
Men (1999, *TFL*)	37.8	33.6	−4.2

Table 5.3 Weekly hours of free time for men

	1965	*1975*	*1985*	*Change in free time*
Men (1989, *AD*)	40	38	40	0.0
Men (1999, *TFL*)	35.7	39.2	40.4	+4.7

8 Because Robinson has not provided documentation with his published articles and did not respond to my requests for documentation, I am not sure how he has dealt with these sample selection issues. *Time for Life* includes some methodological discussion, but does not make it clear exactly how he has treated the sample issues, beyond including rural respondents in 1975 and 1985, and stratifying the sample by employed and nonemployed. It is my understanding from our conversations that for his earlier calculations, he compared the samples with no corrections.

9 Leete and Schor, Mishel *et al.*, Bluestone and Rose, and Bosworth and Burtless have all corrected for output fluctuations in their estimates. For example, using CPS data and correcting with a GDP gap variable, Bosworth and Burtless find a strong positive trend in hours since 1981 for males, and since 1969 for women. They find that during 1967–1989 annual hours of work rose for both men and women aged 25–64 (Bosworth and Burtless 1992: 11 and note 7).

10 The work of Juster and Stafford is particularly notable in this respect. They compared 1965 (an expansion) and 1981 (a serious recession), and concluded that free time was on the rise.

11 These figures underestimate the extent of underemployment because they do not exclude involuntary retirees, whose numbers have also increased, discouraged workers, and prison inmates.

12 Coleman and Pencavel find that annual hours of work have fallen for both white and black males of low educational attainment, and by contrast have risen for those with 16 or more years of schooling. (Other educational categories are not provided, nor do the detailed breakdowns include 1960 and 1970 estimates.) The decline is particularly pronounced for black males with fewer than 12 years of schooling, from 1 953 hours in 1950 to 1 738 hours in 1988 (or 215 hours). By contrast, black male college graduates have increased their annual hours considerably since 1950, from 1 971 to 2 070, or 99 hours. There are similar differences for women. Coleman and Pencavel (1993b) find that the average white woman with fewer than 12 years of schooling experienced a reduction of 317 annual hours of work between 1950 and 1988. College educated white women also had a reduction in total hours between 1950 and 1988, of 44 hours. However, between 1980 and 1988, hours of work rose for this group, by 131 hours. Among black women, the trends mirror those of men. Lesser educated women had a reduction of 230 per year, while those with college degrees increased their hours by 207.

13 Respondents who do work at home should include those hours.

14 Robinson and Godbey claim that Leete and I did not need to look at annual hours because the BLS surveys workers throughout the year, but this is a mistake. We, like almost all economists who study these questions, used the March CPS because it provides the required detail we need for our estimates.

15 In my view, the implausibility of the time diary results is most evident in the case of employed women. Robinson and Godbey find that the average woman with a paying job put in about 6 fewer hours per week in the mid-1980s than she did in the 1960s – despite the fact that women have moved into a wide range of highly demanding professions such as law, medicine, management, and so on. These findings are strongly contradicted by the data from household surveys which find that women's greater labor force attachment and movement into new economic roles has led to higher annual hours of work.

REFERENCES

Bluestone, B. and Rose, S. (1997) "Overworked and Underemployed: Unraveling an Economic Enigma," *The American Prospect* 31: 58–69.

Bond, J. T. *et al.* (1997) *The 1997 National Study of the Changing Workforce*, New York: Families and Work Institute.

Bosworth, B. and Burtless, G. (1992) "Effects of Tax Reform on Labor Supply, Investment, and Saving," *Journal of Economic Perspectives* 6(1): 3–25.

Coleman, M. T. and Pencavel, J. (1993a) "Changes in Hours of Work of Male Employees Since 1940," *Industrial and Labor Relations Review* 46(2): 262–283.

____ (1993b) "Trends in Market Work Behavior of Women Since 1940," *Industrial and Labor Relations Review* 46(4): 653–676.

Fuchs, V. (1986) "His and Hers: Differences in Work and Income, 1959–1979," *Journal of Labor Economics* 4: 245–272.

Gleick, J. (1999) *Faster: The Acceleration of Just About Everything*, New York: Pantheon.

Hochschild, A. (1989) *The Second Shift*, New York: Penguin.

Jacobs, J. A. (1998) "Measuring Time at Work: Are Self-reports Accurate?" *Monthly Labor Review* (December): 42–53.

Jacobs, J. A. and Gerson, K. (1998) "Who Are the Overworked Americans?" *Review of Social Economy* 56(4): 443–459.

Juster, F. T. and Stafford, F. P. (1985) *Time, Goods and Well-Being*, Ann Arbor, MI: Survey Research Center, Institute for Social Research, University of Michigan.

_____ (1991) "The Allocation of Time: Empirical Findings, Behavioral Models, and Problems of Measurement," *Journal of Economic Literature* 29(2): 471–522.

Knulst, W. and van den Broek, A. (1998) "Do Time-use Surveys Succeed in Measuring 'Busyness'? Some Observations on the Dutch Case," *Society and Leisure* 21(2): 563–72.

Leete, L. and Schor, J. B. (1992) *'The Great American Time Squeeze,'* Washington, DC: Economic Policy Institute.

_____ (1994) "Assessing the Time Squeeze Hypothesis: Estimates of Market and Non-market Hours in the United States, 1969–1989," *Industrial Relations* 33(1): 25–43.

Mishel, L., Bernstein, J., and Schmitt, J. (1999) *The State of Working America 1998–99*, Ithaca, NY: Cornell University Press.

Office of Technology Assessment (1988) *'Technology and the American Economic Transition: Choices for the Future*, Washington, DC: Congress of the United States.

Pääkkönen, H. (1998) "Are Busy People Under- or Over-Represented in National Time Budget Surveys?" *Society and Leisure* 21(2): 573–582.

Rifkin, J. (1987) *Time Wars*, New York: Henry Holt.

Robinson, J. P. (1989a) "Time for Work," *American Demographics* (April): 68.

_____ (1989b) "Time's Up," *American Demographics* 13 (July): 33–35.

Robinson, J. P. and Bostrom, A. (1994) "The Overestimated Workweek? What Time Diary Measures Suggest," *Monthly Labor Reivew* 117(8): 11–23.

Robinson, J. A. and Godbey, G. (1996) "The Great American Slowdown," *American Demographics* (June): 42–48.

_____ (1999) *Time for Life: The Surprising Ways Americans Use Their Time*, State College, PA: Penn State Press, 2nd Edn.

Schor, J. B. (1991) *The Overworked American: The Unexpected Decline of Leisure*, New York: Basic Books.

_____ (1998) *The Overspent American: Upscaling, Downshifting and the New Consumer*, New York: Basic Books.

Part II

Empirical and theoretical foundations

Explaining overwork and underemployment

6 Who are the overworked Americans?*

Jerry A. Jacobs and Kathleen Gerson

In recent years, and especially since the publication of Juliet Schor's *The Overworked American* (1991), scholars and ordinary citizens have become increasingly concerned about the issue of working time. Schor's claim that the century-long decline in working time has been reversed in recent years touched a social and cultural nerve. This growing concern about the state of American workers and their families has gained renewed attention with the publication of Arlie Hochschild's *The Time Bind* (1997), which explores the hectic schedules of dual-earner couples who work in one ostensibly family-friendly company.

There is little doubt that workers are facing new and unprecedented challenges in meeting the demands of work and family. The rise of employed mothers and the transformation of family structure and household composition in the closing decades of the 20th century have clearly created a significant time bind for many workers. We argue, however, that this time squeeze is less general and more varied than recent research, and especially the works of Schor and Hochschild, have implied. To understand the dynamics of change and its diverse consequences, we need to move beyond a focus on the average worker to examine the entire distribution of working time among a varied group of workers.

In addition, we believe it is essential to distinguish between workers' behavior and their desires. We thus supplement standard data on the length of the work week with information on workers' preferences. Such subjective orientations may be difficult to measure and interpret, but it is surely more misleading simply to accept people's behavior as a reflection of their preferences – the alternative approach taken by many economists. Indeed, our data show that there is a notable mismatch between the hours many Americans put in on the job and the work schedules they would like to have.

Finally, we argue that the demographic dimensions of social change are crucial to understanding the emergence and shape of current time binds. The rise of dual-earner and single-parent families, both of which rely on employed women, has reduced the amount of unpaid familial support at home and thus increased the pressure on many American workers. As a result, employed women and men are experiencing increased time binds even though, as individuals, they may not be putting in longer hours at the workplace than did workers in earlier generations.

THE OVERWORKED AMERICAN? TRENDS IN THE WORK WEEK SINCE 1970

Despite the image of the overworked American, the average length of the work week does not appear to have changed appreciably in recent decades. To the contrary, the American worker is putting in about the same amount of time on the job, on average, as did his or her counterpart thirty years ago. American men are working about 42 or 43 hours per week for pay, while American women are working about 36 or 37 hours per week on the job. The stability in these averages, however, masks some important shifts in the variation around the average. While the average has remained largely unchanged since 1970, both long and short work weeks have become increasingly prevalent.

Table 6.1 Trends in hours worked last week, 1970–1997, by sex and by occupation: non-farm wage and salary workers

	Mean hours all jobs (s.d.)	*Percent working less than 30 hours per week*	*Percent working 50+ hours*
Men			
1997	42.5 (14.1)	9.6	25.2
1970	43.5 (10.6)	4.5	21.0
Women			
1997	36.7 (12.2)	20.5	10.8
1970	37.0 (9.6)	15.5	5.2
Men			
Professional, managerial and technical:[a]	44.6 (13.1)	7.7	34.5
Other occupations:	40.6 (12.9)	13.5	20.0
Women			
Professional, managerial and technical:[a]	39.1 (12.4)	15.1	17.0
Other occupations:	34.4 (12.1)	26.7	6.8

Source: Authors' estimates based on Current Population Survey data, 1997.

Note

a 1997 data only.

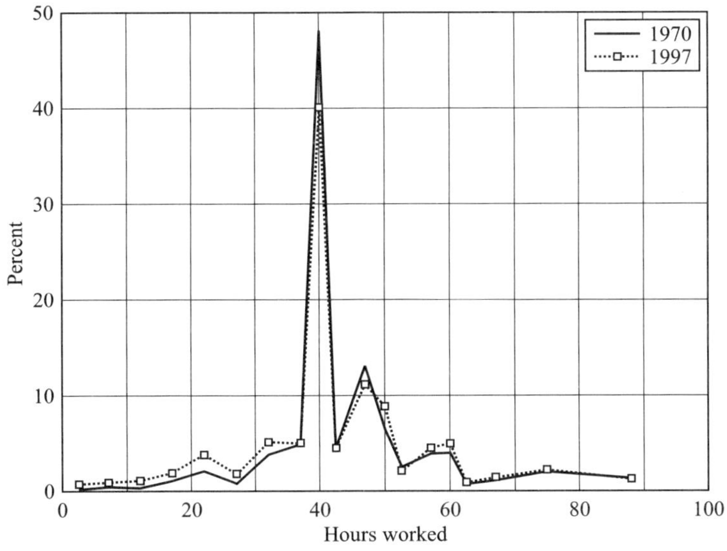

Figure 6.1 Full distribution of working hours per week for men for the years 1970 and 1997.

Schor (1991) and Bluestone and Rose (1997) have noted the trend toward a bifurcation in working time. Yet both of these studies focused on the average worker rather than on the trends at the extremes of the distribution, and on annual hours rather than on the average work week. These studies thus document the increasing number of weeks worked per year by American women as their labor force participation has become increasingly steady. Nevertheless, from the perspective of daily life, a shift among women from 39 to 44 weeks per year does not provide compelling support for the notion of a vast increase in overwork.[1]

Using data from the Current Population Survey (CPS), Table 6.1 compares working time in 1970 and 1997.[2] A large and reliable data series, the CPS has been quite consistent in design and administration since the 1960s, and thus is arguably the best source for examining historical trends in the length of the work week.[3] The data pertain to non-farm wage and salary workers employed for at least one hour in the survey week.

The findings in Table 6.1 suggest stability in the average work week, but they also demonstrate that the percentage of men and women working long and short work weeks has increased during this period. In 1997, one-quarter of men (25.2 percent) worked 50 hours per week or more, as did one in ten women (10.8 percent). At the other extreme, one in ten men in the labor force worked 30 hours per week or less, as did one-fifth of working women.

Figures 6.1 and 6.2 present the full distribution of working time in 1970 and 1997 for men and women. While the 40 hour work week remains the modal

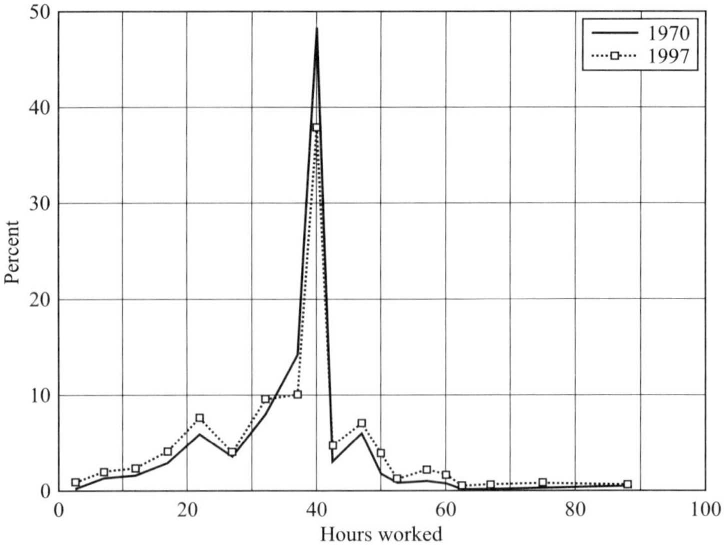

Figure 6.2 Full distribution of working hours per week for women for the years 1970 and 1997.

pattern, with nearly 40 percent of men and women reporting working this standard time in 1997, it has become less typical than it was 30 years ago. For men and women, the 40 hour standard has declined by about 10 percentage points, with increases at both the high and low ends of the spectrum. These results are consistent with those of Rones, Ilg, and Gardner (1997), who also report a growing dispersion in working time.

These data do not make a compelling case for arguing that the length of the work week has increased sharply. Choosing different years can produce a small increase or a small decline, but there is little evidence of a general and marked upward trend in the average length of the work week.[4] More support can be found instead for a modest increase in the bifurcation of working time among workers.

Long work weeks are most common among professionals and managers (see Table 6.1, bottom half). Over one in three men (34.5 percent) who work in professional, technical, or managerial occupations work 50 hours or more per week, compared to one in five (20.0 percent) of men in other occupations. For women, the comparable figures are one in six for the professional and managerial positions versus less than one in fourteen for other occupations.

These occupational differences manifest themselves in sharply graded educational differentials. Nearly two in five American men with four or more years of college education work 50 hours per week or more, compared to less than one in eight men with less than a high school degree. Among women, nearly one in five college-educated American women work 50 or more hours per week, compared to less than one in twenty with less than a high school degree. While these educated workers are more likely to pay attention to and become involved in national discussions about the contours of working time, they actually represent only one part of a larger and more complex puzzle of transformations in work commitment. Their experiences are better understood as one aspect of a growing segmentation of the labor force rather than as representing a general increase among all workers in time spent on the job (Coleman and Pencavel 1993a,b).

While a complete analysis of the forces that are promoting a bifurcation of working time into too-long and too-short work weeks is beyond the scope of this chapter, it is important to note that both benefits and costs create incentives for employers to move in this direction. Firms can lower their total compensation costs by hiring part-time workers with no benefits, thus increasing the proportion of workers at the low-end of the hours distribution. Firms can also lower their total compensation costs by pressuring a fixed number of full-time employees to work as many hours as possible. This is especially true of those who are salaried, and in many cases applies also to hourly workers entitled to overtime pay.

INTERNATIONAL COMPARISONS

Are Americans merely replicating worldwide trends, or is the emergence of a sizeable group of workers who are devoting very long hours to their jobs peculiar to the American context? By comparing work patterns in the United States to those in other countries, we can shed additional light on the question of overwork in America. In the international context, as in the United States, the distribution of working time rather than the length of the average work week emerges as the interesting story.

For this analysis, we rely on the Luxembourg Income Study (LIS), an internationally comparable archive of micro-level data sets gathered from a large number of industrialized countries. These data sets, based principally on household surveys, contain detailed information at both the individual and household level on a range of demographic, labor market, and income variables. The LIS data provide more comparability than many other cross-national comparative sources. They include much larger samples and consequently are more reliable than Wright's Comparative Class Structure survey data (Wright, Baxter, and Birkelund 1995). They also make micro-level analyses possible, unlike the official data published by OECD. We use eight data sets from the third, and most recent, wave (1989–1992) of LIS data sets and one (Luxembourg) from the second wave (1985).[5]

Figure 6.3 compares the average length of the work week for nine industrial countries. For men, the average work week in most countries hovers around 40 hours per week, with only the Netherlands having a particularly

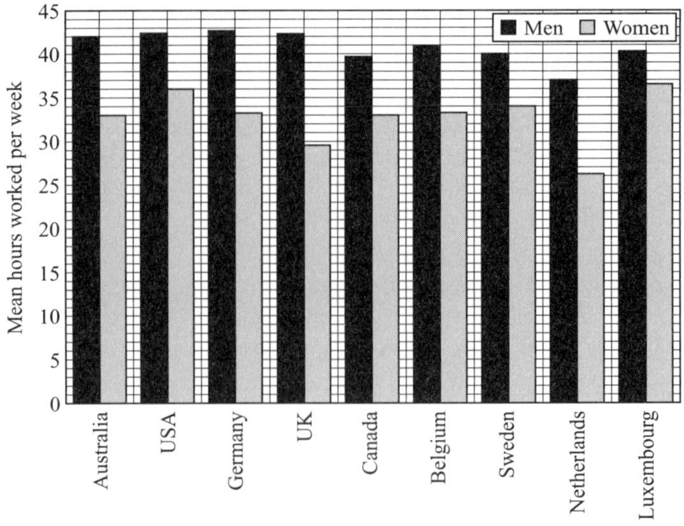

Figure 6.3 Average work week in hours for men and women for a cross-section of nine countries.

short work week. The United States is at the higher end of the sample countries, but it does not stand out markedly from the others in terms of the average length of the week. When it comes to the number of workers putting in very long hours, however, the United States does stand out (see Figure 6.4).

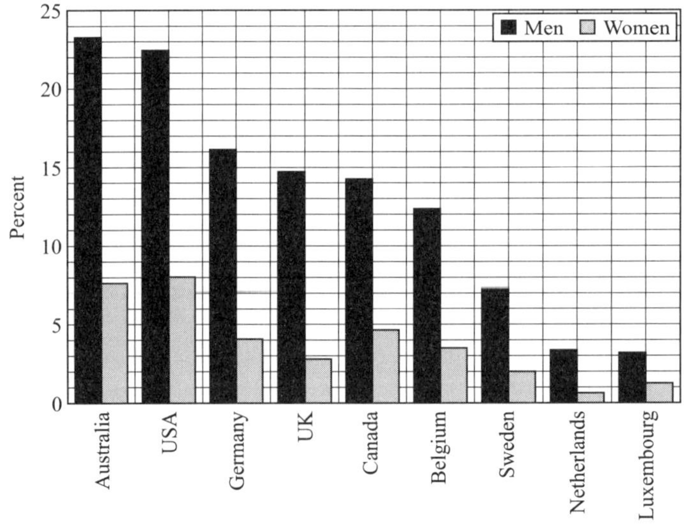

Figure 6.4 Percentage of the workforce (male and female) exceeding 50 hours per week for a cross-section of nine countries.

For men, the United States and Australia have the highest proportion working 50 or more hours per week. The proportion of men working such long hours does not exceed 20 percent in any of the other countries. The variation between countries, moreover, is remarkable. The rates of men working long hours fall between 10 percent and 20 percent in Germany (16.1 percent), Canada (14.3 percent) and Belgium (12.4 percent). Even more noteworthy are three other countries where fewer than one in ten men works 50 hours per week or more: Sweden (7.3 percent), the Netherlands (3.5 percent), and Luxembourg (3.3 percent).

Variation in women's working hours across countries is also quite dramatic. American women, like American men, have among the longest work weeks in the nine countries. The proportion of women working part-time is also among the lowest, and the proportion working 50 hours or more per week is among the highest. The Netherlands again stands out as having the shortest work week. The average woman in the Netherlands works 26.3 hours per week, and nearly half (49.7 percent) work under 30 hours per week (Plantenga 1996).[6]

These international comparisons suggest two conclusions. First, they show that it is possible to maintain a high and growing standard of living with a very different work profile than is evident in the United States. The steady improvements in productivity (OECD 1998; Freeman 1994) and the recent surge in the price of stocks in Europe counters the notion that European labor practices are hopelessly inefficient. While European countries have experienced high unemployment and low job growth in recent years, this may be due to tight monetary policies rather than stodgy labor practices. Whatever the ultimate verdict on the efficiency question, these findings clearly demonstrate that our work patterns are neither inevitable nor inherent in post-industrial economic development. The United States model represents just one of many approaches exhibited by other affluent societies.

Second, the United States stands out more in terms of those working very long weeks than in terms of the average work week. Again, we find that a bifurcation in working time for women and men emerges as a major trend in the American context – and one that is not being replicated in most other affluent societies.[7]

COMPARING ACTUAL AND IDEAL WORK TIMES

While a notable segment of the American labor force is putting in very long hours at the workplace, average working hours have not increased substantially. Yet there are strong reasons to conclude that more people are *feeling* overworked – even among those who are not working excessively long days or weeks. Most families can no longer rely on the unpaid support of a woman at home, yet the structure of work has not changed sufficiently to accommodate the transitions in workers' private lives. A focus on historical trends in actual time spent at paid work misses this more fundamental shift in workers' lives, which may lead them to feel overworked, squeezed, and overburdened in new ways. Since most national surveys do not gather information on workers' desired work week, it has been difficult to address the subjective aspect of change.[8]

In this vacuum, economists such as Kneisner (1993) have argued that since most workers are currently working a few minutes less than were their counterparts in 1950, they do not feel overworked. Such a conclusion ignores the widespread changes that have taken place in family structure over this period and disregards the personal experiences and perspectives of contemporary workers. Regardless of the historical trajectory in working hours, we need to understand how Americans feel about their current work commitments in light of their obligations and responsibilities outside the workplace.

To examine the links between workers' actual and ideal working time, we analyze information from the 1992 National Study of the Changing Workforce, a national probability sample of 3381 employed men and women aged 18 through 64 based on hour-long telephone interviews.[9] The data are weighted to reflect the characteristics of the US labor force as estimated by the March 1992 Current Population Survey (Galinsky, Bond and Friedman 1993). Conducted by the Families and Work Institute, this survey is distinctive because it asks a wide range of questions about workers' values and preferences, and it focuses on the links, tensions, and conflicts between work and family. Since respondents were asked to reveal their ideal as well as their actual working hours, we can examine whether the Americans' overall level of work activity actually reflects the workers' desires. We can thus ascertain whether variation in preferences across groups of workers corresponds to variations in actual work levels.[10]

Respondents in the Changing Workforce survey were asked how many hours per week they usually worked on their principal job and on any additional jobs they held. Here we examine hours worked on all jobs together.[11] To discover ideal work hours, respondents were also asked: Ideally, how many hours, in total, would you like to work each week? Using this information on both actual and ideal hours, we were able to construct a measure of the gap between a worker's usual working time on all jobs and his or her ideal hours.

In Table 6.2, which compares ideal to total hours worked for employed women and men, it becomes clear that most American workers experience a significant gap between how much they work and how much they would like to work. Many wish to work less than they actually do, while a notable group would like to work more. While approximately one-third of respondents reported that their actual and ideal hours corresponded precisely, nearly half indicated that their usual work week was longer than their ideal hours, and an additional one in six reported that they would prefer to work more than they currently do. (The unemployed should also be added

Table 6.2 Comparison of total hours worked and ideal hours, by sex

	Men (n = 1 300)	*Women (n = 1 539)*
Total hours usually worked (all jobs)	45.77[a]	39.71
Ideal hours	40.26[a]	34.82
Difference (ideal – actual)	−5.51	−4.89
Percentage wanting to work less	50.06	45.58
Percentage ideal equals actual	33.78	37.61
Percentage wanting to work more	17.16	16.84
Percentage wanting to work at least 5 hours less	45.36	41.25
Percentage wanting to work at least 10 hours less	32.39	32.40
Percentage wanting to work at least 20 Hours Less	15.30	13.19

Source: Author's analysis of the National Survey of the Changing Workforce.

Note

a The difference between men and women is statistically significant, $p < 0.01$. None of the other sex differences in Table 6.2 is statistically significant at the conventional $p < 0.05$ level.

to this group of "underworked" Americans, but the Changing Workforce survey only includes information on currently employed individuals.)

The vast majority of those who expressed a preference for shorter working hours wished to work at least 5 hours less per week than they currently do. Nine in twenty of the total sample (90 percent of those wanting to work less) preferred to work at least 5 fewer hours per week. Nearly one-third of the total sample (32 percent of both men and women) expressed the desire to work 10 hours less per week, and about one in seven of the total sample wanted to work at least 20 hours less per week.

While women on average work about 6 fewer hours per week than men, the gap between women's and men's actual and ideal hours is quite similar. Men reported a preference for working 5.51 fewer hours, and women wished to work 5.14 fewer hours – a difference that is not statistically significant. If both groups were able to enact their preferences, the gender gap in hours worked (which is about 6 hours per week) would thus not change significantly.

These findings suggest that, whether or not they are actually working more than earlier generations, the majority of contemporary employed Americans feel overworked – at least compared to their ideals. There is little indication that those putting in long hours are doing so because they prefer work over family and personal pursuits. Nevertheless, a notable group of workers would like to work more. Most of these workers, however, wish to extend relatively short work weeks rather than to put in excessive hours at the workplace.[12]

In Figures 6.5 and 6.6 we gain a clearer picture of how the gap between ideal and total working hours is linked to actual working time. Figures 6.5 and 6.6 compare ideal and actual working times for men and women

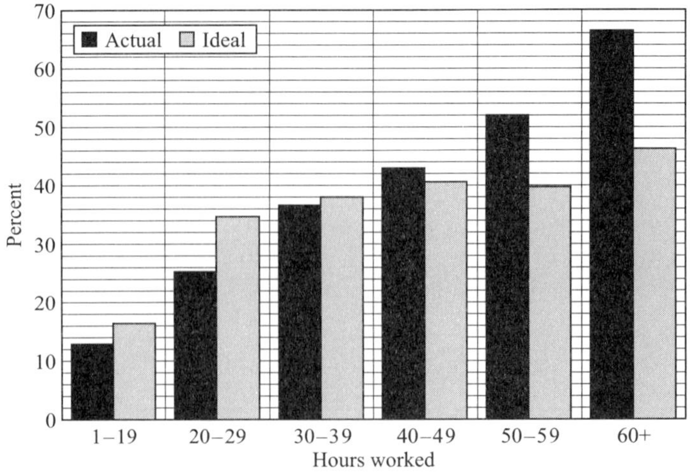

Figure 6.5 Comparison of ideal versus actual working hours for men in 1992.

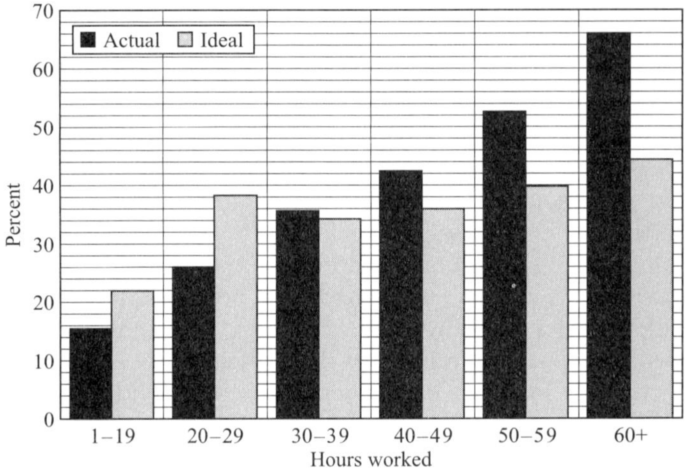

Figure 6.6 Comparison of ideal versus actual working hours for women in 1992.

workers. They show that those working few hours on average prefer to work more, while those working very long weeks on average prefer to work less. The great majority of both men and women who work over 50 hours per week would prefer shorter schedules. Indeed, over 80 percent of those working over 50 hours per week indicated a preference for fewer hours. The excess work was substantial: those putting in between 50 and 60 hours per week preferred working 12 hours less, while those working over 60 hours wished to work a full 20 hours less. While the preferences of individuals vary, we found that only 6.4 percent of women and 15.8 percent of men expressed a desire to work more than 50 hours per week. Yet roughly one in four men and one in ten women actually put in that much time at work.

These findings further illustrate the ways in which social change involves an increasingly bifurcated labor market. This growing time divide has implications not only for how working time is distributed across jobs and workers but also for how workers feel about their work arrangements. Those at the top of the occupational hierarchy are more likely to feel overworked, while those in less attractive and less rewarded occupational positions are more likely to need and desire to work more. These findings also raise questions about how employers are structuring employment options. Since personal "tastes" do not explain why some people are putting in very long work weeks and others very short ones, it appears that employers are organizing work schedules for reasons other than the needs and preferences of employees and their families.

DEMOGRAPHIC CHANGE AND THE EMERGENCE OF TIME BINDS

The growing dispersion in working time is compounded by a second trend – the changing demographics of the labor force. In 1970, the male breadwinner was still the predominant family arrangement. While employed women represented a growing fraction of the labor market, dual-earner couples were still in the minority. By 1997, dual-earner couples had become much more prevalent than the traditional male breadwinner arrangement.

Since 1970, the proportion of couples with only a male breadwinner in the labor market declined from a bare majority in 1970 (51.4 percent) to just over one-quarter in 1997 (25.9 percent). At the same time, the percentage of dual-earner couples rose sharply, from just over one-third of married couples (35.9 percent) in 1970 to nearly three in five (59.5 percent) in 1997. The dual-earner couple is more common today than was the male-breadwinner couple in 1970. The percentage of married couples in which only the wife is employed increased sharply from a low base (from 4.6 percent in 1970 to 7.2 percent in 1997).

Table 6.3 presents the combined time on the job of couples in 1970 and 1997. Married couples are grouped into four mutually exclusive types: (1) male breadwinners, in which the husband is employed and the wife is not; (2) dual-earner couples, in which both partners are employed; (3) female-breadwinner couples, in which only the wife works; and (4) "non-employed couples," in which neither partner works for pay. This analysis of CPS data from 1970 and 1997 includes only married couples in which both partners were aged 18–64.

Table 6.3 Joint hours of paid work by married couples, by employment type, 1970 and 1997

	1970	*1997*
Total, all couples	52.5	62.8
Male breadwinner	44.4	44.7
Dual earner	78.0	81.3
Wife only works	35.5	36.9
Neither works	0.0	0.0

Source: Authors' estimates based on Current Population Survey data.

The average couple is working 10 more hours per week for pay than was the case in 1970 (62.8 hours of paid employment, compared with 52.5 hours in 1970). However, this change signals a shift from single-breadwinner to dual-earner couples rather than a change in the experiences within these groups. Male breadwinners are working just about as much as they did 30 years ago, and so are women who are the sole earners in their families. Only a modest increase has occurred in the work week of dual-earner couples (from 78.0 hours to 81.3 hours per week).[13] The principal cause of the 10 hours per week increase in time on the job for couples is thus the rise in number of dual-earner couples and the decline of male-breadwinner marriages.

These shifts have had important consequences for the working time of married couples. Even though individual workers are averaging about the same time in the labor market as did their predecessors, most couples' joint work week – the number of hours husbands and wives combine to spend in the labor market – has increased dramatically. These changed circumstances have created a time crunch at home and left American workers feeling more pressed. Put simply, women and men alike feel squeezed because they are less likely to be able to rely on someone at home devoted exclusively to family concerns, not because the work week of individuals has expanded.[14]

POLICY CONSIDERATIONS

Jobs that require very long hours are not family friendly. Parents should be able to spend some time with their children every day, for the emotional and intellectual development of the child as well as for the sake of the parents. Extra-long jobs also inhibit gender equity. These jobs require parents to choose between work and family, with women more likely to give up career prospects in favor of family needs. Extra-long jobs also threaten our civil society. Participation in community clubs and activities is undermined by 50 or 60 hours per week jobs. The nation should see the promotion of a balance between work and the rest of life not as simply a private choice between employers and employees, but as a matter of great importance to the public interest.

Public policy needs to promote a level playing field with respect to working time, so that firms do not have an incentive to shorten or extend the work week unduly. One way to accomplish this goal is to require firms to provide proportional benefits to part-time workers. Those working part-time would then receive protections and support commensurate with their contributions. In addition, employees should be provided with flexible benefits packages so that they can use them in the ways they find most useful. Workers could then cash in the benefits they prefer not to use in other forms.

What should be done about long work weeks? First, there should be recognition that very long work weeks are a mixed blessing. The praise we tend to heap on hard-working men and women needs to be balanced by a recognition of the costs to families and communities of expecting such long hours in many occupations and professions. Second, since long work weeks are especially prevalent in professional and managerial positions, the Fair Labor Standards Act needs to be extended to cover professionals and managers. In that way, employers would incur additional costs when they require their professional and managerial staffs to work more than 40 hours per week. This would gradually reduce long work weeks and encourage employers to expect long hours only when they are efficient or absolutely necessary.

Finally, we need to recognize that the 40-hour work week was created for the male-breadwinner family. Since the demographics of the workforce have changed dramatically and irreversibly, the time has come to re-examine this standard. We believe that there is a strong case to be made for adopting a 35-hour work week as the more general standard. This would ease the time crunch on working parents, provide more time for nurturing children, create the possibility of more gender equity in parenting, and provide more time for workers in all types of families to participate in their communities. A 35-hour work week would certainly not be required or expected of everyone, just as the 40-hour work week is not now mandatory. It could, however, become a social and cultural standard, just as the 40-hour work week emerged as the standard in the early decades of the 20th century. As the 21st century dawns, widespread transformations in family and domestic life cry out for a shorter rather than a longer standard week for individual workers.

CONCLUSION

Even though the average work week has not changed dramatically in the USA over the last several decades, a growing group of Americans are clearly and strongly pressed for time. These workers include employees who are putting in especially long hours, often against their own fondest desires, and people in dual-earner and single-parent families who cannot rely on a support system anchored by a stay-at-home member. In the context of these dramatic social shifts in Americans' private lives, the lack of change in the structure of work and the rise of highly demanding jobs, especially at the upper levels of the occupational hierarchy, present dilemmas and problems for many workers. Increasingly, women and men alike face challenging work without the "wives" once relied on by upwardly mobile husbands in highly demanding positions.[15] Yet employers have not responded to these changed realities, assuming that devoted workers have or should have unpaid partners able to devote themselves full-time to the myriad of domestic tasks on which not only family life but even successful careers depend. In this context, it is little wonder that many workers feel they are working harder than ever.

A "time bind" has clearly emerged in the contemporary United States, but it has different roots and a different profile than analysts such as Hochschild and Schor have suggested. Working parents in dual-earner couples have always faced a time bind, and the principal change over the last 30 years has been a marked growth in the number of these families. Moreover, a time squeeze due to excessive hours in paid employment is not a universal phenomenon; rather these are concentrated among professionals and managers who are especially likely to shape the terms of public discussion and debate. Although there are also less affluent workers who put in substantial overtime or who work at two (or more) jobs, this group actually represents a smaller proportion of blue-collar workers than do the overworked Americans among professionals and managers. These trends suggest that while it is important to address the new challenges and insecurities facing American workers and their families, we should be careful to move beyond generalizations to focus on the variety of dilemmas that workers are facing.

NOTES

* Reprinted with permission from *Review of Social Economy*, Winter, 1998.

1 We believe that the increase in the number of weeks worked per year reported by Schor is not primarily an independent development but rather a by-product of the increased labor force participation and the increased continuity of work among women.

2 Robinson and Bostrom (1994) raised questions about the validity of self-reports on the length of the work week in data sets such as the Current Population Survey. However, Jacobs (1998) finds that the standard self-report question about the length of the work week is remarkably reliable and free of systematic bias. A more conservative measure of the dispersion of working time relies on data pertaining to how many hours per week the respondent typically worked last year. Unfortunately, that question was not included in the 1970 CPS and thus cannot be used in this study.

3 There were small changes in the wording of labor force questions in 1993, but these had little effect on the issues explored here. Trends over the period 1970–1990 display much the same pattern as those documented here between 1970 and 1997. The wording of the questions has thus had little effect on this time series.

4 Robinson and Godbey (1997) present a time series of weekly hours worked by each sex stretching from the late 1950s until the early 1990s. There are year-to-year fluctuations but the entire series varies within a remarkably tight range, from 41 hours to 43 hours for men and 34 hours to 36 hours for women. The averages may change slightly if one restricts the analysis, as we do here, to non-farm wage and salaried employees, but again for this group there have been no sharp changes in the length of the work week.

5 The years to which the data pertain, the names of the original surveys, and the sample sizes are presented in Gornick and Jacobs (1998). More detailed information on LIS and on the individual data sets is available in LIS Working Paper #7, The LIS/LES Information Guide (de Tombeur 1995).

6 It would be interesting to know if the trend toward bifurcation in working hours is occurring in Europe as well as in the United States, even if the European countries have not reached the levels found in the USA. Figart and Mutari (1998) suggest that the move toward flexibility in working time is sharpening the gender gap in working time, perhaps as part of a broader bifurcation in working time. On the other hand, the movement in France and elsewhere toward a shorter work week would point in the opposite direction.

7 New figures from the OECD (1998) also show the USA with the fifth largest proportion of workers putting in long hours among the twenty countries included in the analysis, trailing Australia, Japan, Portugal and the UK. The OECD results show the UK ahead of the USA on long hours by men, whereas our results show the reverse. The difference between the two may be due to the different cutoff points (45 hours for the OECD report versus 50 hours for our analysis) and to differences in data sources.

8 Although the CPS asks part-time workers whether they would like to work full-time, it does not ask them how many hours they would like to work. It also does not ask full-time workers whether they would prefer longer or shorter schedules.

9 This topic is explored in greater detail in Jacobs and Gerson (1998a).

10 The first tabulations from the 1997 Families and Work Institute Survey have recently been released (Bond, Galinsky and Swanberg 1998). However, the data were not available for secondary analysis at the time this paper was being completed.

11 For an examination of dual-job holders, see Jacobs and Gerson (1997).

12 This survey also asked workers if they would prefer to work less even if they would have to take a cut in pay. Specifically, the question read "Would you be willing to give up a day's pay each week for an extra day of free time?" Over one-quarter of respondents (28.8 percent) responded "yes" to this question.

To learn about the value of job flexibility, respondents were also asked, "Would you be willing to sacrifice career advancement to have (more) flexibility in scheduling your starting and ending times?" About one-quarter (24.7 percent) of respondents answered "yes" to this question. The fundamental problem with all of these questions is that the *ceteris paribus* conditions are hard to specify, and thus the hypothetical alternative may be hard for workers to imagine. Specifically, substantial cuts in working time are sure to impede career progress. Thus, taking a day off does not simply reduce pay for that one day but, if done on a regular basis, could jeopardize career security and progression for years or even decades to come.

13 In a more detailed exploration of these data, we found that about half of this increase was due to the fact that couples in 1997 were slightly older than those in 1970, had completed more years of schooling, and had fewer children. Taking these factors into account, dual earner couples in 1997 worked for pay about an hour and a half more than did their counterparts in 1970. See Jacobs and Gerson (1998b).

14 In this chapter we do not address whether dual earner couples in 1997 are doing as much housework as their counterparts were in 1990. We expect that analyses underway of the 1995 national time diary data will shed light on this question.

15 For the classic analysis of the phenomenon of the "two-person career," in which a husband's corporate success depends on the support of a full-time wife, see Kanter (1977).

REFERENCES

Bond, J. T., Galinsky, E., and Swanberg, J. E. (1998) *The 1997 National Study of the Changing Workforce*, New York: Families and Work Institute.

Bluestone, B., and Rose, S. (1997) "Overworked and Underemployed: Unraveling an Economic Enigma," *The American Prospect* 31: 58–69.

Coleman, M. T. and Pencavel, J. (1993a) "Changes in Work Hours of Male Employees, 1940–1988," *Industrial and Labor Relations Review* 46(2): 262–283.

_____ (1993b) "Trends in Market Work Behavior of Women Since 1940," *Industrial and Labor Relations Review* 46(4): 653–676.

de Tombeur, C. (ed.) (1995) *LIS/LES Information Guide*, Luxembourg Income Study, Working Paper Number 7, Luxembourg: Centre d'Etudes de Populations, de Pauvrete et de Politiques Socio-Economiques (CEPS), Revised Edn.

Figart, D. M. and Mutari, E. (1998) "Degendering Work Time in Comparative Perspective," *Review of Social Economy* 56(4): 460–480.

Freeman, R. B. (ed.) (1994) *Working Under Different Rules*, New York: Russell Sage Foundation.

Galinsky, E., Bond, J. T., and Friedman, D. E. (1993) *The Changing Workforce: Highlights of the National Study*, New York: Families and Work Institute.

Gornick, J. C. and Jacobs, J. A. (1998) "Gender, The Welfare State, and Public Employment: A Comparative Study of Seven Industrialized Countries," *American Sociological Review* 65(5): 688–710.

Hochschild, A. R. (1997) *The Time Bind: When Work Becomes Home and Home Becomes Work*, New York: Metropolitan Books.

Jacobs, J. A. (1998) "Measuring Time at Work: An Assessment of the Accuracy of Self Reports," unpublished manuscript, Department of Sociology, University of Pennsylvania.

Jacobs, J. A. and Gerson, K. (1997) *The Endless Day or the Flexible Office? Working Hours, Work – Family Conflict, and Gender Equity in the Modern Workplace*, New York: Report to Alfred P. Sloan Foundation.

_____ (1998a) "The Overworked American Debate: New Evidence Comparing Ideal and Actual Working Hours," in T. Parcel and D. B. Cornfield (eds), *Work and Family: Research Informing Policy*, Thousand Oaks, CA: Sage Publications.

_____ (1998b) "The Time Bind: An Empirical Assessment," unpublished manuscript, Department of Sociology, University of Pennsylvania.

Kanter, R. M. (1977) *Men and Women of the Corporation*, New York: Basic Books.

Kneisner, T. J. (1993) "Review Essay: The Overworked American?" *Journal of Human Resources* 28(33): 681–688.

OECD (1998) "Flexibility of Working Hours: Latest Trends and Policy Initiatives," in *Employment Outlook 1998*, Paris: OECD, Chap. 5.

Plantenga, J. (1996) "For Women Only? The Rise of Part-time Work in the Netherlands," *Social Politics* 3(1): 57–71.
Robinson, J. P. and Bostrom, A. (1994) "The Overestimated Workweek? What Time Diary Measures Suggest," *Monthly Labor Review* 111(8): 11–23.
Robinson, J. P. and Godbey, G. (1997) *Time For Life: The Surprising Ways Americans Use Their Time*, University Park, PA: Pennsylvania State University Press.
Rones, P. L., Ilg, R. E., and Gardner, J. M. (1997) "Trends in the Hours of Work Since the Mid-1970s," *Monthly Labor Review* 120(4): 3–14.
Schor, J. B. (1991) *The Overworked American*, New York: Basic Books.
Wright, E., Baxter, J., and Birkelund, G. E. (1995) "The Gender Gap in Workplace Authority: A Cross-National Study," *American Sociological Review* 60: 407–435.

7 The incentive to work hard

Differences in black and white workers' hours and preferences

Linda A. Bell[1]

US workers work longer per year than workers in the other major OECD countries. Although the USA once had led the developed world in a reduction in work hours post World War II to the early 1970s, it now leads the developed world in "workaholism." Despite relatively long hours at work, however, a greater proportion of US workers are likely to say that they want to work even longer hours than are workers in other countries (Bell and Freeman 1995, 1997).

To explain this workaholism, some researchers (Schor 1991; Hochschild 1997) claim that a new workplace culture and the demands of work in the home have created a climate that encourages work over leisure. Our research (Bell and Freeman 1995, 1997) emphasizes the presence of economic incentives that lead to long hours of work. Specifically, a higher degree of US inequality in wages enhances the rewards to working longer hours, while a relatively weak social safety net raises the penalties to slack work. The notion of these differing incentives is supported here by empirical evidence at both the micro and macro economic levels.

The literature that documents the long US work hours has paid little attention to differences that exist between demographic groups in their weekly work hours or in their stated preferences for work. For example, although the shorter average annual hours of black men can be explained by being both more likely to face unemployment and for a longer duration (Freeman and Holzer 1986), it has been more difficult to explain the shorter weekly hours of black men. Similarly, previous studies of workers' preferences regarding work time, using the May 1985 Supplement to the Current Population Survey (CPS) (Shank 1986; Bell and Freeman 1995), have neglected the significant differences in preferences that exist by race. While black men and women work shorter annual work hours than otherwise comparable white men and women, a greater share of African-Americans than whites desire additional work hours (Bell 1998).

This chapter starts by documenting the work hour preferences of workers by race, highlighting the differences between black and white workers, using the May 1985 CPS. Then, more recent data from the merged CPS outgoing rotation group files in 1995 are used to judge the extent to which such differences in hours and preferences persist over time.[2] The goals in this chapter are to illustrate the significant differences in black and white workers' work hours and their preferences for work in the USA, and to offer explanations for these differences. The May 1985 Supplement provides not only useful detailed information on work hours, wages, and incomes, but also very useful observations on work preferences that can be used to contrast workers' actual and desired work hours.

In sum, the findings support the notion that black and white workers differ significantly in both their work hours and work hour preferences, in ways that persist over time. In addition, there is strong evidence in support of the theory that wage inequality is an important determinant of workers' hours. Black and white workers both appear to supply and desire a larger number of work hours when there is a greater degree of wage inequality within an occupational category. Finally, there are significant differences by race in their work hours response to overall inequality. Black workers respond to occupational wage inequality measured for a sub-group of black-only workers, but respond much less to the occupational wage inequality measured across all workers or a sub-group of white-only workers.

The racial component to the hypothesized link between hours-inequality represents a potential challenge to competitive labor market theory, which implies that the incentives to work long hours should be identical for otherwise similar workers and independent of race. A neoclassical explanation for this link might be that the measure of wage inequality among blacks is capturing some unobservable characteristics of black individuals or the jobs in which they are concentrated. A second explanation, more compelling for social economists, is that labor markets are at least partly segmented by race, such that black workers perceive wage inequality within the black only sub-group to be a more relevant indicator of their potential future earnings gains from work harder via longer hours.

The first section of the chapter documents the fact that blacks and whites work different hours and have different preferences for work. I then set up a model for evaluating differences in preferences for work and explore the extent to which these differences can be explained by standard competitive labor market variables. The chapter proceeds to evaluate differences in the actual work hours of blacks and whites and their determinants and offers some conclusions based on this work.

WORK HOURS AMONG BLACK WORKERS

Table 7.1 uses 1990 US Census data to document the basic fact that blacks and whites in the USA work different annual hours. Panel A looks at black-white differences overall, whereas panels B and C evaluate differences for men and women separately. The first row of each panel gives the average of the usual hours worked per week in 1989 as reported in the Census. The

Table 7.1 Work patterns, blacks and whites (1990 Census data)[a]

	White	*Black*	*% Difference*
Panel A: All			
1. Average hours per week[b]	40.37	39.05	3.27
	(0.01)	(0.04)	
2. Average weeks per year[c]	46.84	45.56	2.73
	(0.01)	(0.04)	
3. Average annual hours per worker[d]	1923	1808	5.98
	(0.78)	(2.35)	
4. Employment/population ratio[e]	0.646	0.522	9.91
5. Average annual hours per adult[f]	1242.26	943.78	24.03
Panel B: Male			
1. Average hours per week[b]	43.46	40.56	6.66
	(0.02)	(0.052)	
2. Average weeks per year[c]	47.89	46.01	3.93
	(0.01)	(0.06)	
3. Average annual hours per worker[d]	2105	1894	10.02
	(1.02)	(3.45)	
4. Employment/population ratio[e]	0.747	0.661	11.51
5. Average annual hours per adult[f]	1572.44	1251.93	20.38
Panel C: Female			
1. Average hours per week[b]	36.60	37.72	−2.97
	(0.02)	(0.05)	
2. Average weeks per year[c]	45.55	45.16	0.86
	(0.02)	(0.06)	
3. Average annual hours per worker[d]	1701	1731	−1.73
	(1.12)	(3.18)	
4. Employment/population ratio[e]	0.578	0.584	−1.03
5. Average annual hours per adult[f]	983.18	1010.90	−2.74

Notes

a Standard errors in parentheses under means.

b 1990 Census data for individuals reporting at least one usual weekly hour of work in 1989.

c 1990 Census data for individuals reporting at least one usual weekly hour of work in 1989.

d Mean of average hours per week × average weeks per year.

e Bureau of Labor Statistics data reported from 1997 for adults 20 years of age and older.

f Product of row 3 × row 4.

second row lists the average of the usual weeks worked. Row 3 is the product of the first two rows and gives the annual hours worked per worker as reported in the US Census. Note that whereas black men work roughly 7 percent fewer hours per week and 4 percent fewer weeks per year than white men, black women work 3 percent more hours per week and roughly the same weeks per year as white women. Annual hours per worker (row 3 in each panel) are 10 percent lower for black men and about 2 percent higher for black women.

Black men are more likely to be unemployed and for longer periods of time than white men (Freeman and Holzer 1986). Accordingly, it makes sense to adjust the above numbers for differences in employment probabilities across the two groups. Indeed, the employment to population ratios for black and white men (row 4) suggest that the numbers in the first three rows of the table may underestimate the true hours gap. Row 5 of the table is the product of annual hours per worker and the employment to population ratios, and gives the annual work hours per adult for each of the groups. The most striking thing is the 20 percent difference between annual hours for adult black and white men. The differences in actual work hours between women are small in any case.[3] The differences between black and white work hours are therefore a male-only phenomenon.

DIFFERENCES IN WORK HOUR PREFERENCES BY RACE

Do the differences between black and white work hours reflect differences in black and white attitudes towards work? Are blacks less likely to want to work long hours and is that why they record fewer hours of work? In order to explore this issue, I looked at data from the May 1985 Current Population Survey (CPS) supplement, the only source of such comprehensive information for blacks and whites.[4] In these data the following question was asked of all individuals:

> "If you had a choice, would you prefer to work the same number of hours and earn the same money, fewer hours at the same rate of pay and earn less money, or more hours at the same rate of pay and earn more money?"

Since the CPS question asks about usual hourly earnings (exclusive of overtime pay), it reveals workers' hours preferences at their normal pay rate. Responses to this question have been detailed elsewhere (Shank 1986; Bell and Freeman 1995), but again, little attention has been paid to differences across race.[5]

Table 7.2 tabulates the responses of black and white US workers to the above question on preferences. While a majority of both black and white workers are satisfied with their hours worked, more black workers (both men and women) are dissatisfied with their work hours, since the proportion wanting hours to stay the same is smaller in all cases. The key reason for this is that black workers are more likely to want to work longer hours than white workers. This gap is substantial. This is true among all workers, full-time workers, and both male and female workers. The differences in Table 7.2 between black and white desires for more work in all cases are statistically significant. Note that 41 percent of black males and 27 percent of white males working full-time desire more work, at their same rate of pay. Note as well that at higher levels of actual hours, more workers of all races are satisfied with their hours of work, fewer workers desire more work, and slightly more workers desire less work. Shank (1986) attributes this to a "backward bending labor supply curve" in the USA, and it is consistent with evidence on worker preferences in the UK (Stewart and Swaffield 1997).

Table 7.2 Preferences for work (May 1985 CPS Supplement)[a]

	Percentage of workers preferring:		
	More work	*Same work*	*Less work*
Panel A: All workers			
All workers	27.61	64.61	7.78
	(0.40)	(0.46)	(0.24)
White workers	26.56	65.51	7.93
	(0.423)	(0.49)	(0.26)
Black workers	38.67	55.87	5.46
	(1.46)	(1.56)	(0.65)
White male workers	30.23	63.78	5.98
	(0.61)	(0.69)	(0.31)
Black male workers	44.92	50.56	4.52
	(0.23)	(0.24)	(0.90)
White female workers	25.05	65.42	9.53
	(0.58)	(0.69)	(0.40)
Black female workers	34.15	59.71	6.13
	(2.86)	(2.07)	(0.92)
Panel B: Workers working at least 20 weekly hours			
White workers	24.95	66.67	8.38
	(0.43)	(0.51)	(0.27)
Black workers	37.53	56.73	5.74
	(1.49)	(1.61)	(0.69)
White male workers	27.85	66.06	6.09
	(0.62)	(0.70)	(0.33)
Black male workers	44.02	51.31	4.66
	(2.33)	(2.40)	(0.93)
White female workers	21.82	67.33	10.85
	(0.60)	(0.73)	(0.45)
Black female workers	32.68	60.78	6.54
	(1.92)	(2.15)	(0.98)
Panel C: Workers working at least 35 weekly hours			
White workers	22.71	68.64	8.66
	(0.45)	(0.54)	(0.30)
Black workers	34.70	58.78	6.52
	(1.55)	(1.71)	(0.77)
White male workers	26.55	67.14	6.32
	(0.63)	(0.72)	(0.34)
Black male workers	41.16	53.70	5.14
	(2.42)	(2.55)	(1.03)
White female workers	17.77	70.56	11.66
	(0.62)	(0.81)	(0.52)
Black female workers	29.62	62.78	7.59
	(1.99)	(2.30)	(1.12)

Note

a Frequency of response in each category. Standard errors in parentheses under means.

What meaning should be attached to the finding that disproportionate larger shares of black workers wish to work more hours than they are currently working? In a static competitive labor market equilibrium, with no adjustment costs or constraints, all workers would work up to the number of hours that equate the marginal rate of substitution of work for leisure to the wage they receive. They would report no desire to change their hours of work. In a dynamic setting, with "shocks" that may disturb this equilibrium, some workers will want to work more and some will want to work less, but the numbers in each category should more or less balance out. Apparently, however, a higher proportion of black workers are constrained by the labor market in their desire to work, and thus are in "disequilibrium," because a smaller percentage of blacks are satisfied with their actual work hours and a disproportionate share want more work hours.

Standard labor supply models link individual work hour preferences to workers' wage rates and their non-labor income. Whereas changes in market wages have an ambiguous effect on work time, because of the opposing income and substitution effects, more non-labor income unambiguously reduces desired work time, if leisure is considered a normal good. Competitive theory thus could explain the gap in black versus white preferences if social- or family-based financial resources are more limited for blacks than whites. Alternatively, the gap may be linked to occupations and industries in which blacks are disproportionately concentrated, perhaps for reasons traced to past or current discrimination. Finally, black workers may simply place a higher marginal valuation on an extra hour of work for cultural or other difficult to explain reasons.

Tables 7.3 moves in the direction of evaluating the causes for the high black worker disequilibrium in hours choices by isolating the preferences of blacks and whites for work after accounting for income (panel A) and education (panel B). In the top panel of Table 7.3, workers are grouped according to their race and income quartile. Statistics for the top (quartile I) and bottom (quartile IV) of the income distribution are retained. The data show that consistent with competitive theory, both black and white workers in the higher income quartiles are less likely to want to work more hours than black and white workers in the lowest income quartile – an income effect. Surprising are the persistent and statistically significant differences between blacks and whites in their preferences for greater work. Indeed, for all income quartiles when comparing black and white workers, blacks are disproportionately more likely to say they desire additional work hours, and this is true for full-time workers (working 35 or more hours per week) as well.

The bottom panel of Table 7.3 looks at black–white differences within educational categories. Since family income is poorly reported in the CPS[6] and since educational attainment is correlated with both wage and family income,[7] education is a reasonable "instrument" for family income in the above context. Reported here are data for the cohort of very educated

Table 7.3 Preferences for work by income status and education (May 1985 CPS Supplement)[a]

	Percentage of workers preferring:		
	More work	*Same work*	*Less work*
Panel A: Preferences by income quartile			
White workers, quartile I (top)	17.67	73.59	8.73
	(0.71)	(0.91)	(0.52)
Black workers, quartile I (top)	24.53	68.55	6.92
	(2.86)	(3.56)	(1.65)
White workers, quartile IV (bottom)	38.74	56.36	4.90
	(0.91)	(0.95)	(0.39)
Black workers, quartile IV (bottom)	49.49	46.42	4.10
	(2.64)	(2.61)	(0.97)
White full-time workers, quartile I	15.86	75.19	8.96
	(0.80)	(1.06)	(0.62)
Black full-time workers, quartile I	21.62	69.37	9.01
	(3.28)	(4.27)	(2.25)
White full-time workers, quartile IV	30.61	62.91	6.48
	(1.04)	(1.15)	(0.55)
Black full-time workers, quartile IV	42.11	52.63	5.26
	(2.79)	(2.90)	(1.20)
Panel B: Preferences by education			
White workers	18.16	71.41	10.43
College/college plus	(0.78)	(1.01)	(0.62)
Black workers	28.33	65.83	5.83
College/college plus	(3.62)	(4.20)	(1.84)
White workers	26.56	65.71	7.74
High school	(0.69)	(0.80)	(0.41)
Black workers	40.36	53.71	5.93
High school	(2.37)	(2.49)	(1.09)
White full-time workers	16.17	73.00	10.83
College/college plus	(0.80)	(1.06)	(0.67)
Black full-time workers	25.66	68.14	6.19
College/college plus	(3.62)	(4.31)	(1.96)
White full-time workers	23.80	68.18	8.03
High school	(0.74)	(0.87)	(0.46)
Black full-time workers	36.40	56.54	7.07
High school	(2.50)	(2.72)	(1.28)

Note

a Frequency of response in each category. Standard errors in parentheses under means.

workers and the cohort of high school graduates. As is clear from the table, the preference gap between blacks and whites has little to do with differences in educational attainment since blacks are more likely to want more work than whites in the two educational categories reported here for both full- and part-time workers. Note that the pattern holds true regardless of the educational category. In sum, the suggestion from Table 7.3 is that the "income effect" alone – where the black–white difference is driven by lower income blacks needing more work – is not likely to explain the gap in preferences.

EXPLAINING RACIAL DIFFERENCES IN PREFERENCES

A more comprehensive way of evaluating the effect of various demographic and non-wage income factors on the black-wage gap in work hour preferences is applying a multiple regression that controls for the various factors that might affect the desire for work. Data on preferences are particularly useful, given the well-known pitfalls of estimating models of labor supply using work hours as the dependent variable, when it is clear such work hour choices are often constrained.[8]

Because the responses to the work preference question in the 1985 Supplement are "more," "less," or "the same," the model can not be estimated as a linear regression. Instead, a probit model is used, where the dependent variable is coded equal to 1 for workers who indicate that they wish to work more hours, and responses indicating a preference for the same or fewer hours are coded to zero. Parameter estimates are presented in Table 7.4, columns 1–6; the corresponding estimates of the impact of the independent variable on the probability of the worker wanting more hours (evaluated at the mean of each of the independent variables) are given in columns $1'$–$6'$. Columns 1–$3'$ of Table 7.4 summarize the results for all workers and columns 4–$6'$ repeat the analysis for men only.[9] Included in the regression are variables to capture labor market status (actual work hours), labor supply parameters (wages and income), and various demographic (education, marital status, age, union status, sex) and occupational and industry controls. All continuous variables are in natural log form.

Columns 1 and $1'$ look at the effects of race alone and show that without controlling for any additional factors, blacks are 8.2 percent more likely to respond that they wish to work more hours at their current wage than are whites. Columns 2 and $2'$ control for the key labor supply parameters known to influence work hours choice, namely the hourly wage and family income. Although the impact of a higher wage on work hours is theoretically ambiguous, due to a substitution and an income effect that work in opposite directions, the impact of higher family income on work hours is unambiguously negative. The estimates show that blacks are still 4.6 percent more likely to respond that they desire more work hours after controlling for these factors. Columns 3 and $3'$ further control for actual working hours, differences in demographic factors such as education, age, marital status, sex, and union status, as well as for detailed occupation and industry. The results show that after accounting for the types of factors that may influence work hours choices, blacks remain statistically more likely than whites to desire more work – to be dissatisfied with their current work hours. Note the importance of the coefficient on work hours which is negative and significant in all specifications. This indicates that workers are less inclined to desire additional work the more hours they are actually at work, and that this is true even after controlling for demographic and occupational

Table 7.4 Preferences for work, probit regressions (May 1985 CPS Supplement, all workers). Dependent variable equals 1 if individual desires more work[a]

	All workers						*Men only*					
	(1)	*(1′)*	*(2)*	*(2′)*	*(3)*	*(3′)*	*(4)*	*(4′)*	*(5)*	*(5′)*	*(6)*	*(6′)*
Black	0.24 5[b]	0.082[b]	0.142[b]	0.046[b]	0.199[b]	0.064[b]	0.303[b]	0.107[b]	0.179[b]	0.061[b]	0.245[b]	0.083[b]
	(0.043)	(0.015)	(0.045)	(0.015)	(0.047)	(0.016)	(0.064)	(0.024)	(0.067)	(0.024)	(0.070)	(0.025)
ln family income			−0.208[b]	−0.065[b]	−0.200[b]	−0.061[b]			−0.158[b]	−0.052[b]	−0.148[b]	−0.047[b]
			(0.020)	(0.006)	(0.021)	(0.006)			(0.029)	(0.010)	(0.031)	(0.010)
ln hourly wage			−0.314[b]	−0.098[b]	−0.164[b]	−0.050[b]			−0.387[b]	−0.127[b]	−0.188[b]	−0.060[b]
			(0.026)	(0.008)	(0.035)	(0.011)			(0.037)	(0.012)	(0.050)	(0.016)
ln hours					−0.361[b]	−0.109[b]					−0.356	−0.114[b]
					(0.035)	(0.011)					(0.058)	(0.018)
Education[c]					Yes	Yes					Yes	Yes
Married					−0.091[b]	−0.028[b]					0.041	0.013
					(0.030)	(0.009)					(0.044)	(0.014)
Female					−0.219[b]	−0.066[b]						
					(0.035)	(0.011)						
Union					−0.067	−0.020					−0.117[b]	−0.036[b]
					(0.041)	(0.012)					(0.054)	(0.016)
Age dummies					Yes	Yes					Yes	Yes
Occupation					Yes	Yes					Yes	Yes
Industry					Yes	Yes					Yes	Yes
log likelihood	−6 422.1	−6 422.1	−6 013.8	−6 013.8	−5 654.0	−5 654.0	−3 324.6	−3 324.6	−3 110.4	−3 110.4	−2 935.2	−2 935.2
N	11 527	11 527	11 116	11 116	11 108	11 108	5 735	5 735	5 544	5 544	5 538	5 538

Notes

a Derivatives are evaluated at the means of the independent variables in columns 1′, 2′, 3′, 4′, 5′, 6′. Unreported intercept included in all regressions.

b Indicates statistical significance at the 0.05 level with standard errors in parentheses.

c Education categorical variables included as follows: less than high school, some high school, some college, college graduate, college graduate plus. Omitted category is high school graduate.

characteristics likely to influence these choices. This is an important variable to include in the preference equation since by its inclusion we can conclude that black–white preference differences are independent of actual working hour differences as so measured.

Columns 4–6′ of the table repeat the analysis, this time restricting the sample to men only. By omitting women the analysis is rid of many of the hard-to-measure differences that may influence women's choices about work and work hours. The results show similar if somewhat stronger evidence that black men are constrained in their work hour choices. Black men are more likely to respond that they desire more work hours even after controlling for labor supply side and demographic factors likely to influence the desire for work. In sum, the data show clear and real differences in black and white preferences for more work.

It is of course possible that differences in work preferences reflect the particular cultural way in which blacks and whites answer questions of this type and not, in fact, true differences in tastes. It would be useful to have additional corroboration from other surveys or at different points in time to evaluate this possibility. Unfortunately, I know of no additional data of this type to corroborate the data findings on preferences.

EXPLAINING DIFFERENCES IN ACTUAL WORK HOURS

Reconciling differences in black–white preferences for hours worked is difficult since competitive theory predicts that all else equal black and white work hours choices should be the same. Since differences in preferences do not appear to be due to differences in actual work hours, wages, income, or demographics, what could be causing it?

Standard static labor supply theory predicts that in equilibrium, workers will work up to the number of hours where the marginal rate of substitution between work and leisure is equal to the wage they receive. In this vein, differences in work hour preferences would be explained if black workers working the same number of hours as white workers value an extra hour of work more than their white, and otherwise the same, coworkers. The fact that black workers actually work *shorter* annual hours per week and per year while indicating a preference for working longer hours suggests that they are constrained in their ability to choose and work their optimal number of hours.

Dynamic labor supply theories (concerned with optimal contracts designed to motivate workers) stress the shape of the opportunities frontier facing workers and the distribution of the workers opportunities over time. Tournament models focus on the link between pay and effort rather than pay and output (Lazear and Rosen 1981; Green and Stokey 1983; Malcomson 1984), where relative wages determine the level of effort. In the rat-race model (Landers, Rebitzer and Taylor 1996), workers signal that they are of high quality by working long hours since employers use hours worked as a best indicator ("signal") of future productivity. Workers are therefore rewarded for long hours by promotion and high wages.

The hours-inequality model of Bell and Freeman (1995, 1997) links hours worked to wage dispersion in the relevant labor market cell and builds on the insights from both rat-race and tournament models in stressing the incentives for greater effort created by an unequal payoff in wages. While tournament and rat-race models are more specific in terms of the types of labor market to which the theory applies (such as the labor market for professional workers), the hours-inequality model is easily generalized to labor markets for both high and low skilled workers. It is therefore better suited to application in this context.

The two main arguments in the hours-inequality model are first that an increase in hours (effort) increases the worker's rank in the percentile wage distribution at the workplace, and second that any incremental advance in worker rank will translate into higher wage gains the more unequal is the wage distribution. Workers respond to the greater gain/loss implicit in a wider distribution of earnings by working more hours, since the marginal expected future earnings from this additional effort are necessarily larger (Bell and Freeman 1995, 1997).

How might the hours-inequality model help to explain differences in black and white work hours and work hour preferences? If the expected wage gain for an extra hour of work is not the same for black and white workers, then overall occupational wage inequality measures may not be relevant for black workers, because their future wage opportunities may differ from whites who dominate in calculation of the overall measure. Instead, black workers may respond to higher variation in black-only wages by working longer hours if they perceive this as an indicator of future earnings opportunities, but may not respond (or be less responsive) to greater variation in white wages (or in wages overall). The empirical test is to evaluate the link between the hours of black and white workers and various measures of wage inequality, and to test the extent to which black or white workers' hours respond differently. If labor markets are competitive then otherwise similar black and white workers should respond to a common measure of wage inequality in their relevant job cell.[10] If black and white workers respond differently then at least two explanations may be offered. First, race-specific measures of earnings inequality may better capture unmeasured characteristics of the individual or sorting by job-type. Second, such an association would prevail if labor markets were racially segmented such that the distribution of white wages in the occupational cell does not adequately signal the future wage opportunity frontier available to black workers. While both explanations are consistent with and enhance the body of empirical support for the Bell–Freeman hours–wage inequality hypothesis (1995, 1997), only the first explanation is consistent with neoclassical labor market theory.

EFFECTS ACROSS DIFFERENT OCCUPATIONS

In order to evaluate the behavior of black and white workers and the response of work hours to wage inequality, workers are grouped into categories of "non-competing labor markets" by the detailed occupational classification to which they are assigned in the CPS. In each of the forty-two, two-digit non-agricultural CPS occupations, I calculate the standard deviation of the natural log of hourly earnings, which is the measure of wage inequality used in the statistical analysis. This wage inequality measure is calculated in the overall occupation cell, and subsequently for black-only and white-only workers in the cell as well. The analysis in Bell (1998) is updated, using both the 1985 and 1995 merged outgoing rotation group CPS files, and thereby exploiting the larger sample frequencies of the merged data. Making use of significant hours differences across cells, the hypothesis tested in Bell and Freeman (1995, 1997) is that the incentive of workers to put in more hours is intensified by the dispersion of pay in the job market in which they work. This chapter expands upon the hypothesis in testing the degree to which blacks and whites respond similarly to various incentives.

Do black-only and white-only measures of occupational wage inequality display significant variance to justify such an approach? Table 7.5 answers this question by listing the top ten occupations with the greatest wage variation for both black-only and white-only calculated dispersion, and the bottom ten with the least variation. As is clear from the table there are sizeable differences in the rankings and occupational variances across the two measures that may be important in explaining black and white work hour and preference for work differences in certain occupations, although broadly the two measures are not statistically independent.[11]

Tables 7.6 and 7.7 summarize the basic relationship for black workers and black male workers using a regression that links the mean of actual hours in each occupation cell to the mean and standard deviation of white and black wages in each cell. Recall that standard labor supply theory predicts an ambiguous association between mean wages and mean hours depending on the relative parameter magnitudes of the income and substitution effect. The hours-inequality hypothesis (Bell and Freeman 1995, 1997) predicts that the standard deviation of wages will be positively associated with hours, since higher wage inequality implies a greater reward for effort. While a positive association between mean wages and hours is not a necessary condition for the hours-inequality model, such a correlation would be consistent with the Bell–Freeman theory since it implies that workers respond to a higher payoff in wages by working harder. In this discussion I chose to focus on a large subset of more permanent workers (workers that usually work at least 20 hours per week) since these workers are the group more likely to respond behaviorally in a way consistent with the incentive driven story of the hours-inequality model. It is worth noting that using occupational means of hours and wages necessarily avoids the ratio bias

Table 7.5 Occupational wage variation: black and white workers (1995 CPS merged outgoing rotation file)

Black occupational wage variation rank (standard deviation of ln hourly earnings)	*White occupational wage variation rank (standard deviation of ln hourly earnings)*
Highest wage variation occupations	
Health diagnosing occupations (0.730)	Health diagnosing occupations (0.732)
Natural scientists (0.674)	Private household services (0.656)
Sales reps., finance and bus. services (0.651)	Sales reps., finance and bus. services (0.622)
Teachers, except college and university (0.633)	Teachers, college and university (0.578)
Fabricators, assemblers and inspectors (0.628)	Other professional specialty occupations (0.577)
Private household service occupations (0.593)	Personal service occupations (0.575)
Other professional specialty occupations (0.565)	Other executive, administrators, managers (0.574)
Other executive, administrators, managers (0.562)	Fabricators, assemblers and inspectors (0.564)
Health assessment and treating (0.560)	Sales reps., commodities, except retail (0.559)
Lawyers and judges (0.552)	Supervisors and proprietors, sales occupations (0.544)
Lowest wage variation occupations	
Cleaning and building service occupations (0.416)	Other transportation occupations (0.454)
Computer equipment operators (0.402)	Motor vehicle operators (0.453)
Construction laborer (0.399)	Food service occupations (0.439)
Sales workers, retail and personal services (0.398)	Health assessment and treating occupations (0.422)
Health technologists and technicians (0.391)	Engineers (0.408)
Engineering and science technicians (0.390)	Engineering and science technicians (0.407)
Secretaries, stenographers, and typists (0.389)	Health technologists and technicians (0.405)
Supervisors-adm. support (0.379)	Financial records, processing occupations (0.405)
Financial records, processing occupations (0.378)	Secretaries, stenographers, and typists (0.398)
Sales related occupations (0.340)	Health service occupations (0.389)

Table 7.6 Work hours and earnings inequality regressions by occupational cell, 1985. Dependent variable: mean of ln weekly hours in detailed occupational cell by group as indicated[a]

	(1) 20+ hr	(2) 20+ hr	(3) 20+ hr	(4) 35+ hr	(5) 35+ hr	(6) 35+ hr
Panel A: 1985 merged outgoing rotation group CPS data, all black workers, $N=42$						
Std. ln black hr earnings	0.124 (0.089)		0.238 (0.137)	0.320 (0.047)		0.297 (0.076)
Std. ln white hr earnings		0.086 (0.092)	−0.168 (0.153)		0.256 (0.063)	0.034 (0.089)
Mean ln hr earnings	0.150 (0.020)	0.149 (0.021)	0.147 (0.020)	0.039 (0.010)	0.053 (0.013)	0.040 (0.011)
Adj. R^2	0.578	0.545	0.580	0.605	0.393	0.596
Panel B: 1985 merged outgoing rotation group CPS data, black male workers, $N=42$						
Std. ln black hr earnings	0.167 (0.065)		0.183 (0.073)	0.286 (0.047)		0.208 (0.063)
Std. ln white hr earnings		0.077 (0.094)	−0.050 (0.101)		0.368 (0.081)	0.178 (0.098)
Mean ln hr earnings	0.139 (0.020)	0.128 (0.022)	0.136 (0.021)	0.041 (0.017)	0.056 (0.021)	0.052 (0.018)
Adj. R^2	0.543	0.461	0.534	0.472	0.316	0.502

Note

a Means of ln hours and ln wages and standard deviation of ln wages measured across 42 non-agricultural occupational cells as reported in the CPS.

problem that affects the coefficient on the level of earnings for individuals and possibly the coefficient on inequality as well.[12]

Table 7.6 uses the 1985 merged CPS data and distinguishes between all black workers (panel A) and black male workers (panel B). The first 3 columns of both panels treat workers who report that they typically work at least 20 hours, and the last 3 columns treat workers who report that they typically work full-time. Columns 1 and 4 use the standard deviation of the natural log of wages measured across black-only workers in the occupation as the relevant measure of inequality, and show a significant and positive effect of inequality and hours consistent with the theory in Bell and Freeman (1995, 1997). Columns 2 and 5 repeat the analysis using a white-only measure of calculated occupational inequality and show mixed results, with the white inequality measure insignificant and positive for the group of workers reporting 20 plus hours of work, but significant and positive for the full-time group. Columns 3 and 6 include both measures of occupational inequality, and show that where both measures are included the black-only inequality measure dominates in nearly all cases. With the exception of a sub-group of black male workers working full-time, black hours seem more closely linked

Table 7.7 Work hours and earnings inequality regressions by occupational cell, 1995. Dependent variable: mean of ln weekly hours in detailed occupational cell by group as indicated[a]

	(1) *20+ hr*	*(2)* *20+ hr*	*(3)* *20+ hr*	*(4)* *35+ hr*	*(5)* *35+ hr*	*(6)* *35+ hr*
Panel A: 1985 merged outgoing rotation group CPS data, all black workers, $N=42$						
Std. ln black hr earnings[b]	0.193 (0.114)		0.362 (0.145)	0.183 (0.050)		0.041 (0.057)
Std. ln white hr earnings[b]		−0.036 (0.139)	−0.309 (0.171)		0.263 (0.049)	0.247 (0.065)
Mean ln hr earnings	0.162 (0.029)	0.177 (0.028)	0.154 (0.028)	0.042 (0.013)	0.045 (0.011)	0.042 (0.011)
Adj. R^2	0.510	0.475	0.537	0.392	0.534	0.551
Panel B: 1995 merged outgoing rotation group CPS data, black male workers, $N=42$						
Std. ln black hr earnings[b]	0.142 (0.077)		0.175 (0.082)	0.165 (0.056)		0.155 (0.055)
Std. ln white hr earnings[b]		−0.036 (0.139)	−0.113 (0.101)		0.176 (0.080)	0.142 (0.077)
Mean ln hr earnings	0.140 (0.023)	0.150 (0.023)	0.140 (0.023)	0.071 (0.019)	0.076 (0.020)	0.066 (0.019)
Adj. R^2	0.544	0.506	0.547	0.387	0.377	0.424

Notes

a Means of ln hours and ln wages and standard deviation of ln wages measured across 42 non-agricultural occupational cells as reported in the CPS.

b Standard deviation in natural log of hourly earnings (standard deviations reported in parentheses under coefficient estimates).

to black-only inequality measures. Note that there is a positive and significant association between average hours worked and average wages in all cases.

Table 7.7 repeats the analysis using the 1995 data. The black-only earnings inequality measure dominates for the group of all and male-only black workers working 20 plus hours, but not among the full-time group. Instead, for full-time workers, both black-only and white-only measures of inequality are positively linked with mean hours. Note that the black-only inequality variable is insignificant in the all workers specification that includes both inequality terms (column 6, panel A), consistent with the notion that otherwise similar black workers and white workers face the same marginal expected gain to an extra hour of work.

The results using occupational means suggest that black workers respond to greater black-only earnings inequality by supplying greater hours on average, and that they are less likely to be responsive to white-earnings inequality measures (or to overall occupational inequality), especially true for the less than full-time. Can this explain the difference in black and white worker hours?

Table 7.8 Explaining differences in black and white work hours by occupational cells (1985 and 1995 merged outgoing rotation group CPS data). Dependent variable: difference in usual weekly hours for black-only and white-only workers working 20+ hours[a]

	1985	*1995*
Difference in hourly earnings [b,c]	0.115	0.286
	(0.043)	(0.059)
Difference in earnings variation[c,d]	−0.026	0.233
	(0.057)	(0.084)
N	41	42
Adj. R^2	0.135	0.414

Notes

a The difference in the mean of white-only and black-only usual weekly hours in the detailed occupational cell.

b The difference in the mean of white-only and black-only earnings in the detailed occupational cell.

c Standard errors in parentheses under coefficient estimates.

d The difference in the white-only and black-only standard deviation of ln earnings in the detailed occupational cell.

To test this, I calculate for each of the 42 two-digit non-agricultural occupational cells in the sample the difference in mean white and black hours (using a sub-sample of workers working 20 plus hours), and link this to the difference in mean white and black earnings and earnings inequality measures. Formally:

$$(\mathrm{hrs_w} - \mathrm{hrs_b}) = a + b_1(\mathrm{hrearn_w} - \mathrm{hrearn_b}) + b_2(\sigma_{\mathrm{hrearn,w}} - \sigma_{\mathrm{hrearn,b}})$$

Table 7.8 gives the results of this test for both the 1985 and 1995 data. As is clear from the table, the differences in mean earnings and earnings inequality measures for white-only and black-only workers explain the differences in work hours in the 1995 data, but not in the 1985 data. Note that in both the 1985 and 1995 data the differences in mean hours between the black-only and white-only sub-groups of workers are positively associated with differences in mean earnings. This is consistent with the notion that incentives drive hard work, and may reflect unmeasured differences in the characteristics of black and white workers within the occupational cell.

TESTS FOR INDIVIDUALS

Finally, I explore the link between inequality and hours worked for black and white workers using the 1985 and 1995 data for *individuals* who work 20 or more hours rather than the occupational averages. In these calculations each individual is given one occupational level variable – the standard deviation of natural log of hourly earnings – and his or her own estimated hourly earnings

Table 7.9 Individual hours-inequality regressions, 1985 and 1995, black workers working 20+ hours (1985 CPS merged outgoing rotation group files, non-agricultural workers working 20+ hours only). Dependent variable = ln usual hours[a]

	1985						1995					
	(1)	(2)	(3)	(4)	(5)	(6)	(7)	(8)	(9)	(10)	(11)	(12)
ln hourly wage	0.010 (0.003)	0.062 (0.003)	0.097 (0.003)	0.061 (0.003)	0.101 (0.003)	0.062 (0.003)	0.074 (0.003)	0.027 (0.002)	0.074 (0.003)	0.027 (0.002)	0.077 (0.003)	0.049 (0.003)
Std. ln black hourly wage[b]	0.150 (0.026)	0.161 (0.030)	0.470 (0.044)	0.220 (0.047)			0.247 (0.022)	0.141 (0.019)	0.281 (0.028)	0.094 (0.024)		
Std. ln white hourly wage[c]			−0.378 (0.043)	−0.079 (0.049)	−0.010 (0.025)	0.097 (0.031)			−0.064 (0.033)	0.092 (0.030)	0.144 (0.026)	0.161 (0.029)
Education[d]		Yes		Yes		Yes		Yes		Yes		Yes
Age 25–40		0.027 (0.003)		0.027 (0.003)		0.027 (0.003)		0.017 (0.002)		0.017 (0.002)		0.029 (0.003)
Married		0.021 (0.003)		0.021 (0.003)		0.021 (0.003)		0.008 (0.002)		0.008 (0.002)		0.017 (0.003)
Female		−0.034 (0.003)		−0.034 (0.003)		−0.035 (0.003)		−0.036 (0.003)		−0.036 (0.003)		−0.039 (0.003)
Union		0.003 (0.003)		0.003 (0.003)		0.003 (0.003)		−0.010 (0.003)		−0.010 (0.003)		0.000 (0.004)
Industry controls		Yes		Yes		Yes		Yes		Yes		Yes
Adjusted R^2	0.077	0.133	0.082	0.133	0.075	0.132	0.064	0.093	0.064	0.094	0.058	0.119
N	15 559	15 559	15 559	15 559	15 560	15 560	14 556	14 049	14 556	14 049	14 556	14 556

Notes

a Standard errors in parentheses under coefficient estimates.

b Standard deviation of ln hourly earnings for black-only workers across 42 detailed occupational groups.

c Standard deviation of ln hourly earnings for white-only workers across 42 detailed occupational groups.

d Educational categorical variables: less than high school, some high school, some college, college graduate, college plus. Omitted category is high school graduate.

and hours worked. Included as well are measurable characteristics of the individual associated with their human capital accumulation (education and age), marital status, union status, and sex, as well as industry controls at the two-digit level. The advantage of this framework is that it allows me to control directly for characteristics of the individual likely to be associated with both effort (usual weekly hours) and earnings and to control for the possibly important effects of industry. The disadvantage of the individual level data is that high/low hours due to measurement error produce a low/high wage, thereby inducing a negative correlation. In addition, if the hourly earnings variable suffers from classical measurement error then the variance of earnings inequality will be overstated as well.

In Table 7.9 the regressions are estimated first for individual black workers using the 1985 data (columns 1–6) and then using the 1995 data (columns 7–12). Included are specifications using the black-only inequality measure, the white-only inequality measure, and both the black- and white-only measures to test the robustness of the overall effect and the sensitivity to the presence of possible multicollinearity in the black-only and white-only measures.[13] Table 7.9 shows that in the preponderance of cases the link between hours and earnings inequality for black workers is strongest with the black-only measure, and often it is insignificant or wrong-signed when using the white-only measure. The other variables are correctly signed and stable to specification.

The suggestion from the individual level regressions confirms the existence of a black-hours–black-earnings inequality link that may explain a part of the black-hours gap discussed in the first section of this chapter. The reason why black workers are more responsive to black-only inequality measures is, unfortunately, difficult to ascertain without detailed data on attitudes, and worker and job characteristics not available here. The presence of such an association is consistent with the notion that greater inequality within a job classification does elicit greater effort (more hours) from workers.

CONCLUSION

This chapter has documented several important facts about black and white work hour differences. First, black men work 20 percent fewer annual hours than white men – the differences between black and white women in work hours are small. Second, in response to questions on preferences for work, a greater proportion of black than white workers are in disequilibrium, desiring more hours than they are actually working. The racial gap in the ability to obtain one's preferred number of work hours is not related to differences in actual hours worked, wages, or family income, and is independent of demographic factors likely to influence labor supply behavior.

The analysis confirms the existence of a strong link between individual black worker hours and earnings inequality measured at the occupational level, consistent with the Bell and Freeman (1995, 1997) results for US and German workers overall. Moreover and importantly, black workers are more responsive to black-only measures of earnings inequality than to earnings inequality measures overall. One interpretation of this is that the black-only inequality measure is a better signal to black workers about the expected future gain from working hard today. The reasons why this would be so are difficult to ascertain. The black-hours–black-inequality association may be caused by unmeasured characteristics of the black workers or the job-types that black workers hold that are correlated with both hours and inequality and that differentiate black workers in the sample. Alternatively, the existence of such a link is consistent with the notion that black and white workers compete in labor markets that are at least partly racially segmented. Unfortunately, while it is difficult to reconcile these two very different explanations with empirical tests, both are wholly consistent with the incentive-driven notions that motivate the hours-inequality theory.

NOTES

1 Bell acknowledges research support from the Haverford College Faculty Support Fund and the research assistance of Lily Xiaoli Qiu. This paper builds on the theory developed in joint work with Richard Freeman, and portions of this chapter have been extracted from several joint co-authored articles as referred to in the text.
2 These data were provided by the National Bureau of Economic Research (NBER). The CPS question on work hours preferences has not been asked of workers since the May 1985 survey. Although these data are over a decade old, there is still rich information contained in the responses of workers to this question.
3 The figures do not account for differences in overtime hours between blacks and whites. Since fewer blacks work overtime than whites, according to the May 1991 CPS, the numbers listed above understate if anything the magnitude of the differences between black and white work hours.
4 Similar questions on preferences for work were asked in the 1991 International Social Survey Programme Data. Although these data can be used to corroborate evidence from the CPS, there are too few observations in the sample to use these data to assess black and white worker differences. Similar questions on preferences have been asked of workers in other countries, and the US stands out in the respect of workers wanting more hours. For example, see Stewart and Swaffield (1997) for the patterns of overwork in the UK, and Lang and Kahn (1997) for the differences in European worker responses, based on both the European Union and ISSP Surveys.
5 See Bell (1998) on this subject, based on Clement (1997), as an exception.
6 Family income is given by ranges of income brackets and is calculated at the mean of each category. In addition, family income is capped at a maximum in the top range, so potentially large differences in the high end of the income distribution will be missed.

7 Not only is there a well-established wage premium received by workers for additional years of education, but also individuals whose parents have higher education levels are more likely to pursue additional education beyond high school (see for example, Kane 1994).

8 It is well established that workers' hours of labor supply are "constrained" in the sense that workers can not literally "choose" their own hours of work (Kahn and Lang 1997). In addition, the hourly earnings variable may be endogeneous in a regression model with work hours as the dependent variable. Estimates of average hourly earnings for workers not paid by the hour are computed in the CPS by dividing their usual weekly earnings by their reported usual weekly hours, or elsewhere by using reported annual earnings and annual hours.

9 Since the gap in *actual* work hours is so wide for black men relative to white men, while their *preferences* for work hours differ little, black men are clearly the group most "constrained" in their ability to supply their labor.

10 The degree of wage inequality measured across the major occupational classifications is higher for black men than white men, on average. This might explain a part of the difference in their hours preferences, noted above.

11 The Spearman rank-order correlation coefficient of 0.573 means the two series cannot be regarded as independent of one another, as might be expected given the nature of wage-determination in labor markets.

12 To the extent that the variance of the earnings distribution is correlated with the mean, the coefficient on the inequality term will be biased upward in the regressions for individuals, but not in the regressions on moments.

13 The correlation coefficient between the black-only and white-only inequality measures in the individual level data was in the range of 0.7–0.8 in all specifications.

REFERENCES

Bell, L. (1998) "Differences in Work Hours and Hours Preferences by Race in the US," *Review of Social Economy* 56(4): 481–500.

Bell, L. and Freeman, R. (1995) "Why Do Americans and Germans Work Different Hours?" in F. Butler, W. Franz, R. Schettkat, and D. Soskice (eds), *Institutional Frameworks and Labor Market Performance*, London: Routledge, Chap. 5.

_____ (1997) "Working Hard," in *Changes in Working Time in the United States and Canada*, Kalamazoo, MI: Upjohn Institute.

Clement, M. (1997) "Empirical and Theoretical Findings About the Relationship between Wage Variance and Hours Worked," unpublished undergraduate thesis, Haverford College.

Freeman, R. and Holzer, H. (1986) "The Black Youth Employment Crisis: Summary of Findings," in R. Freeman and H. Holzer (eds), *The Black Youth Employment Crisis*, Chicago: The University of Chicago Press.

Green, J. and Stokey, N. (1983) "A Comparison of Tournaments and Contracts," *Journal of Political Economy* 91(3): 349–364.

Hochschild, A. (1997) *The Time Bind*, New York: Metropolitan Books.

Kahn, S. and Lang, K. (1997) "Hours Constraints and the Wage/Hours Locus," *Canadian Journal of Economics* 29: S71–75.

Kane, T. (1994) "College Entry by Blacks since 1970: The Role of College Costs, Family Background, and Returns to Education," *Journal of Political Economy* 102(51): 878–911.

Landers, R., Rebitzer, J., and Taylor, L. (1996) "Rat Race Redux: Adverse Selection in the Determination of Work Hours in Law Firms," *American Economic Review* 86: 3229–3248.

Lang, K. and Kahn, S. (1997) "Hours Constraints: Theory, Evidence and Policy Implications," in *Changes in Working Time in the United States and Canada*, Kalamazoo, MI: Upjohn Institute.

Lazear, E. and Rosen, S. (1981) "Rank Order Tournaments as Optimum Labor Contracts," *Journal of Political Economy* 89(5): 841–861.

Malcomson, J. (1984) "Work Incentives, Hierarchy, and Internal Labor Markets," *Journal of Political Economy* 92: 486–507.

Schor, J. B. (1991) *The Overworked American*, New York: Basic Books.

Shank, S. (1986) "Preferred Hours of Work and Corresponding Earnings," *Monthly Labor Review* (November): 40–44.

Stewart, M. B. and Swaffield J. K. (1997) "Constraints on the Desired Hours of Work of British Men," *The Economic Journal* 107: 520–535.

8 Driven to spend

Longer work hours as a byproduct of market forces

David George

The claim that the American worker has experienced an increase in the work week over the past thirty years is more complex than it initially appears. That some suffer from the opposite problem of underwork is beyond dispute.[1] That paid work time per family has risen much more than paid work time per worker (with the rise in two-income households) is likewise beyond dispute. And that any rise in waged work time has represented not a net rise in overall work time but substitution of paid work for "household production" adds still more complications.[2]

The importance of these added complexities is obvious, as the other chapters in this book make clear. The focus of the present chapter, however, can proceed without any attempted resolution of these complications. My attention will focus primarily on the economically advantaged half of the population for whom layoffs and decreased work time are much less of a threat. Somewhat surprisingly, it is this group that is most inclined to work long hours. As Jacobs and Gerson (1998: 447) report, among professional, managerial, and technical employees, 34.5 percent of men and 17.0 percent of women work more than 50 hours per week, while for those in all other occupations, the figures are 20.0 percent, and 6.8 percent, respectively.[3]

Whether similar figures from thirty years ago would be higher or lower is not of any immediate significance. My starting point is the observation that few would have predicted that work weeks of this length would have become so common. With rising wages (something that professionals, managers, and technical employees *have* enjoyed), the dominant assumption was that leisure would significantly increase.[4] In the pages that follow, attention will be given to three different explanations of why leisure has remained as scarce as it has.

1. *The minimalist explanation.* It is tempting to attribute the mistaken belief that leisure time would rise to a mistaken assumption about the average individual's labor supply curve. The conventional wisdom certainly seems to have been that with affluence would come a greater demand for leisure. Implied was that any *decrease* in demand for leisure prompted by its higher relative price (the substitution effect) would be more than offset by an *increase* in demand for leisure that affluence would bring (the income

effect). The minimalist explanation simply treats the latter effect, contrary to popular belief, as insufficient to offset the former. If correct, the typical worker in the professional and managerial occupations has a labor supply curve that slopes upward rather than bends backward.[5]

2. *The "work-and-spend" explanation.* According to Juliet Schor (1991), the gain in the power of employers over the last thirty years has forced workers to the right of their labor supply curves. This has led, she argues, to higher incomes than planned and rising material expectations. By this account, what started as superfluous overwork has become, with the passage of time, work that is required if these changing tastes are to be satisfied.[6]

3. *The "spend-and-work" explanation.* Reversing the order of causation, Brack and Cowling (1983) treat a rising demand for goods caused by modern marketing and advertising as the initiating event. A voluntary (rather than *required*) decision to work longer hours is thus interpreted to have followed from this prior event.

In the section to follow I will show that while the differences between the "work-and-spend" and "spend-and work" explanations might appear to be merely superficial, the latter (and, I believe, stronger) explanation appears to have much weaker normative implications.[7] Within the prevailing consensus of neoclassical or mainstream economics – a consensus increasingly embraced by the wider culture – the act of restraining choice that forms part of the "work-and-spend" model is judged to be harmful to workers while the act of merely persuading agents to spend more that describes the "spend-and-work" model is not. The chapter's final section will attempt to solve this normative impasse with the help of metapreferences.

"WORK-AND-SPEND" VERSUS "SPEND-AND-WORK"

Table 8.1 summarizes time allocation changes uncovered by Schor. Note that the rise in hours at paid labor ("market hours") was made possible by both a decline in household labor time and a decline in leisure. Figure 8.1 summarizes Schor's thesis that the reversal of the century-long decline in work time can be attributed mainly to the increased power of employers (1991: Ch. 3). By her analysis, the annual employee work time favored by employers exceeds what is optimal for most employees, and decline in union membership density has resulted in a movement in the direction favorable to employers.

As Figure 8.1 shows, Schor's typical agent was once able to exercise more discretion over how much to work. Point A shows the agent as on her supply curve in 1969, working 1 200 hours per year. Point B summarizes Schor's prediction that, if free to choose, the agent would have moved along her backward bending labor supply curve, supplying fewer hours annually. According to Schor, however, this desire has been ruled out by rising work time requirements imposed by employers, and the typical agent is spending

Table 8.1 Allocation of time per year, entire population[a]

Year	*Market hours per year*	*Household hours per year*	*Leisure hours per year*
1969	1 199	1 227	3 414
1987	1 316	1 157	3 367

Note

a Estimates of "market hours" and "household hours" are from Juliet B. Schor (1991), *The Overworked American* (Basic Books), p. 36. "Leisure hours" are author's calculation, based on assumption of 16 hours per day to devote to the activities shown.

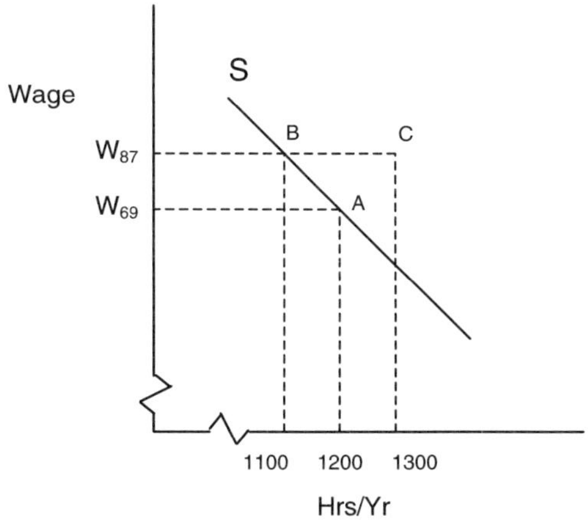

Figure 8.1 Schor's interpretation of the rise in hours worked.

more time in paid employment, as shown by point C, well to the right of the supply curve. (The horizontal distance between points C and B measures the difference between required and desired work time, and is not intended to reflect actual estimates but roughly to reflect the message conveyed by Schor.) Now if this had been the end of the story, two predictions would have followed, neither of which has been observed.

First, a widening gap between the required work time and workers' desired work time would be expected to lead to an increase in the rates of saving. Income that is unexpected or that exceeds one's optimal income level is income for which one would be expected to have fewer than average immediate uses. As an example of this, Japan's high savings rates in the 1980s were attributed by some to its rapid growth, the argument being that it takes time for consumption habits to catch up with sudden increases in incomes (see Rosser and Rosser 1996: 141). Besides saving more because of few immediate uses for one's higher income, the overworked worker might also be expected to save more for strategic, far-sighted reasons. After all, an employer's ability to require employees to work longer than they wish per week or per year does not translate into an employer's ability to require longer hours worked per lifetime. With some discretion over the age of retirement, one can respond to imposed overwork by saving more now so as to be able to afford an earlier retirement.[8,9]

Contrary to what these considerations might lead us to expect, there has been no rise in savings in the USA over the period considered by Schor. Well before the dramatic drop in savings in the late 1990s brought on in large measure by the booming stock market's effect on perceived wealth, savings rates were falling. By one calculation, rates went from approximately 8 percent of disposable income in the 1970s to around 4 percent of disposable income by the late 1980s. By another estimate, the decline was less, from an average of about 10.7 percent in the early 1970s to 8 percent in the 1980s (US Bureau of the Census 1993: Table 700, 448; Table 696, 445). Considerable empirical work would be necessary to draw any firm conclusions, but this certainly casts doubt on the claim that there has been a shift away from a historical period when work time accorded well with the desire of workers to a time when employers were likely to impose longer than desired work hours.

There is a second prediction that would follow from the imposition of longer work hours with workers' tastes unchanged. If people are indeed forced to work more than they would wish (if they are to keep their jobs) we would expect them to indicate a preference for fewer hours when asked. Jacobs and Gerson (1998: 452) provide evidence consistent with this prediction, as the ideal work week for both males and females was found to be approximately 5 hours less than what was actually worked. The study used in reaching this conclusion, however, did not ask respondents to imagine their hourly compensation as fixed, suggesting that some may not have appreciated that the reduction in hours would not be without cost. In a survey described by Bell (1998: 446), in contrast, respondents were asked to assume that more work would mean proportionately more earnings and less work proportionately less. More than three times as many respondents expressed a preference for *more* hours (27.6 percent) than expressed a preference for *less* (7.8 percent). A study of Canadian workers by Kahn and Lang (1991) came up with similar results. Only 4.4 percent of respondents working more than forty hours desired to work less, while 19.5 percent desired to work more. Each of these two latter studies thus suggests a pattern that runs counter to what was reported by Jacobs and Gerson and counter to what the Schor model, absent any further development, would have predicted.[10]

Schor was not oblivious to findings such as these that cast doubts upon the model thus far described. She mentions a rise in "moonlighting" during the 1980s (1991: 31) and goes on to extend her model to make it consistent with such unequivocally *voluntary* increases in work time. To have offered no reply would have given the upper hand to an orthodox interpretation of the observed trends, namely, that the typical labor supply curve is such that higher wages have resulted in more hours from the average worker.[11] By the "work-and-spend" cycle that she presents, workers eventually find outlets

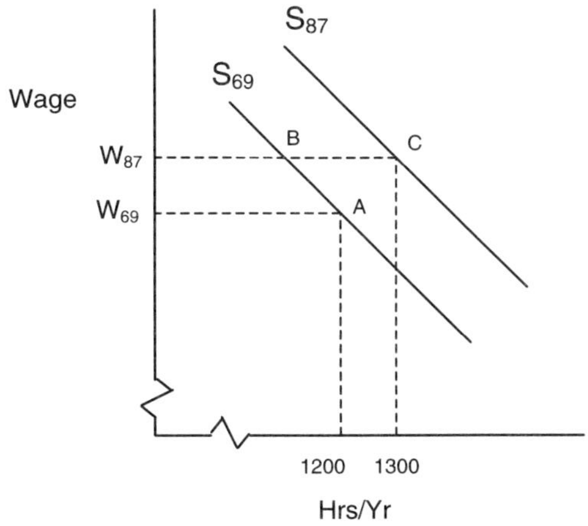

Figure 8.2 Change in labor supply following imposed increase in hours worked, or changes in hours worked following rise in labor supply to accommodate changed tastes.

for their higher than optimal incomes. The increased material needs, in turn, cause the "overwork" to become necessary if changing tastes are to be adequately satisfied. Figure 8.2 summarizes this next stage in the Schor model. By placing a constraint on the worker that forces her to the right of her labor supply curve, the employer inadvertently causes the curve itself to shift rightward until it comes to include the "dictated" point.

The worker thus adapting to a necessary decrease in leisure thus bears a resemblance to the wolf adapting to the unattainability of grapes.[12] Schor's focus reflects a clear interest in labor markets in which employers are few enough to exercise market control, and thus it is not surprising that she chooses to attribute the rise in the work week to decisions imposed by these employers. Indeed, her ability to link increased work and spending with a net social welfare loss – the losses suffered by some exceeding the gains realized by others – might seem to require that an exogenous, imposed event be identified. While normative evaluations require straying outside the bounds of standard normative analysis, they nonetheless still seem possible.

To illustrate, consider the plight of the "Uncle Tom" type of slave. The reality of being held as someone's slave likely resulted in some actually preferring enslavement over freedom. But clearly, though formal welfare theory would be unable to assess whether one undergoing such a change in his preferences is becoming better or worse off, at a less formal level there would be a general consensus that becoming a slave leaves one worse off. While having one's labor–leisure choice set restricted is less dramatic and more morally complex than "being enslaved," learning to prefer the dictated hours of work because of the consumption it makes possible does not alter the intuition that, all things considered, the agent has been made worse off.

What if, however, the shift in one's labor supply curve is the *cause* of one's working more rather than a reaction to *having* to work more? Almost a decade before Schor's book came out, Brack and Cowling (1983) suggested that the former of these causal changes was the correct one. For them, the cycle was not "work and spend" but rather "spend and work." By this alternative version of events (well summarized, with the appropriate rewording, by the already considered Figure 8.2), workers did not experience increased preferences for marketed goods because of the greater income that came with working longer hours. Instead, they found it necessary to work longer hours as more extensive and more effective marketing efforts raised the amount of marketed products that were desired. For the ambitious young salaried professional, the Brack and Cowling account seems the more insightful. As Eastman (1998) reports, management students believe that working long hours is a prerequisite for promotion. For a respondent believing that the failure to work the long hours would result in their firing, there would be little difference in the subjective experience of what they faced and what a wage worker *required* to work longer hours faced. For the respondent believing that the choice of fewer hours would result in fewer promotions, not firing, the situation is indeed different. A voluntary choice of longer hours would signify a desire for future income and status. The desire for future spending (and status) would have preceded the decision to work more.

The difference between this "spend-and-work" version of events and the "work-and-spend" version might on the surface appear trivial, since each claims that increases in work time and increases in the desires for purchasable goods have occurred since the 1960s.[13] It is more difficult, however, to reach any welfare conclusions on the basis of the "spend-and-work" version, since no shrinkage of the agent's choice set would have occurred. According to "work-and-spend," previously available options have been taken away which in turn has changed preferences. For "spend-and-work," in contrast, all that has happened is that acts of persuasion have occurred. And as Galbraith (1958) long ago discovered, it is hard to convince the public and harder still to convince economists that there is anything to be said against mere "acts of persuasion."[14] Wayne Twitchell well captures the prevailing attitude with his comment that "the idea that consumerism creates artificial desires rests on a wistful ignorance of history and human nature, on the hazy, romantic feeling that there existed some halcyon era of noble savages with purely natural needs" (1999: 283).

Marketing and advertising have clearly been on the rise over this century and, if at all effective, would lend support to the "spend-and-work" version over its competitor. Brack and Cowling report a doubling of real advertising expenditures per capita from 1920 to 1976 (1983: 289). Taken by itself this is not particularly striking, especially when it is considered that real economic output per capita grew equivalently. As they point out, however, advertising was becoming less informative and more persuasive, and enormous economies of scale accompanied the advance of radio and television which resulted in the same real monetary outlay buying much more exposure than in the pre-electronic age (1983: 294). Regardless of whether these trends have continued since the 1970s, there has been a more recent development that should not be overlooked. Professional services that previously shunned advertising (education, law, and medicine, most notably) have chosen to market themselves in ways that were not even imagined just twenty years ago.

But before the increase in marketing and advertising can be taken to support the thesis that decisions to spend more preceded decisions to work more, another question needs to be considered. Does advertising raise *total* real expenditures or just the distribution of expenditures? At one extreme is the position that advertising tends to be self-canceling, a "prisoner's dilemma" that firms experience, each finding it rational to advertise, but none increasing market share by doing so since all are doing likewise. Standing at the opposite extreme is the view that relative share is radically altered by advertising, leading to either more or less concentration in the typical industry.[15]

Robert Solow (1968) expresses the conventional view that advertising can be said to have an effect only if it alters the relative mix of goods that consumers select.[16] Such a view overlooks one critical point. Regardless of whether the relative share of the pie enjoyed by firms is constant or changing, the size of the overall pie is in all likelihood growing. As Offe and Heinze (1996) argue, with advertising's advance has come an increase in the *overall* demand for commodities. Since "household production" and "leisure" are not purchased commodities there has been no equivalent rise in the persuasive forces trying to convince agents to use their time in these other ways.[17] This asymmetry of persuasive forces would thus be expected to have led, *ceteris paribus*, to a rise in labor supply and a corresponding drop in the demand for other uses of one's time.[18]

Summarizing where matters stand, two explanations of the trend toward longer work weeks have been contrasted. The "work-and-spend" version treats the rising power of firms qua employers as the precipitating event, while the "spend-and-work" version treats the rising persuasive influence of firms qua marketers of products as the precipitating event. Against either of these critical analyses stands a "minimalist" neoclassical economics position which attributes the observed changes in work time to nothing more than movement along stable labor supply curves, albeit supply curves that may have counterintuitive positive slopes. At this stage, the "spend-and-work" interpretation has something in common with and something at odds with each of the competing interpretations. Like "work-and-spend" (and unlike the minimalist) it assumes that there have been significant labor supply shifts. But *like* the minimalist (and *unlike* "work-and-spend") it is unable to attach much normative significance to the events that it portrays. This is because while "work-and-spend" treats the increase in labor supply as a reaction to a clear welfare reducing event (a requirement that workers work more than they would wish), in the "spend-and-work" version the increase in labor supply is nothing more than a by-product of a rise in the marketing efforts of business. In the section that follows, metapreferences will be called upon to perform the normative function of assessing this version of events.

A NORMATIVE ASSESSMENT OF INCREASED WORK TIME

If a person has been persuaded to desire more products and has freely chosen to work longer hours to make fulfillment of these desires possible, how can such a person be described as "overworked"? One strategy has been to reconceptualize the person as in fact consisting of two (or even more) selves and to speak of one of these selves as being in conflict with the other(s).[19] Such an approach falls short in reaching normative conclusions. It would not be possible to speak of a person who has freely chosen, say, a 60 hour work week as one who is "overworked," but would instead be necessary to speak of "part" of the person as overworked and another part as facing "underwork" if a lessened work week were to prevail.[20]

This normative stalemate can be overcome by instead modeling the conflicted agent as one experiencing a discord between the action that she prefers (and thus does) and the action that she would prefer to prefer. According to the philosopher Harry Frankfurt (1971), the capacity of humans to have preferences about their preferences is what most sets them apart from animals. As I have argued previously (George 1984, 1993, 1998), if preferences are subject to change but preferences for preferences – "metapreferences" – are stable, market forces are ill equipped to create the optimal preferences that agents would prefer having.[21] This conclusion follows from a straightforward application of the externalities argument. When a seller causes an agent to have a preference change for the worse (as judged by the agent) the seller is not liable for the act and thus is not required to bear the cost that his action has imposed on another. As a result of this, the seller, if a profit-maximizer, would overindulge in such preference-worsening actions. Conversely, when a seller causes an agent to have a preference change for the better, the seller receives no payment for this favorable "re-shaping" and thus would underindulge in such actions as judged from an efficiency standpoint.

This is not to say that actions of sellers fully determine what preference will prevail. All that is being claimed is that a seller's actions may result in a preference for the seller's product taking hold and not being fought by the agent. Such passivity on the agent's part needs no explanation if the preference is one she wishes to have. But even if unpreferred it would often be what the agent finds worth "living with," given the costs that would be necessary to alter the preference.

This particular type of externality differs from most in not involving any third party. To see this, consider a more typical sort of externality, such as air pollution that follows from the production of certain products. The first-party (producer) sells to the second-party (consumer) while third-parties (everyone else) suffer dirtier air as a result. Now while the consumer also suffers from the pollution, this does not influence her decision to purchase the product since she must bear this cost regardless of whether or not she buys. In the case of the present unusual kind of externality, the creation of a worse preference, there really are no third-parties in the picture. The second-party (the consumer) experiences a change in her preference, a change which she must bear irrespective of whether or not she buys the seller's product. Given the change in tastes created by the seller, it is suddenly in the consumer's interest to buy the product.[22]

While I have chosen to make the above point in terms of preference change for the worse, it is just as applicable to the reverse case, where there is an improvement in preferences, as judged by the agent experiencing the change. And this draws attention to a critical point, stated above but worth restating. From the argument that there is inefficiency in the production of preferences, it does not follow that the tendency for agents to be experiencing preference change toward more hours of work and fewer hours devoted to other activities is necessarily a change for the worse. It is entirely possible that agents are, on average, happy with this shift. If so, the market's failing would be in not taking the process far enough. Sellers would be engaging *insufficiently* in the process of changing agents' preferences in this direction since they (the sellers) receive no compensation for the act of favorable preference change.

It is thus a purely empirical question: are there more agents who are dissatisfied with their preferences for time allocation who would like to have a preference to give more time to work? Or, are there more dissatisfied agents who would prefer to prefer less work time? The relatively recent introduction of the term "workaholic" does suggest that there is a significant number of workers who would prefer having the preference to work less. If "workaholism" is meant to have attributes in common with the word from which it appears to derive, "alcoholism," it becomes apparent that for those afflicted, the Schor interpretation is inadequate. Certainly one who is *forced* to drink heavily is not an alcoholic. Rather, an alcoholic is better understood as one who is acting on a preference that she would rather not have. Such an agent has a preference to drink heavily but a metapreference to not do so.

Figure 8.3 presents the same labor supply shift as appeared in Figure 8.2. Since the concern now is not in comparing two labor supply decisions over time but in comparing two potential decisions at a single time, only a single wage is now shown. Let L stand for "less" and M for "more," with the former representing the time that the agent would have allocated to work if her pre-advertising labor supply preference continued to prevail, and the latter representing the time in paid employment given her post-advertising labor-supply preference.

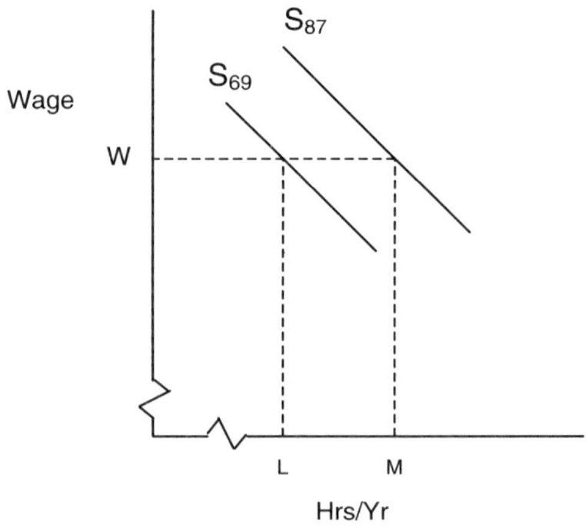

Figure 8.3 Change in work time caused by change in taste.

The shift in the labor supply curve indicates that the agent's preference has changed from (L pref M) to (M pref L). For her to describe herself as a workaholic would suggest that she has a preference she does not prefer (but which, given that she has it, she rationally acts on). In other words, the agent's discontent could reveal her metapreference to be:

(L pref M) pref (M pref L)

Although she would prefer to have a preference to work less (and to act on that preference) she has instead a preference to work more.

The overworked American of this variety becomes a more complex figure than that offered to us by Schor. She is not the victim of employer hegemony, ordered to work more than she wishes or not work at all. Rather, she is one who works as much as she prefers, but is in the grip of preferences that she wishes were otherwise.

CONCLUDING REMARKS

The substitution of marketed products for home-produced goods has been going on for more than a century. Since the process predates the rise of sophisticated marketing, it is easy to overlook the extent to which such marketing has hastened the process in more recent years. The replacement of *leisure* by work time is of more recent vintage. But with expenditures on advertising and marketing far outstripping growth in GDP, an increased desire to earn the income that permits greater satisfaction of material desires should come as no great surprise. I have not intended to deny that some insights might be offered from the most recent and best known explanation for rising work time, that offered by Schor that focuses on the rising power of employers.

It has been my claim, however, that too little attention has been given the explanation that locates the major cause for greater work in the rise in advertising and marketing. To describe the current state as one of "overwork" is clear-cut if workers would prefer to work less but are not given that option (the Schor version) but becomes problematic when simple taste shifts best explain the trend. As developed in the chapter's final section, to the extent that market forces create unpreferred preferences to work more, a clear-cut market failure has occurred.

In attempting to offer some policy suggestions, it becomes necessary to contrast the very *general* rise in consumption that has been my main focus with the rise in *competitive* consumption that has been the concern of Hirsch (1976), and Frank (1999), and has formed a part of Schor's extended model (1998). The conditions that exacerbate competitive consumption are complex. While the way in which sellers appeal to potential buyers undoubtedly contributes to zero-sum "show-off" consumption, it is consumers heaping negative externalities on each other that is the heart of the problem. Collective action might take the form, as Frank (1999) suggests, of taxing these goods at a more than average rate.

Matters are more complex for the more general sort of "overconsumption" that I have attempted to highlight. The profligate consumer who must work long hours to meet his/her escalating needs is not necessarily like the one who is engaging in too much competitive consumption. Indeed, casual empiricism suggests that much of the unpreferred consumption of the workaholic is not at all a means of "showing off." The sorts of items for which the modern consumer tends to have preferences that he dislikes are not generally items that increase status. Working to finance a smoking habit, a junk-food habit, a gambling habit, or a restaurant habit, is not working to finance consumption that gains one status. It is, rather, working to satisfy preferences that, all things considered, the agent would rather not have and as often as not wishes to keep others unaware about.

The "downshifters" described by Schor (1998: ch. 5) attempt to voluntarily spend less and thus work less. However, it is the invidious consumption problem that they are seeking to overcome, and they hope to be able to do this by creating groups of like-minded people. In contrast to this, efforts to overcome unpreferred preferences seem less capable of voluntaristic solution. Following Frank, taxation policy holds some promise, but it would likely be more difficult to agree about which goods deserve to be taxed (and which, possibly, subsidized). Collective action to raise leave-time to limit the work week, while a device for stemming competitive consumption, would not appear to work as well for the problem I have isolated. If the marketing juggernaut has indeed created preferences for high consumption, then long work hours can indeed be a wise strategy.

A step that must precede public action is a growth in public understanding that unbridled persuasion can be harmful. The hold of the classical liberal view of human freedom is strong and by all indications growing. To restrict persuasion violates a core principle of a sizeable chunk of the population. There are exceptions, to be sure. Pressure on television producers to mold healthy preferences in children is continually growing. So too is pressure on tobacco companies to abstain from creating tastes for cigarettes. But widely accepted restraints on persuasion nearly always involve products directed at children or products for which there is physiological evidence of addiction. It becomes much harder to make a case for limiting the creation of tastes for less physically threatening products and activities that are nonetheless items their owners would have preferred not to prefer. A first step in correcting for market inefficiency in the shaping of tastes must thus be the project of convincing contemporary society that the evaluation of tastes is a coherent and legitimate exercise. Only then will the spreading legitimization of market forces be slowed and will concrete steps emerge for the efficient channeling of the forces of preference creation. And only then will private desires to work long hours be lessened.

NOTES

1 For attempts to make sense of the simultaneous existence of overemployment and underemployment, see Bluestone and Rose (1998; and chapter 2 in this volume) and Jacobs and Gerson (1998; and chapter 6 this volume).
2 And as Golden (1999: 8) emphasizes, to divide non-waged time between "household production" and "leisure" still fails to take into account the many ways, some more pleasant than others, in which this "leisure" time way be used.
3 No attempt will be made here to assess the accuracy of the work time estimates, but it is worth considering briefly Haight's (1997) insight of how biases could operate in an upward or downward direction, depending on the sort of work one does. The heroic hunter had an incentive to underestimate the time required to capture his prey and might gain status by boasting how little time was required. The modern bureaucrat (to take one example) has no similar trophy to testify to her accomplishments and thus has an incentive to indicate that her amorphous accomplishments took more time than they actually did. Haight well captures these biases within a single agent when he notes that "A professor might not mention the time spent on a single-authored publication, while simultaneously exaggerating the time spent on a committee" (1997: 35).
4 For a survey of attitudes toward increased leisure and predictions of its social effects, see Cross (1993).
5 For that part of the population experiencing a drop in real hourly compensation, the decision to work more would be consistent with a backward bending curve. As noted above, however, my focus will not be on this part of the population.
6 A decade prior to this Rothschild (1982) similarly argued that preferences could shift toward commodities and away from leisure when the work week was longer than workers preferred. He differed from Schor in not attributing the longer than optimal work week to the power of employers but rather to a failure of hours to adjust downward because of "requirements of factory discipline and short-term rigidities in working-time arrangements" (1982: 214).

7 For increases in consumption that are invidious, this conclusion would not hold. An invidious "spend-and-work" interpretation carries with it the implication that agents might benefit from collective action aimed at discouraging the demand for "positional" goods. My focus will be on increases in goods which an agent wishes to own and consume independently of whether others are aware of his ownership and consumption. See Hirsch (1976), Schor (1998), and Frank (1999) for more on the problem of "invidious" consumption. Still other causes might contribute to an increase in labor supply include: (1) the decline in physically demanding work that may have raised the optimal work hours for the average worker, as suggested by Gramm (1987) and, (2) the drop in the price of goods relative to time-intensive leisure activities. Regarding the third, Axe and Golden (1991: 315) attribute the high price of leisure in Japan as a contributing factor to that nation's high average workweek.

8 In the long run, such a strategic reaction to overwork would have no aggregate effects on savings. The greater savings of overworked workers would be precisely matched by the greater negative savings of the retired. In the short run, however (which we are still in if Schor's argument that overwork is a relatively recent phenomenon is correct), there would be a rise in savings. The currently working (i.e., the newly "overworked"') would be saving more while the currently retired would not have experienced overwork and would not be dissaving more in their retirement years.

9 Bluestone and Rose (1998: 439) suggest that moonlighting is often undertaken as a form of insurance against the effects of future layoffs. By the Schor model presented to this point, forced overtime work would be expected to cause increased rates of savings so as to allow voluntary early retirement. If Bluestone and Rose are correct, the words "forced" and "voluntary" would have to be reversed ("'voluntary overtime work would be expected to cause increased rates of savings so as to prepare for forced early retirement").

10 Perhaps more revealing would be data on trends in overemployment and underemployment. Kahn and Lang found no upward trend in those reporting that they were overworked but their data, unfortunately, end in the mid-1980s.

11 For a strong development of this sort of position, see Stanley Lebergott (1993). Lebergott dismisses pessimistic versions of drifts toward materialism, and interprets this century's changes in what is consumed, what is produced for oneself, and how much leisure is enjoyed as nothing more than rational reactions to price changes.

12 An exactly opposite reaction is also a possibility. Forcing one having a "grass is always greener" disposition to work 50 hours when 40 is preferred would strengthen rather than weaken the desire to work 40 hours. For more on this, see Elster (1983).

13 For an interpretation of the increase in work hours that occurred in the 18th century, see Wisman (1989). After noting that "History provides an almost infinite variety of techniques which brute force has called upon to straighten out the backward-bending supply curve of labor" (1989: 99), Wisman proceeds to describe these efforts as primarily the doings of government in the service of the capitalists. Like Schor, he saw workers as eventually internalizing the directive to work more, but not because of an increased appetite for goods, but rather because of the rise of Protestantism and the associated work ethic (1989: 102–103).

14 While it is difficult to find development of Galbraithian notions of consumer manipulation among economists, similar work is still possible to find in other spheres. See, for example Leach (1993) and Shorris (1994) for particularly polemical looks at the spread of consumer culture.

15 Schudson (1984) offers a different position. According to him, advertising has no effect on sales and is sustained primarily as a means for a firm to signal to other firms that it has "arrived."

16 See Schweickart (1996: 112–118) for a good critique of Solow's claims about advertising.

17 There is the separate issue of how the use of one's time away from the workplace might be used. Game and Pringle (1983: 120) argue that the market changes the nature of household production as well, with shopping, in particular, claiming an increasing chunk of time (cited in O'Hara (1995: 99)).

18 The process being described need not be limited to instances in which a purchased item (e.g., professional entertainment) fully replaces its self-produced equivalent (e.g., friends entertaining each other). It is also possible for sales efforts to lead buyers to increase their demand for add-ons that raise the price but ask less in the way of effort. As I have sought to show elsewhere (George 1997: 48–56), colleges, to the extent that they perceive of their students as customers, face temptations to get students to substitute higher tuition payments that purchase painless learning for lower tuition payments that require some "learning for self" (e.g., study time).

19 See, for example, Schelling (1996), and Laibson (1997).

20 Laibson (1997: 465–468) constructs a model in which one of the "multiple-selves" might actually take action that leaves all of the selves better off, but the conclusion holds only if certain stringent conditions are met.

21 For other work on metapreferences, see Jeffrey (1974), Sen (1974, 1977), Majumdar (1980), van der Veen (1981), McPherson (1982), Hirschman (1985), and Lutz (1993). None of these authors makes any assumptions about the stability of metapreferences vis-à-vis preferences. As a consequence, none is able to draw the normative conclusions mentioned here. Interestingly, Aaron interprets Becker (1992) to have claimed that "while preferences may be altered and formed, 'meta preferences' are stable" (Aaron 1994: 6).

22 Not all "regret" over one's preference can be attributed to discord between the regular preference and metapreference. For more on this, see George (1993: 325).

REFERENCES

Aaron, H. A. (1994) "Distinguished Lecture on Economics in Government: Public Policy, Values and Consciousness," *Journal of Economic Perspectives* 8: 3–21.

Axe, B. A. and Golden, L. (1991) "The Augmented Labor Supply Function: Worktime Evidence from Japan," *Eastern Economics Journal* 17: 305–317.

Becker, G. S. (1992) "Habits, Addictions, and Traditions," *Kyklos* 45: 327–346.

Bell, L. A. (1998) "Differences in Work Hours and Hours Preferences by Race in the U.S.," *Review of Social Economy* 56(4): 481–500.

Bluestone, B. and Rose, S. (1998) "The Macroeconomics of Work Time," *Review of Social Economy* 56(4): 425–441.

Brack, J. and Cowling, K. (1983) "Advertising and Labour Supply: Workweek and Workyear in U.S. Manufacturing Industries, 1919–76," *Kyklos* 36: 285–303.

Cross, G. (1993) *Time and Money: the Making of Consumer Culture*, New York: Routledge.

Eastman, W. (1998) "Working for Position: Women, Men and Managerial Work Hours," *Industrial Relations* 37(1): 51–66.

Elster, J. (1983) *Sour Grapes: Studies in the Subversion of Rationality*, Cambridge: Cambridge University Press.

Frank, R. H. (1999) *Luxury Rever: Why Money Fails to Satisfy in an Era of Excess*, New York: The Free Press.

Frankfurt, H. G. (1971) "Freedom of the Will and the Concept of a Person," *The Journal of Philosophy* 68: 5–20.

Galbraith, J. K. (1958) *The Affluent Society*, New York: New American Library.

Game, A. and Pringle, R. (1983) *Gender at Work*, Sydney: Allen & Unwin.

George, D. (1984) "Metapreferences: Reconsidering Contemporary Notions of Free Choice," *International Journal of Social Economics* 11(3/4): 92–107.

_____ (1993) "Does the Market Create Preferred Preferences?" *Review of Social Economy* 51: 323–346.

_____ (1997) "Working Longer Hours: Pressure from the Boss or Pressure from the Marketers?" *Review of Social Economy* 55(1): 33–65.

_____ (1998) "Coping Rationally with Unpreferred Preferences," *Eastern Economic Journal* 24(2): 181–194.

Golden, L. (1999) "Integrating Social Economics into Analysis of the Labor Market Causes and Consequences of Work and Leisure as an Application," in E. O'Boyle (ed.), *Teaching the Social Economics Way of Thinking*, Edward Mellen Press, 423–454.

Gramm, W. (1987) "Labor, Work and Leisure," *Journal of Economic Issues* 21(1): 167–188.

Haight, A. D. (1997) "Padded Prowess: A Veblenian Interpretation of the Long Hours of Salaried Workers," *Journal of Economic Issues* 31(1): 29–38.

Hirsch, F. (1976) *Social Limits to Growth*, Cambridge, MA: Harvard University Press.

Hirschman, A. O. (1985) "Against Parsimony: Three Easy Ways of Complicating Some Categories of Economic Discourse," *Economics and Philosophy* 1: 7–21.

Jacobs, J. A. and Gerson, K. (1998) "Who are the Overworked Americans?" *Review of Social Economy* 56(4): 442–459.

Jeffrey, R. C. (1974) "Preferences among Preferences," *Journal of Philosophy* 71: 377–391.

Kahn, S. and Lang, L. (1991) "The Effect of Hours Constraints on Labor Supply Estimates," *Review of Economics and Statistics* 73: 605–611.

Laibson, D. (1997) "Golden Eggs and Hyperbolic Discounting," *The Quarterly Journal of Economics* 112(2): 443–477.

Leach, W. (1993) *Land of Desire: Merchants, Power, and the Rise of a New American Culture*, New York: Vintage Books.

Lebergott, S. (1993) *Pursuing Happiness: American Consumers in the Twentieth Century*, Princeton, NJ: Princeton University Press.

Lutz, M. A. (1993) "The Utility of Multiple Utility: A Comment on Brennan," *Economics and Philosophy* 9: 145–154.

Majumdar, T. (1980) "The Rationality of Changing Choice," *Analyse and Kritik* 2: 172–178.

McPherson, M. S. (1982) "Mill's Moral Theory and the Problem of Preference Change," *Ethics* 92: 252–273.

Offe, C. and Heinze, R. G. (1996) "Beyond the Labor Market: Reflections on a New Definition of 'Domestic' Welfare Production," in C. Offe (ed.), *Modernity and the State*, Cambridge, MA: MIT Press: 121–146.

O' Hara, P. O. (1995) "Household Labor, the Family, and Macroeconomic Instability in the United States: 1940s–1990s," *Review of Social Economy* 53(1): 89–120.

Rosser, J. B. and Rosser, M. V. (1996) *Comparative Economics in a Transforming World Economy*, Chicago: Richard D. Irwin.

Rothschild, K. W. (1982) "A Note on Some Economic and Welfare Aspects of Working-Time Regulation," *Australian Economic Papers* 21: 214–218.

Schelling, T. (1996) "Coping Rationally with Lapses from Rationality," *Eastern Economic Journal* 24(2): 252–269.

Schor, J.B. (1991) *The Overworked American: The Unexpected Decline of Leisure*, New York: Basic Books.

_____ (1998) *The Overspent American: Upscaling, Downshifting, and the New Consumer*, New York: Basic Books.

Schudson, M. (1984) *Advertising, the Uneasy Persuasion: Its Dubious Impact on American Society*, New York: Basic Books.

Schweickart, D. (1996) *Against Capitalism*, Boulder, CO: Westview Press.

Sen, A. K. (1974) "Choice, Orderings and Morality," in S. Korner (ed.) *Practical Reason*, New Haven, CT: Yale University Press: 54–67.

_____ (1977) "Rational Fools: A Critique of the Behavioural Foundations of Economic Theory," *Philosophy and Public Affairs* 6: 317–344.

Shorris, E. (1994) *A Nation of Salesmen: The Tyranny of the Market and the Subversion of Culture*, New York: W. W. Norton.

Twitchell, J. B. (1999) *Lead Us Into Temptation: The Triumph of American Materialism*, New York: Columbia University Press.

US Bureau of the Census (1993) *Statistical Abstract, 1993*. Washington, DC, Bureau.

Van der Veen, R. J. (1981) "Meta-Rankings and Collective Optimality," *Social Science Information* 20: 345–373.

Wisman, J. D. (1989) "Straightening Out the Backward-Bending Supply Curve of Labour: From Overt to Covert Compulsion and Beyond," *Review of Political Economy* 1: 94–112.

9 Natural, social, and political limits to work time

The contemporary relevance of Marx's analysis

Paul Burkett

More than 130 years after Karl Marx chronicled the British struggle over the working day, prolonged work times are still impeding the human development of workers and communities, even in the advanced capitalist countries (see other chapters in this volume). From a Marxist perspective, the work time issue sheds important light on the limits of capitalism. Marx argued that capitalist development is based on the exploitation of workers, i.e., their performance of surplus labor (labor over and above that required to maintain the producers at their current level of subsistence) under conditions of competitive commodity production for profit (capital). However, Marx recognizes that there are definite limits to capital's exploitation of human labor power.[1] Like the limits to capital's use of natural conditions as conditions of monetary accumulation, the limits to capital's exploitation of labor power are not fully determined by capital itself. In both cases the limits involve certain material characteristics not subject to alteration by the specific social form of production. The limits to capital's exploitation of labor and nature are, however, elastic limits, this elasticity being due partly to the natural characteristics of labor power and extra-human nature, and partly to the social definition of the limits themselves. According to Marx, capital has a built-in tendency to take undue advantage of this elasticity, as the pressures of competitive monetary accumulation stretch human and extra-human natural forces to the breaking point – necessitating social restraints on capital's exploitation of the two basic sources of wealth (Burkett 1999: ch. 10).

The present chapter considers this problem from the standpoint of work time and its natural, social, and political limits. Marx's analyses of work time, child labor, and the struggle over the working day are shown to contain important insights for those interested in developing an explicit worker–community perspective on work time issues. By "worker–community perspective," I mean one that promotes the further development and empowerment of human beings capable of managing their highly socialized system of production so as to make it more healthy and sustainable in human, social, and environmental terms. Such a perspective is not simply "laborist" in the traditional sense but also emphasizes the cooperative-democratic management of economic and political life by the community as a whole (socialism) on local, regional, national and ultimately global levels (Burkett 1999: chs. 13, 14). Marx's analysis of work time can help us understand the barriers capitalism poses to the development of a worker-community centered economic system, and the corresponding connections between work time initiatives and other popular struggles.

Marx's perspective also offers a path beyond a troublesome dichotomy in the contemporary literature on work time. On one side, neoclassical analyses basically treat changes in work times as natural outcomes of labor market forces – specifically workers' preferences for wage income versus leisure (labor supply) and the technological, managerial, and competitive constraints faced by firms (labor demand). This approach tends to yield the conclusion that the work time outcomes generated by private market forces are efficient, and that any efforts at altering these outcomes through government policy will be both difficult and costly (see, for example, Fitzgerald 1996; Roche, Fynes, and Morrissey 1996).[2] On the other side, advocates of reduced work time have disputed the simple equation of market outcomes with efficiency and competitiveness. Part of their response has been to treat long and/or inflexible work times as a kind of market failure whose correction through enlightened government regulations and tax/subsidy schemes could actually enhance the productivity and competitiveness of firms and entire national economies (see, for example, Schor 1991: 153–155; Boden 1999: 71, 82).

As sensible and practical as this response may seem, however, it shares one shortcoming with the neoclassical approach: it tends to draw attention away from the class-based dynamics that underpin work time changes and struggles in both private-market and government-policy arenas. Both approaches have the effect of focusing work time debates on the relative merits of free market forces versus enlightened (or unenlightened) policy-making, which tends to submerge the central roles of class exploitation, class struggle, and autonomous worker–community movements in the whole work time dynamic. Marx's analysis, with its emphasis on capitalism's built-in tendency to extend work time in the absence of a direct confrontation with the power of capital by workers and communities, can help restore these crucial class elements in what threatens to become just another technocratic policy debate among economists.

The next section sketches Marx's treatment of human labor and labor power as natural and social forces. This sets the stage for Marx's basic analysis of capital's tendency to overstretch the natural and social limits to work time. Marx's discussion of child labor is then reconsidered from the standpoint of capital's exploitation of the specific natural and social characteristics of young labor power. The chapter then outlines Marx's argument that the capitalistic extension of adult and child work time poses a threat to labor power as a "common pool" element of society's natural wealth. In Marx's view, this threat can be alleviated only through "general political action" to protect society's life-forces – an action in which the working class and socialist visions play central roles. This demonstrates the relevance of Marx's approach for contemporary work time struggles.

LABOR AND LABOR POWER AS NATURAL AND SOCIAL FORCES

Marx emphasizes that production is both a material and a social process. Accordingly, he often characterizes both labor and labor power as natural and social forces (1967: v. III, 813; v. I, 239). While insisting that human laboring capacities are socially developed, organized, and utilized, Marx still emphasizes that "labour ... is only the manifestation of a natural force, human labour power" (1966: 3).

Labor power is a natural force insofar as it is subject to the physical and biological laws governing all of nature. For example, it "exists only as ... a definite quantity of human muscle, nerve, brain etc," and as such it is subject to "wear and tear and death" and must therefore "perpetuate [itself] by procreation" (Marx 1967: v. I, 171–172). Hence, in order "to maintain and reproduce itself, to perpetuate its physical existence, the working class must receive the necessaries absolutely indispensable for living and multiplying" (1976: 57). These "natural wants, such as food, clothing, fuel, and housing, vary according to ... climatic and other physical conditions" (1967: v. I, 171). In addition, the worker's "means of subsistence must ... be sufficient to maintain him in his normal state as a laboring individual" (1967: v. I, 171). Clearly "free time to dispose of" is a natural means of subsistence of this sort, since a laborer "whose whole lifetime, apart from the mere physical interruptions by sleep, meals, and so forth, is absorbed by his labor ... is less than a beast of burden" (1976: 54).

Labor and labor power are social forces insofar as: (1) labor contributes to the material reproduction of human beings in and through society; (2) the reproduction and evolution of labor power is itself a social process. As per the first aspect, Marx analyzes each form of production in terms of the specific social relations through which a "natural law" of human production is fulfilled: namely, the necessity of a "distribution of social labour in definite proportions," enmeshed with natural conditions, so as to ensure a "volume of products corresponding to the different [individual and collective] needs" (Marx to Kugelmann, 11 July 1868, in Marx and Engels (1975: 196)). Given this requirement, the labor of any individual or group is a social force insofar as it *participates in a social division of labor* (Marx 1976: 30). In this very specific sense, labor power is a central part of *society's* life-forces.

At the same time, the social division of labor shapes and channels the development of human laboring capacities. After all, in the process of production "not only do the objective conditions change ... but the producers change, too, in that they bring out new qualities in themselves, ... transform themselves, develop new powers and ideas, new modes of intercourse, new needs and new language" (Marx 1973: 494; 1968: 288). The kinds of needs and capabilities generated in the production process will be conditioned jointly by the social relations among producers (both within and among individual workplaces) and the material characteristics of the production process itself. In this sense, too, labor and labor power are both natural *and* social forces.

Most directly, labor power is a social force insofar as the family within which labor power is reproduced is itself a fundamental social relation (Marx and Engels 1976: 48–49). The place of the family in conditioning the development of society's laboring class is apparent from Marx's analysis of the determination of the value of labor power under capitalism. In *Capital*, Marx suggests that "the number and extent of ... so-called necessary wants, as also the modes of satisfying them, are themselves the product of historical development, and depend therefore to a great extent ... on the conditions under which ... the class of free laborers has been formed" (1967: v. I, 171). Elsewhere Marx reiterates that the "traditional standard of life" of the laborer involves "not mere physical life, but ... certain wants springing from the social conditions in which people are placed and reared up" (1976: 57).[3]

CAPITAL AND THE NATURAL AND SOCIAL LIMITS TO WORK TIME

The importance Marx ascribes to labor power's character as a natural and social force is evident from his analysis of work time. Specifically, Marx suggests that because work time is subject to "physical and social bounds," capital's "tendency ... to obtain the greatest possible quantity of living labour time" is itself "held in check in part by physical conditions, and in part by social obstacles" (1967: v. I, 232; 1988: 180).

In Marx's view, capital has a built-in tendency to dissolve all social obstacles to the extension of work time, including those posed by non-capitalist cultural relations (e.g., the numerous non-work days due to holidays prior to capitalism (Schor 1992: 46–47)), extant gender and family relations limiting the employment of women and children (see next section), and non-capitalist modes of manufacturing labor such as guilds. In the process, capital takes advantage of the downward flexibility of the laborer's needs – a flexibility basic to labor power's character as a socially reproduced force (Marx 1977: 1068).[4] In order to convert more of "the active existence of the human being" into surplus labor, capital exploits the elasticity of the worker's need for "time for satisfying his intellectual and social wants, which are conditioned by the general state of social advancement" (Marx 1991: 493; 1967: v. I, 232). Marx refers to such reduction of free time as a contraction of the worker's "space for development," and argues that it represents an "appropriation of the *life*, the mental and physical life, of the worker" (1991: 493; emphasis in original).[5]

However, Marx's recognition of the social elasticity of the limits to work time is not to be confused with a denial that an absolute natural limit exists. This "ultimate limit is given by the physical force of the labouring man," so that "if the daily exhaustion of his vital forces exceeds a certain degree, it cannot be exerted anew, day by day" (1976: 57). Marx argues that, in the absence of external restraints, the forces of monetary accumulation and competition impel capital "to go beyond the natural limits of labour time" and to "produce thus ... not only the deterioration of human labour-power by robbing it of its normal, moral and physical, conditions of development and function," but also "the premature exhaustion and death of this labour-power itself" (Marx 1991: 493; 1967: v. I, 265).

In Marx's view, moreover, workers are degraded as human beings whenever their work times, wages, and/or work conditions are such as to hamper their biological, intellectual, and social development. Obviously, such a "state of degradation" takes place whenever insufficient free time "reduces the sound sleep needed for the restoration, reparation, refreshment of the bodily powers to just so many hours of torpor as the revival of an organism, absolutely exhausted, renders essential" (Marx 1976: 54; 1967: v. I, 265). In other words, the worker is degraded as a human (natural and social) being insofar as extensive and intensive work time *tends* to reduce her or his existence to that of immediate survival and nothing more – the lowest common denominator of all living organisms. The process of degradation clearly begins *before* the worker's existence deteriorates to this least common denominator in purely biological terms (see Burkett 1999: 53–54). In this sense, Marx's analysis maintains its relevance even for situations such as the contemporary United States economy, where many workers find themselves trapped in an increasingly intensive struggle for "middle class" survival even though their immediate physical subsistence is not (in most but by no means all cases) directly threatened.

Also of contemporary importance is Marx's treatment of how capitalism alters the social definitions of day and night so as to further stretch the natural limits to work time. For Marx, nightwork itself, regardless of the total length of daily work time, entails an unnatural "signification of 'day' and 'night' " which exploits the flexibility of the worker's need for a healthy metabolism with nature (1988: 223). Insofar as work is best undertaken in the daytime, "the *day* itself can be characterized as the natural measure of labor's duration" (1988: 181, emphasis in original). With capitalism, however, "the mere circumstance that fixed capital – factory buildings, machinery, etc. – lies idle during pauses in the labour-process," becomes a motive "for an unnatural prolongation of the labour-process and for day-and-night work" (1967: v. II, 238). Thus, under the sway of capital accumulation and competition, "all bounds of ... day and night were broken down," and even "the ideas of day and night" became "confused" so far as work time was concerned (1967: v. I, 278). In our current era of 24-hour retailing (itself necessitated largely by the long daylight work hours of many workers), Marx's analysis is increasingly relevant for non-manufacturing laborers.

NATURAL AND SOCIAL ASPECTS OF CHILD LABOR

In Marx's analysis, the abuse of labor power's natural and social elasticity is an integral aspect of capital's employment of children. To Marx, the degradation of human beings was evident not only from "the physical deterioration" of the children employed by capital, but also from the "moral degradation caused by [this] capitalistic exploitation" (1967: v. I, 397, 399). Marx describes "the intellectual desolation" of child laborers as "a state of mind clearly distinguishable from that natural ignorance which keeps the mind fallow without destroying its capacity for development, its natural fertility" (1967: v. I, 399).

Natural and social degradation are thus inseparable aspects of capitalist child labor in Marx's view. The employment of children involves capital taking advantage of labor power's "natural diversity" in order to lower its wage bill and obtain more pliant labor forces (1967: v. I, 519). But capital's exploitation of children also means that the dominant social conceptions of what comprises an able-bodied worker, and even of childhood and adulthood as such, have to be modified. Hence "according to capitalistic anthropology, the age of childhood ended at 10, or at the outside, at 11" (1967: v. I, 280). At the same time, Marx points out how child labor implicates particular material and social processes *within* the capitalist economic framework.

Marx notes, for example, how the employment of children was encouraged by capital's mechanization of production, since "in so far as machinery dispenses with muscular power, it becomes a means of employing labourers of slight muscular strength, and those whose bodily development is incomplete, but whose limbs are all the more supple" (1967: v. I, 394). Such "mechanical workshops" further promoted child labor via a relative reduction in the demand for "skilled labour, the learning of which can only be begun at a more mature age, and then can only be brought to the required level of virtuosity through long years of apprenticeship" (1991: 493). Marx argues that the worker's physical and mental development is lowered to a sub-natural path when capital "takes control of [the] mind and body when it is still in an *immature* state," the problem being that such "machine labour does away with the all-round exertion of the muscles," and "offers no opportunity for physical activity; nor does it allow any mental activity" (1991: 494; emphasis in original). Marx's basic reasoning here applies just as well to the weaning of children on video games and computer terminals, in preparation for their future life as exploited laborers.

Marx also observes that when child labor is generalized to a certain extent, it automatically becomes a normal, involuntary means of supporting the family. When children "emerged as competitors of the other workers," parents were, in effect, forced into "conducting a slave trade," as they "endeavor[ed] to recover by the *sale of children* what the adult worker loses through the competition of child labor" (1991: 492; emphasis in original). In other words, capital takes advantage of the lower physical subsistence requirements of individual children (and of discrimination against women and children) to gain "economies of scope" from employment of multiple family members when the value of labor power is determined on a family rather than an individual basis. As Marx phrases it (using the example of a "traditional" family with two children), the employment of children (and of women) "spreads the value of the man's labour power over his whole family" in such a way that capital "raises the degree of exploitation" (1967: v. I, 395). Marx notes further that this extension of the family's wage-labor time entails a replacement of domestic activities with purchases of commodities, so that "the diminished expenditure of labour in the house is accompanied by an increased expenditure of money." In this way, the extent and quality of home life are reduced while "the cost of keeping the family increases, and balances the greater income" (1967: v. I, 395). In short, Marx's analysis of work time and child labor helps us understand the structural roots of the "time squeeze" on working-class households trapped in a treadmill of work and consumption (Schor 1991: Chapter 5).[6]

CAPITAL AND LABOR POWER AS A COMMON POOL RESOURCE

Marx's analysis thus points to a built-in tendency of capitalism to impede the human development of workers by extending the wage-labor time of "every member of the workman's family, without distinction of age or sex" (1967: v. I, 394). In Marx's view, this tendency has a broader social significance stemming from the role of human labor power as a social life-force. From the standpoint of the reproduction and development of society, labor power is a common pool resource – one with definite (albeit elastic) natural limits. Capital vitiates this life-force both materially and socially when it plunders it as a condition of private monetary accumulation.

In treating labor power as a common pool resource, Marx often draws a parallel between capital's extension of work time beyond the limits of human recuperative abilities, and capital's overstretching of the regenerative powers of the land. In explaining legal restraints on work time, for example, Marx suggests that

> the limiting of factory labour was dictated by the same necessity which spread guano over the English fields. The same blind eagerness for plunder that in the one case exhausted the soil, had, in the other, torn up by the roots the living force of the nation. (1967: v. I, 239)

Capital's plunderings of labor power and the land each involve the extraction of short-run gains at the expense of long-run sustainability:

> Anticipation of the future – real anticipation – occurs in the production of wealth in relation to the worker and to the land. The future can indeed be anticipated and ruined in both cases by premature overexertion and exhaustion, and by the disturbance of the balance between expenditure and income. In capitalist production this happens to both the worker and the land. ... What is shortened here exists as power and the life span of this power is shortened as a result of accelerated expenditure. (Marx 1971: 309–310)

Capital's exploitation of labor power and the land thus entails a twofold theft of limited natural forces. Just "as a greedy farmer snatches increased produce from the soil by robbing it of its fertility," so capital "usurps the time for growth, development and healthy maintenance of the body" and "steals the time required for the consumption of fresh air and sunlight" (1967: v. I, 265). Marx's treatment of the over-extension of work time as a robbery of natural forces is reflected in his description of capital as a social-material parasite which, "vampire-like, only lives by sucking labour, and lives the more, the more labour it sucks" (1967: v. I, 233).[7] What is being robbed here is more than the labor power of private individuals: it is "the prime energy" or "the vital power of the people," nothing less than the "reserve fund for the regeneration of the vital force of nations" (1967: v. I, 269; v. III, 813).

In short, what capital plunders is labor power considered, just like the land, as natural wealth of present and future society. From capital's limited perspective on wealth, however, "a succession of unhealthy and short-lived generations will keep the labour market as well supplied as a series of vigorous and long-lived generations" (Marx 1976: 57). Indeed, the availability of labor power despite the unnatural extension of work time is supported by capital's "constant absorption of ... physically uncorrupted elements from the country," i.e. by the "surplus-population" set free by the capitalization of agriculture and the competitive ruin of handicraft industry domestically and globally (1967: v. I, 269, 642). Capitalistic employment of children (see last section) should also be located in this context of capital's striving to "leap over the *natural* limit formed by one individual's living, working day ... by positing *another* working day alongside the *first* at the same time – by the spatial addition *of more simultaneous working days*" (1973: 400; emphases in original).[8] The supply of exploitable labor power is also replenished by capital's tendency, through mechanization and intensification of labor, to "set free, render disposable a definite number of labour capacities," i.e., to "eject them from ... different spheres of production as superfluous labour power" (1994: 186). As Marx indicates, "capitalist production can by no means content itself with the quantity of disposable labour-power which the natural increase of population yields," but rather "requires for its free play an industrial reserve army independent of these natural limits" (1967: v. I, 635).

By increasing the capitalistically employed portion of the global population, and producing redundant laborers through mechanization and rising productivity, capital temporarily evades labor power's natural limits by in effect "increasing the mass of living labour capacities which forms the basis for exploitation by capital; the animate material from which surplus value is extracted" (Marx 1994: 10–11). However, this evasion is obtained only at the cost of a broader and deeper exploitation and despoliation of the natural forces of (employed and unemployed) labor power. From the perspective of individual competing capitalists, the supply of exploitable labor power appears to be unlimited and in any case exogenous with respect to their individual efforts to plunder it. Yet the exploitation of the laboring class by capital as a whole vitiates and threatens the reproduction of this basic human-social life-force. Marx treats this dynamic in terms of a "tragedy of the commons" model developed by analogy with speculative bubbles in the stock exchange:

> What experience shows to the capitalist generally is a constant excess of population, i.e., an excess in relation to the momentary requirements of surplus-labour-absorbing capital, although this excess is made up of generations of human beings stunted, short-lived, swiftly replacing each other, plucked, so to say, before maturity. ... Capital that has such good reasons for denying the sufferings of the legions of workers that surround it, is in practice moved as much and as little by the sight of the coming degradation and final depopulation of the human race, as by the probable fall of the earth into the sun. In every stock-jobbing swindle every one knows that some time or other the crash must come, but every one hopes that it may fall on the head of his neighbor, after he himself has caught the shower of gold and placed it in safety. *Après moi le déluge*! is the watchword of every capitalist and of every capitalist nation. Hence Capital is reckless of the health or length of life of the labourer, unless under compulsion from society. (1967: v. I, 269-270)

In sum, by overstretching the natural and social limits to work time, by producing a permanent reserve army of unemployed, and by broadening its exploitation of labor power spatially, sectorally, and inter-generationally, capital is able to continue accessing exploitable labor power – but only at the expense of a worsening threat to the reproduction of this labor power as a natural and social force. This process can only be halted by a "compulsion from society" – one which rejects capital's treatment of labor power as a mere condition of monetary accumulation.[9]

THE POLITICAL LIMITS TO WORK TIME

This brings us to the political limits to work time in Marx's view, specifically his suggestion that the social protection of labor power from capital's "unnatural extension of the working-day" must "take on the form of a class struggle, and thereby call forth the intervention of the state power" (1967: v. I, 266; 1988: 184). Marx's reasoning is as follows:

> As to the *limitation of the working day*, in England, as in all other countries, it has never been settled except by *legislative interference*. Without the working men's continuous pressure from without that interference would never have taken place. But at all events, the result was not to be attained by private settlement between the working men and the capitalists. This very necessity of *general political action* affords the proof that in its merely economic action capital is the stronger side. (1976: 59; emphases in original)

There are several interrelated arguments in this well packed statement. To begin with, Marx asserts that effective regulation of work time cannot be achieved privately. Here and elsewhere, Marx treats a sustainable working day (one consistent with a day-to-day rejuvenation of the natural and social force of labor power) as a kind of public good. This jibes with Marx's recognition of labor power as a limited common pool resource from the standpoint of society's reproduction and development. Even neoclassical economics recognizes that public goods may be undervalued by unregulated markets, due to the forces of competition and the so-called "free rider" problem. However, Marx's analysis of this public good problem is informed by the class relations of capitalism (Burkett 1986). As such, it recognizes that the degree of undervaluation of labor power's daily reinvigoration (i.e., of the worker's free time) depends on the relative bargaining power of capital and labor as a whole. Here, Marx suggests that without "legislative interference" in response to "general political action" and "continuous pressure" by workers, the overall balance of class forces – as conditioned by capital's control over the means of employment and the reproduction of a reserve army of unemployed ("its merely economic action") – will tend to favor capital over labor, the result being "an unlimited and reckless extension of the working-day" (1967: v. I, 298).

Marx's case for the necessity of *general* working-class pressure and state action to impose safeguards against excessive work time is thus based on the combined importance of the class-biased economic dynamics of capitalism *and* the social character of labor power as natural wealth. This is the holistic reasoning behind Marx's otherwise inexplicable suggestion that "the measureless demands of capital could never be held in check by the isolated efforts of the worker," so that "the determination of what is a working day, presents itself as the result of a struggle, a struggle between collective capital, i.e. the class of capitalists, and collective labour, i.e. the working class" (1988: 184; 1967: v. I, 235).

Up until this point, it has been presumed that capital's interests lie in the prolongation of work time to the greatest possible extent. Yet Marx also recognizes that, from a long-term perspective, there are certain ways in which limitations on work time appear to be rational even for capital. Aside from the long-run threat it poses to capital's required supply of exploitable labor power, unlimited work time may place upward pressure on wage costs by augmenting workers' subsistence consumption requirements. Beyond a certain boundary, the extension of work time

> shortens the length of life of the individual labourer, and therefore the duration of his labour-power, [so that] the forces used up have to be replaced at a more rapid rate and the sum of the expenses for the reproduction of labour-power will be greater; just as in a machine the part of its value to be reproduced every day is greater the more rapidly the machine is worn out. *It would seem therefore that the interest of capital points in the direction of a normal working day.* (1967: v. I, 266; emphasis added)

Moreover, the "external costs" of unregulated work time may afflict capitalists and workers alike. Marx mentions how, "as a result of ... excesses" in work time, "there broke out epidemics whose devastating effects were equally threatening to capitalists and workers," so that "the state ... was compelled to introduce normal days in the factories" (1988: 216). Legal caps on work time may also "free the capitalist from some of the brutality natural to a man who is a mere embodiment of capital, and ... give him time for a little 'culture'" (1967: v. I, 302). The question thus arises as to why Marx places so much stress on *working-class* pressure as a condition for effective regulation of work time. After all, one could agree, based on public good and externality arguments in economics, that "it is only government compulsion that can limit labour time," while disagreeing with the view that "the rebellion of the working class itself" is "the main driving force" in the imposition of such compulsion (Marx 1988: 226; 1991: 386). Indeed, Marx himself notes that British work time legislation was "made by a state ... ruled by capitalist and landlord" (1967: v. I, 239). Why the need for, and what is the significance of, explicit *working-class* pressure?

Marx's answer seems to be twofold. First, this is one case where the individual and collective interests of workers correspond more effectively to the interests of the whole present and future society than do the long-term or the short-term interests of capital. The underlying basis of workers' general political action to limit work time is the close affinity between, on the one hand, workers' interest in their own sustainable and healthy reproduction, and, on the other hand, the historical progress of society in terms of the development and fulfillment of human needs and capabilities. By contrast, even from the long-run perspective, capital as such (money seeking more money) requires restraints on work time solely to ensure a supply of exploitable labor power, with no necessary concern for the present and future wealth of society holistically considered. Clearly the working-class standpoint is better situated to take the leading ideological position in any "reaction on the part of society, the very sources of whose life are menaced" by competing capitalists' "immoderate lengthening of the working-day" (Marx 1967: v. I, 409).

The second key aspect here is that the social regulation of work time contradicts the basic principles of capitalist competition. Such regulation represents an encroachment of collective social planning into territory previously ruled by capital and its market forces. Although work time legislation may be supported by individual socially enlightened capitalists, capital as a whole organized politically at the level of the state generally will not restrict the sphere of market-oriented decision-making in favor of explicit social decision-making on behalf of labor unless pressured to do so by the working class. In this sense, work time legislation is a great victory not only for workers under capitalism, but also for socialism. As Marx says with reference to the English Ten Hours Bill:[10]

> besides its practical import, there was something else to exalt the marvellous success of this working men's measure. ... This struggle about the legal restriction of the hours of labour raged the more fiercely since, apart from frightened avarice, it told indeed upon the great contest between the blind rule of the supply and demand laws which form the political economy of the middle class, and social production controlled by social foresight, which forms the political economy of the working class. Hence the Ten Hours Bill was not only a great practical success; it was the victory of a principle: it was the first time that in broad daylight the political economy of the middle class succumbed to the political economy of the working class. (1974: 79)

So concludes Marx's analysis of how capital's tendency "to go beyond the natural limits of labour time ... forcibly compels even the society which rests on capitalist production ... to restrict the normal working day" (1991: 386). For Marx, work time legislation does not manifest the "modernization" or "humanization" of capitalism as such. Rather, it represents an anti-capitalist development within capitalism – an incursion of explicit social decision-making into areas previously reserved for capital and the market. The imperative for "general political action" to limit work time stems from the fact that capital requires human (and extra-human) life-forces only as conditions of monetary accumulation, whereas workers, like society as a whole, obviously have a more holistic interest in these life-forces as conditions of present and future human development. In this sense, work time legislation prefigures a new system of socially planned production in which the needs of the producers and their communities within and across generations take precedence over the needs of capital with its profit-driven supply and demand forces.

CONCLUSION

Marx's analysis suggests that it is a grave error to treat work time changes as either natural outcomes of capitalist market forces or as simply the result of enlightened (or unenlightened) state policies in some class-neutral sense.

Legal restraints on wage-labor time are a contingent political outcome of class struggle, and they remain susceptible to the competitive and political pressures exerted by capital accumulation. Indeed, the historical reduction of the work week has already been reversed in the USA (see other chapters in this volume), while in Japan long work times have produced a growing problem of "exhausted and weakened working people" – one threatening Japan's "social foundation in terms of the necessity to reproduce a healthy labor force" (Itoh 1994: 29, 46). Moreover, capitalists often respond to legislated reductions in work time by stepping up their efforts to mechanize and *intensify* workers' labor – thereby instigating further conflicts over work time, wages, and work conditions.[11] In short, the work time question can be permanently resolved in favor of human development only when workers and communities finally wrest full control over social production away from capital.

Marx's approach also indicates that insofar as progressive work time initiatives are couched in class-neutral terms of economic efficiency and competitiveness, they are unlikely to achieve lasting successes or to resonate with other progressive struggles both within and across countries. In this respect, Marx's analysis is especially relevant to the contemporary US economy, where many households find themselves on a "treadmill" of work and consumption that will be effectively slowed only by a grassroots working-class movement for reinvigorated unions and state policies to reduce the length and increase the flexibility (from the worker's standpoint) of wage-labor time (Hochschild 1997; Geoghegan 1999). Here as elsewhere, work time struggles will succeed only insofar as they directly confront the overall power of capital and the market over human production and development. This broadening of work time struggles will no doubt begin with explicit links to the more proximate worker–community movements – especially the living wage movement (Pollin 1998; Samuel 1999), the struggle for universal and comprehensive health care as a basic human right (Yates 1994: 130-131), and the movement to enhance the status of so-called contingent workers (part-timers, temps, and other contracted labor) (Moody and Sagovac 1995: 49–52). Ultimately, work time initiatives must be part of a movement for a cooperative-democratic and sustainable economic system appropriate to 21st century human beings living and working in a world of highly socialized labor and large-scale natural resource use.

NOTES

1 Human "labour-power or capacity for labour is to be understood [as] the aggregate of those mental and physical capabilities existing in a human being, which he exercises whenever he produces a use-value of any description" (Marx 1967: v. I, 167). In short, labor power is the ability to work, whereas labor is the work activity itself. For a full explanation of these concepts, see Burkett (1999: Chapter 4).

2 West (1983) takes the neoclassical approach to its logical extreme. He argues that not only differences in work time among different workers in general, but even

instances where low wage rates force workers to accept longer hours in order to raise their wage packets above the bare physical minimum, should be treated as voluntary reflections of workers' individual preferences (274–275). See Nyland (1989: 538–540) for a critical discussion of neoclassical preference-based approaches to work time.

3 Marx and Engels (1976: 48) go so far as to say that "to begin with" the family "is the only social relation" – adding that "later, when increased needs create new social relations and the increased population new needs," the family relation becomes "a subordinate one."

4 Capitalism's tendency to reduce the satisfaction of workers' need for free time works alongside a partially opposed tendency to *expand* workers' needs in the realm of consumption – partly through the commodification of need satisfaction in general. For an analysis of this tension see Burkett (1999: 163–172).

5 The over-extension of wage-labor time at the expense of workers' social needs continues in the USA today, where there is a growing popular awareness that home and community life are being vitiated by a "time squeeze" on working-class households (Eckel 1998; Weinstein 1999). The long work times of Japanese workers are such that in "a recent survey of Tokyo families, 10 percent of parents said they did not talk to their spouse at all, and another 51 percent said they spent 30 minutes or less in conversation with each other each day" (Anonymous 1999: 48).

6 In uncovering the sources of working-class "time squeeze," Marx endorses neither the extant distribution of domestic tasks between men, women and children nor the social undervaluation of the labor and leisure time of women and children relative to male time (see, for example, Schor 1992). Indeed, Marx emphasizes that "modern industry, by assigning as it does an important part in the process of production, outside the domestic sphere, to women, to young persons, and to children of both sexes, creates a new economic foundation for a higher form of the family and of the relations between the sexes" (1967: v. I, 489–490). Marx and Engels castigated the "slavery latent in the family ... where wife and children are the slaves of the husband," and which features an "unequal distribution, both quantitative and qualitative, of labour and its products" (1976: 38, 52). Such familial exploitation is also discussed in the *Communist Manifesto* (Marx and Engels 1968: 49–50). For further details of Marx's perspective on gender-based exploitation and women's labor under capitalism, see Lebowitz (1992: 112–118) and Chattopadhyay (1999).

7 In addition to its other appearances in *Capital* (Marx 1967: v. I, 256, 302), the vampire analogy is used in the Inaugural Address of the International Working Men's Association, where Marx speaks of "British industry, which vampire-like, could but live by sucking blood, and children's blood too" (1974: 79). Marx similarly cites a "were-wolf hunger for surplus-labour" as driving capital to "over-step not only the moral, but even the merely physical maximum bounds of the working-day" (1967: v. I, 265; cf. *ibid*: 243).

8 Any such expansion of employment is profitable for capital "if the length of the working-day and the necessary labour-time, and therefore the rate of surplus-value are given," in which case "the amount of surplus-value depends on the *number* of workers simultaneously employed by the same capital" (Marx 1968: 410; emphasis in original).

9 West (1983) mentions Marx's "public-good argument whereby legislation would reduce free riding upon the common pool of labour," but strangely dismisses it as not "plausible" (277). Stranger still is West's notion that Marx both assumed and empirically asserted a uniformity of individual work times across industries (268–269).

10 Following thirty years of struggle, Lord Shaftesbury's Act limiting daily work time for women and children textile workers to ten hours was finally passed in June 1847 (Thompson 1966: 299–300, 336–349; Marx 1974: 78).

11 See Marx (1967: v. I, 409–417; 1976: 54–55; 1991: 386; 1994: 23). Nyland (1986: 522–524; 1989: 540–543) provides an excellent overview of this element in Marx's analysis.

REFERENCES

Anonymous (1999) "Japan's Unruly Classrooms," *The Economist* (June 26): 48.

Boden, R. J. (1999) "Flexible Working Hours, Family Responsibilities, and Female Self-Employment," *American Journal of Economics and Sociology* 58(1): 71–83.

Burkett, P. (1986) "Critical Notes on the 'Free Rider Problem' in Collective Action," *Forum for Social Economics* 29–43.

_____ (1999) *Marx and Nature: A Red and Green Perspective*, New York: St. Martin's Press.

Chattopadhyay, P. (1999) "Women's Labor Under Capitalism and Marx," *Bulletin of Concerned Asian Scholars* 31(4): 67–75.

Eckel, S. (1998) "Are We Losing the Right to Have a Personal Life?" *Terre Haute Tribune-Star* (November 21): A8.

Fitzgerald, T. J. (1996) "Reducing Working Hours," *Federal Reserve Bank of Cleveland Economic Review* 32(4): 13–22.

Geoghegan, T. (1999) "Unions Can Save the Workaholic," *New York Times* (September 6): A17.

Hochschild, A. R. (1997) "Time in the Balance," *The Nation* (May 26): 11–15.

Itoh, M. (1994) "Is the Japanese Economy in Crisis?" *Review of International Political Economy* 1(1): 29–51.

Lebowitz, M. A. (1992) *Beyond Capital: Marx's Political Economy of the Working Class*, New York: St. Martin's Press.

Marx, K. (1966) *Critique of the Gotha Program*, New York: International Publishers.

_____ (1967) *Capital*, vols I–III, New York: International Publishers.

_____ (1968) *Theories of Surplus Value*, Part 2, Moscow: Progress Publishers.

_____ (1971) *Theories of Surplus Value*, Part 3, Moscow: Progress Publishers.

_____ (1973) *Grundrisse*, New York: Vintage.

_____ (1974) "Inaugural Address of the International Working Men's Association," in D. Fernbach (ed.) *The First International and After*, New York: Random House: 73–81.

_____ (1976) *Value, Price and Profit*, New York: International Publishers.

_____ (1977) "Results of the Immediate Process of Production," in K. Marx, *Capital*, vol. I, New York: Vintage: 948–1084.

_____ (1988) "Economic Manuscript of 1861–63, Third Chapter," in K. Marx and F. Engels, *Collected Works*, vol. 30, New York: International Publishers: 9–346.

_____ (1991) "Economic Manuscript of 1861–63, Continuation," in K. Marx and F. Engels, *Collected Works*, vol. 33, New York: International Publishers: 9–252, 372–501.

_____ (1994) "Economic Manuscript of 1861–63, Conclusion," in K. Marx and F. Engels, *Collected Works*, vol. 34, New York: International Publishers: 7–354.

Marx, K. and Engels, F. (1968) "Manifesto of the Communist Party," in K. Marx and F. Engels, *Selected Works in One Volume*, London: Lawrence and Wishart: 35–63.
_____ (1975) *Selected Correspondence*, Moscow: Progress Publishers.
_____ (1976) *The German Ideology*, Moscow: Progress Publishers.
Moody, K. and Sagovac, S. (1995) *Time Out! The Case for a Shorter Work Week*, Detroit: Labor Education and Research Project.
Nyland, C. (1986) "Capitalism and the History of Worktime Thought," *British Journal of Sociology* 37(4): 513–534.
_____ (1989) "The Income and Fatigue Explanations for Worktime Change," *Journal of Industrial Relations* 31(4): 538–551.
Pollin, R. (1998) "Living Wage, Live Action," *The Nation* (November 23): 15–20.
Roche, W.K., Fynes, B., and Morrissey, T. (1996) "Working Time and Employment: A Review of International Evidence," *International Labour Review* 135(2): 129–157.
Samuel, L. (1999) "Living Wage Campaigns Become a Movement," *Labor Notes* (July): 1, 10–11.
Schor, J. B. (1991) *The Overworked American: The Unexpected Decline of Leisure*, New York: Basic Books.
Thompson, E. P. (1966) *The Making of the English Working Class*, New York: Vintage.
Weinstein, M. M. (1999) "Time Isn't Money If You Are a Parent Badly in Need of Both," *New York Times* (May 27): C2.
West, E. G. (1983) "Marx's Hypotheses on the Length of the Working Day," *Journal of Political Economy* 91(2): 266–281.
Yates, M. D. (1994) *Longer Hours, Fewer Jobs*, New York: Monthly Review Press.

10 Revising the labor supply curve

Implications for work time and minimum wage legislation

Robert E. Prasch

The theory of supply and demand holds a venerable place in economics. In the contemporary professional and textbook literature, it is used to determine the price of every variety of commodity from theater tickets to corn, oil, votes and labor. It is no exaggeration to state that the supply and demand theory of price determination is one of the most widely accepted economic principles of our day. However, problems arise when a theory as abstract as supply and demand is too readily applied to situations in which it may be inappropriate. Indeed a long-standing, if somewhat eclipsed, literature within economics has argued that the application of the supply and demand theory to the labor market is an important instance in which such an error is made (Lester 1941, 1947; Galbraith 1997; Prasch 1998b, 1999; Power 1999; Prasch and Sheth 1999).

This chapter[1] will argue that labor, considered as a commodity, embodies at least one quality that differentiates it from other commodities. The point is best illustrated through a couple of examples. When the price of a representative commodity falls, suppliers are supposed to substitute out of the business of providing that particular item, and devote their productive capacity to the provision of some other item. Typically, this substitution is thought to occur with zero transaction costs. Now this idea is not necessarily without merit. Indeed, it is reasonable to suppose that a low price for minivans will induce automobile manufacturers to supply more trucks or sedans. But what of the aggregate labor market? Or the market for unskilled labor?

We know that most people depend upon the sale of their labor for the bulk of their income and, indeed, their livelihood. Can we plausibly conclude that a low wage will induce more than a minority of people to substitute into leisure and forgo any effort to earn a living? What percentage of the population can live off the bounty of the land, or depend upon savings or inheritance? While this is the implication behind the standard presentation of the labor supply curve, it is not a plausible representation of the dilemma faced by the overwhelming majority of people in the workforce. To summarize, mainstream economics has long presumed that all economic agents can exist outside of the market system, and therefore retain a credible threat to withdraw from any and all exchanges (Levine 1980; Prasch 1995).[2]

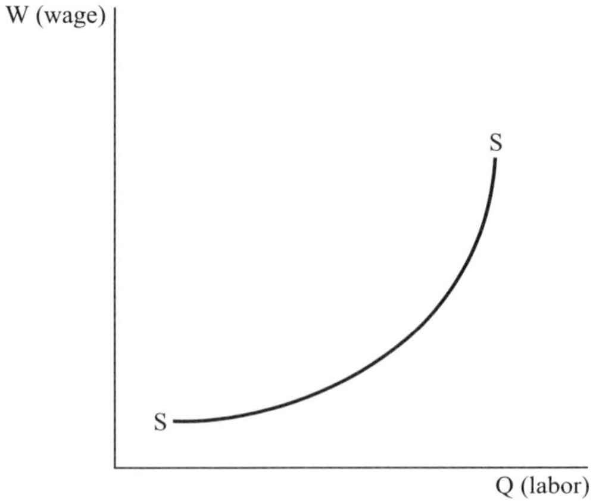

Figure 10.1 Typical labor supply curve.

Empirically, there are grounds to believe that low wages lead to the *theoretically* counterintuitive response of a larger quantity of labor supplied (Bluestone and Rose 1998b: 28–30; Gordon 1996: ch. 4; Mishel, Bernstein, and Schmitt 1999: 307–314). If this is the case, then the standard view of the labor market, specifically the shape of the labor supply curve, must be revised. With a more plausible specification of the relationship between income and the value of leisure, we can develop a more accurate model of the labor market, without necessarily losing the primary merit of the received model – its simplicity. But this issue is about more than economic theory. What is at stake is an improved understanding of the unique complexities of labor market dynamics, and the distinct possibility that labor market legislation, such as the minimum wage, can improve its performance.

THE NEOCLASSICAL LABOR SUPPLY SCHEDULE

The upward sloping factor supply curve holds a prominent place in textbook discussions of the labor market and the distribution of income. As one among several productive "factors," the labor supply schedule is constructed from the aggregate of labor–leisure tradeoffs made in the community (see Katz and Rosen 1991: 133–150; Taylor 1998: 326–329). A typical labor supply function, sloping upward to the right, is depicted in Figure 10.1.

Despite the near-consensus view presented in contemporary textbooks, there is some dissatisfaction with the conclusions that are typically drawn from this model. First is the problem posed by our actual experience with

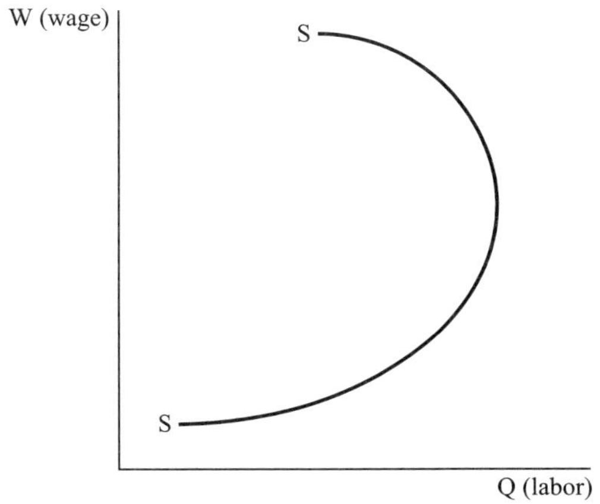

Figure 10.2 Backward-bending labor supply curve.

labor markets. Over the years, numerous empirical studies have supported the idea of a labor supply schedule that is either vertical or sloping downward to the right (Lester 1941: 104–108; Kaufman 1994: 60–62; Dessing 1999). Second, the labor supply curve is thought to be "backward-bending" at higher levels of wages. Microeconomic theory suggests that at high wages, and consequently high income levels, the representative worker will wish to purchase more of all "normal goods." Since leisure is considered to be a good with properties like any other normal good, high wages can lead to the apparently counter-intuitive result of a lower quantity of labor being supplied to the market. This modified labor supply curve is shown in Figure 10.2.

With increased levels of income, people will wish to purchase additional units of the good "leisure." Hence the tendency to substitute out of leisure time into labor time, that would be induced by higher wages, is offset by the income effect that follows from these high wages. In technical language, economists say that at high wage levels the income effect "dominates" the substitution effect.

Despite this theoretical innovation, a problem remains. The labor supply schedule depicted in Figure 10.2 suggests that, at lower wage levels, the quantity of labor supplied will decrease as wages decline. Yet the empirical studies referenced above do not support this formulation. In addition, recent American experience, which features the conjunction of stagnating wages and increased work hours for the bulk of the population, undermines the received view of the labor supply schedule (Schor 1991: chs. 1–3; Gordon 1996: ch. 4; Mishel, Bernstein, and Schmitt 1999: 307–314). Studies of labor supply from the Third World also fail to support this conclusion (Dessing 1999). Therefore, we need to reassess the labor supply curve.

INTERSUBJECTIVE COMPARISONS OF UTILITY

Economists typically dismiss attempts to compare the utility that any two persons may experience from any given level of consumption. They claim that it is inherently subjective. At least in theory, they support British economist Lionel Robbins' famous contention that utility, and the intensity of preferences, are inherently subjective, and that we can never know how intensely one person may enjoy a particular good, or set of goods, relative to any other person (Robbins 1984: ch. 6). According to the textbooks, the intensity of any individual's relative preferences is considered to be beyond the economist's knowledge (Katz and Rosen 1991: 59; Taylor 1998: 116–117).

While this position is readily advanced when consumer sovereignty or the distribution of income is under examination, it is quickly set aside when economists are constructing or applying favored theories. For example, every economist who engages in a cost–benefit analysis is *de facto* violating this rule (Lutz 1993: 7–11). So long as the winners and losers from some new regulation or distribution of income, wealth, or opportunity are not identical, then some implicit comparison of the weight of their preferences has been built into the calculation (typically it is presumed that their preferences are of even weight). Another example occurs when economists conclude that there are substantial gains to be made from a policy of free trade even if some people will lose their jobs or otherwise incur costs. Again, implicit weights are given to the relative intensity of the preferences of those who win or lose from such policies.[3]

Economists make an additional evaluation of inter-subjective preferences when they construct the labor supply schedule. There is an implicit assessment of the relative value of leisure to individuals, and to the aggregate of individuals, in the labor market. Specifically, it is presumed that the marginal utility of leisure to the person who consumes it is necessarily positive, even at the lowest levels of income. In other words, leisure is an end in itself and additional hours of leisure will always retain a positive value independently of the level of a person's income.

Given this assumption concerning the subjective value of leisure, an additional hour of leisure is always an addition to the consumer's utility, even if it is a very modest addition. But this assumption is not explicitly argued for. Rather, it is implicit in the structure of the assumptions underlying the model of the labor market. In addition, it represents another case of economists violating their own injunction against commenting on another person's preferences. This error is compounded when a labor market supply schedule is constructed through an aggregation of everyone's individual labor supply curve.

In light of the almost habitual violation on the part of professional economists of Robbins' injunction against making intersubjective comparisons of preferences, it is reasonable to ask if any economic policies can be advanced without them. The fact is that much of economic theory, and virtually all economic policies, depend upon generalizations, comparisons, and the aggregation of the preferences of various groups of people. In place of an often-violated rule against these practices, this chapter will argue explicitly for the merits of the constructions and generalizations that it employs.

INCOME AND THE MARGINAL UTILITY OF LEISURE

Given that comparisons between the preferences of individuals do, and must, take place in the course of economic analysis and policy discussions, it is incumbent upon the researcher to make a defensible case for the preferences that they specify in their models. In this chapter, I maintain that the received position on the relationship between income and leisure is inaccurate.

Economists typically posit a positive relationship between income and the marginal utility of leisure. This seems very plausible. It is also plausible to argue that, as incomes rise, people will place a higher value on an additional hour of leisure, and often are willing to trade off some of their income for more leisure time. However, while the received theory recognizes that a person with a lot of leisure on their hands may place a low marginal value on additional leisure time, additional leisure is always taken to be a good thing. Consistent with their attitude toward all other goods, the received theory presumes that more leisure is better at all levels of income. It is this latter assumption that I wish to challenge. Specifically, I would like to argue that under certain conditions, additional leisure is not a desirable commodity, and could even be perceived to be disagreeable.

This claim is based on three main stylized facts that I take to be broadly acceptable once one reflects upon the relationship between leisure and income in a world without non-labor income. First, "leisure" is a "joint product" of free time and purchasing power. Therefore, the "quality" of leisure hours cannot be assumed to be constant for any individual, or even across two individuals. For example, if I enjoy the perfect margarita on my spacious deck overlooking the ocean in front of my Malibu, California, beachfront home, my leisure is more fulfilling than if I spend the same quantity of time drinking a cheap bottle of beer in a dark and dingy apartment.

Second, in the economics literature, "leisure" is an omnibus term for time not spent working for wages. Often it includes time spent on duties and chores that can more accurately be termed "personal work" (Mincer 1963; Prasch 1997). Cleaning the house, paying taxes, and washing dishes all fall into this category. By contrast, the wealthy can afford to pay for someone else to attend to their personal work, so they can devote a larger percentage of their non-work hours to the pleasures that are usually implied by the word "leisure." Indeed, as a partial response to this problem, and as a reflection of the changing distribution of income, we now see the emergence of firms that, for a fee, will attend to the personal work of others (Levine 1997: 114–118).

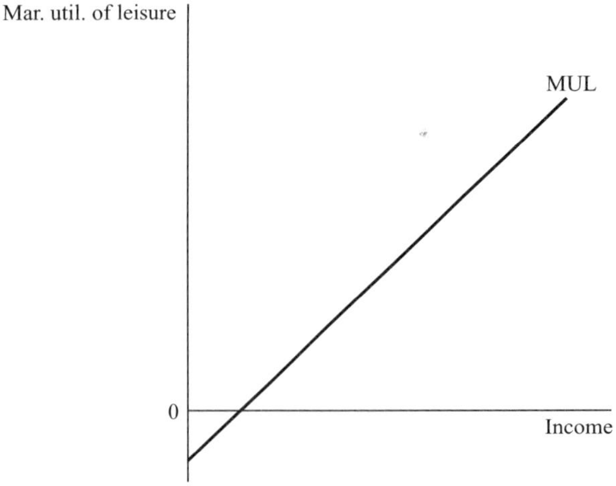

Figure 10.3 Marginal utility of leisure and its increase with income.

To the extent that the wealthy can substitute money for personal work, they can derive more utility from their non-work hours.

Third and finally, it is a misuse of language to assert or imply that the destitute individuals living upon the sidewalks of our major cities are in some sense deriving pleasure from their leisure. For many poor or low-income persons additional free time is often a burden, not a boon. The fact that so many retirees are willing to go back to work for very low pay is partial evidence for this conclusion.

If the three propositions presented above are accepted, and a linear function is assumed for convenience, then the line depicting the relationship between income and the marginal utility of leisure will not originate at a positive number when income is zero (as conventional understandings of this relationship would imply). Rather, it is more accurately depicted in Figure 10.3, in which the marginal utility of additional leisure time falls below zero at lower levels of income.

In Figure 10.3, the marginal utility of leisure experienced by a representative individual increases with their income. Again, what is different about the characterization presented here is the idea that, at sufficiently low levels of income, the marginal utility of leisure actually becomes negative. In other words a destitute person, who spends her leisure looking for work, or negotiating with the bureaucracy of an increasingly intrusive and judgmental welfare state, or listening to her children plead for food, may perceive her "leisure" hours to be both long and painful.

I wish to reiterate at the outset that this generalization is constructed upon the three stylized facts discussed above. It is not based upon some concept of "refined taste," or any other aspect of snobbery. Rather it acknowledges that

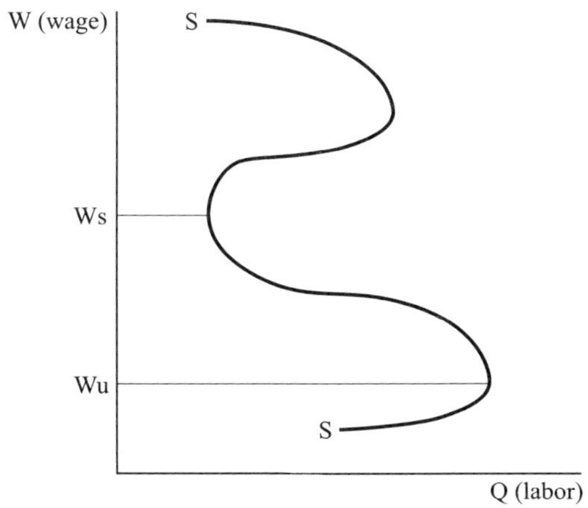

Figure 10.4 Revised labor supply schedule showing second bend.

the poor face a diminished quantity and quality of choices during the hours that they are not working for wages. It simply affirms that because the wealthy have more money, they have more choices and are burdened with less personal work.

REVISING THE LABOR SUPPLY CURVE

If it is the case that the marginal utility of leisure becomes negative when a person's income falls far enough, then at low wage levels, economic agents (be it a person or a family) will be willing to work additional hours – even at these low wage levels. The premise is that this extra effort will enable that person or family to achieve the income that is necessary to appreciate more fully the hours of leisure that remain. Graphically, the result is a second "bend" in the labor supply schedule as depicted at wage level Ws in Figure 10.4. The level of wages at which this second bend takes place will be termed, in honor of the classical economists, the "subsistence wage."[4]

Despite the above modification of the relation between income and the marginal utility of leisure, it remains the case that, over an extensive range of values, lower wages are associated with the supply of a lower quantity of labor. This upper part of the labor supply curve is consistent with the received theory and the behavior of many overworked middle- and upper-middle-class Americans (see Hochschild 1997). However, Figure 10.4 is also consistent with the observation that once the real wage (W) falls below the subsistence wage (Ws), the quantity of labor supplied will again begin to rise, even though the real wage continues to fall.[5] This will occur until the total hours of work required to maintain a socially acceptable standard of living are unsustainable. When the real wage falls far enough (to Wu), the hours

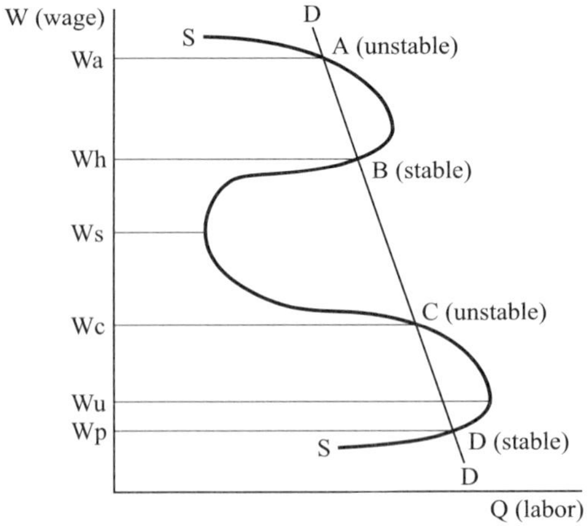

Figure 10.5 Labor demand schedule with downward slope to the right.

worked will once again decline as the primary worker and his or her family abandon their attempt to maintain a standard of living consistent with effective membership in civil society and the workforce. At wage rates below this level we can anticipate a collapse in the quantity of labor supplied as that family drops out of the regular workforce.

MULTIPLE EQUILIBRIA IN THE LABOR MARKET

If Figure 10.4 is an accurate formulation of the labor supply curve, then it follows that the labor market may be characterized by multiple equilibria. To illustrate this point, let us stay with the conventional depiction of factor demand functions and assume that the labor demand schedule slopes downward to the right as depicted in Figure 10.5.[6]

The revised presentation of the labor supply schedule, taken in conjunction with the standard labor demand schedule, indicates that there may now be four points where the supply and demand schedules cross each other. Two of these equilibrium points are stable and two are unstable. All four are of interest.

Suppose we accept the standard presentations of labor market dynamics, and agree that if the quantity supplied is greater than the quantity demanded the real wage will fall, and when the quantity demanded is greater than the quantity supplied, the real wage will rise. Then Figure 10.5 demonstrates that when the market wage is higher than Wa the wage will continue to rise. If the real wage is just below Wa it will fall until the system achieves a new equilibrium at the wage Wh. It follows that point A is an unstable equilibrium.

As we have seen, if the wage is just below Wa, a new equilibrium will be achieved at point B. At wage levels between Wh and Wc, the wage will tend to rise until it is consistent with the equilibrium at point B. It follows that point B is an equilibrium that is locally stable. Given a typical labor demand schedule, and the stability conditions of point B, the range between Ws and Wa is consistent with the self-regulating labor market of the principles textbooks – and the typically *laissez-faire* policy recommendations that often follow from those presentations.

Wages below Ws are interesting since they capture some of the novel aspects of the revised labor supply curve. All along the range from Ws to Wu families will want to supply additional labor hours in their attempt to sustain a minimally acceptable standard of living. At wage levels below Wc this tendency becomes self-reinforcing as their willingness to work additional hours exerts downward pressure on the market wage – which continues to fall thereby inducing additional work effort. In effect we have a classic vicious circle wherein falling wages induce additional work effort that, in turn, further reduces wages. Until the wage falls to Wp, which is the second stable equilibrium in this system, the quantity of labor supplied is continually greater than the quantity demanded.

The lesson is that inordinately low wages will continue to decline as a direct result of their already low level. This dynamic is, of course, generated by the fact that working poor families are toiling ever-longer hours in their attempt to maintain a socially acceptable standard of living. Once the market wage falls to Wu the hours of labor required to achieve subsistence become unsustainable. At wages below Wu the family is forced to abandon a subsistence standard of living and cut back on its labor supply.

These low-wage dynamics present an example of a positive feedback system, or "vicious circle," at work in the economy (Prasch 1998a). In such a case, market dynamics push the wage level ever-further away from the range that is consistent with a self-regulating labor market. At low wage levels the system features destructive competition among those who supply labor and must earn their living exclusively from their labor.

Point D, which is consistent with a wage level below the subsistence wage, is another locally stable equilibrium point. Such a point might describe the labor market caught in a "poverty trap." Maryke Dessing (1999) surveys numerous empirical studies of low-wage labor markets in developing countries that are consistent with the revised labor supply schedule depicted in Figure 10.5. The equilibrium at point D is also consistent with what economists of the Progressive Era referred to as "Sweated labor" (Prasch 1998b; Power 1999).[7]

IMPLICATIONS FOR ECONOMIC THEORY

Whatever one might make of the "realism" of the revised labor supply schedule presented above, one result still stands out: the conventional depiction of the labor market is fragile, in the sense that a small and highly plausible modification of one of its premises dramatically changes our understanding of labor market dynamics. This simple modification has profound implications for the shape of the labor supply schedule even as it induces dramatic changes in the equilibrium and stability properties of the model, along with the policy proposals that flow from the theory of the labor market. It follows that the conventional case against minimum wage legislation is severely undermined.

Underlying the argument of this chapter is the idea that the received understanding of the labor supply function, which results from the interaction between a derived demand for goods on the part of workers, and a positive demand for "leisure" as an end in itself, is something other than a convenient simplification. Rather, it is an abstraction that is reductionist – in the sense that it results in a misunderstanding of labor market dynamics.

Since the revised labor supply schedule in Figure 10.5 features two stable equilibrium points, reflecting high and low wage levels respectively, the proposed model is broadly consistent with the literature on segmented labor markets (Edwards, Reich, and Gordon 1975; Harrison and Sum 1979; Gordon, Edwards, and Reich 1982). However, in juxtaposition to this literature, the presentation in this chapter does not require some external constraint to maintain a low-wage labor market. Depending upon where on the graph one starts, path dependence, which in this case is generated spontaneously by market forces, will drive the system to one of the two stable equilibrium points. Once achieved, neither of these equilibria requires any additional structure to be maintained; the market takes over, and will ensure the stability of the system if no other disturbances, for good or ill, occur. In addition, as previously mentioned, the downward-sloping labor supply schedule at lower wage levels is consistent with the observation that, in the face of declining wages, many American families are working longer hours in order to maintain their standard of living (Gordon 1996: ch. 4; Bluestone and Rose 1998b: 28–30; Mishel, Bernstein, and Schmitt 1999: 307–314).

Given the existence of two stable equilibrium points, there is no *a priori* reason to believe that the equilibrium at point D has superior efficiency or welfare properties to the equilibrium at point B. Moreover, we can not characterize either equilibrium as that place where the wage is uniquely equal to the marginal product of labor. These results are both true despite the fact that the low-wage equilibrium at point D is determined in a completely free market setting. In addition, both equilibria are locally stable in the sense that once they are achieved, the market embodies no internal mechanism or force that exerts a tendency towards change. In this sense, the revised labor supply schedule presented in this chapter refocuses the decision facing policy-makers in a way that social economists are prepared to discuss. Since neither equilibrium is the unique result of market forces, it is the proper role of ethics, working in conjunction with economic theory, to provide the answer to society's choice of labor market policies. The ethical dimension that is valued by social economists would dictate that policy should be devoted to bringing about the high-wage equilibrium.

CONCLUSION AND IMPLICATIONS FOR ECONOMIC POLICY

If we accept the revised theory of the labor market presented in this chapter, a number of implications follow for the conduct of economic policy. The first is that at wage levels above Wa, the market is dynamically unstable in an upward direction. Quantity demanded will continue to exceed quantity supplied at every wage level. Since the quantity of labor supplied will continue to fall as the wage continues to rise, there is no reason to believe that any equilibrium will ever be achieved. The theory posits that these high wages will move continuously upwards. This story is certainly consistent with the pay of American CEOs since 1980.[8] In such a state of affairs, there is a *prima facie* case for a progressive income tax on all wages over Wa. Moreover, and despite the touching concern of the "supply-side" school of economists, such a tax should not result in a decline in the quantity of labor supplied. Indeed a tax directed towards the highest incomes could help to stabilize the labor market, while increasing the quantity of labor available to the market.

Second, and of more importance, a minimum wage set just above Wc would contribute to labor market stability, even as it enhances general prosperity. This result is consistent with much of the recent theoretical and empirical research on the dynamics of the minimum wage (Brosnan and Wilkinson 1988; Card and Krueger 1995; Prasch 1996; Prasch and Sheth 1999). If the mandated wage is set slightly above Wc, the quantity of labor demanded will be greater than the quantity supplied, and the market process will ensure that wages will rise to the locally stable equilibrium at point B.

Third, although such policies can be administratively complex, the revised labor market schedule has important implications for regulating the length of the standard workweek under the US Fair Labor Standards Act (FLSA). Policies to explore would include expanding the set of jobs subject to FLSA wage and hours coverage – agricultural and domestic workers come immediately to mind. In addition, a simple, obvious, and easily monitored expedient is available that could lessen the annual workload while making more time available for family life and community activities. This simple expedient is to declare several more national holidays. We should ensure that these holidays cover everyone, not just the employees of banks and the Postal Service. I would begin by suggesting that we have five more national holidays. Moreover, if the public opinion polls that indicate that people are feeling the strain of overwork are accurate, then such a program should be politically viable (of course this assumes a political system that responds to the needs of voters).

We should also note that this chapter presents an implicit critique of the positivist tradition within contemporary economics, which has long eschewed cases of multiple equilibria. In opposition to that tradition, I would maintain that the existence of multiple equilibria within the labor market model presented in this chapter is its strength, not a "flaw." A theory of the labor market that features multiple equilibria affirms some interesting insights that have, over the past several decades, been neglected by the mainstream of labor economists: namely the reality of segmented labor markets and the stabilizing properties of minimum wage and hours legislation. These are compelling arguments, especially when taken in conjunction with the themes of economic justice that social economists have so long advanced (see Prasch and Sheth 1999). The above model, which illustrates the contingency of any given equilibrium wage, and the potential for multiple outcomes, captures some of the underlying complexity of real world labor markets. It also illustrates the opportunities that are available to enlightened public policy.

NOTES

1 The author would like to thank Falguni A. Sheth, Lonnie Golden, Deborah M. Figart, Maryke Dessing, Anne Mayhew, Mathew Forstater, Jonathan Powers, and Ann Davis for their comments and assistance at various stages in the writing of this chapter.

2 Elsewhere I have labeled this assumption "the Lockean preconception" since it recalls John Locke's State of Nature where subsistence can be acquired by anyone who is willing to put forth an effort to gather the earth's bounty (Locke 1947: ch. 5). In various guises, this assumption plays a crucial role in the formation of the analytical and policy conclusions that are typically derived from mainstream economic theorizing (Prasch 1996: 394–395).

3 Discussions of economic policy often include a dodge called "Hicks–Kaldor compensation," which is a hypothetical restoration of the losses incurred by those who are harmed by a given policy change. Nevertheless, so long as it is clear that such compensation will never be paid, an implicit inter-subjective comparison of utility is being made whenever an economist proposes a policy change.

4 One could also argue that this second bend in the labor supply curve is based upon the representative worker's need to achieve a minimum level of subsistence. However, I believe that the presentation offered here is more general and, for this reason, has several advantages over the "classical" approach to this issue.

5 A number of scholars, including Arlie Hochschild (1997), Barry Bluestone and Stephen Rose (1998a), and Lonnie Golden (1998) have each pointed out that more educated and higher income workers tend to work longer hours than less educated and lower income workers. This fact is in contrast to the tendencies depicted in Figure 10.4. There are several answers to such an observation. First, most measurements are of employer records, and do not capture the long hours of those who hold multiple jobs. Second, if we take our economic agent to be the family rather than the individual or even the household, the dynamics begin to change, especially when we consider the fact that the children of the wealthy are often in school or college and less likely to be working. Third, Figure 10.5 may accurately capture *desired* working hours, even though the actual hours of labor

obtained by the working poor may be constrained for two reasons: they are more likely to be among those Americans that the Federal Reserve is likely to disemploy in the course of its "fight against inflation," *and* their ability to trade off duties at home (raising children, laundry, etc.) in exchange for more hours on the job is constrained, relative to the rich, by their lower incomes. Finally, the jobs the working poor get are often more seasonal or pro-cyclical than the wealthy.

6 Of course, the famous "reswitching controversy" of the 1950s and 1960s demonstrated that we have no reason to believe that the demand for labor schedule has this shape. Indeed, all of the participants in that debate finally concluded that neoclassical economic theory cannot determine the shape of factor demand curves (see Harcourt 1972; Hunt and Schwartz 1972: Pt. 3; Garegnani 1990; Kurz 1990). However, I do wish to note that not all of the participants agreed on how best to interpret the results of this debate.

7 After the first drafts of this research had been written and circulated, I learned that another scholar, Maryke Dessing, had developed an analysis of, and analyzed the stability properties behind, a labor supply curve remarkably similar to that presented in Figure 10.5. But important differences remain. Dessing developed her analysis to explain the dynamics of low wage markets in developing countries. My own analysis grew out of my interest in the various arguments in favor of a minimum wage legislation advanced by American economists of the Progressive Era (see Prasch 1998b, 1999, 2000).

8 I note that it is merely consistent since this market is institutionally complex. A partial development of the author's views on this subject are presented in Prasch (1998c).

REFERENCES

Bluestone, B. and Rose, S. (1998a) "The Macroeconomics of Work Time," *Review of Social Economy* 56(4): 425–441.

_____ (1998b) *The Unmeasured Labor Force: The Growth in Work Hours*, Public Policy Brief No. 39, Annandale-on-Hudson, NY: The Jerome Levy Institute.

Brosnan, P. and Wilkinson, F. (1988) "A National Statutory Minimum Wage and Economic Efficiency," *Contributions to Political Economy* 7: 1–48.

Card, D. and Krueger, A. B. (1995) *Myth and Measurement: The New Economics of the Minimum Wage*, Princeton, NJ: Princeton University Press.

Dessing, M. (1999) "Implications for Minimum Wage Policies of an S-Shaped Labor Supply Curve," manuscript in possession of author, International Center for Trade and Sustainable Development, Geneva.

Edwards, R., Reich, M., and Gordon, D. M. (eds), (1975) *Labor Market Segmentation*, Lexington, MA: D. C. Heath.

Galbraith, J. K. (1997) *Dangerous Metaphor: The Fiction of the Labor Market*, Public Policy Brief No. 36, Annandale-on-Hudson, NY: Jerome Levy Economics Institute.

Garegnani, P. (1990) "Quantity of Capital," in J. Eatwell, M. Milgate, and P. Newman (eds), *The New Palgrave: Capital Theory*, New York: Norton.

Golden, L. (1998) "Working Time and the Impact of Policy Institutions: Reforming the Overtime Hours Law and Regulation," *Review of Social Economy* 56(4): 522–541.

Gordon, D. M. (1996) *Fat and Mean: The Corporate Squeeze of Working Americans and the Myth of Managerial Downsizing*, New York: Free Press.

Gordon, D. M., Edwards, R., and Reich, M. (1982) *Segmented Work, Divided Workers: The Historical Transformation of Labor in the United States*, New York: Cambridge University Press.

Harcourt, G. C. (1972) *Some Cambridge Controversies in the Theory of Capital*, Cambridge: Cambridge University Press.

Harrison, B. and Sum, A. (1979) "The Theory of Dual or Segmented Labor Markets," *Journal of Economic Issues* 13(3): 687–706.

Hochschild, A. R. (1997) *Time Bind: When Work Becomes Home and Home Becomes Work*, New York: Henry Holt.

Hunt, E. K. and Schwartz, J. G. (eds) (1972) *A Critique of Economic Theory: Selected Readings*, Baltimore, MD: Penguin.

Katz, M. L. and Rosen, H. (1991) *Microeconomics*, Boston: Irwin.

Kaufman, B. E. (1994) *The Economics of Labor Markets*, New York: Dryden, 4th Edn.

Kurz, H. (1990) "Debates in Capital Theory," in J. Eatwell, M. Milgate, and P. Newman (eds), *The New Palgrave: Capital Theory*, New York: Norton.

Lester, R. A. (1941) *Economics of Labor*, New York: Macmillan.

_____ (1947) "Marginalism, Minimum Wages, and Labor Markets," *American Economic Review* 37: 135–148.

Levine, D. P. (1980) "Aspects of the Classical Theory of Markets," *Australian Economic Papers* (June), 1–15.

Levine, R. (1997) *A Geography of Time*, New York: Basic Books.

Locke, J. (1947) *The Second Treatise of Civil Government*, New York: Hafner.

Lutz, M. (1993) "Social Economics and Economics Imperialism," *Forum for Social Economics* 23(1): 1–12.

Mincer, J. (1963) "Market Prices, Opportunity Costs, and Income Effects," in C. Christ *et al.* (eds), *Measurement in Economics: Studies in Mathematical Economics and Econometrics in Memory of Yehuda Grunfeld*, Stanford, CA: Stanford University Press.

Mishel, L., Bernstein, J., and Schmitt, J. (1999) *The State of Working America 1998–1999*, Ithaca, NY: Cornell University Press.

Power, M. (1999) "Parasitic-Industries Analysis and Arguments for a Living Wage for Women in the Early Twentieth-Century United States," *Feminist Economics* 5(1): 61–78.

Prasch, R. E. (1995) "Toward a General Theory of Exchange," *Journal of Economic Issues* 29(2): 807–828.

_____ (1996) "In Defense of the Minimum Wage," *Journal of Economic Issues* 30(2): 391–397.

_____ (1997) "The Overburdened Consumer: The Economics of Technological Change in the Service Sector," working paper, Department of Economics, Vassar College.

_____ (1998a) "Complexity and Economic Method: An Institutionalist Perspective," in D. Colander (ed.), *Complexity and the History of Economic Thought*, New York: Routledge.

_____ (1998b) "American Economists and Minimum Wage Legislation During the Progressive Era, 1912–1923," *Journal of the History of Economic Thought* 20(2): 161–175.

_____ (1998c) "Review of *The Winner-Take-All Society*, by R. H. Frank and P. J. Cook," *Eastern Economic Journal* 24(2): 244–246.

_____ (1999) "American Economists in the Progressive Era on the Minimum Wage," *Journal of Economic Perspectives* 13(2): 221–230.

_____ (2000) "John Bates Clark's Defense of Mandatory Arbitration and Minimum Wage Legislation," *Journal of the History of Economic Thought* 22(2): 251–263.

Prasch, R. E. and Sheth, F. A. (1999) "The Economics and Ethics of Minimum Wage Legislation," *Review of Social Economy* 57(4): 466–487.

Robbins, L. (1984) *An Essay on the Nature and Significance of Economic Science*, New York: New York University Press, 3rd Edn.

Schor, J. B. (1991) *The Overworked American: The Unexpected Decline of Leisure*, New York: Basic Books.

Taylor, J. B. (1998) *Economics*, New York: Houghton Mifflin, 2nd Edn.

Part III

Innovations in working time and public policy

11 Working time reductions, employment consequences and lessons from Europe

Defusing a quasi-religious controversy

Gerhard Bosch

Analysis of working time reduction has become a quasi-religious controversy. This chapter attempts to defuse it by surveying across countries not only "whether" but "how" hours reduction has been implemented, and the conditions under which it has created employment gains. In most industrialized countries 120 years ago, average working time was around 3 000 hours per year. Since then, average working time has declined by almost 50 percent (Table 11.1). Hourly productivity in the USA, for example, is now approximately thirteen times higher and wages have risen ninefold, if we take gross domestic product per capita as a rough indicator of the evolution of wages, in the absence of any other data. From the perspective of our great-grandfathers, therefore, Americans work "part-time" hours for nine times the wage they once earned. The pattern of development has been broadly similar in the other developed industrial economies.

However, workers work not only shorter hours today but also in a different way. The sharp growth in productivity, out of which the ninefold increase in wages has been financed, has been mainly achieved only through the introduction of completely new forms of work organization and plant utilization. The labor process has been intensified through scientific management methods, such as Taylorism. Machine utilization times have been extended by reducing stoppage times and increasing operating hours (Foss 1984; Anxo *et al.* 1995). Shorter average working times per worker have not proved to be an obstacle to increased capital stock utilization. Different forms of shift organization have been developed. In continuous (i.e., 7-day) production plants, such as in the steel, textiles and chemical industries, two-shift systems were the norm in the last century. At the beginning of the 20th century there was a change to three-, after the Second World War to four-, and in recent years to five-shift systems.

Thus the reduction of working time over the past 100 years has not only constituted a form of redistribution, but has also, through its effects on work organization and operating hours, provided much of the impetus behind productivity growth and economic growth. It is true that working time reductions have been forced on business and industry from outside largely through legislation and collective agreements; however, they have also caused firms

Table 11.1 The evolution of working time, hourly productivity and gross domestic product per capita (1870–1992)

	USA	*Germany*	*Japan*	*France*	*UK*
Working time	−46.3%	−46.9%	−36.3%	−47.6%	−50.0%
Hourly productivity	+1287.6%	+1734.7%	+4352.2%	+2127.9%	+918.8%
Gross domestic product	+918.6%	+998.3%	+2632.0%	+967.1%	+501.7%

Source: Maddison (1995).

to introduce more productive forms of work organization. As a result, shorter working times have become integral to the improved efficiency in modern systems of work organization.

It is generally taken for granted that, without reductions in working time, the productivity gains of the past 150 years would have led to high and persistent levels of unemployment (Hicks 1946: 301; Drèze 1986: 36). However, what is regarded as self-evident over the long term is, ironically, controversial in the short term. Some analysts are prepared to accept the role of work sharing in reducing unemployment over the long term. However, they argue that such reductions have no place in the armory of medium- and short-term employment policy. Rigidities in work organization or higher wage costs are frequently adduced as evidence in support of this position (Drèze 1986: 44). But how is working time to be reduced in the long run, if the time is never right for initiating such a reduction?

Working time can be reduced not only to improve worker welfare but also to create jobs, by distributing a volume of work more evenly over a greater number of people. The high rates of unemployment in many countries indicate that full employment cannot be achieved through economic growth alone and that working time reduction must continue to be an important element in employment policy, along with growth and innovation policy. There is no theoretical justification for productivity gains to be distributed solely in the form of higher wages and not also as shorter working times. On the contrary, when wages are rising, additional hours of leisure are likely to become more valued by individuals than additional income.

Like any other employment policy instrument, working time reductions have been used either successfully or unsuccessfully. The mere fact that a reduction in working time in a given country has not led to increased employment cannot be adduced as evidence that hours reductions cannot work. There may have been particular conditions, such as excessive wage increases, conservative management or shortages in the labor market, that undermine its effectiveness. Under different conditions, working time policy can be very successful.

All too frequently, debate in this area is reduced to quasi-religious exchanges of articles of faith between opponents and advocates of working time reduction. These wars of religion can be defused only if discussion focuses not only on the "whether" but also on the "how" of working time reduction. This applies to collective reductions in working time as much as to individual reductions through part-time working. Thirty years ago, discussions of cuts in working time generally focused only on the reduction of the standard working time of full-time workers. This is no longer possible because of the increase in part-time work. A considerable share of reduction in the annual average working hours is now a result of the increased importance of part-time employment. The Netherlands, for example, has become the first truly part-time economy in the world.

This chapter provides an analysis of the conditions of success and failure of reductions of the standard working time in Europe in the last 20 years, and goes on to survey the effects on average hours of an increase of part-time on employment. Then the link is explored between work organization and working time. It is at the micro level of the plant or establishment that working time patterns are influenced by the emerging forces of globalization, introduction of new technologies or expansion of the service sector. Some conclusions are drawn from these empirical findings for developing appropriate working time policies.

REDUCTIONS IN WEEKLY WORKING TIME IN EUROPE: THE CONDITIONS FOR SUCCESS IN BRINGING ABOUT EMPLOYMENT GAINS

Weekly working time has been reduced in many European countries since the end of the 1970s. The initial pace was set by Belgium, which is still, with Denmark, Germany and the Netherlands, one of the countries with the shortest collectively agreed average working times. Other countries followed in Belgium's wake. This includes the UK (39-hour week in the engineering industry in 1981), France (legislation introducing the 39-hour week passed in 1982), the Netherlands (38-hour week introduced in many industries between 1983 and 1986) and Germany, where below 40-hour standards were initiated in 1985 after major strikes in the engineering and printing industries.

The developments of the past 15–20 years have left their mark on working time statistics. In Belgium, Denmark and Germany, annual working time for full-time employees fell between 1983 and 1993. As Figure 11.1 shows, collective working time reductions came more or less to a standstill in France after the introduction of the statutory 39-hour week in 1981. In the USA, working time increased, although contractual working time remained unchanged, while overtime increased. In the UK despite reductions in contractual working time, the actual annual working time of full-timers has increased because of a rise in the volume of overtime worked. In other words, working-time reductions in the UK have not eased the labor market situation but have simply led to increased use of overtime.

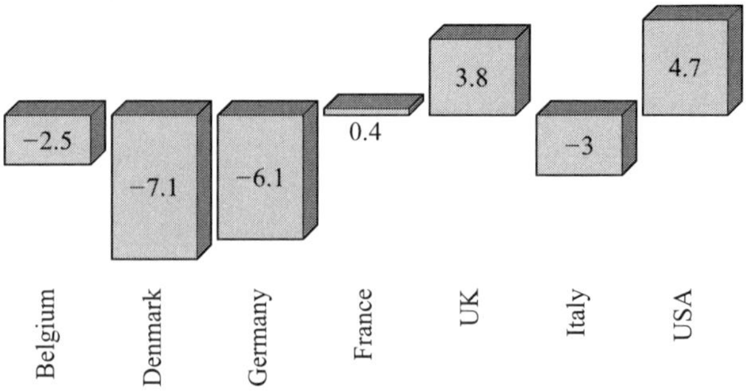

Figure 11.1 Changes in annual hours of full-time employees for the period 1983–1993 (percentages). (Source: OECD, 1998.)

Numerous studies of the employment effects of these working time reductions have been carried out in the various countries. The major challenge in all empirical studies of the employment effects of working time reductions lies in the difficult task of distinguishing between the influence of the three factors of growth, productivity and working time on employment. It is impossible to make a clear distinction on either the macro- or micro-economic level. However, the range of expected employment effects can be narrowed down by ensuring that the assumptions on which any estimates are based are as theoretically and empirically well founded as possible. Using a range of different methodologies (regression analyses, company surveys and case studies, macroeconomic simulations and decompositions) most studies conclude that working time reductions have positive employment effects of 25–70 percent of the arithmetically possible effect (Cette and Taddei 1994; Bosch and Lehndorff 2001). Only a few studies find zero (Hunt 1996) or even negative effects (König and Pohlmeier 1987). Thus the employment effects of working time reductions are better than their reputation would suggest.

Table 11.2 presents the findings of six company surveys in the EU of estimated employment creation following collective hours reduction. The results are heavily influenced by who asks the questions and who answers them. Nevertheless, it has to be said that none of the surveys known to us has concluded that the collective working time reduction in question has had no employment effect, or even a negative one. One difficulty with company surveys can also be that they merely produce snapshots. However, firms' reactions to changes in external conditions are usually delayed, with the lags varying depending on the specific impetus and the form of reaction. French, Dutch and German studies have also drawn attention to delays in adjusting manning levels to shorter working times. The immediate reaction of many firms to working time reductions was to intensify the work process in a way that could not be sustained over the medium term. As has been estimated by means of macroeconomic simulations, the ensuing productivity increase fell gradually from an initial 75 percent to about 50 percent (de Lange 1989; Cette

Table 11.2 Company surveys on the employment effects of collective working time reductions (selection)

Country	*Working time reduction*	*Nature of investigation*	*Employment effects found*
France	39-hour week 1982	Company survey carried out in 1983 by the government statistical service INSEE	26% of firms, new recruitment; 11%, reduction in job losses; 59%, no change in employment
Netherlands	Industry-wide collective agreements on 38-hour week (shorter in some cases) 1982–1985	Company survey carried out by *Loontechnische Dienst*	15% of firms, new recruitment (with employment effect of about 20–25%); 3.5%, existing jobs safeguarded; 78%, no change in employment
Germany	Reduction of working week in 3 stages to 38.5, 37.5 and 37 hours (engineering industry)	Surveys of works councils at each stage by IG Metall (about 5 000 plants)	Employment effects of 70%, 58% and 70%, respectively
Germany	First stage in the reduction of weekly working time to 38.5 hours in 1985 (engineering industry)	Company survey by engineering employers' association (about 5 000 plants)	Employment effect of 21% (plus 14% extra overtime, which was later reduced)
Germany	Reduction of weekly working time to 39 hours (public service)	Established and staff council survey by market research institute Infratest	Employment effect of 52%
Germany	First stage of reduction in weekly working time to 38.5 hours in 1985 (printing industry)	Survey of works councils by IG Druck trade unions (450 plants)	Employment effect of 66%

Sources: ATOS (1997), Cette and Taddei (1994), and Seifert (1991).

and Taddei 1994; Stille and Zwiener 1997). Thus the employment effects of working time reductions in the countries mentioned here were distributed over the economic cycle. Consequently, a dynamic approach has to be adopted if the employment effect of a cut in working time is to be assessed adequately.

In evaluations of the employment effects of any fiscal, financial or labor market policy measures, it is now assumed that positive effects on employment can be achieved only under certain conditions: the timing has to be right and implementation adroit. Analysis of working time reduction measures, however, is still dominated by undifferentiated, over-generalized statements. Working time reductions are examined in isolation rather than as an instrument that is always used under concrete and historically very variable conditions. In what follows, we will attempt to sift out, from the European studies conducted in the last two decades, the conditions that are decisive for the success or failure of working time reductions as an instrument of employment policy. Six conditions emerge as being particularly important (see also Bosch 1999).

1. Wage compensation. In both public and academic debate, there is a perception that working time reductions without any reduction in total (monthly) wage compensation is a means of sharing the cake out twice, effectively increasing wage rates on top of the normal pay rise. If this were the case, working time reductions would indeed give rise to exceptional cost increases. However, if working time reductions and pay increases are negotiated as a total package, then the compensatory increase for the working time reduction can be offset by lower pay rises. If, as a result of this holistic approach, the increase in costs does not outstrip the gains in productivity, then unit wage costs will remain constant. If the aim is to reduce working time quickly and in larger steps than can be achieved by offsetting any rise in unit wage costs against the expected gain in productivity, then the compensatory wage increase will have to be abandoned altogether. If longer-term package deals can be agreed on, however, then larger cuts in working time can be combined with wage increases while at the same time ensuring cost neutrality.

Longer-term package deals of precisely this kind were put together in the German engineering industry and in the Netherlands, when working time reductions were introduced there. In these cases, workers financed the working time reductions themselves by accepting smaller wage increases. In Norway in 1986, working time was cut, first in the engineering industry and then throughout the economy, from 40 hours to 37.5 hours per week. However, this working time reduction was accompanied neither by wage negotiations timed to coincide with it nor by agreements on more flexible forms of working time organization. This discrepancy must have contributed a good deal to the rise in overtime and inflationary pressures in Norway (Bosch 1997b). Empirical experiences with the relationship between reductions in working time and labor costs have been summarized by Cette and Taddei (1994: 45) as follows: "Historically ... all the compromises achieved have ultimately ended in the same financing mechanism: over the long term, the bill is ultimately always paid for by productivity gains, even if at the outset the negotiating partners have always been much exercised by the needlessly mythical question of wage compensation."

2. Changes in work organization. In both manufacturing and services, work organization in firms was based on the 8-hour day. This traditional form of working time was assumed, almost unconsciously, to be the self-evident foundation of work organization. This is the main reason why traditional forms of work organization became second nature to both employees and firms. Larger reductions in working time generally have to be accompanied by changes in work organization and new standards like the 7-hour day or the 4-day week have to be introduced. If the old standard will be maintained the firms have to rely on overtime and the working time reductions will not have any positive employment effects. In all countries where there have been considerable cuts in weekly working hours, firms have initially stuck to their old system of work organization and have not sought to make changes until difficulties have become apparent.

The flexibilization arrangements agreed in Germany already in the 1980s have, for example, been used in various ways only with a time lag in the 1990s. There has been a shift from a rigid 8-hour day to flexible annualized working hours (Bosch 1997a). Through the introduction of new shift systems, operating hours in Germany rose from 60.6 hours per week in 1984 to 71.8 hours in 1996, and Germany now has the highest share of shift-workers in Europe, after Luxembourg (Bauer *et al.* 1998). Company reorganization is facilitated by medium-term, step-by-step plans, which give firms time to plan for organizational changes. The French government is aware that companies need time and expertise for organizational change. To facilitate this learning process the French announced the goal of working time reduction from 39 hours to 35 hours some years before it becomes obligatory for firms. The state also subsidized companies that reduced working hours earlier as well as consultants for small and medium size companies that wanted to change their work organization to reduce the work week.

3. Shortages of skilled labor in the labor market. Contrary to all fears, shortages of skilled labor did not occur in Germany between 1984 and 1992, although there was an upturn in the economy during the same period as well as a considerable reduction in working time. The volume of overtime worked even fell, from 80.2 hours per employee in 1980 to 65 hours in 1992. The most important reason for this happy state of affairs was the expansion of initial and further vocational training in the 1980s. Because of the political pressure that had been exerted, many firms declared themselves prepared to intensify their training efforts in order to facilitate the integration of the large age cohorts into working life. By a fortunate coincidence, the same period had also seen more unemployed people receiving further training through active labor market policy measures. When the working time reductions were being implemented, fewer firms complained of shortages of skilled workers than at the beginning of the 1980s (Stille and Zwiener 1997: 29). The situation in the UK is completely different. There, 64 percent of employees have had no formal vocational training, compared with only 26 percent in Germany (OECD 1995: 53). One reason for the large volume of overtime worked in the UK is undoubtedly the inadequate supply of skilled workers in the British labor market. As one British trade unionist remarked to the author: "We don't have skill shortages, we call it overtime." Thus an active training policy is an indispensable supplement to working-time policy.

4. Fixed costs per employee. If high fixed costs are paid on a per capita rather than hourly basis, then firms obviously have an increased incentive to utilize their employees' labor as extensively as possible. This fixed cost problem can be seen in the USA, for example, where health insurance and pension schemes are agreed at the company level and paid for per capita rather than on the basis of hours worked. It is proven that working time is longer in those firms that operate their own insurance schemes than in those that do not (Cutler and Madrian 1996). Most countries in Western Europe have statutory social welfare systems. Contributions are usually proportional to earnings, or the systems are financed out of taxation, so that this fixed cost problem is relatively insignificant for full-time employees. A similar fixed cost problem occurs when firms invest in their employees' human capital. The higher this investment is, the greater employers' incentive is to extend "brain operating times," particularly since employees' knowledge and skills go out of date quickly because of the rapid pace of technological change. In recent years, working times for highly skilled employees have increased in many countries. In 1996, highly skilled white-collar workers in Germany worked an average of 46.3 hours per week, 1 hour longer than in 1984, although their contractual working time had fallen by 2.5 hours (Wagner 1998). If skilled workers continue to be overburdened in this way, there is a risk that many "brains" will be able to function for only 10–20 years, rather than a full working life. Moreover, if brains are made to work for excessively long periods, then they often cease to function properly.

5. The evolution of earnings. The decreasing rate of real wage rises in most industrialized countries has reduced the scope for implementing cuts in working time and wage increases simultaneously. This is particularly the case if a majority of workers in the entire earnings distribution have experienced real wage stagnation or reduction relative to those at higher wages. Under such conditions employees tend to opt first for wage increases, and it becomes more difficult for trade unions to gain acceptance for working time reductions. Real wage increases, which were running at 4.9 percent per year in Germany in the 1960s, fell in the 1980s to 0.8 percent per year and to 0.4 percent per year between 1990 and 1995. The fact that real wages in Germany in the 1980s and 90s rose by less than the OECD average (OECD 1998: 165) was also related to the significantly higher level of working time reductions. Thus even in economically difficult periods there is scope for a solidaristic working time policy, in order to prevent redundancies, for example.

Changes in earnings inequality are portrayed in Figure 11.2. In the USA the median real wage for men fell between 1979 and 1995, and thus inequality rose. In terms of purchasing power, a German worker in the lowest earnings decile earns approximately 2.2 times (a British worker only 1.3 times) as much as his American counterpart. If real wages are declining, workers try

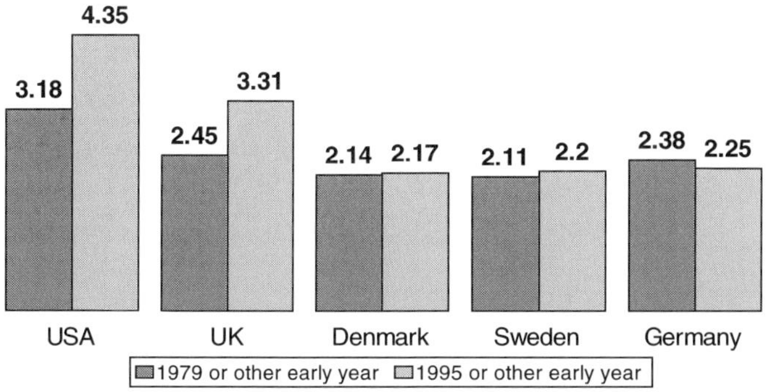

Figure 11.2 Levels and changes in earnings inequality among advanced OECD countries (measured by the ratio of the 90th to the 10th decile, male earnings, 1979–1995). (Source: Freeman, 1997.)

to increase their working hours to maintain their household income. Since trade union members are concentrated primarily in the lower and middle income groups, increasing earnings inequality makes it more difficult for unions to find support for a policy of collective working time reductions. One fundamental precondition for the working time policy pursued in Germany and Denmark, for example, was a stable and realatively equal earnings distribution. Neo-liberal policies of income differentiation undermine attempts to redistribute working time because employees are unwilling to accept reductions in their hours.

6. *The standardization of working hours.* If actual working hours are to be redistributed by changing standard hours, then the standards have to strongly influence actual hours worked. If actual hours are destandardized and standard hours have lost their determining power, decisions on actual working hours are individualized and no longer influenced by laws or collective agreements. Such a situation can be observed in the UK (Figure 11.3(a)). In the relatively flat distribution of working time for men and women, there are no peaks in the distribution of average actual working time. The reduction of standard working hours in the British engineering industry in the 1980s did not influence actual working hours. In Denmark or Germany, working hours of men and less of women are more concentrated around a mode (Figure 11.3(b,c)).

Further, as a result of the general working time reductions of recent years, this peak point in both Denmark and Germany has shifted to the left. In Denmark, we can see that following the working time reduction more women are working full-time than before. Shorter standard working hours for men and women seem to be a possibility for establishing a new gender contract based on full-time work for both partners and sharing household work. To redistribute working hours, the work actually done has to be recorded and remunerated. Increasingly, however, firms are either going

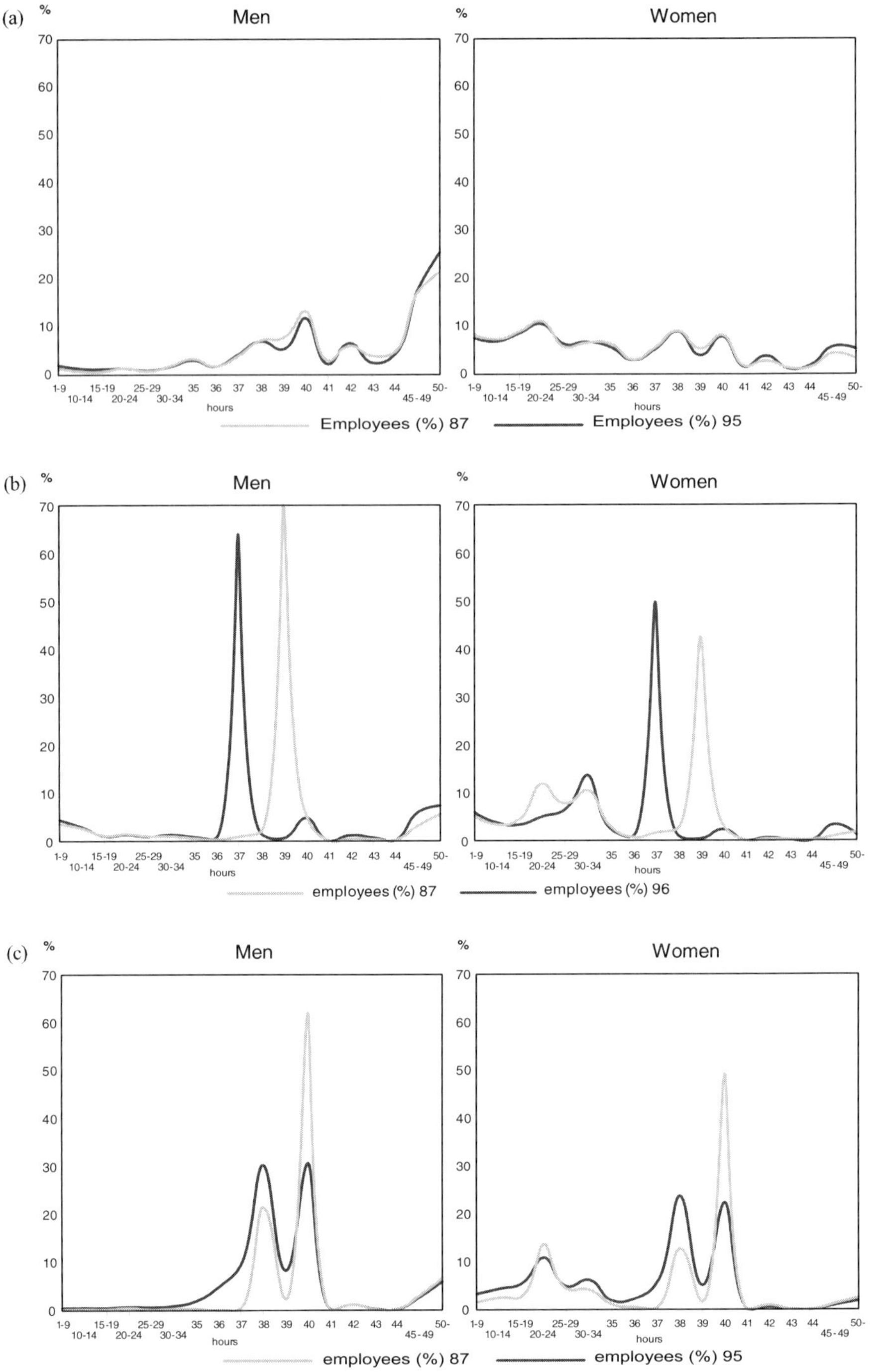

Figure 11.3 Distribution of usual weekly working hours for employees: (a) UK, 1987 and 1995; (b) Denmark, 1987 and 1996; (c) Germany, 1987 and 1995. (Source: Eurostat.)

over to employment contracts that do not stipulate any working time and provide simply for the payment of a flat-rate salary, particularly for more highly skilled employees, or are abandoning the practice of recording actual working times in full. Working time that is not recorded and paid for cannot be redistributed. One problem with many flexible working time systems is the elimination of recorded overtime, even though employees work longer hours than are stipulated in their contracts. In most European countries (with the exception of the UK) only a minority of employees is currently affected by such informal working time structures, although this could change in the future.

However, in an analysis of the conditions under which a working time policy might produce positive employment effects, the general political conditions should not be ignored. The most important of these is the acceptance of working time reductions by the employees, works councilors and trade unionists, the State and employers. Acceptance of reductions does not imply unbridled joy, but rather viewing them as a challenge or an unavoidable condition that cannot be circumvented, not even by powerful employers or employer associations. For example, when BMW introduced a 37-hour week at its Munich plant, it also put in place a new shift system; at the same time, it made firm plans for the next two union-agreed stages of working time reduction by laying down clear targets for their implementation. It has been clear to employees for a long time that the company is serious about cutting working time. If firms in Germany assume that they can avoid making any reduction in working time, they will fail to come to grips with new working time systems. They can reach such a judgment if their employees prefer to work longer hours and the works councilors and trade unionists become less powerful.

NEW FORMS OF WORK SHARING: PART-TIME WORK AND ELECTIVE WORKING TIMES

About 30 years ago, working time reduction meant nothing more than the reduction of standard working time for full-time employees through shorter weekly working times or extended holidays. Today, individual working time reductions in the form of part-time work or temporary leave of absence have become more important. The most important reason for such individual reductions in working time is the rise in female participation rates, particularly among married women in all industrialized countries (Pott-Buter 1993). In many cases, women are no longer merely secondary earners, but significant joint earners or even the main breadwinners, albeit to date in only a small minority of households.

However, if there are several earners in a family, then the most important shortcoming of part-time work, that it does not provide sufficient income to live on, no longer applies for many workers. This brings completely new

Table 11.3 Frequency of dual-earner, single-earner and no-earner households for couples with children, 1996

	Dual earners	*Single earners* (*men*)	(*women*)	*No earners*
Portugal	67.1%	27.3%	3.8%	2.0%
Germany, East	64.0%	26.8%	5.5%	3.8%
Belgium	61.6%	30.3%	2.5%	5.6%
UK	61.0%	26.3%	3.3%	9.3%
Austria	60.6%	32.0%	4.8%	2.7%
France	57.3%	33.3%	4.1%	5.4%
Netherlands	52.4%	39.8%	2.6%	5.2%
Germany, West	50.8%	40.5%	3.5%	5.1%
Ireland	39.0%	45.4%	4.1%	11.6%
Spain	32.7%	53.5%	4.1%	9.6%
EUR 13	51.4%	38.6%	3.4%	6.5%

Source: Eurostat (1996), Labour Force Survey.

social models and working time systems on to the agenda. The traditional breadwinner model is no longer the dominant household model in European countries (with the exception of Spain), as the female participation rate continues to rise and there are two earners in most households with children (Table 11.3).

As a replacement for the male, single breadwinner model, the Dutch trade unions, for example, are discussing a proposal that each partner in a household should work 75 percent of standard full-time hours. In the Scandinavian countries, the assumption is that both partners will work full-time, although their working lives will typically be interrupted by periods of parental or training leave or their working time temporarily reduced by spells of part-time work. These two models can be combined to offer a menu of individual working time reductions, so-called elective working hours.

However, not all trade unions regard such elective part-time working hours as a desirable instrument for redistributing work. In this respect, the policies adopted by the American and Dutch trade unions are pulling in opposite directions. In the USA, the Teamsters took strike action against the private courier company United Parcel Service (UPS) in support of their demand for more full-time jobs, while the Dutch trade unions are calling for more part-time work. In the USA, the part-time rate (i.e., part-time as a proportion of total employment) has been reduced from 16.4 percent in 1979 to 13.4 percent in 1998, while in the Netherlands it rose in that period from 16 percent to 30 percent (OECD 1993 and 1999). Employment in the Netherlands grew by 34 percent between 1980 and 1995, even more than in the USA (25.9 percent). In the Netherlands, this growth was achieved by redistributing an unchanged volume of work, while in the USA working time increased and the volume of paid work expanded. The share of part-timers who would like to work longer hours is greater in the USA than in the

Netherlands. These examples suggest that part-time work is not a useful instrument of job creation that can be applied across different national situations.

The following five conditions are important for achieving a voluntary reduction of working time. The first is that hourly pay differentials between full-timers and part-timers must be low. If the difference in rates of pay between full-timers and part-timers is more than 100 percent, as it is at UPS ($20 per hour compared with $8–9), and part-timers are not covered by health insurance and pension schemes, then volunteers for reduced working hours will be very thin on the ground. In the Scandinavian countries or the Netherlands, hourly rates for part-timers are exactly the same as for full-timers.

Second, the difference in male and female wage rates must be reduced. In the UK the average hourly pay for full time working men was in 1996 was £9.39 and for part-time working women £5.44 (Department for Employment and Education 1996). This difference is exacerbated if the husband is working in the manufacturing industry and gets an overtime supplement of time-and-a-half while the wife is working part-time and will not get overtime supplements for additional hours worked. The household has the choice between £14.1 and £5.44 for an additional working hour, with the well-known result for the distribution of working hours between men and women in the UK that we observed in Figure 11.3(a).

Third, income tax and social security systems should be neutral in their effect on the distribution of hours. Currently, systems in many countries encourage overtime. In Italy, no social security contributions have to be paid in respect of overtime, so that the cost of overtime to employers is less than that of normal working time, despite the 25 percent premium paid to workers. In Germany, married couples are still taxed jointly. In the so-called "spouse-based splitting" system, a couple's joint income is divided in two and the two halves are taxed separately. In this system, women who enter the labor market often have to pay very high marginal rates of taxation immediately. In Sweden or Austria, separate taxation for married couples has been introduced. This increases the incentives for women to work by lowering their marginal tax rates but reduces the incentives for overtime working by raising marginal tax rates on these additional hours worked (Anxo *et al.* 1999; Dingeldey 1999). The reduction of the gender gap in pay and the individualization of tax systems in Sweden is one of the reasons for the more equal distribution of working hours in this country.

Fourth, the distribution of household incomes must be made more equal. As income becomes more concentrated in the upper income households, the share of households that can afford to reduce their working hours likely falls. Household incomes in the Netherlands, where the part-time rate is high, are far more equally distributed than in other countries. In the USA in the early 1990s, households in the top decile of the income distribution earned approximately six times as much as those in the lowest decile, while in the

Netherlands they earned only 2.9 times as much. This clearly explains the high level of acceptance for the Dutch policy of encouraging part-time work (Atkinson, Rainwater, and Smeeding 1994).

Finally, the damage that can be done to workers' careers as a result of voluntary reduction of work must be reduced. Those willing to reduce their working hours are all too often reckoned to be less ambitious. It is hardly surprising, therefore, that very few employees at Bayer or BMW in Germany have availed themselves to date of the provisions available on elective working hours contained in company agreements, even though both firms offer their employees an exemplary range of options from which to choose their individual working times.

Both the Netherlands and the Scandinavian countries have brought about a cultural change. This has virtually reduced the bias against working part-time hours. Employees' rights to reduce their working hours have been strengthened. In the Scandinavian countries, both the fathers and mothers of small children have a right to work part-time, with the option of returning subsequently to a full-time job. This stands in complete contrast to the mere lip-service paid to calls for increased part-time working in Germany or the UK, where the workplace culture is still firmly rooted in full-time work.

WORKING TIME NEEDS TO BE MODERNIZED AS WELL AS REDISTRIBUTED

An increasingly significant obstacle to recommending working time policy is the differing patterns in which working time has evolved in various industrialized countries. The joint international "convoy" that for 100 years traveled, albeit at differing speeds, towards the goal of the 8-hour day and then the 40-hour week has now broken up into several individual groups operating independently and with little radio contact. In those countries in which the labor market has been deregulated and income inequalities have increased, working time has become longer. The burden of work on households in the USA and the UK, for example, is considerably higher than in Germany or the Netherlands. Average annual working time for all people of working age (including part-timers and the economically inactive population) in the USA is 465 hours longer than in Germany and 558 hours longer than in the Netherlands (Figure 11.4). Despite the significantly higher volume of work, the question of income inequality has taken center stage while, with the increasing burden of work, the redistribution of work has virtually disappeared from the policy agenda. This divergence can be seen in multinational companies, where the working time cultures collide with each other. American and Japanese managers have difficulty understanding and accepting international forms of working time organization based on shorter working times.

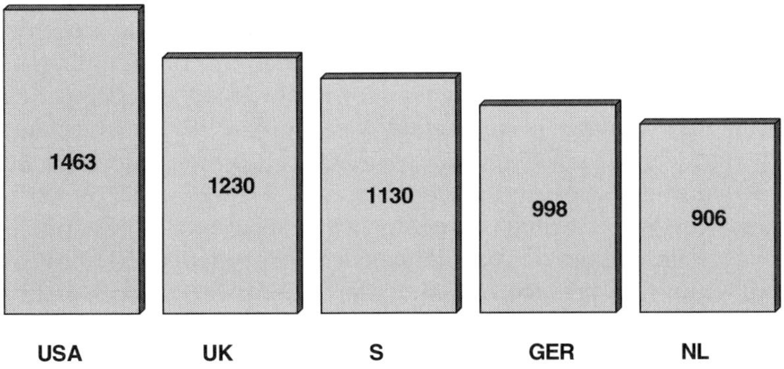

Figure 11.4 Average annual working time in hours per person of working age (including the economically inactive population) for 1996. (Source: OECD, 1997, and author's calculations.)

Cultural differences of this kind can be observed in the merger between Daimler Benz and Chrysler. German works councilors and trade unionists are trying to restrict overtime. The American and Canadian collective agreements, however, contain the following clauses on overtime: "Any right to decline overtime or Saturday or Sunday work that this Memorandum of Understanding confers to any employee may be exercised only by each individual acting separately and individually, without collusion, conspiracy or agreement with, or influence of, any other employee or employees or the Union or pursuant to any other concerted action or decision . . . No employee may seek to prevent others from accepting overtime. Violation by any employee of the terms, purpose or intent of this Paragraph shall subject him/her to discipline" (UAW/Chrysler "1996 Production and Maintenance Agreement. Memorandum of understanding on overtime in US Plants"). Other collective agreements in the North American automobile industry even contain the following provisions: ". . . However, the fact that a few employees have arranged in the course of ordinary social relationships to attend, for example, a sporting event or wedding shall not in itself be considered evidence of concerted activity." (Agreement between Ford Motor Company of Canada Limited and National Union, C.A.W. September 24, 1990: 239).

Since the efficiency of the various working time regimes in a global economy is a criterion for selection in the world market, advocates of working time reductions are under increasing pressure to come up with innovative and economically efficient forms of working time organization. There is a need not only to redistribute work but also to *modernize* work organization to improve efficiency and at the same time to manage shorter working hours. The extensive management literature on work organization of recent years has almost completely ignored the importance of working time questions and concentrated on other topics, such as the advantages of a less rigid division of labor in reintegrating production and quality control, for example. In contrast to the Taylorist forms of work organization, working time in these systems is not strictly prescribed from above; rather, there is some scope for decentralized decision-making. In order that such systems, once implemented, do not result in increased working time for want of fixed time structures, rules governing the trading of contractual working time have to be negotiated. Such rules should cover the transparency of working time accounts and the procedures to be applied when the specified upper limits on working time are exceeded as well as agreements to initiate recruitment procedures once a certain volume of overtime has been exceeded. Such rules can be successfully put into practice only in a climate of trust and cooperation between management and the bodies representing employees' interests, and should therefore be negotiated between employers and unions.

However, the pressure to modernize comes not only from firms but also from employees who want more freedom to choose and are also seeking a better balance between work and family. "Modern" working time regimes have both to create the conditions under which the "flexible firm" can flourish and also take account of employees' new working time requirements. This twofold modernization has to be achieved if working-time reductions are to be actively sought, or at least accepted by employers and employees. Many firms have devised creative working time systems in recent years, and much can be learned from such endeavors.

WORKING TIME POLICY IN THE FUTURE

Four main conclusions on the future of working time policy can be drawn from the analysis presented here. First, shorter working times are an indicator of prosperity. Those who enjoy them have to be in a position to afford them. If material conditions deteriorate, the question of sufficient or unequal earnings comes to the fore again and the labor supply increases. This fundamental link between income and working time is often not recognized. In Germany, the influential Committee on Future Issues, for example, thinks it can simultaneously introduce a low-wage sector and expand part-time working (Kommission 1997). However, these two objectives are incompatible because employees' working time preferences will change if their wages fall. Thus, neo-liberal policies, that tend to raise income inequality, represent the biggest obstacle to achieving further reductions in working time.

Second, both collective working time reductions and elective shorter working time options can create additional employment. However, such employment effects will not happen automatically. The necessary conditions under which employment expands must be created. These conditions include an active training policy, wage increases in line with productivity gains, the standardization of actual hours worked, the reduction of differences in hourly rates for full-timers and part-timers, better social security for flexible working lives, a change in the deep-seated full-time culture in the workplace and social security contributions that are proportional to the paid hours of work. Many of these conditions can be met only if a consensus can be forged between the social partners, as in the Netherlands or in Scandinavia.

Third, all working time reductions must, at the plant level, pass through the eye of the needle of "work reorganization." A new work organization has to be based on a new working time standard and should allow more flexibility for elective working hours. At the same time it has to improve efficiency. Only such organizations will remain competitive in a global economy in which many competitors are using longer working hours.

Finally, reducing or redistributing working hours via increasing the proportion of workers working part-time may be difficult to sustain in the long run. The high part-time rate in the Netherlands, for example, seems to be a historically specific episode. Dutch women traditionally had one of the lowest participation rates in industrialized countries. Part-time is for them the first step of entering the labor market. With better general and vocational education and a changing institutional framework (more public child-care) they will tend to increase their working hours. The higher integration of women in the labor market in the Scandinavian countries is the most important reason why the part-time rate is slowly declining there. Thus, a work-sharing policy that relies only on increasing part-time jobs might in the end create a "part-time-trap" (Lehndorff 1998). Part-time work opportunities should be brought much closer to the current nature of full-time work. Consideration should also be given, however, to new ways of linking collective and individual elective working times. In the future we need short and life long flexible working patterns for men and women as it was proposed by Gösta Rehn (reprinted in 1977) as early as in the 1950s.

REFERENCES

Anxo, D., Bosch, G., Bosworth, D., Cette, G., Sterner, T., and Taddei, D. (eds) (1995) *Work Patterns and Capital Utilisation: An International Comparative Study*, Dordrecht: Kluwer.

Anxo, D. *et al.* (1999) *Households Income Distribution and Working Time Patterns: An International Comparison*, Gelsenkirchen: Institut Arbeit und Technik.

Atkinson, J., Rainwater, L., and Smeeding, T. (1994) "Income Distribution in OECD Countries: The Evidence from the Luxembourg Income Study (LIS)," paper presented at the American Economic Association Meeting, Boston, MA, December.

ATOS Beleidsadvies en -onderzoek bv (1997) *Reduction of Working Hours in the Netherlands 1988–1995*, study contract concerning company policies with regard to the reduction of working time: Amsterdam: ATOS.

Bauer, F., Bosch, G., Bundesmann-Jansen, J., Gross, H., Stille, F., and Wagner, A. (1998) *Betriebszeiten 1996: Ergebnisse einer repräsentativen Betriebsbefragung zu Betriebs- und Arbeitszeiten im verarbeitenden Gewerbe*, Düsseldorf:

Ministerium für Arbeit Soziales und Stadentwicklung, Kultur und Sport des Landes Nordrhein-Westfalen.

Bosch, G. (1997a) "Annual Working Hours: An International Comparison," in G. Bosch, D. Meulders, and F. Michon (eds), *Working Time: New Issues, New Norms, New Measures*, Brussels: Dulbea, 13–36.

_____ (1997b) "Flexibility in the Norwegian Labour Market in a Comparative Perspective," in A. H. Steen and J. E. Dolvic (eds), *Making Solidarity Work?* Oslo: Scandinavian University Press: 211–247.

_____ (1999) "The Reduction of Working Time, Pay and Employment," in B. Marin *et al.* (eds), *Innovative Employment Initiatives*: Aldershot: Ashgate.

Bosch, G. and Lehndorf, S. (2001) "Working Time Reductions and Employment: Experiences in Europe and Economic Policy Recommendations," *Cambridge Journal of Economics*, in press.

Cette, G. and Taddei, D. (1994) *Temps de travail, Modes d'Emplois: vers la Semaine de 4 Jours*, Paris: Editions La Découverte.

Cutler, D. M. and Madrian, B. C. (1996) *Labor Market Response To Rising Health Insurance Costs: Evidence On Hours Worked*, Working Paper 5525, Cambridge, MA: National Bureau of Economic Research.

de Lange, W. (1989) *Configuratie van Arbeit*, Zutphen: Thieme.

Department for Employment and Education (1996) *New Earnings survey*: London

Drèze, J. H. (1986) *Work-Sharing: Why? How? How Not ...*," Paper No. 27, Brussels: Centre for European Policy Studies.

Dingeldey, I. (1999) *Work, The Family and the Tax and Social Security System: The Rewards and Penalties Of Various Patterns Of Household Economic Activity and Working Time: A Comparative Study of Ten European Countries*: Gelsenkirchen: Institut Arbeit und Technik.

Eurostat (1996) *Erhebung über Arbeitskräfte*, Luxemburg.

Foss, M. (1984) *Changing Utilization of Fixed Capital. An Element in Long-Term Growth*, Washington, DC: American Enterprise Institute for Public Policy Research.

Freeman, R. B. (1997) *When Earnings Diverge: Causes, Consequences, and Cures for the New Inequality in the U.S.*, Commissioned by the Committee on New American Realities of the National Association, Washington, DC.

Hicks, J. (1946) *Value and Capital*, Oxford University Press, 2nd Edn.

Hunt, J. (1996) *Has Work-Sharing Worked in Germany?*, Working Paper 5724, Cambridge, MA: National Bureau of Economic Research.

Kommission (1997) *Maßnahmen zur Verbesserung der Beschäftigungslage*, vol. III, Bonn: Kommission für Zunkunftsfragen der Freistaaten Bayern und Sachsen.

König, H. and Pohlmeier, W. (1987) "Arbeitszeit und Beschäftigung: eine ökonometrische Studie", in Bombach, G. (ed.), *Arbeitsmärkte und Beschäftigungs – Fakten, Analysen, Perspektiven*, Tübingen, Mohr, Siebeck.

Lehndorff, S. (1998) "From 'Collective' To 'Individual' Reductions In Working Time? Trends and Experience with Working Time in The European Union," *Transfer* 4(4): 598–620.

Maddison, A. (1995) *L'Économie Mondiale 1820–1992, Analyse et Statistiques*, Paris: OECD.

OECD (1993) *Employment Outlook*, Paris: OECD.

_____ (1995) *Economic Surveys – United Kingdom*, Paris: OECD.

_____ (1997) *Employment Outlook*, Paris: OECD.

_____ (1998) *Employment Outlook*, Paris: OECD.

_____ (1999) *Employment Outlook*, Paris: OECD.

Pott-Buter, H. (1993) *Facts and Fairy Tales: About Female Labor, Family and Fertility*, Amsterdam: Amsterdam University Press.

Rehn, G. (1977) *Towards A Society Of Free Choice*, Stockholm: Swedish Institute For Social Research; in J. Wiatr and R. Rose (eds) *Comparing Public Policies*, Wroclaw: Ossolineum.

Seifert, H. (1991) "Employment Effects Of Working Time Reductions In The Former Federal Republic of Germany," *International Labour Review* 130(4): 495–510.

Stille, F. and Zwiener, R. (1997) *Arbeits- und Betriebszeiten in Deutschland: Analysen zu Wettbewerbsfähigkeit und Beschäftigung*, Berlin: DIW-Sonderheft.

Wagner, A. (1998) "Working Time Of High-Level White Collar Workers In Germany. An evaluation of the SOEP", International Working Party on Segmentation Theory 20th Conference in Trento, Italy, July.

12 The "lump-of-labor" case against work-sharing

Populist fallacy or marginalist throwback?

Tom Walker

The persistence of high rates of unemployment in Europe, coupled with longer average work hours among many workers in the predominantly English-speaking countries, has revived interest in policies to redistribute working time. A common reaction by mainstream economists to the idea of redistributing hours of work is to contend that proposals such as work-sharing, which are intended to spark job growth, are based on the mistaken belief that there is only a fixed amount of work to be done. That assumption is sometimes called the "lump-of-labor" fallacy. Alternatively, the notion has been labeled a "lump-of-work" or "lump-of-output" fallacy.

The dismissive phrase has become an article of faith among many in the economics profession, despite the fact that advocates of reduced work time have, for more than a century, repeatedly disavowed the alleged belief in a fixed amount of work. Advocacy of work time redistribution as a remedy for unemployment is based not on an *idée fixe* but on the defensible proposition that current work arrangements are less than ideal and that substantial improvement in the allocation of work is both desirable and practicable.

This chapter briefly examines the sources of the lump-of-labor claim and its role in scholarly and public policy debates regarding work-sharing. The closer look presented here shows the claim has never been an authoritative tenet of economic thought but has persisted as an uncritical relic of textbook lore, cobbled together from disconnected and incompatible fragments of archaic economic doctrine. To put it bluntly, the lump-of-labor fallacy is a counterfeit – the economists' equivalent to the Piltdown man hoax, which for four decades caused the skull of a modern man and the jawbone of an orangutan to be regarded as the missing link in human evolution.

As if to show that Gresham's law – that bad money drives out good – also governs economic discourse, the claim of a lump-of-labor fallacy has displaced genuine analysis regarding the complex relationship between the hours of work, employment and productivity. For example, S. J. Chapman's 1909 theory of the hours of labor, which was described by pre-eminent British economist J. R. Hicks as "the classical statement of the theory of hours in a free market" (1932: 102n.), is today rarely acknowledged by mainstream economists (Nyland 1989). Yet that theory suggests a compelling rationale, examined later in this chapter, for the redistribution of work time: shorter hours reduces fatigue, allows for greater efficiency and consequently lowers per unit costs. Those productivity gains provide a basis for employment growth beyond just the short term reallocation of existing work.

What difference could a lapse of scholarly memory make to policy? It is suggested here that the claim of fallacy has enforced a taboo that has effectively kept redistributing working time off the public policy agenda in Canada, the United States and the United Kingdom. Bosch (1998) has noted the unsatisfactory nature of the debate on working time, which "all too frequently becomes bogged down in quasi-religious exchanges of articles of faith between supporters and opponents of reduced working time" (1998: 1). The subtitle of a paper by Freeman (1998), "Work-Sharing to Full Employment: Serious Option or Populist Fallacy?" also hints at the stigmatization haunting the topic.

Moreover, deference to the illegitimate fallacy and the resulting eclipse of genuine theory may be facilitating the continuation of ill-considered policies that erect fixed employment cost barriers to the voluntary reduction of the hours of work – with the unintended consequence of encouraging long hours of work and contributing to more precarious employment. Those perverse policy incentives may also be inflicting a more general slowdown of productivity growth, stifling employment and wage gains. Workable policy and voluntary responses to the regime of high fixed costs and long hours of work can be developed, but the stigma of a lump-of-labor fallacy discourages serious consideration of those options by policy makers.

ONE LUMP OR TWO?

A customary practice of scholars is to introduce their work by situating it in relation to previous work in the field. It is noteworthy therefore when the author of an econometric study of working time reductions frames her findings not in relation to other econometric studies but as a retort to an amorphous popular belief. The first paragraph of Hunt's (1996) research paper, "Has Work-Sharing Worked in Germany?" exemplifies the claim of a lump-of-labor fallacy:

> There is a wide-spread popular belief that unemployment can be reduced by reducing the number of hours worked per person. The reasoning is usually based on what is sometimes called the "lump of work fallacy": labor input is seen as fixed, and it is believed that if each worker works fewer hours, this work can be spread over more workers, and employment will rise. This is known as work-sharing. However, if restrictions on hours make labor less attractive to employers, they will substitute to other inputs, and there will also be a scale effect reducing use of all inputs (1996: 1).

Hunt's opening paragraph displays a number of rhetorical features that are characteristic of the lump-of-labor charge: (i) the work-sharing concept is identified as a "wide-spread popular belief" – implicitly contrasting it with more substantive expert knowledge; (ii) advocates of work-sharing are alleged to assume that the amount of work to be done is fixed – no evidence is offered in support of the allegation, which is hedged by qualifiers such as "usually" and "sometimes;" and (iii) the concluding *coup de grace* relies on the use of technical jargon to suggest a rigorously "scientific" result opposite to what the naive popular belief might predict.

In a later version of the paper, Hunt dropped the reference to a lump-of-work fallacy but retained the allegation of a "widespread popular belief ... based on the idea that labor input is fixed" (1999: 117). In yet another paper, Hunt reprised the assertion that "popular confidence in the ability of work-sharing to increase employment is based on the idea that the amount of work that needs to be done is fixed" (1998: 340).

Commenting on Hunt's 1998 article, Katz (1998) developed the same theme with minor variations. He referred to a vaguely attributed belief – this time by "many individuals" – that cuts in the work week can reduce unemployment (1998: 373). According to Katz, most advocates of that belief, which he referred to as the lump-of-output fallacy, implicitly assumed a fixed level of output and consequently an unchanged total number of hours of work. Like Hunt, Katz concluded his tale with vague allusions to imperfect substitution and econometric estimates. Katz credited Layard, Nickell, and Jackman (1991) as his source for the expression "lump-of-output fallacy."

In their explanation of the fallacy, Layard *et al.* adhered to the convention that work-sharing advocates assume a fixed amount of work, but in other respects they presented quite a different argument from Hunt as to why work-sharing cannot alleviate unemployment (1991: 502–505). In the Layard *et al.* version, the cut in hours initially might lower unemployment but only at the cost of increased inflation. If this were the case, they argued, there could be one of two sets of consequences. One possibility is that inflation would be tolerated – in which case it would have been better to cut unemployment by expanding output through fiscal stimulation. Another is that government will act to curb inflation by allowing unemployment to rise back up to its prior level – in which case everyone will end up worse off because output will have been lowered with no gain in employment.

In contrast to Hunt, who had explained the fallacy in terms of the micro-economic behavior of the firm, Layard *et al.* explained it as a failure to anticipate an eventual macroeconomic policy response from the government. In restating Layard's argument, Katz left it unclear whether the eventual spoiler of the expected employment gains was the firm or the state: "A reduction in the unemployment rate is likely to increase the bargaining power of incumbent workers and lead to wage increases that reduce the employment gains" (1998: 374).

Although the Hunt and Layard versions each offer partial explanations of why a work-sharing strategy may not be effective under different specified circumstances, they both digress from the conspicuous charge of fallacy. The differences between the two versions highlight their improvised and incomplete status. Neither version establishes why advocacy of work-sharing must, *necessarily*, rest on a belief in a fixed amount of work. Because that claim is unsubstantiated – indeed, cannot be substantiated because it is incorrect – the subsequent "explanations" of why such a belief is fallacious are gratuitous.

Surveying the various instances where the lump-of-labor fallacy is invoked, it becomes clear that the *ad hoc* quality of explanation is yet another characteristic feature. Those who use the phrase and allege that work-sharing advocates assume a fixed amount of work seem to sense that there is something missing in the argument, so they tack on an explanation borrowed from somewhere else in the economists' bag of tricks. What is really missing, though, is evidence for the charge, a logic for the "implied" assumption and an authoritative source for the legendary fallacy.

STALKING THE ELUSIVE FALLACY

Although it has been described as one of the best-known fallacies in economics, "which first-year students are taught to refute" (Anon 1996), the lump-of-labor fallacy is omitted by most economics reference books. Three economics dictionaries that do include entries for the lump-of-labor fallacy are the *Oxford Dictionary of Economics*, the *Routledge Dictionary of Economics* and the *Canadian Dictionary of Business and Economics*. All three dictionaries define the fallacy as a belief in a fixed amount of work, but they diverge when it comes to explaining how it deviates from economic reality.

The *Oxford Dictionary of Economics* claims that the lump-of-labor view "ignores the possibility that the demand for labour may depend on the relation between wage rates and the value of work to employers" (Black 1997: 281). The Routledge volume points out that the view "suggests that macroeconomic policy is limited in its ability to stimulate an economy" (Rutherford 1992: 276). The *Canadian Dictionary of Business and Economics* avers that the fallacy "ignores the possibilities for new consumer wants and new industries in stimulating growth and creating more jobs" (Crane 1993: 385). All three entries associate the lump-of-labor fallacy with proposals for shorter hours of work. None of them explains why such proposals imply a belief in a fixed amount of work. Nor does any of them cite an authority for the oddly named fallacy.

With the notable exception of Samuelson's famous introductory textbook, *Economics* (see Samuelson and Nordhaus 1998: 239–240), contemporary economics textbooks omit discussion of the lump-of-labor fallacy. An introductory economics textbook widely used in the 1920s, 1930s and 1940s, Bye's *Principles of Economics*, dutifully featured an exposition of the fallacy (1927: 48–51). Neither Bye nor Samuelson presented evidence for the charge of a belief in a fixed amount of work, and their respective explanations of its economic consequences differed. The longevity of Bye's textbook, first published in 1924, and Samuelson's, which was a staple in first-year courses from the 1950s through the 1970s lends credence to the description of the lump-of-labor fallacy as something first-year students were taught to refute. Evidently, though, students were only taught to refute the fallacy as alleged, not to question the authenticity or cogency of the allegation.

NOT A SIMPLE SUM IN ARITHMETIC

The claim of a lump-of-labor fallacy can be traced back to the 1890s – a time of widespread agitation in England and the United States for the 8-hour day – when the phrase appeared in an article about piece-work by David Schloss (1891a):

> The basis of this belief, which is in a large measure responsible for the unpopularity of piece-work, is that noteworthy fallacy to which I desire to direct attention under the name of "the theory of the Lump of Labour."
>
> In accordance with this theory it is held that there is a certain fixed amount of work to be done, and that it is best in the interests of the workmen that each shall take care not to do too much work, in order that thus the Lump of Labour may be spread out thin over the whole body of work-people (1891a: 324).[1]

In an earlier article, Schloss (1891b) had used the same expression, "the lump of labour," not in connection with a reputed theory or fallacy but simply as a rustic specimen of working class slang. From the perspective of its current usage, the most interesting thing about Schloss's seminal discussion of "the theory of the lump of labour" is that he avowed it had *nothing to do* with the question of the length of the working day (1891a: 325). Schloss himself expressed sympathy toward proposals for an 8-hour day, which he held to be both economically and socially desirable.

No mention of a lump of labor occurs in any of the prominent articles or books of the day addressing the issue of the 8-hour day, such as *The Eight Hours Day* by Sidney Webb and Harold Cox or John Rae's *Eight Hours for Work* (Webb and Cox 1891; Rae 1894). In the latter book, though, Rae vigorously attacked the idea that shorter hours could offer a cure for unemployment. Rae's full argument stands in ironic contrast with those of contemporary opponents of shorter work time. Rae strongly supported the call for an 8-hour day on the grounds that it would make industry more efficient. His argument against shorter hours *as a cure for unemployment* was based primarily on his conviction that shorter hours would result in the same (or lesser) number of workers performing the same (or greater) amount of work in a shorter time (1894: 181). His sharp polemic against an alleged economic fallacy was a secondary theme that echoed a venerable employers' complaint, which held that workers, and especially trade unions, conspired to restrict work effort:

> ... and (2nd) from yielding to the gross but evidently very seductive economic fallacy, which leads so many persons to think that they will all increase the wealth they individually enjoy by all diminishing the wealth they individually produce, and to look for a great absorption of the unemployed to flow from a general restriction of production, the very thing which in reality would have the opposite effect of reducing the demand for labour, and throwing multitudes more out of employ (1894: 181).

Rae summarized his analysis of the 8-hour day and the unemployed with the conclusion that "the most trusted and popular argument in favour of the eight hours day constitutes really its only serious practical danger" (1894: 216).

The bulwark of Rae's argument was his demonstration that the redistribution of work time was not "a simple sum in arithmetic" (Rae 1894: 179). Although this part of his argument was compelling, it was not original. The same point had been eloquently presented several years earlier by Francis Amasa Walker (1890: 808). Walker had confined his case to disputing only the more simplistic slogans of 8-hour day agitators. Rae, however, tried to stretch the rebuttal to cover the economically sophisticated arguments of shorter hours advocates such as Sidney Webb and Harold Cox (1891: 103–115). Rae curtly dismissed Webb and Cox's analysis, expressing incredulity that the unemployed should "obtain employment from capital which only comes into being as the result of their employment" (Rae 1894: 215).

Rae's dismissal of Webb and Cox was both feeble and bizarre. At face value, it was nothing more than a blunt reaffirmation of the discredited wages-fund doctrine of classical political economy, which held that wages could only be paid out of a pre-existing fund of circulating capital that was fixed in the short term (on the wages-fund doctrine and controversy, see McNulty 1980: 76–80, 111–117). Even Rae's conclusion that reductions in work time combined with restrictions on work effort would result in more, rather than less, unemployment was subsequently shown by Beardsley to rely on the wages-fund doctrine and its underlying assumption that the relative shares of wages, profit and rent are immutable (1895: 452–455).

Rae's reversion to the wages-fund doctrine was as much an enigma as it was an anachronism. In an earlier book, he had described the doctrine as "dead and buried" in its original form and "little more that a stately truism" in its revised, more flexible formulation (1891: 491). Adding to the heap of self-contradiction, Rae's polemic against the restriction of work effort revolved around yet another version of the wages-fund doctrine. John Wilson (1871) had been explicit 20 years earlier when he berated a "Unionist reading of the Wage-fund theory." In Wilson's account, the trade unions put this theory into action through "the enforcement of all sorts of arbitrary restrictions on the combined workmen with the avowed object of securing that the work to be done shall be divided among as many (Unionist) hands as possible" (1871: 243).

Rae's attempt to show that reducing the hours of work would not relieve unemployment thus relied on variously affirming and denying the self-same doctrine, depending on where he was in the course of the argument and who was presumed to be speaking. Given the equivocal nature of Rae's argument, it is not surprising that it never become solidly established as economic theory. But his conclusion evidently appealed to the prejudices of employers' associations and newspaper editorialists in the early 1900s, in whose hands Rae's extraordinary inconsistency even lent itself to a "salami tactics" of isolating and refuting – with distinctly different arguments – one facet after another of the case for the 8-hour day.

The lump-of-labor case against shorter work time thus emerged as a hodgepodge of borrowed working-class slang, middle-class prejudice and archaic economic doctrine. The original expression had nothing to do with working time. It was grafted to an argument against shorter hours as a remedy for unemployment that was Byzantine in its self-contradictions. Most bewildering and disheartening is that this odd collection of remnants has eclipsed the coherent and formerly acclaimed theory of hours presented in 1909 by Sir Sydney Chapman.

S. J. CHAPMAN'S THEORY OF THE HOURS OF LABOR

Chapman revisited the issue of the hours of labor in his presidential address – delivered in Winnipeg, Manitoba – to the British Association for the Advancement of Science, Section on Economic Science and Statistics (1909). That analysis came to be considered the "classical statement of the theory of 'hours' in a free market" (Hicks 1932: 102n.; Nyland 1989). Arthur Pigou restated Chapman's argument in *Economics of Welfare* (Pigou 1952; 462–469). Alfred Marshall referred to Chapman's analysis as authoritative, as did Lionel Robbins (Marshall 1961: 695; Robbins 1929: 25). Concluding his footnote reference to Chapman and Pigou, Hicks declared, "There is very little that needs to be added to the conclusions of these authorities." Very little, perhaps, other than the strange occurrence that although Chapman's argument has never been challenged, economists today are oblivious to its major conclusions. Most are unaware not only of the theory's authoritative status but even of its existence.

Unlike Rae, Chapman saw no particular danger in workers' views – "fallacious or otherwise" – about the mechanics of distribution (Chapman 1909: 365). On the contrary, Chapman suggested that such attitudes probably had protected workers "against the injurious consequences of short-sightedness."

Chapman began his discussion of the hours of labor by reviewing the mass of evidence that reductions in the hours of work had not led to proportionate declines in output. Chapman attributed the phenomenon to the fact that as production methods become more intensive, workers require more leisure time to fully recover from the fatigue of work. He emphasized that in modern industry fatigue was increasingly psychological, resulting from the demands of modern industry for specialization and mental concentration as well as from the workers' attitude toward leisure rather than from the strictly physiological demands of the work. When the hours of labour were reduced, the better-rested workers were often able to produce as much or more in the shorter hours than they had previously in longer hours.

The total value of the output from standard working days of different lengths would thus initially increase as the day became longer but eventually the total output – not only the output per hour – would decline as the standard day became too long to allow the worker to recover sufficiently from fatigue. Beyond a certain point, each additional hour of work would continue to add a quantum of output to the current day's total output but only at the expense of reducing the next day's hourly pace. What that point was, Chapman maintained, depended on the intensity of the specific production methods and thus would vary in response to changes in those methods.

Having established the idea of an optimal length of standard working day that would maximize output, Chapman next turned to the questions of whether such an optimal length would likely be established by the workings of a free market and whether the optimal length of day for output coincided with the optimal length from the perspective of the workers' welfare. His conclusions in both cases were negative.

From the perspective of the employer, Chapman argued, the optimal length of day for output could only be achieved if all employers acted in enlightened accord. This is because the maintenance of the long-term optimum would always require some short-term restraint. A single employer could never be entirely certain of reaping the benefit of that restraint. Another firm could always potentially offer a small wage premium and hire away the first firm's well-rested workers. For employers, the optimal output work time would thus be a form of investment without equity:

> The reforming employer would run the risk of paying the whole cost of the labour value created by shorter hours and getting little in return; other employers might secure and exhaust the new labour value and no permanent good would be effected (1909: 361).

From the perspective of the worker, the optimal length of day could, for all practical purposes, be considered to be shorter than the optimal length of the day for output. Chapman considered three elements in assessing the optimal day for the worker: 1, the wage, which Chapman assumed for the purpose of analysis to exactly equal the worker's marginal productivity; 2, the marginal value of leisure, which Chapman assumed to vary in response to changes in the level of wages; and 3, the disutility of work, which Chapman assumed to also be a function of the length of the working day – during some intermediate period of the working day, Chapman assumed that work could often be experienced as pleasurable.

Chapman maintained that in forming their ideal of a working day, workers' would disregard the effects of changes in work time on efficiency, and hence on wages. As a consequence they would tend to prefer a working day longer than would be prudent in the long run, even though it would not be as long as that preferred by employers acting competitively. Thus the exclusive concern of both employers and workers with immediate self-interest would bias the preferences of each toward longer than optimal hours (1909: 367).

In the two decades following Chapman's address, his demonstration of market failure in the determination of working time led to systematic empirical study of the relationship between fatigue and work intensity. According to Nyland (1989), however, attention to the question of work intensity faded during the 1930s and after, largely because "the fact that work time had both a temporal and intensive character made it difficult to utilize marginal productivity theory to determine the return on various factors of production" (1989: 33). As a simplifying abstraction, economists assumed that the given working day was of optimal length. Eventually, the hypothetical – and *antithetical* – status of that assumption came to be overlooked. Economists negligently reverted to a pre-Chapman faith that unencumbered market forces would spontaneously lead to the establishment of an optimal length of work time.

THE LUMP-OF-L MODEL: AN IMPERFECT SUBSTITUTE

A production function describes mathematically the transformation of economic inputs – such as labor, machinery and raw materials – into outputs. Economists who criticize work-sharing sometimes represent the "best-case scenario" for work-sharing by a model of the production function in which labor services (*L*) equal the number of workers (*N*) times the average hours worked by each worker (*H*) (see, for example, Hoel 1986; Hart 1987; Freeman 1998; Katz 1998).[2] The model is written as $L = f(NH)$. According to the critics, the assumptions underlying the model are that hours per worker and numbers of workers are perfect substitutes, hourly wages are constant, there are no fixed costs of employment, workers are homogeneous and productivity is unaffected by the length of work time. It is easy to show that the stated assumptions are unrealistic and to conclude from that demonstration that the employment effects of a reduction in work time would certainly be considerably less than anticipated by the model, and often could be negative.

However, there is also an unstated and ultimately damning assumption at the core of the demonstration. It is an assumption made by the critics of work-sharing, not by its advocates. As mentioned earlier, mainstream neoclassical economists in the 1930s abstracted from the question of work intensity central to Chapman's theory of hours. That simplifying abstraction, and the failure of economists to consistently think back from their abstractions to a more realistic form, led eventually to the implicit assumption that free labor markets would establish an optimal working day or week. Movement away from that presumed optimum could then be assumed to generate suboptimal outcomes for both output and welfare. The model where workers and hours are perfect substitutes thus represents the "best-case scenario" only if we also assume – contrary to theory and much evidence, but in accord with the simplifying abstraction of the neoclassical economists – that the given working time arrangements are optimal for output and for the welfare of the currently employed.

Advocates of shorter work time do not assume that current working time arrangements are optimal. Thus they expect that policy efforts to redistribute working time can improve productivity and the welfare of the currently employed as well as create new jobs. Those expectations are more likely to be based on observation of current conditions in the labor market than they are on an understanding of Chapman's theory of hours. However, unlike the simplifying abstraction of the neoclassical economists, those observations are consistent with Chapman's theory.

If we assume, following Chapman, that for any given interval (day, week, year or lifetime) there is some hypothetical length of work time that would optimize total output per worker (O) and another, lesser length that would optimize hourly productivity (P), then current average hours of work (H) must occupy one of five positions in relation to those two optima:

1. greater than the output optimum ($P < O < H$)
2. equal to the output optimum ($P < H = O$)
3. between the output optimum and the productivity optimum ($P < H < O$)
4. equal to the productivity optimum ($P = H < O$)
5. less than the productivity optimum ($H < P < O$)

For purposes of analysis, the second case, where current hours of work equal the output optimum, can be merged with the third case where current hours lie between the output and productivity optima. Table 12.1 summarizes the net employment effects implied by a reduction in work time for the four remaining scenarios, now labeled A through D.

According to Table 12.1, scenario C, the perfect substitute model, is not the only one that offers grounds for expecting a positive employment effect.

Table 12.1 Projected net employment effect of a reduction in work time

Scenario	*Initial condition*	*Redistributed*	*Unit labor cost*	*Demand induced*
A	$P < O < H$	None	Lower	Gain
B	$P < H \leq O$	Gain (less than C)	Lower	Gain (less than A)
$C = f[NH]$	$P = H \leq O$	Gain	No change	None
D	$H < P < O$	Gain (loss)[a]	Higher	Loss

Note

a There could be a net loss of jobs if there was an increase in moonlighting that exceeded the gain from redistributing hours.

Furthermore, there is nothing in the analysis to suggest that scenario C would necessarily create more jobs in total than either scenario A or scenario B. It would, hypothetically, redistribute more work time from hours to employment. However, both A and B also imply labor cost savings, and thus the potential to create additional jobs through the effect those lower costs would have on the demand for labor. That reduction in unit cost could translate into a wage increase, partially compensating for lost income from reduced work time, or product price cuts, which could be expected to result in a greater quantity of product demand and therefore a demand-induced employment gain, or some intermediate mix of wage increases and price cuts.

The plausibility of scenarios A and B can be tested by supplying estimates for the variables. In his analysis of long-term productivity trends, Denison (1962) estimated the optimum output week to be close to the level of average weekly hours performed in 1929, 48.6 hours. He further suggested that small reductions in work time below that level would be partially offset by gains in productivity until a point of maximum hourly productivity was reached, which he projected to be 33.9 hours. Below that point, he suggested, a further reduction in work time would result in a more than proportionate fall in output. About 60 percent of workers in Canada and the USA currently work weekly hours in the range between Denison's estimated productivity optimum of 33.9 hours and his output optimum of 48.6 hours (Statistics Canada 1997; US Bureau of Labor Statistics 1999). Table 12.2 integrates Denison's estimates into the projections of net employment effects.

The estimates presented in Table 12.2 can be used to project the changes in total output and hourly output per worker that may be expected to result from a given reduction in work time.[3] Using Denison's estimates, for example, a 10 percent reduction in the average work week for full-time workers, from 42 hours to 37.8 hours, would result in a 5.6 percent loss of output per worker. Output in the reduced work time would be partially offset by a 4.9 percent gain in hourly productivity. To maintain the same total output as before the change would require that full-time employment be expanded by 5.9 percent. That is not to say overall employment would expand by that amount, because the change would represent a reduction in work time mainly for those who currently are working more than 37.8

Table 12.2 Estimates for *O* and *P*

Scenario	*Denison estimates*	*Redistributed*	*Unit labor cost*	*Demand induced*
A	$H > 48.6$	None	Lower	Gain
B	$H \leq 48.6$, $H > 33.9$	Gain (less than C)	Lower	Gain (less than A)
$C = f[NH]$	$H = 33.9$	Gain	No change	None
D	$H < 33.9$	Gain (loss)	Higher	Loss

hours per week and not across the entire workforce. Nor would the change necessarily induce a large drop in the nominal unemployment rate, since a considerable proportion of the newly created full-time employment might be filled by augmenting the hours of people currently working only part-time.[4] The productivity gains would be large enough to cover the growth in fixed employment costs resulting from expanded employment and provide for a moderate wage increase to partially offset income lost from reduced hours of work.

Since the 1960s economists have warned that reducing the hours of work would increase labor costs, given the presence of fixed costs of employment (see Oi 1962; Ehrenberg 1971; Hart 1987). Such an increase in labor costs, it is often feared, could lead to negative employment effects from shorter work time. While it is true that with fixed costs a reduction in hours would raise the average *hourly* cost of labor, the hourly cost is not the relevant point of reference for labor costs – the cost per unit of output is (Pfeffer 1998). If hourly productivity increases more than hourly labor costs, the net result is a decrease in unit labor costs. Again using the above example, if we assume that 20 percent of total labor costs are fixed per person costs, the 5.9 percent expansion in full-time employment would translate into a 1.2 percent rise in the hourly labor cost – less than a quarter of the estimated 4.9 percent productivity gain.

There is one catch. The hourly cost increases would occur immediately, while the productivity adjustment could be realized only over a period of time. Furthermore, the larger the projected productivity gains, the longer would be the period of adjustment needed to achieve them. If we assumed that the gains would be forthcoming instantaneously, the case for shorter hours would appear deceptively strong. However, if we acknowledge, with Chapman, that the productivity gains take time to present themselves, the presence of high fixed costs of employment significantly increases the investment required to make the transition. How long it would take to pay back that investment would depend on the ratio of fixed costs to variable costs, the timing and size of wage increases, the size of the productivity gains and the time it takes to achieve them.

Fixed employment costs thus do impose a formidable hurdle to reducing working time. But the hurdle does not result from increased unit labor costs, it reflects the cost of adjustment and the risk inherent in investing in potentially mobile workers. Those barriers could be reduced or overcome, either by government action to convert currently fixed costs to variable costs, as suggested by Golden (1992), or by labor–management cooperation to phase in work time reductions with wage increases keyed to productivity gains. In looking for ways to surmount the barriers to adjustment, it is important to understand that the magnitude of those fixed employment costs is not an artifact of the free market.

THE INJURIOUS CONSEQUENCES OF SHORT-SIGHTEDNESS

Ninety years ago, when he warned against the injurious consequences of short-sightedness, Chapman had in mind the short-sightedness of employers acting selfishly and the short-sightedness of workers who neglected the effects of long hours both on their immediate enjoyment of life and on their long-term earning capacity. Today, there is growing evidence that rather than correcting for the short-sightedness of employers and workers, public policy may be making matters worse by offering perverse incentives that favor longer hours of work and precarious employment.

Although fixed employment costs are sometimes portrayed as immutable barriers to shorter work time, they are "fixed" only in the relative sense that in the short term they are less responsive to changes in work hours than are variable costs. Fixed costs vary considerably over the long run. As has been noted in public consultations in both Canada and the United States, much of the growth in fixed labor costs can be traced to government policies (Osberg 1997; US National Commission for Manpower Policy 1978). Osberg pointed out that in Canada the design of federal payroll taxes, which require contributions on income only up to an amount somewhat below the median income level, along with tax exemptions for employer-paid fringe benefits, encourage firms to increase overtime hours rather than hire new employees (1997: 155–156).

In Canada, during the period from 1976 to 1995, there has been a polarization of the hours of work away from a standard 35-to-40-hour week. In 1995, 54 percent of the work force put in between 35 hours and 40 hours a week, compared to 65 percent in 1976 (Statistics Canada 1997). During roughly the same period, payroll taxes doubled as a percentage of GDP, from 3 percent in 1970 to 6.3 percent in 1992 (Picot *et al.* 1995: Table 4, 3.13). Because of upper limits on the amount of earnings subject to taxation, the impact of this increase fell disproportionately on those earning median incomes. By targeting the highest rates of payroll tax close to the median income level, policy makers may also have been inadvertently targeting the median arrangements for hours of work – the standard 35-to-40-hour week.

Policy needs to pay attention not only to the presence of fixed costs but to the trend and history of their growth. Golden (1992) found that the growth of fixed labor costs in the post-war US economy tended to lengthen the average work week, reduce aggregate employment and raise the incidence of layoffs. Furthermore, an unintentional policy bias in favor of long hours may lead to employment losses both immediately and in the long term. The immediate loss comes from providing perverse incentives to employers that maldistribute the available work. Ironically, the full extent of short-term employment losses may be concealed statistically by the proliferation of part-time and precarious employment. The long-term effect may be to impair productivity growth, and thus to inhibit the demand driven expansion of employment and augmentation of wages. Ultimately, unemployment, underemployment and overwork themselves add to the cost of social support and medical services, thus contributing to an upward spiral of the fixed component of employment costs.

CONCLUSION

The character of the lump-of-labor case against work-sharing may be summed up by contrasting mainstream economists' longstanding trepidations toward reducing the hours of work with their usually confident embrace of other labor-saving innovations, such as computers, machinery or power technology. Strange as it may seem, the reduction of work time is a labor-saving device, albeit a uniquely worker-friendly one.

Over the long run, the way that shorter work time creates jobs is no different from that of any other aid to efficiency, whether it be a mechanical loom or a silicon chip. In the past, reducing the hours of work has created jobs by lowering the costs of production and thus by making the products of industry more affordable to consumers. Unlike other labor-saving devices, though, limiting the hours of work can also create jobs in the short term by redressing current imbalances in the distribution of work. Also unlike other labor-saving devices, progressively reducing the hours of work makes a priceless good, free time, directly available to workers in ever greater abundance. The claim of a lump-of-labor fallacy is an unwarranted rationalization that obstructs serious discussion of the benefits of shortening work time.

NOTES

1 Schloss's article on piece-work was reprinted in his *Methods of Industrial Remuneration* (1894). In a review of the French translation of the book, F. Y. Edgeworth (1902) referred to Schloss as the expositor of the fallacy.
2 See, however, Feldstein (1967), who described and criticized the model more generally as the *traditional* specification of the production function for labor.
3 The estimates in this section are based on linear interpolation of values between the two optima. That is, given an output optimum, defined as one unit per hour at O hours per week, and a productivity optimum at P hours ($O > P$), the

output for any H hours, located between O and P, is calculated as: $O - (((O - H - 1)/2 + 1)(O - H)/(O - P))$. For example, given the Denison estimates for O and P, the estimated output at 42 hours would be $48.6 - (((48.6 - 33.9 - 1)/2 + 1)(48.6 - 42)/48.6 - 33.9)) = 46.89$ or 96.5 percent of the optimal output at 48.6 hours. The estimated output at 37.8 hours would be $48.6 - (((48.6 - 33.9 - 1)/2 + 1)(48.6 - 37.8)/48.6 - 33.9)) = 44.27$, or 91.1 percent of the optimal output.

4 The conversion of some part-time positions to full-time may be expected, as a secondary effect, to contribute a small further rise in productivity and hence reduce slightly the short-term employment gains (but potentially expand the long-term gains).

REFERENCES

Anon (1996) "Cranks and Proud of It," *Economist* 338(7949), 20 January: 86–87.

Beardsley, C. (1895) "The Effect of an Eight Hours' Day on Wages and the Unemployed," *Quarterly Journal of Economics* 9(4): 450–459.

Black, J. (1997) *Oxford Dictionary of Economics*, Oxford: Oxford University Press: 281.

Bosch, G. (1998) "The Reduction of Working Time, Pay and Employment," paper given at United Nations/DESA, New York.

Bye, R. T. (1927) *Principles of Economics*, New York: Alfred A. Knopf.

Chapman, S. J. (1909) "Hours of Labour," *The Economic Journal*, 19(75): 353–373.

Crane, D. (1993) *Canadian Dictionary of Business and Economics*, Toronto: Stoddart: 385.

Denison, E. F. (1962) *The Sources of Economic Growth in the United States and the Alternatives Before Us*, New York: Committee for Economic Development.

Edgeworth, F. Y. (1902) "Review of *Les Modes du Rémuneration du Travail*," *The Economic Journal* 12(46): 259–260.

Ehrenberg, R. G. (1971) *Fringe Benefits and Overtime Behavior: Theoretical and Econometric Analysis*, Lexington, MA: D.C. Heath.

Feldstein, M. S. (1967) "Specification of the Labour Input in the Aggregate Production Function," *The Review of Economic Studies* 34(4): 375–386.

Freeman, R. (1998) "Work-Sharing to Full Employment: Serious Option or Populist Fallacy?" in R. Freeman and P. Gottschalk (eds) *Generating Jobs: How to Increase Demand for Less-Skilled Workers*, New York: Russell Sage Foundation: 195–222.

Golden, L. M. (1992) "Unions, Nonwage Labor Costs, and the Character of Labor Market Adjustment," 1929–1987, *Quarterly Review of Economics and Finance* 32(2): 46–70.

Hart, R. A. (1987) *Working Time and Employment*, London: Allen and Unwin.

Hicks, J. R. (1932) *The Theory of Wages*, London: Macmillan.

Hoel, M. (1986) "Employment and Allocation Effects of Reducing the Length of the Workday," *Economica* 53(209): 75–85.

Hunt, J. (1996) *Has Work-Sharing Worked in Germany?* Working Paper 5724, Cambridge, MA: National Bureau of Economic Research.

_____ (1998) "Hours Reductions as Work-Sharing," *Brookings Papers on Economic Activity* (1): 339–382.

_____ (1999) "Has Work-Sharing Worked in Germany?" *Quarterly Journal of Economics* 114(1): 117–149.

Katz, L. (1998) "Comment and Discussion," *Brookings Papers on Economic Activity* (1): 370–382.

Layard, R., Nickell, S., and Jackman, R. (1991) *Unemployment: Macroeconomic Performance and the Labour Market*, Oxford: Oxford University Press.

Marshall, A. (1961) *Principles of Economics*, London: Macmillan, for the Royal Economic Society, 9th Edn.

McNulty, P. J. (1980) *The Origins and Development of Labor Economics: A Chapter in the History of Social Thought*, Cambridge, MA: MIT Press.

Nyland, C. (1989) *Reduced Working Time and the Management of Production*, Cambridge: Cambridge University Press.

Oi, W. (1962) "Labor as a Quasi-Fixed Factor," *Journal of Political Economy* 70(6): 538–555.

Osberg, L. (1997) "A Personal Reflection on the Collective Reflections," in *Collective Reflection: Report of the Advisory Committee on the Changing Workplace*, Ottawa: Human Resources Development Canada: 143–162.

Pfeffer, J. (1998) "Six Dangerous Myths about Pay," *Harvard Business Review* 76(3): 109–121.

Picot, G., Lin, Z., and Beach, C. (1995) "Recent Trends in Employer Payroll Taxes," *Canadian Economic Observer*, September: 3.1–3.24.

Pigou, A. C. (1952) *The Economics of Welfare*, London: Macmillan. 4th Edn.

Rae, J. (1891) *Contemporary Socialism*, London: Swan Sonnenschein, 2nd Edn.

_____ (1894) *Eight Hours for Work*, London: Macmillan.

Robbins, L. (1929) "The Economic Effects of Variations of Hours of Labour," *The Economic Journal* 39(153): 25–40.

Rutherford, D. (1992) *Dictionary of Economics*, London: Routledge: 276.

Samuelson, P. A. and Nordhaus, W. D. (1998) *Economics*, Boston: Irwin/McGraw-Hill, 16th Edn.

Schloss, D. F. (1891a) "Why Working-Men Dislike Piece-Work," *The Economic Review* 1(3): 312–326.

_____ (1891b) "The Jew as Workman," *Nineteenth Century* 29(1): 96–101.

_____ (1894) *Methods of Industrial Remuneration*, London: Williams and Norgate, 2nd Edn.

Statistics Canada (1997) *Labour Force Update: Hours of Work*, Ottawa: Minister of Industry.

US Bureau of Labor Statistics (1999) Persons at work in agriculture and nonagricultural industries by hours of work, October 1999. Available from: ftp://ftp.bls.gov/pub/special.requests/lf/cpseea23.txt [Accessed 11 November 1999].

US National Commission for Manpower Policy (1978) *Work Time and Employment: A Conference Report*, Washington, DC: USNCMP.

Walker, F. A. (1890) "The Eight-Hour Law Agitation," *The Atlantic Monthly* 65(392): 799–810.

Webb, S. and Cox, H. (1891) The Eight Hours Day, London: Walter Scott.

Wilson, J. (1871) "Economic Fallacies and Labour Utopias," *Quarterly Review* 131(261): 229–263.

13 Better timing?

Work schedule flexibility among US workers and policy directions

Lonnie Golden

The 1990s economic expansion in the USA has gone far to remedy the labor market problems of unemployment and the stagnation of real median wage rates. Yet, it has not yet solved the ill of mal-distributed hours of work. Many workers report a desire for greater flexibility in work hours at their current job, to reduce their work hours even for reduced pay, on a temporary or indefinite basis. Such "overemployment" is apparently growing, while continuing to dwell alongside underemployment among other workers. Both the incidence and extent of overemployment are likely to grow further in the USA as long as the number of dual-income households, family annual hours of work, and employment-to-population ratios continue to climb, and employer demand for hours per employee remains high. The ultimate solution lies in a fundamental restructuring of workplace practices and labor markets to deliver more temporal flexibility in ways preferred by workers.

A major first step toward achieving this would be fostering greater flexibility in the timing of workers' paid work hours each day or week. Worker sovereignty to alter their own daily starting and ending times of work or days worked is well-known to curb pressures on employees imposed by the time and role conflicts that arise when work and non-work responsibilities collide in the same block of time. To be sure, the extent of such daily schedule flexibility has been on the rise. Flexible scheduling of work is now available to over 27 percent of the US work force, up from 15 percent in 1991 (US BLS 1998). While this a noteworthy improvement, polls suggest the supply of such flexible schedules is lagging behind demand. Furthermore, it remains to be seen whether this is an ephemeral feature of a strong business cycle expansion or a permanent structural change in work organization.

The aim of this chapter is to systematically describe many of the current patterns and problems concerning work hours and work schedules. Such an understanding is essential before any country, such as the USA, can develop a coherent, national policy regarding hours of work. The first section creates a nomenclature and framework to analyze the various dimensions of working time and their impacts. It makes subtle but important distinctions between duration, variability, and timing (scheduling) and temporal flexibility of both the duration and timing of work hours. The next section describes the current distribution and differential access to flexible daily work scheduling (i.e., flexitime) by workers' various demographic characteristics and by industry and occupational sector, using 1997 US Census data. These data are then analyzed to estimate the probability that a worker with a given demographic or work characteristic has access to flexitime. The final section discusses the implications for policy. While there are virtually no national policy initiatives designed to directly promote more flexibility in hours or schedules in the USA, there are intriguing labor law reforms proposed that will impact on working time. Some proposals would expand opportunities and supports for temporary leaves. Others would allow private sector workers and employers to agree to future compensatory time in lieu of premium pay for overtime work beyond a 2-week average "standard," while widening the "exemption" of certain classifications of jobs from the overtime regulations.

The key empirical finding is that while many workers are gaining flexibility in the timing of their daily work schedules, access to flexible schedules remains uneven by characteristics of workers such as gender or race and by their jobs such as skill level, job status and hours status. Having flexible scheduling comes at the expense of working long average hours per week, or relocating to part-time or self-employment status or to "unsocial" evening shifts. Thus, workers must "pay" a steep price for greater schedule flexibility with foregone leisure or income. Proposed changes in the Fair Labor Standards Act (FLSA) are apt to be off-target in promoting either reduced overemployment or welfare-enhancing flexibility to the 73 percent of workers currently unable to access flexitime at their current jobs. A nuanced policy of delivering greater time sovereignty for workers must seek first to spread work schedule flexibility to more full-time jobs and to workers currently not sharing it because of their occupation, industry or other personal or labor market characteristics.

DISTINGUISHING DIMENSIONS OF HOURS: DURATION, TIMING, FLEXIBILITY, VARIABILITY

In the standard economists' model of the labor market, workers choose to work a given number of hours per week, given their compensation rate and the constraints imposed on them, including that of the number of hours per week required of the job by their employer. The volume of non-work time is assumed to add to worker well-being ("utility") either by providing self-directed leisure time, or time for self-producing household goods and services. If workers are unable to get as many hours of work and income as they would prefer at their current job, and would be willing to give up some hours of non-work time to get the additional income, they are considered to be underemployed.[1] Conversely, if they would be willing but are unable at their current job to give up some income to reduce their hours of work burden, they are termed overemployed.

The daily *timing* of available time for leisure or household production, in addition to the sheer volume of non-work time, may itself have a profound impact on an individual's well being. The daily and weekly scheduling of work, e.g., shop, office, school, class or store hours, as well as many non-work responsibilities, are often outside the direct control of the individual. To the extent scheduling a given number of hours of work interferes or conflicts with workers' ability to execute their other, non-work responsibilities, well-being is reduced. On the other hand, schedules that ease individuals' transition between work and non-work activities, or allow employees discretion to adjust the timing of work, contributes to well-being.

Also in the conventional economic model, a smoothly operating labor market will guarantee that if workers exhibit greater preference for more flexible schedules, employers will move to accommodate these preferences, so long as workers are willing to accept a lower wage in return, or save employers other costs (see Gunderson and Weiermeir 1988). Economists have devoted too little attention to the actual timing of work hours and the mismatches between employers' assigned schedules and workers' desired schedules, given constraints outside of their work lives (see Hamermesh 1999: 65).

A simple framework shows that workers usually have preferences regarding the time slot or interval I, the block of time in the course of a day over which work is scheduled. Even if their number of actual (H) and desired (H^*) hours are identical in each week over an entire time period, it matters whether the actual I is equal to their desired interval I^* each day. For example, a worker may prefer 8 hours each work day on a regular, predictable, traditional daily schedule. Yet, he/she may be scheduled to work 8 hours, but on a troublesome shift-time, where the starting (I_0) and ending (I_n) times deviate from the worker's preferred work schedule times, denoted by I^*, at starting and finishing times 0 and n. As an illustration, suppose $H = H^* = 8$ for all 5 days of the work week, but the worker's preferred daily schedule changes, having enrolled in a college course, to an earlier schedule, 7 am to 3 pm,

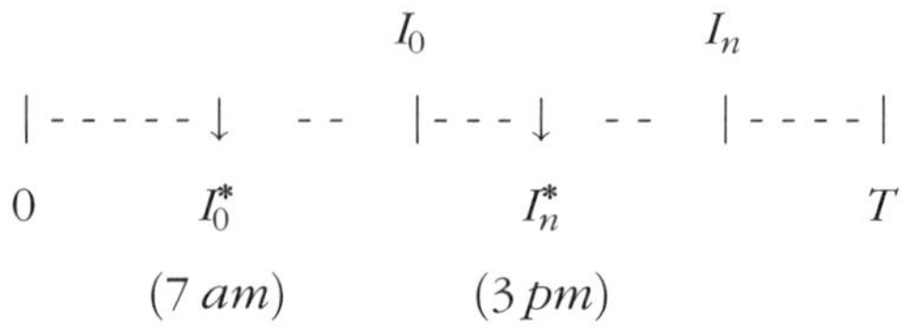

The degree of schedule flexibility can be represented by the expression,

$$\Delta I_t = \lambda(I_t^* - \overline{I_{t-1}}) \qquad 0 \leq \lambda \leq 1$$

The term λ captures the responsiveness of the actual daily I slot, toward the preferred daily schedule I^* in the case when I^* changes and thus deviates from the fixed schedule (I-bar). If λ is 1.0, then a worker has complete schedule flexibility, to accommodate their preference regarding timing. The degree of well-being lost by the worker each day due to an inflexible schedule is represented by the sum of the differences between actual and desired starting times (at 0) and ending times (at n).

Similarly, the degree of flexibility in the duration of hours is the term δ in

$$\Delta H_t = \delta(H_t^* - H_{t-1}) \qquad 0 \leq \delta \leq 1$$

The impact of working time dimensions on worker utility (U) is captured by

$$U = U[Y, L; \delta, \lambda, V]$$

Worker well-being increases not only in income (Y) and leisure time (L) variables, but in the speed with which H and I adjust dynamically toward changes in hours (H^*) or schedules (I^*) desired. Utility decreases in the undesired variability of hours (V).[2] Indeed, workers may be willing to trade off one aspect of working time for another. Workers may tolerate inflexible or unpredictable hours or schedules if these also involve relatively short work weeks. Conversely, they may accept long average work weeks if the daily timing becomes more open to their discretion.

Causes and consequences of work hours and schedules: an overview

Hours of work patterns per individual both determine the total level of market and non-market production, and are determined by it. Actual hours (H) as well as the total and specific uses of non-working, "leisure" time affect the macroeconomy via their effect on aggregate demand (AD) and aggregate supply (AS). The resulting levels of both market and non-market production then feed back into the hours of paid work demanded by employers (H^d) and desired by workers (H^*).[3] Overwork (H^d exceeding H^*), work time inflexibility and time-pressured "leisure" can come back later to haunt the macroeconomy's performance.[4] That is because it reduces the quantity (or quality) of time either for socially productive leisure, such as for parenting, volunteering or life-long learning, or of non-productive leisure, such as recuperation and shopping.

This framework also suggests that if better matches are made between employer required (H^d) and worker desired (H^*) work this may yield higher total production, on balance, even if reduces average actual hours (H). This is because reducing overemployment may stimulate average labor productivity per hour and thus AS. Reducing mismatches between employer scheduled intervals (I^d) desired by workers (I^*) can also improve total output, albeit more indirectly. First, to the extent that flexitime or individualized work schedules promotes productivity via increased work effort, longer term commitments to employment relationships, and less stress, role conflict or "on-the-job" leisure, output per hour or per worker will increase. Second, it removes daily obstacles that would otherwise hamper some opportunities for parenting, meal preparation, volunteering or other non-market goods and services production.

Employers offering of flexitime

Strikingly high proportions of employers report in surveys that they offer flexible work arrangements including flexible schedules. These range across various surveys from 53 percent to as high as 84 percent (Daniels 1997). These estimates are slightly higher than the last BLS survey of (10 345) employers, in 1989, which found flexitime (43 percent) to be the most prevalent type of flexible work arrangement offered as an employee benefit (US BLS 1992). Yet, even this lower estimate greatly overstates the prevalence of flexitime among workers. Polls conducted by consulting groups among client firms may exaggerate the extent to which employers have designed, implemented and promoted formal flexible scheduling programs among all their employees. For one reason, the surveys over-sample large firms which may tend to more widely offer flexitime. In addition, flexitime programs may be made available only to managerial and professional positions, or only temporarily, seasonally or experimentally (Kush and Stroh 1994). Moreover, most of the workers actually receiving flexitime are on informal rather than formal plans (US Department of Labor 1999) – about half the flexitime benefit programs are granted subject to managers' discretion (Romano 1994). Furthermore, a large share of employees (40 percent) fear, much more than hiring managers at firms (10 percent) believe, that using flexitime will damage their career prospects (Galinsky and Bond 1998). Finally, most (59 percent) women workers never ask their employer for flexible arrangements, since they assumed the answer would be no and their careers would be harmed by asking (US Department of Labor 1999).

There is still a great, unsatisfied demand for more flexible schedules (see Galinsky and Bond 1998, 1999). Nearly 92 percent of polled workers say they are concerned with having the flexibility in their work schedule to take care of family needs, including 38 percent of workers saying they are extremely concerned, and 37 percent saying they are very concerned. Workers rank as "important" receiving the flexibility in their work schedules to address family needs, such as emergency time off, unpaid leave, and flexible hours (*Work Trends* 1999). The survey finds that 14 percent of those workers looking for a new job cite more flexibility in the hours and days they can work as the chief reason for their search.

Thus, while access to flexitime has grown, most workers remain insufficiently privileged to take advantage of flexitime programs in practice. While supply of flexible schedules has grown, it has not kept pace with growing demand. This is despite evidence that temporal flexibility for employers in the duration of average work hours appears to be on the rise.[5] The excess demand for flexitime persists for three main reasons: the gradual encroachment of work into what had been typically non-work hours of the day, rising annual hours of work among families, and a dearth of supporting institutions in the workplace or labor market to resolve time conflicts.

There is some evidence that the traditional 9-to-5 work day has been spreading out, with the work day de-standardizing as work increasingly is being performed at the fringes of the traditional day (Presser 1995, 1999; Hamermesh 1999; see Bell and Hart 1998; Fagan 1999 for similar trends in the UK). Having flexitime, however, is quite distinct from a nonstandard schedule. The former is instituted by employers to accommodate worker preference and invariably is viewed by workers as favorable while the latter usually is involuntary. The following sections take advantage of largely neglected CPS supplement questions to focus on the availability of flexible daily work schedules and the underlying determinants of worker access to them, on the assumption that they are a desirable commodity.

FLEXIBLE SCHEDULES: FLEXIBILITY FOR MORE BUT DISTRIBUTION STILL SKEWED

The May 1997 Supplement to the CPS asks 48 000 respondents about the timing of their paid work activity. The total Supplement sample was 88 728 (of 135 116 total in the sample). Over 24 000 individuals administered the supplement questions are employed and thus can be combined with regular CPS observations regarding the employed individuals' detailed industry and occupation classification along with many demographic characteristics. The May 1997 CPS supplement contains a total of 52 "detailed" SIC industry and 45 "detailed" SOC occupation observations for workers, which are then collapsed into 23 "major" industries and 14 "major" occupations. The regular CPS also provides data regarding the length of workers' usual and actual daily hours worked. The supplementary questions begin by asking the typical starting and ending times of their work day for the employed individuals in the surveyed household. They are then asked if they have the ability to vary the starting or ending times of their usual work day (at half-hour intervals). Additional questions are asked regarding whether individuals work on a standard day shift or some other shift time.

The distribution of workers' typical daily starting and ending times are shown in Table 13.1. A surprisingly high proportion of workers, 40 percent, are usually still at work past 5:00 pm (although Table 13.1 does not specify what time each of these workers start their work day). Also, 28 percent of the workforce is at work by 7:30 am (although again it is unclear what time they typically finish their shift). Finally, approximately 10 percent of the workforce

Table 13.1 Distribution of usual starting and ending times of the work day, full-time wage and salary workers (ages 16 and over) in the USA, May 1997

		Beginning time		*Ending time*	
Total	*Time interval at work*	*Number of workers 90 549*	*Percent of workers 100*	*Number of workers 90 549*	*Percent of workers 100*
AM	12:30 to 1:29	84	0.1	569	0.6
	1:30 to 2:29	100	0.1	411	0.5
	2:30 to 3:29	179	0.2	245	0.3
	3:30 to 4:29	421	0.5	181	0.2
	4:30 to 5:29	1 509	1.7	231	0.3
	5:30 to 6:29	6 285	6.9	486	0.5
	5:30 to 5:59	768	0.8	51	0.1
	6:00 to 6:29	5 518	6.1	435	0.5
	6:30 to 7:29	19 099	21.1	1 517	1.7
	6:30 to 6:59	3 085	3.4	216	0.2
	7:00 to 7:29	16 014	17.7	1 302	1.4
	7:30 to 8:29	29 517	32.6	930	1.0
	7:30 to 7:59	8 189	9.0	319	0.4
	8:00 to 8:29	21 327	23.6	611	0.7
	8:30 to 9:29	12 068	13.3	182	0.2
	8:30 to 8:59	5 524	6.1	64	0.1
	9:00 to 9:29	6 544	7.2	117	0.1
	9:30 to 10:29	1 938	2.1	69	0.1
	10:30 to 11:29	762	0.8	92	0.1
	11:30 to 12:29	494	0.5	226	0.2
	AM PM				
PM	12:30 to 1:29	429	0.5	475	0.5
	1:30 to 2:29	868	1.0	1 706	1.9
	2:30 to 3:29	2 014	2.2	7 083	7.8
	2:30 to 2:59	389	0.4	1 804	2.0
	3:00 to 3:29	1 625	1.8	5 279	5.8
	3:30 to 4:29	1 380	1.5	15 903	17.6
	3:30 to 3:59	451	0.5	6 198	6.8
	4:00 to 4:29	929	1.0	9 705	10.7
	4:30 to 5:29	555	0.6	26 719	29.5
	4:30 to 4:59	163	0.2	7 767	8.6
	5:00 to 5:29	392	0.4	18 952	20.9
	5:30 to 6:29	450	0.5	11 867	13.1
	5:30 to 5:59	60	0.1	4 623	5.1
	6:00 to 6:29	390	0.4	7 244	8.0
	6:30 to 7:29	779	0.9	4 187	4.6
	7:30 to 8:29	766	0.8	1 861	2.1
	8:30 to 9:29	415	0.5	1 033	1.1
	9:30 to 10:29	514	0.6	1 058	1.2
	10:30 to 11:29	1 138	1.3	1 786	2.0
	11:30 to 12:29	478	0.5	1 515	1.7
Time varies		6 572	7.3	8 304	9.2
Actual time not available		1 734	1.9	1 913	2.0

Table 13.2 Proportions of full-time wage and salary workers on flexible and shift schedules, in May, 1985–1997, selected years and demographic groups

	Flexible schedules			
	1985	*1989*	*1991*	*1997*
Total	12.4%	11.9%	15.1%	27.6%
Gender				
Men	13.1%	12.9%	15.5%	28.7%
Women	11.3%	10.6%	14.5%	26.2%
Race				
White	12.8%	12.5%	15.5%	28.7%
Black	9.1%	8.2%	12.1%	20.1%
Hispanic	8.9%	9.0%	10.6%	18.4%

cannot specify their typical ending time of day, mainly because it is variable, somewhat greater than the percentage whose daily starting time is variable.

Table 13.2 shows the share of the total full-time work force with the ability to vary their daily schedules increased to over 27 percent. This is considerably higher than it had been in prior survey years, at 15 percent in 1991 and about 12 percent in 1985. A slightly greater proportion of men and whites have flexitime compared with women, blacks and Hispanics, as do workers in the prime child-bearing years. Substantial disparity in access to flexible work schedules exists by industry, and even more by occupational sector. By major industry, proportions range from a high of over 49 percent of the work force in "other professional services" and 42 percent in private households, to a low of about 19 percent in educational services and 13 percent in local government. By detailed occupation and industry data, in Table 13.3, there is even more variation by job type and sector. Even within manufacturing, there are some industries that have higher than average flexible scheduling, such as tobacco manufacturing, primary metals, professional equipment and miscellaneous manufacturing – at least double the rate for workers in textile and leather industries and stone/clay/glass and lumber. Other public administration well exceeds the rate found in hospitals, entertainment–recreation, utilities and other professional services industries.[6] The disparity of flexible scchedules among workers is more stark by occupational classification. The percentage with flexitime ranges from 11 percent (machine operators and tenders) up to over 60 percent for natural scientists and 77 percent for farm operators.

The frequency distribution of flexitime across ranges of usual weekly hours is "U-shaped." Only 22.6 percent of workers reporting usual 40 hours per week exactly have flexitime. This is distinctly lower than the 33 percent of those in both the 41–49 and the 35–39 hours brackets. Also, it is far below the 52 percent with flexitime who report averaging 50 or more hours. It falls well short of the 45 percent and 62 percent working 21–34 and 1–20 hours. Notwithstanding this, worker access to flexitime is positively correlated with usual work week length (with $p = 0.55$).

Table 13.3 Percentage of workers with flexible schedules by detailed industries, ranked

Rank	*% with flexible schedule*	*Detailed industry*	*Detailed occupation*	*% with flexible schedule*
1	63.9	Forestry/fisheries	Farm operators	77.9
2	62.3	Agric–other	Natural scientists	60.2
3	49.4	Other profl services	Lawyers and judges	58.6
4	47.5	Insurance/real estate	Sales reps, finance, bus. service	58.1
5	45.5	Agric services	Mathematical scientists	55.9
6	41.7	Priv household service	Teachers, college and university	54.6
7	39.8	Auto/repair	Forestry occupations	53.8
8	38.1	Human resource admin.	Other professional	50.3
9	37.5	Personal services	Sales reps, commodities, exc. retail	49.8
10	37.3	Business services	Engineers	47.9
11	36.7	Wholesale trade	Managers	47.9
12	35.8	Natl security/internal	Sales supervisors and proprietors	45.7
13	35.4	Entertainmt/recreatn	Sales related occupations	44.4
14	34.9	Construction	Other technicians	44.0
15	34.8	Printing/publishing	Financial records, processing	43.5
16	34.4	Other public admin	Private household service	43.3
17	34.1	Other retail trade	Health diagnosing occupations	42.6
18	33.0	Profl/photo/watches	Managmt related occup.	41.2
19	32.1	Petroleum/coal	Public administration	41.0
20	31.7	Chemicals	Farm workers	36.1
21	31.3	Communication	Personal service occupations	35.5
22	30.7	Miscellaneous manufacturing	Engineering, science technicians	33.1
23	30.5	Social services	Sales, retail & personal services	30.7
24	30.2	Aircraft	Construction trades	30.4
25	29.1	Other transport eqpmt	Supervisors – administrative support	29.3
26	29.0	Eating/drinking	Secretaries, stenographers, typists	27.1
27	28.6	Toys/sporting goods	Motor vehicle	27.0
28	28.2	Health services	Mechanics and repairers	24.7
29	28.2	Banking/finance	Other administrative support	24.3
30	26.3	Machinery-electrical	Health assessment and treating	23.3
31	26.3	Machinery-nonelectric	Food service occupations	22.1
32	26.1	Transportation	Cleaning and building service	21.2
33	24.1	Mining	Health technicians	20.6
34	22.8	Hospitals	Other precision production	19.9

Table 13.3 (Continued)

Rank	*% with flexible schedule*	*Detailed industry*	*Detailed occupation*	*% with flexible schedule*
35	22.2	Utilities	Construction labor	19.5
36	21.8	Lumber	Health service occupations	19.4
37	21.8	Stone/glass	Computer equipment operators	19.3
38	20.8	Furniture	Freight handlers	17.8
39	20.7	Justice/public order/safety	Protective service occupations	16.2
40	19.9	Fabricated metals	Other handlers and laborers	15.1
41	19.3	Educational services	Mail and message distributing	14.4
42	17.7	Food	Fabricators	13.9
43	16.9	Paper	Other	13.6
44	15.8	Motor vehicles	Teachers, except college and university	12.8
45	15.5	Rubber/plastic	Machine operators and tenders	11.1
46	15.4	Tobacco	Armed forces	0.0
47	14.4	Primary metals		
48	13.7	Apparel		
49	13.3	Leather		
50	10.0	Textiles		
51	0.0	Other metals		
52	0.0	Armed forces		

DIFFERENTIAL ACCESS TO FLEXIBLE WORK SCHEDULES

Several characteristics of workers themselves, and their jobs, significantly raise or lower the probability a worker in the sample will have flexitime hours. Whether a respondent reports they "have flexible work hours that allow them to vary or make changes in the time work begins and ends" may depend on four sets of factors: 1, personal characteristics such as gender, race, marital status and age; 2, human capital characteristics such as education level, or attending college; 3, job characteristics, such as the occupation and industry of employment, self-employment status, union membership; and 4, work hours status, such as usually full-time or part-time, actual average duration of weekly hours, working on a nonstandard (non-day) shift time schedule, and having variable work week lengths.[7]

Probit regression estimations were conducted by merging the micro-data from the CPS Supplement with information from the basic CPS questions. The key results of this statistical testing are reported in Table 13.4. The coefficient estimates for each variable, holding all else constant, the degree to which this characteristic changes the probability an individual responds affirmatively that they have the ability to vary their daily work

Table 13.4 Likelihood of having flexible start- and end-times, probit estimates: marginal effect of personal, work and hours characteristics[a]

	Long hours		*Standard hours*						*Shifts*		*Hours vary*	
Variable	*coeff.*	*z-stat.*	*coeff.*	*z-stat.*	*coeff.*	*z-stat.*	*coeff.*	*z-stat.*	*coeff.*	*z-stat.*	*coeff.*	*z-stat.*
Age	−0.0006	−0.19	0.0017	0.60	0.0024	0.82	0.0017	0.60	−0.0007	−0.25	−0.0112	
Age squared	0.0003	8.61	0.0003	7.59	0.0002	7.44	0.0002	7.50	0.0003	8.65	0.0004	11.93
PhD	0.4884	5.16	0.5209	5.49	0.4054	4.28	0.4205	4.44	0.4659	4.94	0.5548	5.81
Master	0.6181	15.21	0.6834	16.70	0.5086	12.26	0.5109	12.30	0.6426	16.02	0.7258	17.61
College	0.4327	13.73	0.4395	13.96	0.3683	11.47	0.3983	12.35	0.4106	13.12	0.4815	15.07
Associates	0.1476	3.69	0.1818	4.54	0.0866	2.14	0.0976	2.41	0.1368	3.42	0.2278	5.61
Some College	0.1374	4.34	0.1558	4.92	0.0580	1.79	0.0728	2.24	0.1515	4.84	0.1995	6.22
High School	0.0935	3.03	0.1205	3.91	0.0285	0.91	0.0329	1.05	0.0485	1.59	0.1267	4.04
Less than H.S.	−0.2013	−5.63	−0.1770	−4.94	−0.2794	−7.68	−0.2824	−7.75	−0.2428	−6.82	−0.1456	−4.01
Nonwhite	−0.5493	−29.25	−0.5508	−29.29	−0.5677	−30.12	−0.5752	−30.54	−0.5276	−27.98	−0.5962	−31.21
Female	−0.0712	−5.13	−0.0858	−6.15	−0.0668	−4.80	−0.0586	−4.20	−0.1093	−7.84	−0.0418	−2.97
Married	0.0773	5.56	0.0749	5.37	0.0818	5.86	0.0935	6.67	0.1062	7.61	0.0787	5.64
College student	0.3824	8.49	0.0452	0.00	0.3695	8.20	0.3570	7.91	0.3540	7.78	0.3932	8.71
Self-employed	1.0091	39.47	1.0130	39.65	0.9894	38.53	1.0120	39.45	1.1109	43.80	1.0148	39.86
Union member	0.0374	0.93	0.0715	1.77	0.0300	0.75	0.0259	0.65	0.0682	1.71	0.0888	2.19
Usual PT	1.2024	29.73	1.1132	27.24	1.1862	29.31	1.1595	28.60	1.1466	28.46	0.6603	15.04
StdDay	−0.2945	−19.70	−0.2449	−16.02	−0.2880	−19.28	−0.2748	−18.37				

Hours 50+	0.1806	10.95	0.0780	4.39	0.1249	7.37	0.0834	4.82			0.1555	8.58
Hours 41–49					−0.2880	−14.05	−0.3184	−15.42				
Hours 40			−0.2205	−15.35							−0.1455	−9.85
Hours 35–39							−0.3330	−12.68				
Hours Vary											0.6796	27.60
Evening									0.1552	4.66		
Night									−0.3628	−6.79		
Irregular									0.8302	30.26		
Occupation:												
Managerial	0.7584	4.87	0.7457	4.78			0.7799	5.04	0.6800	4.35	0.6354	4.04
Professional	0.5699	3.63	0.5624	3.57			0.5794	3.71	0.5147	3.26	0.4281	2.69
Technicians	0.6484	3.96	0.6659	4.05			0.6190	3.80	0.5653	3.44	0.5549	3.35
Sales	0.7492	4.83	0.7066	4.54			0.7613	4.93	0.7121	4.57	0.6014	3.83
AdminSupport	0.1991	1.28	0.1953	1.25			0.1631	1.05	0.1317	0.84	0.0502	0.32
Protective Service	0.1599	1.02	0.1126	0.72			0.1432	0.92	0.1717	1.09	0.1118	0.70
Other Service	0.3403	2.18	0.3409	2.18			0.3093	2.00	0.2943	1.88	0.2130	1.35
Craft	−0.2295	−1.45	−0.2087	−1.32			−0.2542	−1.62	−0.2302	−1.45	−0.2852	−1.79
Operators	0.1527	0.97	0.1360	0.86			0.1489	0.95	0.0987	0.62	0.0366	0.23
Transportation	0.0580	0.37	0.0489	0.31			0.0313	0.20	0.0401	0.25	−0.0249	−0.16
Laborers	0.8608	5.43	0.8287	5.21			0.8401	5.33	0.8387	5.27	0.6538	4.08
Constant	−1.2742	−7.62	−1.2389	−7.39			−1.1943	−7.17	−1.4494	−8.62	−1.1835	−7.00
Pseudo R^2	0.198		0.207		0.226		0.2080		0.2180		0.21	
χ^2	15 200		15 824		23 054		15 953		16 072		16 346	
n	56 982		56 982		88 728		56 982		56 982		56 982	
Log likelihood	−30 618		−30 306		−39 689		−30 241		−30 182		−30 046	

Note

a Dependent variable = 1 if able to vary start or end times of work.

scheduling.[8] The clear pattern that emerges from the empirical tests is that while many personal characteristics either significantly improve or diminish the likelihood of having schedule flexibility, access to such flexibility is also significantly affected by workers' job status and hours status. By usually working a part-time job, putting in very long hours – greater than 50 hours per week – or becoming self-employed, workers can gain more influence over the starting and ending times of work. In addition, workers in certain occupations may be able to gain more access to flexitime, although the number of detailed occupational classifications that significantly improve access to flexitime are exceeded by the number that lessen access to it.

Non-whites clearly have more limited access to flexitime, being about 50–60 percent less likely to be on flexitime work schedules. Being female also significantly reduces the probability of having flexitime, by roughly the same rate. However, women's lack of access appears to be attributable more to their occupational segregation. Access to flexible schedules tends to improve with age, suggesting seniority helps workers gain access to control over the timing of their work day. Finally, married workers are significantly more likely to have flexibility, although the magnitude is small, on the order of about 8 percent. A worker who is also currently attending college is more likely to be on a flexible schedule.

By major occupation type, managerial/professional, technical, sales, service (except household or protective) and handler/laborer positions consistently appear to have greater access to flexitime. However, if a worker's major industry location is taken into account, workers in professional, personal service and machine operator jobs do not gain access to schedule flexibility, because the location of their jobs preclude it. Craft occupations appear to yield less access to such flexibility, although this reduced likelihood is often not statistically significant.

When the major industry of jobs is accounted for, the six detailed occupational classifications that have greater access to flexitime are: other executive/administrative/managerial, freight/stock/material handlers, math and computer science professionals, farm labor and secretaries/typists and (somewhat for) supervisors and proprietors in sales occupations. Interestingly, there are thirteen detailed occupations that, in contrast, yield reduced likelihood of having flexitime coverage. For example, these include health assessment and treating, lawyers/judges, construction trades and construction laborers, fabricators/assemblers/inspectors/samplers and perhaps protective service jobs. Controlling for detailed industry, however, shows that supervisors of clericals, as well as protective service financial records processing, and food and building service and perhaps "other precision production" jobs have reduced access to flexitime.

Table 13.4 also shows that if a worker reports they usually work part-time, this is very positively associated with having flexitime (and the opposite for usually working full-time). A full-time worker's hours status is then broken down into hours ranges (with at least one omitted, to serve as a reference group). Working exactly 40 hours per week is associated with a relatively lower probability of having flexible schedules, on the order of 0.31 percent less likelihood. However, workers reporting to have worked 50 or more hours per week are significantly more likely to have flexible schedules, by an estimated 8–21 percent greater likelihood. Interestingly, this reward to longer hours workers of having more flexibility is not delivered to workers working in the 41–49 hours per week range. Thus, only workers who average 10 or more hours per day have greater chances of being able to alter the starting or ending times of their typical work day. This is reinforced by the fact that among all workers who usually work at least 35 hours, the average work week for those having flexible schedules is over 45.8 hours vis-à-vis 42.7 hours for those without such schedules – a discrepancy of over 3 hours per week to gain flexibility.[9]

Reporting that the usual number of hours cannot be specified because they typically vary week to week is strongly positively associated with having more flexibility in schedule. The Table 13.4 "Hours vary" column shows that having variable hours raises the likelihood of having flexible starting or ending times, by over 0.67 percentage points. This association is even stronger among the part-time workers whose weekly hours vary. Workers appear to be enduring unpredictable work week duration in order to gain an ability to alter their daily starting or ending work times.

Being self-employed rather than a payroll employee more than doubles the likelihood a worker has the ability to vary his/her own start and end times of work. Schedule flexibility is clearly a major draw for becoming self-employed, even though their average duration of hours is relatively longer than that of payroll employees (Boden 1999). Working in government reduces the likelihood of having flexible schedules. This is somewhat surprising given the current legality for state and local governments, if agreed upon by individuals or collective bargaining agents, to substitute compensatory time in lieu of pay for overtime hours. Being a union member may somewhat improve worker access to flextime. This runs counter to assumptions and findings that unionism is associated with less individualized control over work time (for example, Duncan and Stafford 1982).

Working on a "standard" day schedule reduces the likelihood that a worker has a flexible work schedule by between 0.25 and 0.29 percentage points. Those working an evening shift do improve their access to scheduling flexibility, as do those whose shift is irregular, but those working the night shift actually have reduced likelihood of flexible times. Having "hourly" pay status appears to diminish a worker's access to flexible schedules. However, being of "non-hourly worker," such as salaried, status does not appear to be significantly related to the likelihood of having flexitime.

CONCLUSIONS AND IMPLICATIONS FOR A NATIONAL WORK HOURS POLICY

The flexibility of daily work schedules is rising across most types of jobs. But access to flexible starting and ending times remains uneven. It is noticeably higher in occupations and industries marked by higher-skilled work or lower unemployment. Having a flexible schedule is less likely for non-whites, women, unmarried, relatively less-educated and public sector employed individuals, all else constant. The findings suggest that workers can gain greater control over the timing of their daily hours if they are willing to endure very long work weeks (50 or more hours). This may also be achieved if they work regularly on evening or irregular shifts, work an unpredictable number of hours each week, or shift to part-time or self-employment status. Workers desiring greater access to flexitime may have to endure either a sacrifice of foregone leisure time, or transition to a non-standard job status, which is associated with both current and long-term reductions in income (Ferber and Waldfogel 1998). Otherwise, workers wishing to gain more flexible schedules must make longer term mobility decisions such as entering different occupations (managerial, professional, technical, sales, laborer/helper/cleaner and handler jobs and perhaps service (except protective and household)). This suggests workers on full-time "standard" work weeks face a dilemma, forced to sacrifice either compensation or valuable leisure hours to have an adjustable work day length.

Flexibility appears to be occurring mainly in the stretching out of the timing at the beginning and end of the typical work day. With the declining incidence of working a standard work week or work day, it begs the question of what will fill the void left by this destandardization? If indeed there has been a structural change toward longer hours of paid work (demanded and/or supplied) per worker, even if the corresponding increase in schedule flexibility is a permanent rather than a temporary product of a cyclical upturn, then what is the appropriate policy response?[10] A re-standardization that applies a uniform, one-size-fits-all standard work week may compromise too greatly the increasingly diverse interests of today's post-breadwinner model of working households. Since workers clearly harbor a preference for greater variety and adjustability in work duration and schedules, what is needed to better accommodate such households is a fuller continuum of work time and schedule options (see Clarkberg 1999). The early 20th century witnessed the Taylorization of work processes, which viewed the worker as one cog in the production processes' capital, whose productivity could be physically enhanced or exhausted. Twenty-first-century organization and public policy now call for a "tailorization" of work, customizing work hours to workers who are viewed more as whole persons seeking work–life balance according to their rhythms and constraints.

The twofold challenge for policymakers who seek improved flexibility for individuals, working families, organizations and the labor market remains to foster structural changes that, as a first step, allow a greater number of full-time workers on the "standard" work week to vary the timing of their work day. Policy must not simply seek to deliver greater schedule flexibility generally, say through tax incentives to subsidize organizations which adopt flexitime as a tax exempt employee benefit. It must target particularly those sets of workers who are currently not sharing in its wider availability because of their occupation, industry, other personal or labor market characteristics, or because they are currently scheduled for a standard 40-hour work week.

Extending flexitime to more workers at their current jobs and workplaces may be aided by spreading recent, innovative collective bargaining contract provisions, human resource management "best practice" and new national policies. Some recently negotiated collective bargaining contracts include the requirement that each employee must be at the work site for no more than its designated "core hours." Another grants workers the ability to excuse themselves from working compulsory overtime, when feasible, so long as another appropriate employee is available.[11] Progressive private sector best practice workplaces include the "paid time off banking," where firms pool together all vacation, holiday, sick leave and personal times, and allow employees to use the time off at their own discretion for whichever purpose, without diminishing the sum total paid time off in their previously separate compartments. In addition, some employers allow employees to donate to fellow employees in dire need of time off but lacking their own sick leave or vacation time.

The Administration of President Bill Clinton has attempted to make the US Federal Government a public sector model for other public and private sector organizations to follow. This includes the recent decree to allow Federal workers to use their paid sick leave time to attend to their sick children. There also are Administration and Congressional proposals regarding the extension of the Family and Medical Leave Act (FMLA) which would grant workers an entitlement to a number of hours per year for unpaid time off. Very similar legislation has passed at the state level. Massachusetts' Time Off for Small Necessities law allows eligible employees to take up to 24 hours of additional leave in a 12-month period in increments to participate in school activities of a son or daughter or to accompany a son or daughter (or elderly relative) to routine medical or dental appointments.

Finally, there are pending Congressional proposals to reform the Fair Labor Standards Act (FLSA) which standardized the 40-hour work week and requires overtime premium pay for all workers not exempt from its coverage.[12] The main "reform" is to allow payment in the form of future compensatory time off in lieu of cash payment for overtime hours performed by private sector employees, at the premium time-and-a-half rate, if agreed to by individuals or collective bargaining representatives. Employees would be permitted to use their comp time after making a request, provided it does not unduly disrupt the operations of the employer. A similar, US Senate version of the bill contains an additional provision that would change the standard work pay period from 40 weekly to 80 biweekly hours, i.e., to permit more variable work week lengths (with 50 hours permissible in a given week without requiring either premium pay or comp time).[13] Critics maintain that to make reform truly live up to its billing of providing "flexibility for working families" it should include a range of additional amendments, and expand rather than contract the scope of occupations and perhaps industries covered by an hours standard.[14] A policy of using overtime deregulation runs the risk of actually making workplaces more family unfriendly than friendly, thus harming worker "utility" on balance. This is because it is likely to drive up employer demand for average overtime hours per employee (due to the reduced short-run marginal cost of overtime), make work weeks and thus schedules more unpredictable, and does not legally grant workers the added sovereignty they need in selecting the comp time option and the timing of when hours can be used.

Two general tasks remain for a policy designed to improve worker welfare and the social economy. One is to extend much needed and much valued work schedule flexibility to the remaining 73 percent of workers still deprived of basic flexitime at their current jobs. In addition, it should eliminate the need for workers to continue to endure long weekly hours or make the costly transition to part-time or self-employment status to attain work schedule flexibility.

NOTES

1 Multiple-job holding is a sign of underemployment at current jobs. It soared in the 1980s, climbing to 6 percent of the work force in the 1990s (Stinson 1997).

2 See Golden (1999a) for a description of the variability (V) of hours concept.

3 See Golden (1999b) for a diagrammatic presentation of these recursive processes. The range of economic factors that influence the desired hours of labor supply per week is discussed in Idson and Robbins (1991), Bell and Freeman (1995), and Eastman (1998). Forces behind employer demand for hours per week are covered in Gunderson and Weiermair (1988), Schor (1994), Landers, Rebitzer, and Taylor (1996), and Golden (1999a).

4 The incidence of overemployment is rising, now up to between 13 percent and 17 percent (Schor 1994) or perhaps as high as 23 percent of the work force (Golden 1999b), using data from Galinsky and Bond (1998) as compared to earlier US BLS estimates of 8 percent (Shank 1986). In the UK, a country whose work hour pattern and trend resembles the USA, overemployment has been estimated as high as a third of male manual workers, by an estimated 4.3 hours per week (Stewart and Swaffield 1997). The steep rising trend line of average annual hours among all families in the 1980s and its tapering off in the 1990s (Rones, Ilg, and Gardner, 1997; Bluestone and Rose, 1998; Mishel, Bernstein, and Schmitt, 1999) may actually understate the incidence of overemployment, because annual family hours are climbing among middle and higher income families but falling in the lowest income quintile of families.

5 The responsiveness of average work hours to a concurrent fluctuation in the demand for output has been increasing, among US manufacturing industries, since 1979 (Glosser and Golden 1999). Variability of hours is higher among the

contingent and "nonstandard" work force (Belman and Golden 2000) and is likely gaining in part because these types of job have been escalating.

6 The FWI survey of firms (Galinsky and Bond 1998) generally is consistent with this differential pattern of flexitime by industry.

7 Having hours vary is correlated positively with usually part-time status, $p = 0.44$ (but is zero with usually full-time). This suggests part-timers appear to be more prone to having variable work weeks. Having flexitime and variable hours correlate (0.24), as does having variable daily ending times (0.30) – most strongly in sales, crafts and farming occupations.

8 R^2 of the estimated model was in the range of 0.19–0.24, depending on controls used.

9 This discrepancy is larger when actual rather than usual weekly hours are examined.

10 There is an inverse relationship between industry unemployment and flexitime – the correlation coefficient is −0.30. Thus, a labor shortage conditions gives rise to flexitime, while a labor surplus stifles it. Growth in flexitime is partly a cyclical phenomenon.

11 This is the Communications Workers of America agreement with BellSouth Telecommunications, and Newspapers Guild #35 with BNA, respectively. The International Brotherhood of Electrical Workers Local 1245 negotiated flexible start and end times with Pacific Gas and Electric Hayward Administrative Services. Others unions have negotiated voluntary reduced time arrangements, such as that between the Service Employees International Union Local 715 and Santa Clara and San Mateo Counties, CA. Members may request a reduction in their work hours of 1 percent, 2 percent, 5 percent, 10 percent, or 20 percent, for up to six months, while otherwise keeping regular full-time status (*Labor Project for Working Families* 1998).

12 The latest incarnation of the legislation bill is entitled, the "Working Families Flexibility Act of 1999," HR 1380, and is S-4 in the US Senate.

13 Other features of the law include that an agreement to receive comp time must be *before* the work is performed, and by employees who have worked at least 1000 hours for their employer continuously. The employer can cancel the comp time option upon 30 days notice, and employees cannot accrue more than 160 hours of credits.

14 Schor (1994), Economic Policy Institute (1997), Golden (1999a) and Walsh (1999) critique the pending FLSA overtime reform proposals, and propose some provisions designed to be more protective of worker rights and safeguard against potential pitfalls. Congressional proposals include creation of a new, exempt classification of "knowledge workers" (US GAO 1999).

REFERENCES

Bell, D. and Hart, R. (1998) "Working Time in Great Britain, 1975–94: Evidence from the New Earnings Survey Panel Data," *Journal of the Royal Statistical Society* 161 (part 3): 327–348.

Bell, L. and Freeman, R. (1995) "Why Do Americans and Germans Work Different Hours?" in F. Buttler, W. Franz, R. Shettkat and D. Soskice (eds), *Institutional Frameworks and Labor Market Performance: Comparative Views on the U.S. and German Economies*, London: Routledge: 101–131.

Belman, D. and Golden, L. (2000) "Contingent and Nonstandard Work Arrangements in The United States: Dispersion and Contrasts by Industry, Occupation and Job

Type," in F. Carré, M. Ferber, L. Golden, and S. Herzenberg (eds) *Nonstandard Work: The Nature and Challenge of Emerging Employment Arrangements*, Ithaca, NY: ILR Press, in press.

Bluestone, B. and Rose, S. (1998) "Macroeconomics of Work Time," *Review of Social Economy* 56(4): 425–441.

Boden, R. (1999) "Flexible Working Hours, Family Responsibilities and Female Self-Employment: Gender Differences in Self-Employment Selection," *American Journal of Economics and Sociology* 58(1): 71–83.

Clarkberg, M. (1999) "The Time-Squeeze in American Families: From Causes to Solutions," in *Futurework: Trends and Challenges for Work in the 21st Century*, US Department of Labor.

Daniels, S. (1997) "Flexible Hours, Telecommuting Increasing," *National Underwriting* 101(35): 23.

Duncan, G. and Stafford, F. (1982) "Do Union Members Receive Compensating Wage Differentials? Reply," *American Economic Review* 72(4): 868–872.

Eastman, W. (1998) "Working for Position: Women, Men, and Managerial Work Hours," *Industrial Relations* 37(1): 51–66.

Economic Policy Institute (EPI) (1997) *Family Friend or Foe? Working Time, Flexibility and the Fair Labor Standards Act*, Briefing Paper.

Fagan, C. (1999) "The Temporal Re-Organization of Employment and the Rhythm of Household Schedules," paper presented at the 7th International Seminar on Working Time, February 18–20, Gelsenkirchen, Germany.

Ferber, M. and Waldfogel, J. (1998) "The Long-Term Consequences of Non-standard Work," *Monthly Labor Review* 121(5): 3–12.

Galinsky, E. and Bond, J. T. (1998) *The National Study of the Changing Work Force*, New York: Families and Work Institute.

_____ (eds) (1999) *The 1998 Business Work-Life Study: A Sourcebook*, New York: Families and Work Institute.

Glosser, S. and Golden, L. (1999) "Labor Flexibility in U.S. Manufacturing Industries: Emerging Dynamic Patterns of Adjustment in Work Hours and Employment and Their Likely Causes," draft paper, February.

Golden, L. (1999a) "Projected Labor Market Consequences of Reforming the U.S. Overtime Hours Law," in G. De Geest, J. Siegers, and R. Van den Bergh (eds), *Law and Economics and the Labour Market*, Cheltenham, UK: Edward Elgar: 423–454.

_____ (1999b) "Integrating Social Economics into Analysis of the Labor Market: Causes and Consequences of Work and Leisure as an Application," in E. O'Boyle (ed.), *Teaching the Social Economics Way of Thinking: Selected Papers from the Ninth World Congress of the Association for Social Economics*, Mellen Studies Economics Vol. 4, Lewiston: Edward Mellen Press: 423–454.

Gunderson, M. and Weiermair, K. (1988) "Labor Market Rigidities: Economic Analysis of Alternative Work Schedules Including Overtime Restrictions," in G. Dlugo, W. Doron, and K. Weiermair (eds), *Management Under Differing Labour Market and Employment Systems*, Berlin: Walter de Gruyter: 153–163.

Hamermesh, D. (1999) "The Timing Of Work Over Time," *The Economic Journal* 109(452): 37–66.

Idson, T. and Robbins, P. K. (1991) "Determinants of Voluntary Overtime Decisions," *Economic Inquiry* 29(1): 79–91.

Kush, K. and Stroh, L. (1994) "Flextime: Myth or Reality?" *Business Horizons* 37(4): 51.

Landers, R., Rebitzer, J., and Taylor, L. (1996) "Rat Race Redux: Adverse Selection In The Determination Of Work Hours In Law Firms, *American Economic Review* 86(3): 329–348.

Labor Project for Working Families (1998) 6(4), Fall.

Mishel, L., Bernstein, J., and Schmitt, J. (1999) *The State of Working America: 1998/99*, Ithaca, NY: ILR Press; [www.epinet.org/fids05.html].

Presser, H. (1995) "Job, Family and Gender: Determinants of Nonstandard Work Schedules Among Employed Americans in 1991," *Demography* 32(4): 577–598.

_____ (1999) "Toward a 24-Hour Economy," *Science* 284: 1778–79.

Romano, C. (1994) "What is Your Flexibility Factor?" *Management Review* (January): 9.

Rones, P., Ilg, R., and Gardner, J. (1997) "Trends in Hours of Work Since the Mid-1970s," *Monthly Labor Review* 120(4): 3–14.

Schor, J. (1994) "Worktime in a Contemporary Context: Amending the FLSA," *Chicago-Kent Law* 70(1): 157–172.

Shank, S. (1986) "Preferred Hours of Work and Corresponding Earnings," *Monthly Labor Review* 109(11): 40–44.

Stewart, M. B. and Swaffield, J. K. (1997) "Constraints on the Desired Hours of Work of British Men," *The Economic Journal* 107(3): 520–535.

Stinson, J. F. (1997) "New Data on Multiple Jobholding Available from the CPS," *Monthly Labor Review* 120(3): 3–8.

US BLS (1992) "Workers on Flexible and Shift Schedules in 1991," *BLS News*, August 14, US Department of Labor, Bureau of Labor Statistics.

_____ (1998) "Workers on Flexible and Shift Schedules in 1997," *BLS News*, March 26, US Department of Labor, Bureau of Labor Statistics.

US Department of Labor (1999) "Futurework - Trends and Challenges for Work in the 21st Century, Part 3: Work And Family: Flexibility On The Job." Available at www.dol.gov/dol/asp/public/futurework/report.htm.

US GAO (1999) *Fair Labor Standard Act: White Collar Exemptions in the Modern Work Place*, GAO/HEHS- 99-164, Report to the Subcommittee on Workforce Protections, Committee on Education and the Workforce, US House of Representatives, General Accounting Office.

Walsh, D. J. (1999) "The FLSA Comp Time Controversy: Fostering Flexibility or Diminishing Worker Rights?," *Berkeley Journal of Employment and Labor Law* 20: 74–137.

Work Trends: America's Attitudes About Work, Employers, and Government (1999) The John J. Heldrich Center for Workforce Development at Rutgers University and Center for Survey Research at University of Connecticut, 7(1).

14 The social implications of European work time policies

Promoting gender equity?

Ellen Mutari and Deborah M. Figart

Contrary to the assumptions of neoclassical economics, feminist political economists view time spent in the labor force not simply as a disutility but as a means of accessing resources that bestow power in both the public and private sphere. Conversely, non-income producing time is not necessarily leisure; the unpaid work of families is an integral aspect of economic life. Social norms, as well as neoclassical theory, have advocated specialization in one or the other of these economic roles: a male breadwinner supporting a family and a spouse whose primary responsibility was unpaid work in the home.[1] While neoclassical economists view such specialization and trade as efficient, feminist political economists argue that the gender division of labor between paid and unpaid labor promotes inequity between men and women.

Gender relations[2] with regard to work time allocation have undergone periods of both stability and transition. During the post-war period, the standardization of a 40-hour work week in many industrialized countries institutionalized a vision of a full-time worker with limited involvement in domestic and caring labor, especially during weekdays. This organization of work time suited the dominant view of how men's and women's lives should be organized. Recent change and cross-country variation in work time policies afford an opportunity to investigate how the social reorganization of time could promote gender equity and the redistribution of paid and unpaid work. As work time is destandardized, some economies are creating alternatives to the full-time worker as a breadwinner but not a care-giver. However, in other countries a new form of gender inequity has developed. What differentiates gender roles in not *whether* individuals have a job but the *amount of time* spent in paid employment, while women's responsibility for the unpaid work of families remains relatively unchanged. For social economists and other scholars concerned with economic and social justice, these social implications of work time may be as crucial as issues of job creation.

This chapter integrates comparative feminist scholarship on welfare state regimes and an analysis of European work time policies to identify four distinct regimes of work time. Previous comparative studies of regime types, both feminist and mainstream, have concentrated on the state's labor market interventions and provision of social services. Clusters of policies may reflect a strong commitment to free market forces (liberal regimes), a universal guarantee of equal citizenship (social democratic regimes), or a rigid class system perpetuated through a strong state (conservative-corporatist regimes). In *The Three Worlds of Welfare Capitalism*, Gøsta Esping-Andersen (1990) created this typology of welfare state regimes, based upon three dimensions of state policy: state–market relations, degrees of stratification, and the degree of "decommodification" of labor through state provision of what he termed "social citizenship rights." Social citizenship rights are welfare state provisions that provide economic security against the harsh vicissitudes of the market.[3]

As noted by Ann Orloff (1996), feminists have critiqued Esping-Andersen for his singular emphasis on class as the basis of political agency. Not only have feminist scholars documented the gendered impact of social policies, they have also expanded the types of social policy under discussion. Specifically, these researchers have examined state–market relations in the provision of child care and other services that affect the organization of social reproduction and caring labor. However, this feminist scholarship has continued to concentrate on the role of the state in institutionalizing particular models of gender relations.

Our contribution, by focusing on work time, moves beyond the emphasis on state policies to consider other generalized social practices. Work time is indeed circumscribed by regulations affecting maximum hours or part-time employment. In fact, we have chosen to focus on member countries of the European Union (EU) because of recent policy initiatives, described below, to harmonize work time policies. However, work time practices are also defined in other institutional arenas that make up a country's political economy such as the bargaining table, corporate boardrooms, and households.

The comparative method that analyzes regime types has been underutilized in appraising social practices such as work time. A notable exception is a comprehensive study of national work time regimes by Jill Rubery, Mark Smith, and Colette Fagan (1998). These authors examine a range of flexible work time policies and practices in twelve of the member countries of the European Union.[4] The twelve countries are clustered into four (unnamed) groups or "regimes" based on the extent of practices that promote or impede equal opportunities. However, as the authors note, their methodology does not permit weighting of the relative importance of various work time practices nor the societal context that provides meaning for the practices. Therefore, the clusters contain "odd couples" such as Greece and the United Kingdom, both identified as long hours regimes yet diametrically different in the extent of labor force participation and part-time employment among married women. In order to avoid these limitations, we have chosen to narrow our focus to flexibility in the number of work hours and to embed our empirical analysis in a cultural and institutional context drawn from secondary research.

Following an overview of European policy initiatives regarding work time, the ensuing sections present our "work time regime" typology. National institutions and culture continue to differentiate work time practices despite the harmonization of European social policy. First, we examine the gendered organization of working time that combines part-time employment for married women with long hours of work for men. Second, we briefly examine alternative methods of structuring full-time employment. The four work time regimes are: (1) male breadwinner (Greece, Italy, Spain, and Portugal); (2) liberal flexibilization (United Kingdom and Ireland); (3) solidaristic gender equity (Denmark, France, Belgium, and Finland); and (4) high road flexibilization. We also identify a fifth case – countries that are experiencing "transitional flexibilization" – including the Netherlands, Sweden, Germany, Austria, and Luxembourg. We find greater gender equity in countries with shorter work week policies than those with diverse full-time schedules.

THE BIFURCATION OF POLICY

For many countries, the first step toward more flexibility in work hours is greater differentiation, either more short-hours jobs or increasingly long hours for full-time workers. Both part-time and overtime are effective means for employers to adjust total hours worked in order to respond to fluctuations in demand, while restraining labor costs. Increasing current employees' usual hours reduces the relative fixed costs of new hires. Also, part-timers' schedules can be more easily arranged to cover peak hours or temporarily extend hours of operation. Frequently, however, the employer's choice of work hours strategy is associated with the existing gender composition of the firm, industry, or occupation's work force, which may reflect underlying social norms regarding gender roles (Meulders, Plasman, and Plasman 1997; Perrons 1998). The lack of available child care forces most dual-earner families to rely on private resources, encouraging women, the primary care-givers, to accept part-time jobs (Daune-Richard 1998). Further, employers consider social norms associated with the labor pool from which they draw their employees when setting policies such as hours. Discussions of long-hours and short-hours jobs therefore must be linked in order to fully appreciate the gendered nature of contemporary flexibility strategies.

The European Union (EU) has instituted a bifurcated, rather than integrated, policy toward working time flexibility. Two legislative mandates effectively separate the regulation of overtime for full-time employees from the regulation and promotion of part-time employment. The gender implications of overtime regulations have been left unexamined, while discussions of part-time jobs focus primarily on women and other marginalized workers such as young men in school or older men nearing retirement.

The Council of the EU adopted a directive "concerning certain aspects of the organization of working time" on November 23, 1993. The directive was intended to encourage member states to establish policies promoting flexible working time as well as to provide some regulatory standards. The Working Time Directive establishes minimum health and safety standards for the organization of working time, including periods of daily rest, weekly rest, and annual leave, breaks, and maximum weekly working time. Annualization of hours, a policy articulated in Article 6, allows employees to work overtime so long as their weekly hours add up to a national standard that is no more than 48 hours, but averaged over a longer time period (Council Directive 1993).[5] For employer organizations, the annualization of hours option was a priority. The Working Time Directive did not contain strong language on reductions in the standard work week, a priority of the labor movement and some feminist advocates. The language of the directive is silent on its gender and/or family implications.

This was followed by passage of a separate directive regulating part-time work in 1997. Although phrased in gender-neutral language, one of the purposes explicitly stated in the directive is to enable workers to "reconcile professional and family life." The Directive on Part-Time Work (Council Directive 1997) was one of the first directives to be passed under the Social Protocol instituted by the Treaty of Amsterdam earlier that year. The three organizations representing European social partners (employers, unions, and the state as employer in public enterprises) hammered out a "framework agreement" that was then adopted by the European Council of Ministers ("Social Policy State of Play" 1998).[6] The framework agreement, and the ensuing directive, establish a principle of non-discrimination against part-time workers. Employment benefits and social security provisions that are conditioned on employment would have to be extended to part-timers, on a *pro rata* basis where appropriate. There is an exemption where "differential treatment is justified on objective grounds" but it is too soon to determine how this will be interpreted in practice. The directive also contains language encouraging employers to create more part-time jobs and to facilitate transitions between full- and part-time status where possible. The Part-Time Directive was welcomed by many advocates for gender equity who believed that raising the pay and working conditions in part-time jobs is one way to encourage men to choose them (see, for example, Gregory and O'Reilly 1996; O'Reilly and Fagan 1998).

The two working time directives are still in the process of implementation by the fifteen individual member states. The social implications of these twin directives are clearer when their cumulative impact is considered. If implementation of the Part-Time Directive raises the pay and working conditions of part-time jobs while working time reforms lower the hours in full-time jobs, these two directives taken together could create a new model for gender equity in work time. On the other hand, the 1993 Working Time Directive contains a provision allowing annualization of hours, that is, permitting employers to use overtime beyond the EU limits if it is used as part of hours-averaging schemes. This undermines the restrictions on

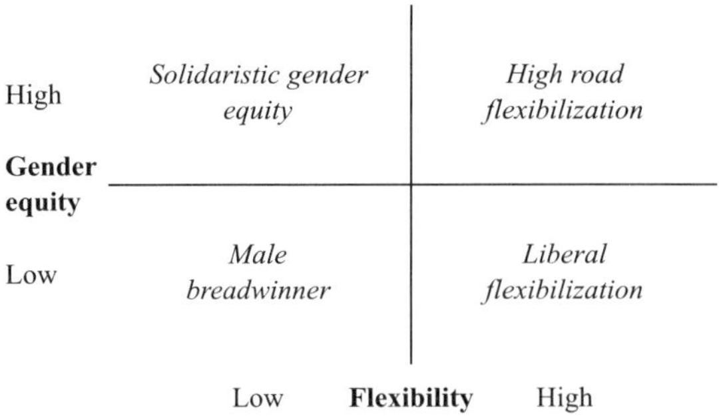

Figure 14.1 Alternative work time regimes.

overtime that were long part of collective negotiations and public policies in countries such as Germany and France (Figart and Mutari 1998). Prior regulations in most member states had already set statutory limits to overtime (ILO 1995: Table 2). However, the new, expanded reference period for calculating average weekly hours could implicitly lower standards and facilitate long work schedules. Countries such as Denmark, for example, are beginning to witness the Anglo-American pattern of long hours for men (Drew and Emerek 1998). There is strong evidence that European unification is pressuring countries to harmonize down, that is, to deregulate their labor markets in the manner of liberal welfare states such as the UK and USA (Plantenga 1997; Bruegel and Perrons 1998; Mazey 1998). Finally, without other measures to redistribute household labor, such as state support for child care, part-time jobs, even under a nondiscrimination policy, are likely to remain the province of women, young men in school, and older men nearing retirement.

EUROPEAN WORK TIME REGIMES

The bifurcation of work time policy could reinforce a gendered organization of work time that is already apparent in some EU countries. We distinguish four types of Work Time Regimes by their degree of *flexibility* and of *gender equity* in the number of work hours (see Figure 14.1). There are three, separate dimensions to flexibility: the proportion of workers working a "standard" work week (defined as the mode of usual weekly hours); the proportion usually working "overtime" (beyond 40 hours); and the extent of part-time work in the labor force. Gender equity also has at least three dimensions. First, the labor force participation rates of men and women should be relatively equal. Second, men and women should be similarly distributed across possible work schedules. Third, long hours jobs should be kept to a minimum so that breadwinners can also be care-givers.

These criteria for gender equity in work hours are grounded in the theoretical work of Nancy Fraser (1997). Fraser distinguishes three approaches to gender equity. A universal-breadwinner model promotes women's employment while reallocating child and elder care to the public sector or the market. The aim is to bring women's lives closer to a male standard. A care-giver-parity model seeks to reduce the costs women bear for maintaining their care-giving roles in the family. Fraser notes that paid family leave and flexible work practices such as part-time employment and flexitime provide support for women's unpaid work. However, Fraser also evokes a third, more comprehensive form of gender equity based on both men and women participating in paid employment and caring labor. She terms this preferred strategy a universal-care-giver model. Our assessment of work time policies is posited on whether they foster this universal-care-giver model of gender equity.

Two work time regimes exhibit low flexibilization of work hours. The male breadwinner work time regime, in the southwest quadrant of Figure 14.1, is low in both flexibilization and gender equity. In these countries, the so-called "male-model" of a long work week is linked with low labor force participation rates among married women and relatively few opportunities for either gender to combine paid employment with caring labor in the home. In contrast, a solidaristic gender equity work time regime creates greater gender equity in the labor market by changing social norms concerning work time. This entails a shortening of the *standard* work week, providing more opportunity for both men and women to participate in the labor market and care-giving, without having to resort to taking a part-time job. We have chosen the adjective "solidaristic" to convey the commonality of men's and women's interests and responsibilities, as well as the solidification of new social norms, in these countries.

The last two work time regimes may be considered the "low road" and the "high road" to labor market flexibility.[7] The low road is characterized by high flexibility with low gender equity. We designate this situation a liberal flexibilization work time regime, found in the southeast quadrant of Figure 14.1. This name reflects the congruence between Esping-Andersen's liberal welfare state regime and a particular approach to flexible work hours. In a deregulated labor market, the institutionalization of flexible work hours tends to reflect and reinforce the prevailing gender norms. Such flexibility is achieved via more short-hours jobs concentrated in female-dominated sectors and positions and longer hours in male breadwinner jobs (Horrell and Rubery 1991; Fagan 1996).

The high road flexibilization work time regime, the northeast quadrant of the figure, would provide the institutional basis for a restructuring of gender relations. The types of work pattern that would constitute high road flexibilization are difficult to document at the macro level. True flexibility from the perspective of the employee would mean the ability to reschedule hours of work in response to personal needs (see Golden, chapter 13 in this volume).

Table 14.1 EU countries and work time regimes

Male breadwinner	*Solidaristic gender equity*	*Liberal flexibilization*	*High road flexibilization*	*Transitional*
Greece	Finland	United Kingdom	(none)	Netherlands
Italy	Denmark	Ireland		Sweden
Spain	France			Germany
Portugal	Belgium			Austria
				Luxembourg

Nevertheless, some characteristics of this work time regime are apparent: ideally, they would entail more options to work shorter hours in order to better facilitate balancing of paid and unpaid labor without sacrificing job quality.

The following sections provide an evaluation of work time practices in European countries and the extent to which they conform to these work time regimes. Each of the 15 EU countries is categorized according to our typology. These categorizations are summarized in Table 14.1. There are four male breadwinner work time regimes, although Portugal deviates somewhat from the pattern. Only the United Kingdom has fully institutionalized a liberal flexibilization work time regime; however, Ireland contains elements of this regime type. None of the EU countries surveyed exemplifies the high road flexibilization work time regime. The best case examples have resisted flexibility in order to advance gender equity, "solidaristic gender equity." These countries are Belgium, Denmark, Finland, and France. The largest group of EU member states, the remaining five, fall into a category of work time regimes in flux. We tentatively refer to these as transitional work time regimes, implicitly moving toward some form of flexibilization. However, we recognize that time series analysis would be needed to conclusively defend this appellation.

LONG HOURS, SHORT HOURS, AND GENDERED WORK TIME

In order to evaluate the degree to which member countries of the EU have adopted short hours for working women and long hours for male workers, we plot in Figure 14.2 the percentage of employed married women working part-time against the percentage of employed men working long hours as a usual practice.[8] We define long hours using a conventional standard of overtime, more than 40 hours per week.

The solid lines demarcating a box in the lower left corner of Figure 14.2 represent the percentages for the European Union as a whole. Thus, 38 percent of married working women in the fifteen member countries held part-time jobs in 1997; 24 percent of male workers reported usual weekly

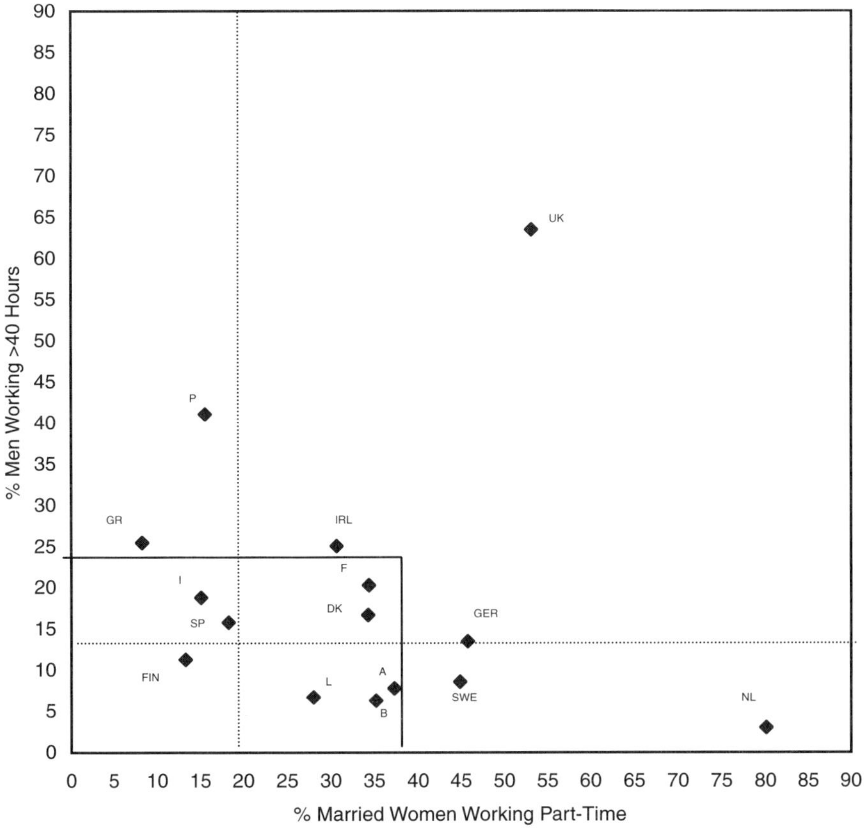

Figure 14.2 Gendered division of work schedules.

hours of work of more than forty hours. Eight countries within the box rank lower than the European average on both indicators: Finland, Spain, Italy, Luxembourg, Belgium, Austria, France, and Denmark. In order to further differentiate those countries relatively close to the average from those with particularly low levels of long and/or short hours, the dotted lines designate 50 percent of the EU 15 average, or 19 percent and 12 percent, respectively.

The four "corners" of the graph in Figure 14.2 are represented by the United Kingdom (high part-time, high overtime), Finland (low, low), Portugal (low, high), and the Netherlands (high, low). The United Kingdom is visually apparent as an outlier, with the highest percentage of male overtime and the second highest percentage of married women working part-time. The UK is a relatively self-regulated or *laissez-faire* market economy and thus a liberal flexibilization work time regime. It clearly epitomizes a gendered division of working time. Although women's labor force participation is relatively high, a gendered division of work time has replaced the traditional male-breadwinner model. Because part-time jobs offer lower pay and less mobility than full-time jobs, the UK has a low female-to-male wage ratio, with women earning on average only 74 percent as much as the average male worker.[9] The closest to the UK model is Ireland. It has historical ties to the United Kingdom, yet is less clearly in the liberal tradition. Overtime is higher than the EU average, however, part-time is a bit lower, perhaps because the labor force participation rate of married women is only 41.5 percent.

Finland emerges as the "best case scenario" in Figure 14.2, avoiding gendered work time strategies by combining low rates of overtime for men with relatively few married women working part-time. Despite relatively low rates of part-time employment, Finland has managed to elicit high labor force participation by women. Rather than using part-time jobs as a means of reconciling work and family, Finland has opted for ample family support services such as child care (Rantalaiho 1997; Pfau-Effinger 1998; Bittman 1999).[10] Gender equity in hours also goes hand-in-hand with a relatively high gender wage ratio of 82 percent. In this regard, Finland represents a solidaristic gender equity approach to work time. In France and Denmark, although not as dramatic as in Finland, both long hours and short hours are relatively moderate phenomena. Belgium is classified as a solidaristic regime on the basis of the discussion in the ensuing section despite being closer to Austria and Luxembourg in Figure 14.2.[11] Since all four countries have active work-sharing movements and relatively short standard work weeks, we label them as examples of solidaristic gender equity work time regimes.

There seems to be a southern European pattern in Figure 14.2. Four countries from this region – Portugal, Greece, Italy, and Spain – are linked by their low rates of part-time employment for married women and long hours for men.[12] Vaiou and Stratigaki (1997: 106) characterize the "Southern pattern" as a bimodal distribution over women's life cycle, as their labor force participation rates decline after marriage and childbirth. The relatively low percentages of married women working part-time result from labor force intermittency. For example, the labor force participation rates of married women are only 39 percent, 36 percent, and 36 percent for Greece, Italy, and Spain respectively. Southern European men generally work long hours to support families, especially in Greece and Portugal. These countries are representative of the male breadwinner work time regime in which male breadwinners support full-time, unpaid care-giving by married women. Working women tend to be single women or others who choose full-time employment.

Gender roles are slightly different in Portugal than in the other three countries. The labor force participation rate of Portugese women is one of the highest in Europe. Even among married women, labor force participation is 56 percent. According to Eurostat data (1995), Portuguese men's wages are the lowest in the EU. The absence of a male breadwinner wage contributes to high rates of married women's labor force participation coupled with long hours for men (see Ruivo, González, and Varejão 1998). Nevertheless, Portugal is closer to the male breadwinner regime than the other models of work time.

The transitional work time regimes combine legislated or negotiated limits on overtime with significant rates of part-time employment among married women. The prototype is the Netherlands, located in the lower-right corner of Figure 14.2. Although the Netherlands also has the highest rates of male part-timers in the EU, 17 percent and primarily young students, this is far less than 68 percent of all women and 80 percent of married women (Eurostat 1998: Table 53). The Netherlands has been at the forefront of efforts to increase the continuity of women's labor force participation over the life cycle by making part-time jobs available for those with family responsibilities. Plantenga (1996) suggests that part-time work has been a compromise strategy, reinforcing occupational segregation and the wage gap. At 71 percent, the Netherlands has the lowest wage ratio in the European Union. At the same time, the Netherlands has maintained the lowest levels of men working long hours.

Four other countries are classified with the Netherlands as transitional regimes, on the basis of high amounts of (female) part-time work and low (male) overtime. Swedish policy has actively promoted part-time employment as a strategy to maintain women's labor force participation over the life cycle. This has been effected through a generous parental leave policy that allows parents to shorten their daily working hours (with a reduction in pay) until the child is school age (Roche, Fynes, and Morrissey 1996; Sanne 1998). Despite a low proportion of men working long hours, hours of work have been increasing since the 1980s due to tight labor markets and relatively strong growth rates (Sanne 1998). The Social Democratic Party and the LO (Sweden's labor confederation) have prioritized efforts to curtail overtime, especially in light of fears that the EU Working Time Directive could facilitate long hours ("Sweden" 1996). Austria and Luxembourg also have extremely low rates of overtime at present; on the part-time axis they fall below the European average, but still have substantial percentages of married women working short hours. As in the other transitional regimes, Germany actively promotes part-time jobs for married women (Blossfeld and Rohwer 1997; Pfau-Effinger 1998). Yet a noticeable percentage of German men work long hours, despite an active movement to shorten the work week.

GENDERED DIVERSITY AMONG FULL-TIME WORKERS

To better identify which counties are creating alternatives to the male model of the 40-hour work week, we turn to a direct comparison of men's and women's employment patterns within full-time work. There is wide variation in patterns of full-time employment in different member states. Nevertheless, these diverse work time practices generally confirm the categorization of

Table 14.2 Distribution of hours of full-time workers in work time regimes

Regime	*Mode (men)*	*Mode (women)*	*Peakedness*
Male breadwinner (Greece, Italy, Spain, Portugal)	40	40	moderate-to-high
Solidaristic gender equity (Denmark, France, Belgium, Finland)	<40	<40	high[a]
Liberal flexibilization (United Kingdom, Ireland)	>40[b]	<40	low
Transitional (Netherlands, Sweden, Germany, Austria, Luxembourg)	40	40[c]	moderate-to-high

Notes

a The exception is Finnish men, whose mode is 40 hours, but with a low peakedness because many men work shorter hours.

b In Ireland, the male mode is 40, however, a substantial proportion of men work longer hours.

c The exception is Germany. German women have a mode of 38–39 hours; both men's and women's distributions have low peakedness.

work time regimes in Table 14.1. To illustrate, we have chosen as archetypes three of the fifteen member countries that best illustrate distinct models of full-time work, and thus three of the work time regimes: Greece, the United Kingdom, and Denmark. These countries differ in the mode of usual weekly hours and the degree of peakedness of the hours distribution. In order to compare each of the member states with these archetypes, a measure of the degree of peakedness of the hours distribution, the kurtosis, was calculated for both men and women in each of these member states. Countries are categorized as high, moderately above, or low relative to the EU average (3.28 for men and 1.56 for women). These findings, along with the mode of weekly hours for women and men, are summarized in Table 14.2.

Greece illustrates the male breadwinner work time regime. In Figure 14.3, the 40-hour work week is standard for full-time workers of both genders. Appreciable numbers of full-timers work long hours, although the male line is above the female line at the longest work schedules. Greece has a traditional gender division of labor, with full-time work structured on the male model of long hours. Overtime is the most prevalent form of flexible work time (Kyriazis 1998: 80). Those women who do participate in the labor force are the ones in need of full-time jobs. The kurtosis, our measure of the peakedness of the distribution, is moderate, 3.38 for men and 5.77 for women. Italy, Spain, and Portugal – the other male breadwinner regimes – similarly institutionalize long hours and a 40-hour norm (see Table 14.2).

The United Kingdom again typifies the pattern of a liberal flexibilization work time regime, high flexibility without gender equity. The relatively deregulated environment in the UK has facilitated the introduction of flexible work practices without necessitating the legislative changes (Perrons and Hurstfield 1998). In Figure 14.4, workers are distributed among a wide variety

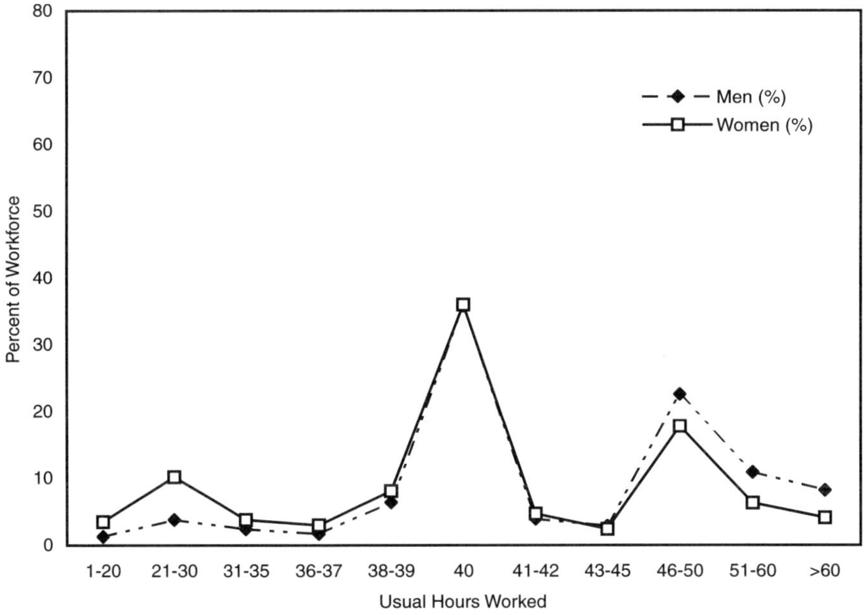

Figure 14.3 Hours distribution of full-time workers in Greece.

of hours groupings. The 40-hour work week is not the peak for either men or women. For women, the mode is 38–39 hours while for men it is 46–50 hours. The flatness of the hours distribution for both women and men is confirmed by the kurtosis of each line: −1.00 for men and 0.34 for women. The hours of men in Ireland are not quite as long, but it is more similar to the UK than other regimes.

Denmark presents a dramatically different pattern, as shown in Figure 14.5. Successful efforts to shorten the work week from 1986 to 1990, mainly through collective agreements, mean that the majority of full-time workers of both genders have a usual work week of 36–37 hours (see also Højgaard 1998; Madsen 1998). The kurtosis is very high: 10.46 and 10.67 for men and women, respectively. Although the genders diverge at the tails according to the usual pattern of male long hours and female short hours, this affects a small percentage of the full-time workforce. With the highest female labor force participation rate in the EU, 59 percent, Denmark facilitates women's economic integration into paid labor. The wage ratio is among the highest in the EU at 83 percent. These are characteristics of a solidaristic gender equity work time regime. The basis for this regime is a redefinition of the concept of full-time work away from the male model of the 40-hour work week. The shape of the distribution in France and Belgium is similar, though the mode of weekly hours is 38–39. Finnish women work slightly shorter full-time hours than men, avoiding ghettoization in part-time jobs.

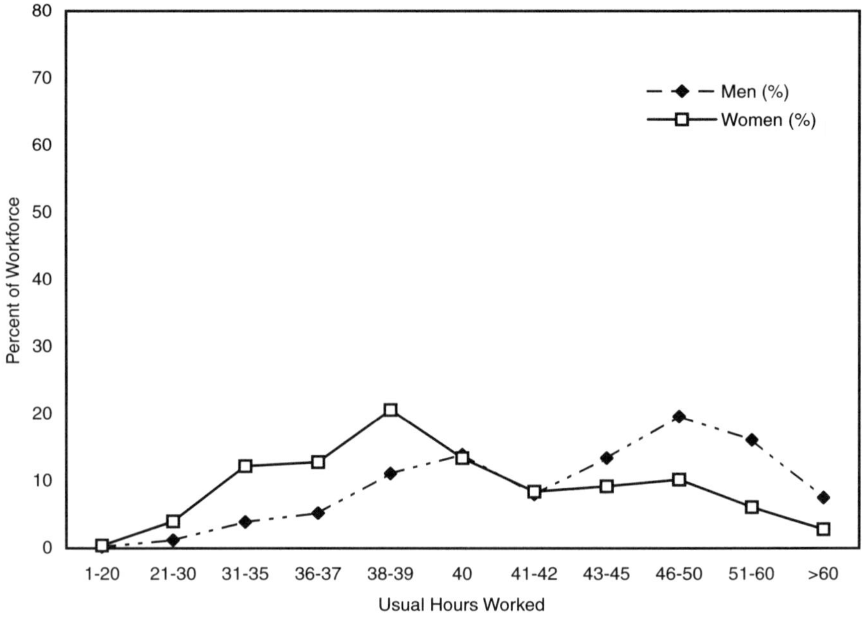

Figure 14.4 Hours distribution of full-time workers in the UK.

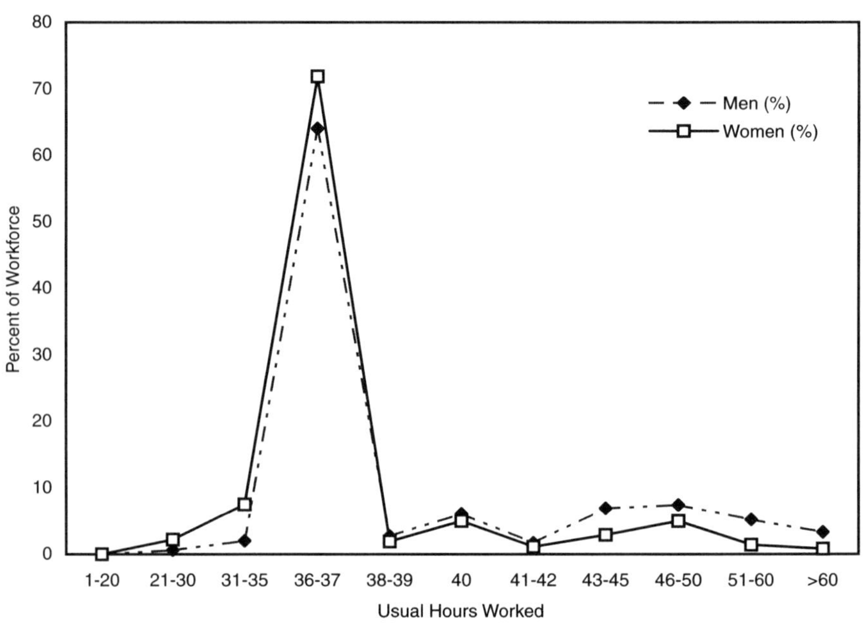

Figure 14.5 Hours distribution of full-time workers in Denmark.

The transitional regimes are more diverse in the patterns of full-time work hours. Among the transitional work time regimes, men and women in Sweden and Luxembourg are more concentrated around the 40-hour mode than in the Netherlands, Austria, or Germany. Therefore, the measure of peakedness varies from low in Germany to high in Sweden and Luxembourg. Full-time women workers in Germany have shorter work weeks, with a mode of 38–39 hours (see Table 14.2).

These findings suggest the importance of standard work hours reductions in achieving gender equity. In general, the countries with shorter work weeks, such as Denmark, have a lower gap between men's and women's labor force participation rates and hours of work. In contrast, the UK model indicates the resulting gender inequities of unregulated labor markets where there have been no institutionalized limits to overtime. Increasing flexibility while promoting gender equity is a difficult feat yet to be navigated by any of the European Union member states.

CONCLUSION

The facilitation of gender equity in the labor force and in the household should be one criterion for evaluating whether particular flexibilization policies facilitate economic and social justice. Reforms that decrease the average work week and increase workers' time sovereignty can indeed facilitate these goals. However, gender equity in flexibilization requires that both men and women are distributed equally or comparably among the possible lengths of usual working hours. Such equity is most likely to occur where working hours are declining. Therefore, the worksharing movement in Europe, originally advocated by labor as a job creation strategy, is also receiving support from feminists as a means of equalizing the responsibility for the unpaid work of families (Bruegel, Figart, and Mutari 1999). Adequate state provision of social care, especially for children and dependent adults, is also critical, so that women's choices of work hours are less constrained.

Flexibilization policies can also be instituted in ways that reproduce gender inequity in the division of labor. Specifically, working time flexibility has come to be identified with a gendered division of work time between short and long hours. Women workers, especially married women with children, are most likely to be concentrated in short-hours or part-time jobs. At the same time, flexibilization has taken the form of increased overtime in male-dominated industries, particularly in some countries (ILO 1995; Lehndorff 1998). When these two types of flexibility are combined – overtime for men and part-time jobs for women – they are likely to reinforce the already skewed division of domestic labor.

Through a comparative analysis of part-time, overtime, and full-time work patterns, we have identified four distinct social organizations of work time.

The male breadwinner work time regime is still dominant in southern Europe. Workers adhere to a male model of long hours and there is little institutional support for the work of families. The low road to flexibility, liberal flexibilization, is characteristic of states with more deregulated labor markets such as the United Kingdom and Ireland. Women's labor force participation is higher than under the male breadwinner model, but with little state support for family life, women are pressured into taking part-time jobs that can accommodate the existing, uneven household division of labor. Even if men wish to accept more responsibility for domestic labor, their longer work hours will impede progress toward gender equity.

Denmark, France, Belgium, and Finland each has some of the characteristics of solidaristic gender equity in work time. Women's labor force participation is relatively high, especially in Denmark and Finland, but Denmark's shorter standard work week results in greater homogeneity in the distribution of full-time work hours by gender. Part-time employment as a gendered strategy is on the decline. France, where the worksharing movement is currently most active at present, also has a shorter work week and fewer disparities between men's and women's schedules. Finland, with its combination of low overtime for men, high rates of full-time employment for women, and generous public support for the work of families has most clearly avoided the inequitable, gendered work time.

A large number of countries seem poised to either follow the low road or create an alternative paradigm. In this regard, work time policies are like other institutional differences between member states. Focusing on the Scandinavian countries, Borchorst (1993) contends that restrictions on public expenditures will undermine the tradition of support for child care, shifting these countries toward the family-based systems of support that dominate in the UK and continental Europe. Plantenga (1997: 100–101) suggests that convergence between welfare state regimes is likely, but the question remains, toward which model? She finds that the deregulated, liberal welfare state model is most clearly in alignment with the current direction of European unification. Mazey (1998) also argues that EU policy has shifted toward deregulation and unfettered markets, in contrast with the more social democratic orientation of the 1970s. Therefore, the diversity of work time regimes that we have identified may turn out to be a passing moment on the way to harmonization down to the low road across Europe.

NOTES

1 For a summary and feminist critique of the neoclassical treatment of household labor supply, see, for example, Blau, Ferber, and Winkler (1998) and Heath and Ciscel (1996).

2 Orloff defines gender relations as "the set of mutually constitutive structures and practices which produce gender differentiation, gender inequalities, and gender hierarchy in a given society" (1996: 52). Gender relations are institutionalized in

the division of labor, compulsory heterosexuality, ideologies about masculinity and femininity, and other social practices.

3 His original welfare state regimes include: (1) social democratic welfare states, chiefly the Nordic countries, (2) liberal welfare states such as the United Kingdom and United States, and (3) conservative-corporatist welfare states of continental Europe. A fourth category has been added to Esping-Andersen's original formulation – rudimentary welfare states primarily in southern Europe (see Plantenga 1997). The framework was updated in Esping-Andersen (1999).

4 The three most recent members – Sweden, Finland, and Austria – are not included in their study that relies upon 1994 data; these three countries joined the EU in 1995.

5 There is a 4-month reference period for calculating average weekly hours, potentially expandable to 6 months. Moreover, member states may allow employers and unions to negotiate collective agreements containing a reference period up to 12 months, according to the fine print in Article 17 of the directive. Finally, member states have the option to ignore Article 6 completely, as long as they ensure that workers have acquiesced to the excess overtime in advance and employers do not subject a worker "to any detriment" for refusing long hours. This option is to be reviewed in 2003.

6 The three signatories to the framework agreement are: UNICE (Union of Industrial and Employers' Confederations of Europe), ETUC (European Trade Union Confederation), and CEEP (European Centre of Enterprises with Public Participation).

7 Analysts contrast two approaches to instituting flexibility: (1) the "low road" or "mean" version that relies upon a cheap, often contingent and disposable, labor force in a deregulated environment; and (2) the "high road" that provides workers as well as employers with control over work schedules and input into the production process (Gordon 1996; Golden 1998).

8 It would be more appropriate to focus on the presence of children, rather than simply marital status, in determining women's employment status. However, the European *Labour Force Survey* only differentiates women working part time by marital status. Overtime by marital status was unavailable. In addition, social norms regarding men's labor market roles are not generally conditioned by their marital status.

9 All wage ratios are authors' calculations based on mean gross hourly earnings data from Eurostat (1995). The special survey calculates wages in Ecus and includes industry and services but not public administration.

10 In discussing the Finnish approach, Michael Bittman asserts that "entitlements to generous parental leave, high quality child care, and to family-friendly hours of paid work are all necessary components of an equitable solution to the difficulties of combining work and family in the twenty-first century" (1999: 40).

11 Rubery, Smith, and Fagan (1998) rate Belgium and Denmark highly in their index of work time characteristics favorable to equal opportunities. France is slightly lower and Finland is not considered because it was not a member of the EU at the time.

12 This grouping is not completely congruent with Esping-Andersen's categorizations. Although Greece, Portugal, and Spain are rudimentary welfare states, Italy is often categorized with the conservative-corporatist countries (see Saraceno 1994).

REFERENCES

Bittman, M. (1999) "Parenthood without Penalty: Time Use and Public Policy in Australia and Finland," *Feminist Economics* 5(3): 27–42.

Blau, F. D., Ferber, M. A., and Winkler, A. E. (1998) *The Economics of Women, Men, and Work*, Upper Saddle River, NJ: Prentice-Hall, 3rd Edn.

Blossfeld, H. and Rohwer, G. (1997) "Part-time Work in West Germany," in H. Blossfeld and C. Hakim (eds) *Between Equalization and Marginalization: Women Working Part-time in Europe and the United States of America*, Oxford: Oxford University Press: 164–190.

Borchorst, A. (1993) "Working Lives and Family Lives in Western Europe," in S. Carlsen and J. E. Larsen (eds) *The Equality Dilemma: Reconciling Working Life and Family Life, Viewed in an Equality Perspective, the Danish Example*, Copenhagen: The Danish Equal Status Council: 167–180.

Bruegel, I., Figart D., and Mutari, E. (1999) "A Feminist Perspective on Full Employment and Work Redistribution," in J. Wheelock and J. Vail (eds), *Work and Idleness: The Political Economy of Full Employment*, London: Kluwer: 69–83.

Bruegel, I. and Perrons, D. (1998) "Deregulation and Women's Employment: The Diverse Experiences of Women in Britain," *Feminist Economics* 4(1): 103–125.

Council Directive 93/104/EC of 23 November 1993 Concerning Certain Aspects of the Organization of Working Time, *Official Journal of the European Communities* No. L 307: 18–24.

Council Directive 97/81/EC of 15 December 1997 Concerning the Framework Agreement on Part-Time Work Concluded by UNICE, CEEP and the ETUC; (1998) *Official Journal of the European Communities* No. L 14: 9–11.

Daune-Richard, A. M. (1998) "How Does the 'Societal Effect' Shape the Use of Part-time Work in France, the UK, and Sweden?" in J. O'Reilly and C. Fagan (eds), *Part-time Prospects: An International Comparison of Part-time Work in Europe, North America and the Pacific Rim*, London: Routledge: 214–231.

Drew, E. and Emerek, R. (1998) "Part-time Employment in a European Perspective," in E. Drew, R. Emerek, and E. Mahon (eds), *Women, Work and the Family in Europe*, London: Routledge: 88–99.

Esping-Andersen, G. (1990) *The Three Worlds of Welfare Capitalism*, Princeton, NJ: Princeton University Press.

_____ (1999) *Social Foundations of Postindustrial Economies*, Oxford: Oxford University Press.

Eurostat (1995) *Statistics on the Structure of Earnings*, New Chronos Database.

_____ (1998) *Labour Force Survey: Results 1997*, Luxembourg: Office for Official Publications of the European Communities.

Fagan, C. (1996) "Gendered Time Schedules: Paid Work in Great Britain," *Social Politics* 3(1): 72–106.

Figart, D. M. and Mutari, E. (1998) "Degendering Work Time in Comparative Perspective: Alternative Policy Frameworks," *Review of Social Economy* 56(4): 460–480.

Fraser, N. (1997) *Justice Interruptus: Critical Reflections on the "Postsocialist" Condition*, London: Routledge.

Golden, L. M. (1998) "Working Hours Determination, Policy and Regulatory Reforms in the US and Other Industrialized Countries," *International Review of Comparative Public Policy* 10: 51–75.

Gordon, D. M. (1996) *Fat and Mean: The Corporate Squeeze of Working Americans and the Myth of Managerial "Downsizing,"* New York: The Free Press.

Gregory, A. and O'Reilly, J. (1996) "Checking Out and Cashing Up: The Prospects and Paradoxes of Regulating Part-time Work in Europe," in R. Crompton, D. Gallie, and

K. Purcel (eds), *Changing Forms of Employment: Organisations, Skills and Gender*, London: Routledge: 207–243.

Heath, J. A. and Ciscel, D. H. (1996) "Escaping the Fate of Sisyphus: Bargaining, Divorce, and Employment in the Patriarchal Family," *Review of Radical Political Economics* 28(1): 1–19.

Højgaard, L. (1998) "Workplace Culture, Family-Supportive Policies and Gender Differences," in E. Drew, R. Emerek, and E. Mahon (eds), *Women, Work and the Family in Europe*, London, Routledge: 140–150.

Horrell, S. and Rubery, J. (1991) "Gender and Working Time: An Analysis of Employers' Working-time Policies," *Cambridge Journal of Economics* 15(4): 373–391.

ILO (1995) *Working Time Around the World, Conditions of Work Digest*, Vol. 14, Geneva: International Labour Office.

Kyriazis, N. (1998) "Greece," in *Flexible Working and the Reconciliation of Work and Family Life – or a New Form of Precariousness: Final Report*, Brussels: European Commission, Directorate-General for Employment, Industrial Relations and Social Affairs: 77–118.

Lehndorff, S. (1998) "From 'Collective' to 'Individual' Reductions in Working Time? Trends and Experience with Working Time in the European Union," *Transfer* 4(4): 598–620.

Madsen, P. K. (1998) "Working Time Policy and Paid Leave Arrangements: The Danish Experience in the 1990s," *Transfer* 4(4): 692–714.

Mazey, S. (1998) "The European Union and Women's Rights: From the Europeanisation of National Agendas to the Nationalisation of a European Agenda?" in D. Hine and H. Kassim (eds), *Beyond the Market: The EU and National Social Policy*, London: Routledge.

Meulders, D., Plasman, O., and Plasman, R. (1997) "Atypical Labour Market Relations in the European Union," in A.G. Dijkstra and J. Plantenga (eds), *Gender and Economics: A European Perspective*, London: Routledge: 75–85.

O'Reilly, J. and Fagan, C. (1998) *Part-time Prospects: An International Comparison of Part-time Work in Europe, North America and the Pacific Rim*, London: Routledge.

Orloff, A. (1996) "Gender in the Welfare State," *Annual Review of Sociology*, 22: 51–78.

Perrons, D. (1998) "Comparative Report/Executive Summary," in *Flexible Working and the Reconciliation of Work and Family Life – or a New Form of Precariousness: Final Report*, Brussels: European Commission, Directorate-General for Employment, Industrial Relations and Social Affairs: 1–42.

Perrons, D. and Hurstfield, J. (1998) "United Kingdom," in *Flexible Working and the Reconciliation of Work and Family Life – or a New Form of Precariousness: Final Report*, Brussels: European Commission, Directorate-General for Employment, Industrial Relations and Social Affairs: 119–161.

Pfau-Effinger, B. (1998) "Culture or Structure as Explanations for Differences in Part-time Work in Germany, Finland and the Netherlands?" in J. O'Reilly and C. Fagan (eds), *Part-time Prospects: An International Comparison of Part-time Work in Europe, North America and the Pacific Rim*, London: Routledge: 177–198.

Plantenga, J. (1996) "For Women Only? The Rise of Part-time Work in the Netherlands," *Social Politics* 3(1): 57–71.

_____ (1997) "European Constants and National Particularities: The Position of Women in the EU Labour Market," in A. G. Dijkstra and J. Plantenga (eds), *Gender and Economics: A European Perspective*, London: Routledge: 86–103.

Rantalaiho, L. (1997) "Contextualising Gender," in L. Rantalaiho and T. Heiskanen (eds), *Gendered Practices in Working Life*, New York: St. Martin's Press: 16–30.

Roche, W. K., Fynes, B., and Morrissey, T. (1996) "Working Time and Employment: A Review of International Evidence," *International Labour Review* 135(2): 129–157.

Rubery, J., Smith, M., and Fagan, C. (1998) "National Working-time Regimes and Equal Opportunities," *Feminist Economics* 4(1): 71–102.

Ruivo, M., do Pilar González, and Varejão, J. M. (1998) "Why is Part-time Work so Low in Portugal and Spain?" in J. O'Reilly and C. Fagan (eds), *Part-time Prospects: An International Comparison of Part-time Work in Europe, North America and the Pacific Rim*, London: Routledge: 199–213.

Sanne, C. (1998) "The Working Hours Issue in Sweden," *Transfer* 4(4): 715–728.

Saraceno, C. (1994) "The Ambivalent Familism of the Italian Welfare State," *Social Politics* 1(1): 60–82.

"Social Policy State of Play" (1998) *European Industrial Relations Review* 288: 14–19.

"Sweden" (1996) *European Industrial Relations Review* 266: 112–113.

Vaiou, D. and Stratigaki, M. (1997) "Women in the South: Diverse Experiences of Work in a Unifying Europe," in A. G. Dijkstra and J. Plantenga (eds), *Gender and Economics: A European Perspective*, London: Routledge: 104–117.

15 History and housework

Implications for work hours and family policy in market economies

Laura Leete

In modern industrialized societies, the history of productive activity can be traced from its current location in stores, factories and offices to its origins in the home, field and shop. While family members once directly produced a variety of basic products needed for their family's survival, most economic activity now takes the form of individuals selling highly specialized labor in the marketplace. At work they participate in the production of some fraction of a complex good or service. In turn, they use their earnings to purchase the array of goods and services needed for their family's consumption – all of which were themselves produced for sale in the market. It seems that this centuries-long process of the marketization of home production is now virtually complete.

While this process has had profound implications for many elements of social organization, the present chapter focuses on just one – the implications of this transition for the economics of child-care and child-rearing. What is highlighted by this discussion is that a number of seemingly disparate social problems have their roots in this transition. Three in particular, the time bind experienced by working parents, the feminization of poverty, and the welfare "crisis," all can be traced to the basic economics of providing child-care in capitalist free-market economies. While the analysis here does not break new ground with respect to policy formulation, it does shed new light on the urgent and inevitable need for more extensive and coherent public policies regarding work hours, family leave and child-care in post-industrialized countries.

HISTORY AND HOUSEWORK

The transition from home to market production – and the accompanying specialization of labor – is widely known to be a long and gradual process. Indeed, this transition may be characteristic of most of human history. Its beginnings might be traced to the first barter transaction between non-family members. Barter eventually gave way to money-financed transactions. Different types of production became increasingly market oriented, from agriculture to crafts to mass-produced industrial production to human services to information to post-information-age technologies. Home production at the beginning of the last millennium consisted of a different set of tasks than home production 1000 years later. Today, the transition continues with the continued marketization of activities that once would have been non-market activities. For example, permanent press clothes and new fabrics have almost eliminated the need for the iron that my mother once wielded with great skill. Family style take-out meals and microwavable food have become commonplace. Now, grocery delivery, laundry pickup, pet taxis, errand and plant watering services are ever more available, as are internet-based businesses that will send appropriate greeting cards to appropriate people on the appropriate days.

The economic forces behind the on-going marketization of home production are commonly understood. Adam Smith (1976) pointed out the gains from specialization and division of labor over two centuries ago. Technological developments have made economies of scale a driving force behind the massive industrialization of the 19th and 20th centuries. Thus, the economic activity that has left the home for the market has often been greeted by huge productivity gains. When products produced at home can be manufactured on a much larger scale, far more output can be produced with a given quantity of inputs. When service providers take on tasks otherwise done at home, specialization and a streamlining of activities can lead to more efficient production. While the parallel between earnings and rising labor productivity is not perfect, as when the earnings distribution becomes more uneven, certainly this rise in labor productivity is at the root of the rising average standard of living in industrialized countries in recent centuries.

The above represents the upbeat version of the story of the transition from home to market. By reaping the advantages of technology, specialization of labor, economies of scale and the efficiencies of money transactions, human beings produce ever more economic output with the same effort. In this story the fact that production simply changes locations – from home to business – and the fact that consumption activity involves an increasing number of market transactions are incidental to the well being of society.

THE ECONOMICS OF PRODUCING CHILDREN

There is, however, one incongruity in this story that has yet to be considered – the production, or rearing, of children.[1] When production methods were simpler and more decentralized, and families produced as work groups in their own homes and farms, economic activity took place in tandem with child-rearing. In an economic sense, child-rearing and the production of other goods at home can be considered as a joint production process. Caring for children requires adequate space, safety, equipment for food preparation, and appropriate conditions for napping. In addition, child-care can be successfully combined only with activities from which one can be frequently interrupted, to which one can give partial attention, and to which one can devote irregular amounts of time. On the basis of these criteria, one might expect that some work tasks would be more efficiently achieved in combination with child-rearing than others. Many of those writing about the history of the gender division of labor in the household have attributed the division of labor between men and women to the need for women's work to be compatible with the task of caring for small children. One might think of this as choosing the appropriate gender division of labor that is intended to maximize household production, given the relationship between performing child-care and other tasks. Since in most societies women have largely been responsible for the most immediate child-rearing tasks, at least with regard to young children, I will not discuss men's home production and its transition to market here.

What is missing from the historical account above is an assessment of how the complementarities between child-rearing and other economic activity have changed over time. Up through the initial stages of the industrial revolution, it was traditionally male tasks, such as butchering, milling and tool making, that shifted away from the home and into the marketplace. Men going to work in coal mines and the introduction of coal burning stoves replaced the traditional male tasks of wood hauling and chopping (Hayden 1981; Boydston 1990; Blau, Ferber, and Winkler 1998). Then gradually over time women's work also shifted. This included the introduction of utilities (electricity, natural gas, water) that replaced stove- or fire-tending, candle making, and water hauling. Then the mechanization of sewing, food processing, and rug making and the advent of refrigeration eliminated many other activities that previously were performed in the home by women (Strasser 1982; Cowan 1983; Boydston 1990). In later years, further development of food processing and freezing and thawing technologies have reduced the need to cook, in the traditional sense of the word. New technologies have also simplified the care of clothing. The development of undertaking and nursing as professional jobs further eliminated tasks traditionally carried out by women in the home. In a multitude of ways, housework shifted into the market, and the paid working time of men, and then women, followed.

In contrast with many other household tasks, however, technological advance has had little impact on the task of caring for children. As with many other service sector functions, productivity gains in caring for children have been limited to date. While the advent of disposable diapers and prepared baby foods has decreased some of the time needed to care for children, many tasks remain unchanged. Feeding, consoling, playing with a child and rocking one to sleep are still labor-intensive tasks for which the productivity gains from technology or economies of scale are limited. And while a 19th century parent might have performed some of the above in conjunction with another economic activity going on in the household, a 21st century parent will find it more difficult to accomplish this while also engaged in modern production activity. First, few work places are suitable for children or even permit their presence. Second, few employers grant their employees the permission or means to divide their attention between children and work. Third, both specialization and technology have changed the nature of modern work tasks so that many of them require more concentration and undivided attention. Even if children are allowed in the workplace, or an employee is able to work in their own home (i.e., teleworking), few parents find that they can effectively give their attention to skilled tasks such as debugging computer programs, providing telephone customer service, conducting meetings or fast-paced production work when young children are present.

All of the above implies an odd social anomaly. Our production technologies, which have brought us great material wealth, have evolved in such a way as to be increasingly incompatible with child-rearing. Many observers have noted that with industrialization, with its decline in agriculture and externalization of home production, the economic contribution of children to their families has waned. However, it has now gone further. Independent of any economic contribution to the family, the absolute, opportunity and relative costs of children and child-rearing have risen.

First, the absolute costs of child-rearing have risen because of the diminished production complementarities with other activities. Production activities with which child-care was once combined are now largely accomplished elsewhere at a place and pace which are not welcoming to children. When individuals care for their children now they do so largely in addition to, instead of in conjunction with, other economic activities.

Second, where child-care might once have been a relatively costless "by-product" of other economic activities, engaging in child-care now entails lowering one's productivity considerably. As the value of market production rises, so does the opportunity cost of engaging in household production tasks. More generally, the relative cost and opportunity cost of child-care have risen no matter where it is provided – home or market – because childcare, as is the case with many time-intensive services, does not lend itself well to the productivity increases experienced by goods-producing activities. Care for a child might require the same amount of time input as it always did, but now that same time entails giving up more of some other good or service that could be produced with ever increasing productivity levels.

While the opportunity costs of many low-productivity growth goods or services have risen over time, the implications of the rising opportunity cost for child-care are somewhat unique. In many other contexts, as relative productivities change, one gives up more of the high-productivity growth good or service in order to consume the same quantity of low-productivity growth good or service. However, the higher-productivity growth of some sectors often creates such a rise in real wealth that it more than makes up for the rising proportion of income that is devoted to expenditures on items involving lower-productivity growth. When opportunity costs are too high, in most cases individuals can simply choose to shift their consumption away from the expensive good. However, in the case of caring for their children, parents can not, and perhaps should not, choose to shift away from this activity. Alternatively, when the costs of goods rise, individuals can choose to consume less of an expensive product or to shift their consumption to a lower quality version of the product. Again, in the context of child-care, neither of these choices would be socially desirable.

Furthermore, in the case of child-care, the more dispersed the distribution of income, the more problematic the rising opportunity cost of child-care. If providers of child-care are paid according to their next best opportunity in society, then these costs can be expected to rise with the average productivity level in the economy. However, if the distribution of workers' earnings is also widening (as it has in recent decades), then increasingly those at the low end of the income distribution find that purchasing child-care encumbers a larger and larger share of their income. These relationships are made clearer with some simple algebra. The share of a family budget spent on purchasing child-care is equal to

$$[(W_c/K) \times N]/W_f,$$

where W_c is the care-giver's wage, K is the number of children per care-giver, N is the number of children in the family, and W_f is total family income. If, for some share of the population W_c is rising relative to W_f, then only by raising K or lowering N can the share of their income spent on child-care be reduced. Raising K implies more children per care-giver. It is clear from the literature on early childhood development that there is a point beyond which this is detrimental to childhood well-being and development (Burchinal *et al.* 1997; Ramey *et al.* 2000). Indeed, for this reason government regulations generally place limits on this parameter. In the USA, all fifty states and the District of Columbia specify maximum child/teacher ratios (by age of child) allowed in state licensed day care centers and group provider homes. Most states also specify age, education, training and experience requirements for child-care providers.[2]

Lowering N by having fewer children can also lead to lower child-care expenditures. With the exception of the post-World War II baby boom, birth rates in industrialized countries have been declining steadily since the industrial revolution (Jacobsen 1994). While lower population growth may be desirable from an environmental standpoint, in some countries (Italy and Japan, for example) exceptionally low birth rates are raising public policy concerns with regard to the adequacy of the labor force to support the retirement of an increasingly "gray" population (see, for example "Decline in Birth Rate a Headache for Italy" 1993).

INSIGHTS FOR MARKET ECONOMIES

The loss of complementarities between child-care and home production, the rising opportunity costs and the implications of those rising costs in conjunction with a more dispersed income distribution have all put parenting tasks in more direct conflict with meeting the work demands of the modern economy. The result is an economic order that places substantial time and financial burdens on parents – an economic order that is hostile to the task of one generation producing the next. Critics might reject this argument on the grounds that the technology of child-rearing has in fact changed so little over time. In fact, this observation – that little has changed in the nursery and the playroom – is precisely at the core of the argument advanced here. What must be recognized is that so much else has changed in the world outside the nursery and the playroom.

In theory, all parents might have the option to revert to the home production techniques of an earlier time, caring for their children and home in the fashion that their grandparents or great-grandparents did. They might ignore the economic forces discussed here and thereby eliminate them. In practice, however, this would be very difficult to accomplish in the modern world. First, few families have access to the natural resources to be truly self-sustaining and independent of the market. Furthermore, modern population densities limit their ability to attempt this. Additionally, as is made clear in the work of Scitovsky (1976), Frank (1985) and Sen (1987), it is extremely difficult for human beings to escape the importance to their psychology of maintaining their *relative* standard of living. What psychologists have long known and economists are just beginning to discover (see, for example, Rabin 1998) is that human needs, wants and sense of dignity are intensely dependent on the standards in the surrounding society. Thus, even if it were economically feasible for parents to engage in a different, less market-oriented lifestyle, basic human psychology makes it difficult for many to take on such a task.

The discussion above sheds some light on a number of seemingly disparate social developments. From these, some observations can be drawn with implications for social welfare. First, the extension of public education since the industrial revolution to both older and younger children represents a gradually growing state subsidization of the cost of rearing children.[3] That society would support such an extensive subsidy of child-care is consistent with the view put forth in this chapter that the costs of that care are a growing burden for families. Furthermore, the fact that the spacing of the births of siblings is generally closer in the United States than it is in many European countries is consistent with the relatively lower public subsidy for child-care for younger children (under age five) being far less in the United States. This is consistent with US parents attempting to minimize the total length of time that would be most "costly" to them, the time during which they have preschool age children.

Second, many observers have pointed to an unexplained anomaly that fertility rates in industrialized countries began dropping long before birth control technologies were revolutionized and before the modern feminist movement helped to change women's attitudes about their roles in society (see, for example, Jacobsen 1994). However, if the costs of raising children have risen gradually over time as work has left the home for the marketplace, then this is entirely consistent with the long gradual decline in birth rates experienced in many countries.

Third, the "time-squeeze" increasingly experienced by working parents (Hochschild 1989; Leete and Schor 1992) and recently discussed in many public forums is a function of the incompatibility between modern economic activity and child-care. As Hochschild (1989: 8) has noted, parents (and particularly mothers) are now working a "second shift" on top of their paid worktime: "As masses of women have moved into the economy, families have been hit by a 'speed-up' in work and family life. There is no more time in the day than there was when wives stayed home, but there is twice as much to get done." Hewlett (1986) also makes an eloquent case for the difficulties faced by American women and their children because of conflicts between paid work and child-care needs.

Finally, the feminization of poverty – the term used to describe the increasing concentration of poverty among single mothers and their children – and the "welfare crisis" experienced in a number of countries in recent decades both can largely be understood as a result of the clashing of forces noted here. While other writers have provided many other careful and cogent analyses of the economic and social forces contributing to growing poverty and welfare dependence (see, for example, Wilson 1987, 1996; Edin and Lein 1997; Mink 1998), a companion view grows out of the discussion here. As home production becomes economically valuable, then a stay-at-home parent becomes a consumption good – a luxury afforded only by higher-income (largely two-parent) families. And as the average productivity and income inequality in industrialized countries both rise, there is a growing class of the lowest wage earners in society that increasingly cannot afford to pay for costly child-care out of their earnings. This phenomenon is particularly exaggerated for single parents, and in the United States, where subsidies for early childhood care are so low and income supports for stay-at-home low-income parents have been diminishing. The more disparate the wage distribution, the more difficult it becomes for those at the low-end of the wage spectrum to find affordable child-care.

IMPLICATIONS FOR FAMILY POLICY

Since the first public kindergarten was opened in St. Louis in 1873 and public schooling slowly began to be extended to five-year-olds, few major steps have been taken in the USA with regard to the provision of child-care and early childhood education. Europeans have generally done a better job of subsidizing early childhood care and education, although there is still much diversity across countries there as well. France has the most extensive system of "public nurseries," but Italy, Sweden, Denmark and Finland have extensive public provision and/or subsidy of high quality daycare and pre-school (Kamerman and Kahn 1978; Hewlett 1986; Bergmann 1996). In industrialized societies, it would seem that the very way in which we organize our work is making it difficult for workers to reproduce themselves. Moreover, it creates an obstacle to low-earnings parents leading economically productive lives, a vicious cycle that threatens to consign an ever-larger number of children to living in poverty. These ought to provide reason to think more seriously about the child-care policy implications of having an economy where production may some day become completely marketized.

In thinking about the broad implications of this chapter regarding various policies related to work hours, there are first a few points worth noting. First, work hours, family and child-care policies are not just "women's" issues. It is not a change in women's attitudes that has created the "problem" of working mothers. While women were the last to leave the home, they were not the only ones to do so. Men preceded them by a century or so. Rather, it is centuries long changes in production technology and the basic economic forces of capitalist market economies that have removed production from the home and changed the nature of work. All parents, men and women alike, face these issues. Second, it is not likely that these events will reverse themselves. As long as human development requires intensive one-on-one relationships and much time for loving contact between child and care-giver, it is likely to remain a low-productivity growth industry. Unless further technological development changes the nature of market work so that it requires less concentrated attention and effort, we are not likely to be able to simultaneously work and care for children with much success.[4]

Market economies have created a time bind for all parents, increasing the difficulty of simultaneously raising children and being economically productive. For those with the least dollars (low-wage earners) or the least free time (working single parents), the constraints become most severe and can easily consign a family to both poverty and welfare dependence. Only 6.9 percent of the US population at a given point in time is children under the age of five (US Census Bureau 1999), and only 22 percent of US families include children under the age of six. However, seeing these families through this challenging segment of their lives and giving young children adequate care and education is essential to the well-being of the entire society. Thus, there is a clear-cut case for public intervention, given that a relatively small public investment would likely lead to immensely better outcomes for society as a whole. If early childhood development is as important to later life outcomes as many researchers now believe, then the public good arguments that are generally applied to free public education (see, for example, Hanushek

1994) apply to early childhood care and pre-school education also, perhaps even in magnified fashion.

The most pressing need is for policies that reduce the incompatibility between parenting and economic activity in industrialized societies. The best policy responses are those that reduce the working hours required of parents and/or those that provide for affordable high quality early childhood care. The first of these could be accomplished with requirements (along the lines of the Family and Medical Leave Act) that parents be allowed to continue working at their current job but with reduced weekly hours on an ongoing basis (for proportionally reduced pay). However, while this could provide a workable alternative for higher income, two-parent families, taken alone it is unlikely to provide a viable financial option for single or low-wage parents. In these cases, the lower earnings that result from low work hours also require a public subsidy along the lines of an expanded earned income tax credit or expanded tax exemptions for families with children.

Flextime and teleworking are two other relatively popular worktime policies that can be expanded to address these issues, but unfortunately they do not address the core cause of work hours problems for parents. Flextime can help two-parent families by allowing for overlapping work schedules and thus reducing the number of total hours of child-care required. It can also help parents match their work hours to child-care availability. But flextime policies do not reduce the overall hours burden that parents now face. Teleworking can eliminate time parents spend commuting, but again does not address the more fundamental issues. Because of the difficulty of effectively combining most types of work with providing care for a child, particularly for young children, teleworking itself provides a child-care solution for only very few parents.

In conjunction with worktime policies, as a society we must also take responsibility for providing affordable high-quality early childhood care and education. It is no longer acceptable at this juncture for the public to assume some collective responsibility for children aged five and over, while neglecting all younger children. A system of high quality publicly subsidized child-care and early childhood education is now called for where it is not yet in place. France, Sweden, Denmark and Finland provide examples that other countries might follow.

The arguments here do not break new ground with regard to the types of policies that might resolve modern work/family time conflicts. Instead, this chapter identifies the ongoing transition of productive activity from home to market in industrialized economies as leading to a fundamental incompatibility between the task of taking care of children and the tasks required by modern day paid work. This conflict is a root cause of a number of related social problems – the increasing time bind for working parents, the feminization of poverty and the vicious cycle of welfare dependence. The continuance of these forces appears to be inevitable, given the current structure of most industrialized, market economies. It is hoped that societies will now come to grips with the inevitable incompatibility between child-care and paid worktime, and will be spurred to find a more comprehensive policy solution to the time conflicts and social problems this is imposing universally.

NOTES

1 In fact, child-rearing may be just one example of a broader class of services that share the issues discussed here.
2 For a summary of state regulation, see The Children's Foundation (1999).
3 In 1890, only 6.7 percent of fourteen to seventeen year-olds were enrolled in school (Van Scotter 1991). By 1997, 96.6 percent of fourteen to seventeen year-olds were enrolled in school (National Center for Education Statistics 1998).
4 Rifkin (1995) has argued that technology will soon release much of the labor force from the need to work altogether.

REFERENCES

Bergmann, B. R. (1986) *The Economic Emergence of Women*, New York: Basic Books.
Blau, F. D., Ferber, M. A., and Winkler, A. E. (1998) *The Economics of Women, Men and Work*, New Jersey: Prentice Hall, 3rd Edn.
Boydston, J. (1990) *Home and Work: Housework, Wages and the Ideology of Labor in the Early Republic*, Oxford: Oxford University Press.
Burchinal, M. R., Campbell, F. A., Bryant, D. M., Wasik, B. H., and Ramey, C. T. (1997) "Early Intervention and Mediating Processes in Cognitive Performance of Children of Low-Income African American Families," *Child Development* 68: 935–954.
Children's Foundation (1999) *1999 Child Care Center Licensing Study*, Washington, DC: The Children's Foundation.
Cowan, R. S. (1983) *More Work for Mother: The Ironies of Household Technology from the Open Hearth to the Microwave*, New York: Basic Books.
"Decline in Birth Rate a Headache for Italy" (1993) *The Cleveland Plain Dealer*, August 29, 18-A.
Edin, K. and Lein, L. (1997) *Making Ends Meet: How Single Mothers Survive Welfare and Low-Wage Work*, New York: Russell Sage Foundation.
Frank, R. H. (1985) *Choosing the Right Pond: Human Behavior and the Quest for Status*, Oxford: Oxford University Press.
Hanushek, E. A. (1994) *Making Schools Work: Improving Perfomance and Controlling Costs*, Washington, DC: Brookings Institution.
Hayden, D. (1981) *The Grand Domestic Revolution: A History of Feminist Designs for American Homes, Neighborhoods and Cities*, Cambridge, MA: MIT Press.
Hewlett, S. A. (1986) *A Lesser Life: The Myth of Women's Liberation in America*, New York: Warner Books.
Hochschild, A. R. (1989) *The Second Shift: Working Parents and the Revolution at Home*, New York: Viking.
Jacobsen, J. P. (1994) *The Economics of Gender*, Cambridge: Blackwell Publishers.
Kamerman, S. B. and Kahn, A. J. (eds) (1978) *Family Policy: Government and Families in Fourteen Countries*, New York: Columbia University Press.

Leete, L. and Schor, J. B. (1992) "The Great American Time-Squeeze: Trends in Work and Leisure, 1969–89", Washington, DC: Economic Policy Institute.
Mink, G. (1998) *Welfare's End*, Ithaca, NY: Cornell University Press.
National Center for Education Statistics (1998) *Digest of Education Statistics*, Washington, DC: Government Printing Office.
Rabin, M. (1998) "Psychology and Economics," *Journal of Economic Literature* 36(1): 11–46.
Ramey, C. T., Campbell, F. A., Burchinal, M., Skinner, M. L., Gardner, D. M., and Ramey, S. L. (2000) "Persistent Effects of Early Intervention on High-Risk Children and Their Mothers," *Applied Developmental Science*, in press.
Rifkin, J. (1995) *The End of Work: The Decline of the Global Labor Force and the Dawn of the Post-Market Era*, New York: Tarcher/Putnam Publishing.
Sen, A. K. (1987) *The Standard of Living*, Cambridge: Cambridge University Press.
Scitovsky, T. (1976) *The Joyless Economy: An Inquiry into Human Satisfaction and Consumer Dissatisfaction*, Oxford: Oxford University Press.
Smith, A. (1976) in E. Cannan (ed.), *An Inquiry Into the Nature and Causes of the Wealth of Nations*, Chicago: University of Chicago Press.
Strasser, S. (1982) *Never Done: A History of American Housework*, New York: Pantheon Books.
US Census Bureau (1999) Population Estimates Program, Population Division. Available from http://www.census.gov/population/estimates/nation/intfile2-1.txt).
Van Scotter, R. D. (1991) *Contemporary World Issues: Public Schooling in America*, Santa Barbara, CA: ABC-CLIO, Inc.
Wilson, W. J. (1987) *The Truly Disadvantaged: The Inner City, The Underclass and Public Policy*, Chicago: University of Chicago Press.
_____ (1996) *When Work Disappears: The World of the New Urban Poor*, New York: Random House.

Index